Decision-Making in Planning and Teaching

Decision-Making in Planning and Teaching

Stephen J. Thompson
University of Akron

Susan N. Kushner Benson
University of Akron

Lynne M. Pachnowski
University of Akron

James A. Salzman
Cleveland State University

New York   San Francisco   Boston
London   Toronto   Sydney   Tokyo   Singapore   Madrid
Mexico City   Munich   Paris   Cape Town   Hong Kong   Montreal

Publisher: Priscilla McGeehon
Acquisitions Editor: Aurora Martinez-Ramos
Production Manager: Denise Phillip
Project Coordination, Text Design, and Electronic Page Makeup: WestWords, Inc.
Cover Designer/Manager: Nancy Danahy
Senior Manufacturing Buyer: Dennis J. Para
Printer and Binder: The Maple-Vail Book Manufacturing Group
Cover Printer: Phoenix Color Corp.

Library of Congress Cataloging-in-Publication Data

Decision-making in planning and teaching / Stephen J. Thompson ... [et al.].
    p. cm.
  Includes bibliographical references and index.
  ISBN 0-8013-3135-8
  1. Teaching—United States—Decision making. 2. Educational planning—United States—Decision making 3. Teachers—Training of—United States. I. Thompson, Stephen J.

LB1025.3.D42 2000
371.102--dc21   00-056718
                                                         CIP

Please visit our website at http://www.awl.com

ISBN 0-8013-3135-8

1 2 3 4 5 6 7 8 9 10—MA—03 02 01 00

Dedications

To my wife Penny, a master teacher of early grade children,
and to our children Kirsten, Tressa, and Trent,
who continually teach me about life and loving.
—Stephen J. Thompson

To my dear husband Mark D. Benson, my best friend and
true companion—and in memory of my loving parents,
Nathan and Nina Nan Kushner.
—Susan N. Kushner Benson

To my husband, Joe, my daughter, Marisa,
And my mother, Marie,
For their love, patience,
And encouragement.
—Lynne M. Pachnowski

To my wife, Robin, who has brought balance and fiber into my life,
and my children, Stephen, David, and Amy, who provide
me with the cognitive dissonance to grow.
—James A. Salzman

Contents

Chapter 6   INTEGRATING INSTRUCTIONAL RESOURCES AND TECHNOLOGY   188

Chapter 7   COLLECTING TEACHING STRATEGIES   223

Chapter 8   SELECTING LEARNING STRATEGIES   263

Chapter 9   PLANNING ASSESSMENT STRATEGIES 303

SECTION IV   ACTING ON THE PLAN   333

SECTION V   LOOKING AT THE RESULTS   355

Chapter 10   EVALUATING STUDENT ACHIEVEMENT 357

Chapter **11**   EVALUATING TEACHING   376

Preface

In writing *Decision-Making in Planning and Teaching*, we have attempted to put in book form the kinds of guidance we provide in our own teacher education classes. For example, with our students we stress that before they think about *what* they will teach, teachers had better consider *whom* they will teach. The relationship is reciprocal, but the attitude of "students first" is at the heart of effective instruction. Thus, in the first chapter, we look at the wonderful but increasingly diverse characteristics of our students before we look in the second chapter at the broad contours of curriculum. Throughout, we refer to students' families, communities, social settings, and other context realities that shape teachers' lesson-making decisions. Similarly, when we teach and learn with our students, we talk directly about decision-making as a constant in every teacher's day and provide experiences in making decisions in simulated situations. Thus, as you study this text, you will see us emphasize the processes of teacher decision-making for young learners in both the organization and content of what you read. Just as we try to engage our students in "thinking like teachers," we've tried to write a book that will not only give you knowledge about best practice but engage you in constructing personal and thoughtful responses to instructional challenges.

The primary audience for this text are pre-service teachers who are preparing to become elementary, middle, and high school teachers. However, it can be a resource for all teachers involved in curricular review and design as well as those who wish to extend their knowledge in preparation for standards and performance-based examinations.

TEXT ARRANGEMENT AND THE IDEAL MODEL

This book is organized around the IDEAL model for problem-solving (Bransford and Stein 1984). The five sections of the book follow the elements of problem-solving and decision making presented by the model: **I**dentifying a challenge, **D**efining a challenge, **E**xploring alternatives, **A**cting on a plan, and **L**ooking at and reflecting on results. Chapters within the sections take up the topics of planning and teaching, but do so within the framework of the IDEAL decision-making processes. Elements of decision-making are not always followed sequentially. For example, while actually teaching (**A**cting on a plan), teachers may simultaneously think about options they might have followed (**E**xploring alternatives). Consequently, you will consider the teaching-learning act in some of its complexities while you are grounded in a decision-making strategy that will help you plan, deliver, and evaluate lessons and larger units.

FEATURES TO AID READING AND STUDYING

We have incorporated features to aid your reading and study of this text. Each section opens with a visual of the IDEAL model, with the feature of the section highlighted to give you an overview of the section's emphasis and its relationship to other elements of decision-making.

In each chapter, you will be introduced to the content through a conversation in which a novice teacher considers the implications of planning for student learning in terms of the content of the chapter. While these introductory stories are short, they should provide you with an anticipatory set for the content that follows and teachers' thinking processes in decision-making. In the "Developing Competence" feature that follows, pre-reading prompts will also encourage you to think about what you may already know about issues and set directions for considering the content which follows.

Within the chapters themselves, we have integrated a series of application-type activities which relate to the topic of the chapter. These are opportunities to actually construct a "product" that can be used in an educational setting such as a script of a lesson, an evaluation checklist, or a multimedia presentation. Embedded in the chapters are key terms which stand for key concepts; pause when you come upon these bolded words and reflect on your understanding of their meaning.

At the end of each chapter, we include reflection questions to encourage you to extend your thinking about the topics just encountered. The final feature places you in the role of teacher as researcher. Here you have the opportunity to consider the implications of others' research for your teaching and to be a classroom researcher yourself.

Our sincere hope is that you will use this book in a deliberate way. With your peers and instructor, we want to challenge you to mentally work with the ideas within, shaping and reshaping them until they make sense. Use the book's organization and features, not as prescriptive directions, but as the suggestions of an ally and friend as you try out approaches to an exciting new task. As you do, you'll see yourself grow as a professional decision-maker in planning and teaching.

We would like to thank our students, first and foremost, who inspired us to even begin this project. We would also like to thank the people at Longman, especially Ginny Blanford, who helped shepherd us through the revision process. We owe a great debt to the many reviewers, whose names we never knew, who prodded us to strengthen the content and sharpen the focus of the final product.

Decision-Making in Planning and Teaching

SECTION I

IDEAL

Identifying the Challenge

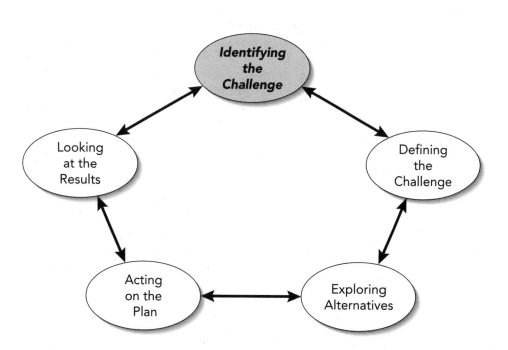

Teachers in the twenty-first century will have many realities with which they will need to deal. They will, first and foremost, have the reality of more diverse groups of students than ever before in the history of our country. That diversity extends from the racial and ethnic mixes of classrooms to the languages that students bring with them and even to new home and family situations from which students come to school. There is also the reality of a society which is holding schools and their teachers more and more accountable for student achievement at a time when many of society's institutions, including schools and churches, are arguably breaking down or losing their importance in the lives of children. Finally, there is the reality of schools themselves. Technology, school-to-work initiatives, partnerships with corporate sponsors, and educational reforms, like shared governance, are changing the ways in which schools have operated for decades. All of these realities pull at teachers in many different ways, and they aren't always pulling in the same direction. All of these factors and more will require that the teachers of the future be accomplished and thoughtful decision-makers, perhaps more so now than at any other time.

What does it mean to be an accomplished and thoughtful decision-maker? Consider that it is estimated that teachers make 4,000 decisions in a single day (Danielson, 1997) and multiply that by the average school year of 180 days. Obviously, many of these decisions can be made rather quickly, and veteran teachers may be weighing the effects of several decisions at any one time. It doesn't take a great deal of concentration to decide to allow Billy to get a pencil from his locker while also letting Serena ask her neighbor a question about an assignment. It does require much greater care in determining which students to group together in a classroom activity or whether to encourage Anthony's parents to have him tested for learning disabilities. Being a strong decision-maker means being "deliberately reflective" in all situations, requiring that you be able to describe the steps in which you engaged in reaching your decision. This means that good decision-makers can consciously follow a decision-making model.

We have organized this book around the theme of decision-making, building our sections on modifications of the IDEAL problem-solving model provided by Bransford and Stein (1984). We have adapted the five stages to reflect what skillful teachers do: Identify the Challenge; Define the Challenge; Explore Alternatives; Act on the Plan; and Look at the Results. If you think about a decision you have made recently, especially if that decision were an important one, you will probably be able to trace your own use of each of these steps. And as you look at each of these phases in arriving at decisions, you should note that there are distinctly different mental activities that you would do at each stage. Note also that there are lines running in both directions from all of the stages. While we have organized the book so that we proceed from Identifying the Challenge all the way to Looking at the Results, we are also aware that making good decisions is seldom a linear process that proceeds from step one through step five. The arrows in both directions indicate that the process of making decisions is a recursive one. That is, as you engage in one mental activity, it may cause you to go back and look at a previous stage; for instance, as you begin to define the challenge, you may discover that the initial issue that you identified is not really the one that you want to deal with at first. At the beginning of each section we will remind you of the IDEAL model and highlight a different stage.

The first of the stages is Identifying the Challenge. As you prepare to become a teacher, you will be facing all of the challenges that we mentioned in the first paragraph and more. For the purposes of this book, however, we are going to focus your attention on the two major challenges that teachers face every day—how to teach *someone something*. Notice that in the order of that statement the word "someone" comes before "something." We want to encourage you always to put your students before the content you are teaching. In chapter 1, we will introduce you to some of the challenges that students bring with them. This chapter provides a brief overview of some of the implications of educational psychology, as well as social and cultural phenomena, on the development and needs of students. Chapter 2 identifies the challenge of analyzing curriculum, the *something* that you will be teaching to your students. We will provide you with an overview of some considerations you will want to make as you think about curriculum in a global manner, as well as a procedure in which you can engage as you consider the "big picture" of making curricular decisions.

CHAPTER **1**

Studying Students

CONVERSATION

The school population of Midtown, USA, has changed a great deal since the 1970s. Close to a major American city, Midtown lost three of its largest industries in the past decade. While some families continue to prosper, more and more families have less discretionary income; many are reaching the end of unemployment benefits and are taking jobs that pay considerably less than they were making in their previous manufacturing positions. As a result, tax levies to support school funding are failing, not because the people of Midtown don't want to support their schools, but because they are stretched so thin that levies are one of the few taxes that they actually have an opportunity to vote on. Growing numbers of immigrants and the working poor, possessing few work skills and performing low-paying jobs, further stretch the schools' meager resources as they try to meet the special needs of students with limited English proficiency and native speakers with other exceptional needs.

None of this really concerned Linda Reyes, a first-year teacher, who was excited when she received her first class list. Twenty-five students who would be hers for the entire year. Twenty-five, she thought, as the number sunk in. Who were these children? What did they like to do? What skills did they bring? What did they lack? She remembered all of the work that she had done in her college course work, and the voice of Dr. Barone intruded into her thoughts: "It's not a class of twenty-five children; it's twenty-five children who make up the class." She and her classmates had always laughed at that, mimicking Dr. Barone in all his seriousness, when they got together for collaborative planning. But now those words, along with the enormity of what she would be doing as she tried to plan instruction, deliver it, and evaluate the students' grasp of the concepts that were outlined in the Graded Course of Study (GCS) she had just been handed, came screaming back into her head.

The meeting with the third-grade teachers from the previous year would surely ease her mind, she had thought. These were all veteran teachers who would tell her exactly where the students had left off, and she would just be able to pick up there. This thought had comforted her as she sat down in the meeting. Now she wasn't so sure. The previous year's achievement tests had shown a range of three grade levels in reading and a little more than that in math skills. Nearly half of these children were below grade level in reading; some still had difficulty with simple addition and subtraction. Five of her students had been tested for learning disabilities and had Individualized Educational Programs (I.E.P.) that she had to accommodate. Two others had just missed being placed in the Gifted and Talented program, so they would provide a different challenge. While she knew that she would have a variety of abilities and skills, she hadn't really thought they would be this varied. She also hadn't really considered some of the personal lives of these children and how this might affect their learning. She had just found out that several students were on the free lunch program, while two others had parents who were going through divorces. These were not the adorably curious and capable students she had imagined in her dreams. Where should she begin?

She decided to begin with Mrs. Karim, her mentor. Mrs. Karim had said to come to her at any time, even if it were just to talk. Linda surely needed to talk right now.

"Where do I start, Mrs. Karim?"

"That's a good question, Linda. Where would you like to start? What challenges seemed to jump out at you as you were listening to last year's teachers?"

"Well the differences in math achievement struck me first. I mean, the GCS says that I should be teaching advanced multiplication, but how can I do that if some of them can't even do simple arithmetic?"

"That certainly is a challenge, isn't it? Now, do you realize what you've just done?"

"What do you mean?"

"What I mean is, you've taken a piece of information, an important piece, and it's gotten your wheels turning. You've identified a challenge that you and your students will face."

"I know it's a challenge, but what do I do about it? What would you do?"

"I always begin with my students. Who are they and what kinds of skills and information do they bring with them to fourth grade? Knowing *where* they are, as you found out with the achievement scores, is one piece of the puzzle. Knowing *who* they are can provide you with insight into how they approach math in school, what motivates them, and how to capitalize on what they can already do. So, how do you suppose you can find out more about these students?"

"Well, I suppose I could try . . ."

DEVELOPING COMPETENCE

In common with most first-year teachers, Linda Reyes has been thrown into a situation in which she feels somewhat overwhelmed. She has been through teacher preparation courses and field work. She has even successfully completed her student teaching. What she hasn't necessarily done is to approach the teaching-learning act in a systematic way, using a problem-solving method to help her think and plan her way through the difficult decisions that teachers make on a daily basis. While veteran teachers are able to focus on multiple sources of information and choose the most important, novice teachers often are bogged down with information overload and may find themselves unable to determine the most significant. Veterans also have large repertoires of strategies and knowledge that they can call upon as they make adjustments in their lessons. While many of these adjustments are done "on the fly," when asked, these teachers can rationalize their decisions in terms of student needs and student achievement. Lacking these resources, novices benefit from careful planning and anticipating the likely outcomes of their decisions.

Developing Competence prompts are intended to help you begin thinking about decisions you might make as teachers. We suggest that, prior to reading each section, you try to answer these questions based on your prior knowledge—what you bring to the text. After carefully reading, you should find that you can answer each of these questions in different ways from your original.

1. Based on your experiences, identify, rank, and defend the reasons that teachers should know about learners' characteristics and the culture of the community from which they come.

2. Name factors that inhibit and those that enhance motivation in students.

3. Explain how understanding multiple intelligences might help teachers when planning learning goals for their students.

4. Predict ways in which socio-economic status, limited English proficiency, and/or culture may affect student achievement in school. Identify ways you can counteract these effects.

5. Compare "mainstreaming" and "inclusion" of students with exceptionalities with regard to *who* teaches *what* to *whom*.

6. Identify and describe the benefits that increased school-home communication provide for students, parents, and teachers.

INTRODUCTION

On the first day of school, students bring with them many things that we can see—book bags, pencils, notebooks, etc.—but they also bring many things that aren't quite so obvious—experiences and characteristics. These experiences and characteristics include cognitive developmental levels, prior knowledge and skills, individual interests and motivations, and various intelligences, as well as community and cultural influences. Together, these are the resources that students use to make sense of the various worlds in which they live. Every child that comes to you will be individually unique and culturally diverse, yet all will act in a variety of settings that provide contextual norms that influence their individual and collective behaviors.

It is these experiences and characteristics that make up the building blocks of all types of learning, in school and out. Because of this, it is essential that teachers get to know what influences students bring with them to school. With this knowledge, they write goals, sequence learning activities, understand and anticipate students' responses, and communicate with parents and professionals. As they plan and teach, teachers sometimes refer to students as a challenge they face.

However, what they actually mean is that students' current experiences, knowledge, and/or strategies are insufficient to facilitate their learning of skills and construction of knowledge.

This chapter looks at the "challenge" of students. We begin by providing a brief overview regarding cognitive psychology and developmental levels of students. We pay special attention to the importance of understanding and assessing prior knowledge and skills, recognizing the impact of cultural and social influences on learning, and the implications of selected theories of motivation and multiple intelligences.

COGNITIVE PSYCHOLOGY AND THE CONSTRUCTION OF KNOWLEDGE

An Ichabod Crane-like task master standing in front of the room casting approving or disapproving looks toward students as they recite their lessons represents one popular and enduring image of teachers. In this view, knowledge is something that teachers possess and that students try to grasp through memorization. The task of the teacher in this view is really quite simple: teachers decide on the content to be learned and evaluate the accuracy with which their students can regurgitate it. Here, depth of understanding is often replaced by accumulation of information. In recent years, cognitive psychologists have challenged this relatively limited view of teaching.

Cognitive psychologists look at people's learning in light of all the processes by which sensory information is reformulated, reduced, enlarged, stored, retrieved, and used. Research in cognitive psychology investigates these covert mental processes. These investigations have led to a different view of learning, which, in turn, require that teachers take a different approach to teaching. Stemming from these investigations, **constructivism** is a psychological theory of learning that "construes learning as an interpretive, recursive, building process by active learners interacting with the physical and social world" (Fosnot, 1996, p. 30). Constructivism is in opposition to behavioral theories, in which students engage in certain acts on the basis of reinforcers and refrain from others on the basis of punishments appropriately applied at the right moments. In the constructivist view, learning is a continuous process of making meaning of the world. Meaning is constructed by individual students as they interact with the materials and activities that teachers provide, as well as within the social context of the classroom within their school and community. Meaning is something that involves constant negotiation within the individual and within the various groups to which individuals belong. As such, real meaning is not something that can be recited to a teacher who determines the correctness of the recitation.

This view puts students at the center of the learning process as all information and activity is filtered through the cognitive structures, prior knowledge, current learning strategies, and socio-cultural understandings that each one brings to class every day. As students are presented with information and engage in experiences, they form the mental structures, sometimes called **schemes,** that allow

Constructivism

Students construct personal meanings by interacting with *ideas* and *materials*

them to participate in even more sophisticated learning. According to Woolfolk (1995), schemes are "organized systems of action or thought that allow us to mentally represent or 'think about' the objects and events in our world" (p. 31). Some schemes are quite simple, such as the ones that students use as they sharpen a pencil or take out a piece of notebook paper. Others are quite complex and may require the combining of a number of simple schemes. Think about the number of simple schemes that combine to form the more sophisticated "driving" scheme. You first engage the "opening the car door" scheme, followed by the "sitting down" scheme, maybe the "adjusting the seat and mirror" schemes before even beginning the "turn the key" scheme, and so on. That you no longer even "think" about all of this is evidence of the power of the organizational functions of the cognitive domain and the formation of schema.

Because schemes are individually formed and filtered through numerous influences, it is no wonder that a teacher can teach the same lesson to two different groups of students and have entirely different reactions to it. This can certainly lend a certain appeal to behavioral learning theories. If learning is merely acquiring a set of behaviors that can be taught using behavioral principles, then teaching is a relatively easy task. All you would have to do is find out what motivates different students, wait until students perform the behavior, and provide them with the appropriate reinforcement immediately after the behavior presents itself. In the constructivist view, learning is much messier and less prescriptive because we can't see what students are doing mentally as they struggle with a problem. However, even though there is not a prescription for teaching according to a constructivist philosophy, Fosnot (1996) offers some general principles that can guide you as you prepare to become "guides on the side" of student learning. These are:

- Learning *is* development. Learners must become comfortable with identifying and defining meaningful problems and finding ways to meet the challenges that problem-solving inevitably brings. In this way, learning can *lead* to development. To do this, however, students must be made to feel comfortable taking risks and applying strategies, like the IDEAL model, to their own learning.

- Disequilibrium facilitates learning. Learners must become comfortable with being uncomfortable. Cognitive discomfort, or disequilibrium, is indicative of growth and learning. As such, students (and teachers) need to view "mistakes" as opportunities for learning and the source of these mistakes as places from which learning can spring.

- Reflection drives learning. Learners need to be taught ways and given time to think about their learning. Given this time and guided by skillful questions, your students will have opportunities to make sense of the activities you provide for them. More importantly, students who reflect on their learning become aware of their meta-cognitive thinking; that is, they come to greater understandings of ways in which they apply learning strategies in different situations and how their own thought processes work.

- Dialogue within a learning community encourages further thinking. Learners need to take responsibility for identifying and supporting their views on topics within small groups and whole class discussions. All members of the class need to be taught to consider opposing points of view and present these as the validity of certain "truths" is considered and defended.

- Constructing meaning encourages the development of cognitive schemes. These structures are "learner-constructed, central organizing principles that can be generalized across experiences and that often require the undoing or reorganizing of earlier conceptions." (pp. 29–30)

COGNITIVE DEVELOPMENT

Jean Piaget and his associate (Piaget & Inhelder, 1969) wrote about stages of cognitive development in which students engage in different mental processes during each stage. In this portion of the chapter, we will look at the four stages of development and, more importantly, the processes that children and adolescents

---

Activity 1.1

As just discussed, students bring a great deal of prior knowledge and influences to school with them. To demonstrate this, choose a poem (or your instructor may choose one for you) with which you are unfamiliar that tells a story. Read the poem all the way through once, then read it a second time and write a summary of what is happening. Consider who are the characters, where are they, what are they doing, and why. After summarizing the poem, read aloud your summaries in a small group. Discuss (or write about) the differences in the summaries. Try to identify what events in your life may have caused you to interpret the poem as you did. What skills did you bring to the act of reading this poem that helped or hindered your summary? How did you feel about doing this assignment and how might that have affected your work?

---

engage in as they move from one stage to the next. We will also provide a brief discussion of Vygotsky's (1962) learning theory, which extended Piaget's theories of cognitive development by adding a sociocultural aspect. Regardless of the grade levels you teach, you will enhance your ability to teach by understanding the cognitive processes your students may already possess or need to acquire to be successful in your class.

Cognition—Organization and Adaptation

Piaget is often cited for his work that identified the four stages of cognitive development, which we will discuss shortly. However, he spent the last fifteen years of his career focusing more of his efforts on how children form their cognitive structures at each of the stages. He theorized that all people have two processes—**organization** and **adaptation**—that they use to make sense of their worlds. As people take in information through their senses, they begin to organize these massive amounts of data into **schemes.** They have many schemes available that are used throughout the day. For instance, you have a "getting ready for class" scheme, an "eating" scheme, a "driving" scheme, and so on. These schemes are so well-organized within your brain that you don't often give them much conscious thought. You have other schemes, too, like studying for a calculus test, that may be called upon in more conscious ways. For the most part, at this stage in your life you have tens of thousands of schemes that you can call upon to complete most of the tasks you face on any given day.

But what happens when your current schemes are insufficient to accomplish a certain task? You feel tense, maybe a bit anxious, certainly uncomfortable. Piaget called this feeling **disequilibrium.** To overcome this feeling, Piaget theorized that people use two complementary processes—**assimilation** and **accommodation**—in order to adapt new information into their schemes. He noticed that even young children try to make sense of their worlds by trying to find ways to incorporate new and different tasks or information into their schemes. The easiest way is to *assimilate* the new information into an already existing scheme. To do that, Piaget noted that sometimes children will ignore an important criteria of that existing scheme in order to make the new thing fit. For instance, if a little boy has grown up with a cat in his house, he will develop a "cat" scheme early on. That scheme will involve cat characteristics, like "four legs," a "tail," and "fur." It also may involve a "meow" sound. That boy will know a "kitty" through this scheme, but what happens when he first sees a dog? He may look at it quizzically at first, but the dog has four legs, fur, and a tail. The little boy's scheme informs him that, though odd looking, this new animal is a kitty. When the dog barks, the boy now has a new bit of disequilibrium with which to deal. If he chooses to ignore the "meow" characteristic of his cat scheme, he will still assimilate this dog into the cat scheme that already exists. After a few encounters with dogs, however, the boy will begin to recognize that there are other ways in which this new animal does not fit into the cat scheme. The boy's first teachers, his parents and other adults, are probably prompting him with the name "doggy." At this point he *accommodates* this new animal into his mental store room by adding a "dog" scheme. When this happens, the boy has regained his cognitive **equilibrium;** that is, his understanding of the world is now back in balance.

Learners assimilate new information into existing schemes

FIGURE 1.1 PIAGET'S STAGES OF COGNITIVE DEVELOPMENT		
Stage	Approximate Age/Grade	Stage Characteristics
Sensorimotor	Birth to 2 years	World of the here and now Know objects through senses Simple motor activities No language; no thought
Preoperational	Early childhood through early elementary years	Use symbol system, including language One-way thinking Inability to conserve
Concrete Operations	Mid-elementary to middle school	Hands-on thinking Ability to conserve Mentally reverses actions Classify and sequence items
Formal Operations	Middle to high school	Imagine multiple worlds Deal with the hypothetical Connect assumptions and implications

Though the previous discussion is overly simplified, it serves to illustrate how children learn as they construct their understandings of the world. Piaget theorized that it is through children's sensory encounters in the world that they organize information into schemes. These schemes provide them with ways of encountering new information. When new encounters create disequilibrium in individuals, children attempt to integrate the new information into existing schemes by either assimilating or accommodating it. As the schemes become more complex, children's cognitive development increases. Through these processes, they move from one stage of cognitive development to another (see Figure 1.1 for a brief summary of the four stages).

Sensorimotor Stage

In the first two years of life, children exist in a world of the "here and now." During this sensorimotor stage, they come to know their environment through the senses of sight, sound, touch, smell, and taste. In the earliest part of this stage, objects such as a cloth animal or a plastic tool are real if a child can experience them through the five senses. Put that same cloth animal out of sight or away from the touch of those same children and the animal ceases to "exist." During this stage, children are intrigued with simple motor activities like throwing a toy ball, jumping through a hoop, or sliding off the couch. Language is simple and generally limited to words for family members, pets, and things that interest individual children.

Preoperational Stage

From early childhood through the early elementary years, children begin the process of moving away from schemes tied to the senses and physical action toward what Piaget referred to as **operations.** Operations are the mental representations of actions, and these are carried out mentally rather than physically. In order to initiate mental operations, children begin to use symbol systems, such as words, pictures, and gestures. During the preoperational stage, children's language ability and use grow geometrically, especially early in the stage. Without any formal grammar instruction, children internalize very sophisticated usage rules and learn to apply them nearly flawlessly according to the models that they emulate. In addition, engaging in play, pretending for instance, provides children with opportunities to form schemes that allow them to interact with the world in a symbolic way. As teachers, watching children play at this stage provides us with some sense of how children perceive the world to be. Think back to your own early experiences with playing "school" or "house." How you behaved in your role as teacher or student, spouse or child, had to do with how you had constructed these roles in your mind, with the schemes you had formed of what it meant to be in these roles.

While certain mental structures, especially those dealing with language, become quite sophisticated, during this stage children's thought is limited by a tendency to engage in one-way thinking. Children have difficulty planning for how to reverse the steps in one of their schemes. For instance, the child who walks to school in the morning but is picked up after school every day would probably have difficulty if told to walk home from school one day. One of the types of reversible thinking with which children have difficulty is **conservation.** Conservation is the principle where changes in appearance do not affect the amount or number of something. The classic experiment that Piaget used was to show a child two identical glasses filled with the same amount of liquid. Then with the child watching, the researcher would pour the liquid into a different container. When asked if the two containers had the same amount of liquid or if one had more, the child who had not yet mastered the operation of conservation said that one has more. The child was unable to mentally reverse the pouring back into the original container. While different types of conservation tasks are mastered at different ages, in general terms the inability to master these tasks is one of the indicators of children who are still within the preoperational stage.

Concrete Operations Stage

From elementary to middle school, children's thinking is characterized by this "hands-on" stage. During this time, children become more consciously aware of the physical stability of the world. Mastery of conservation tasks, the principle of **compensation,** is one of the ways in which this understanding is formed. Children become aware that changes in form, as in the example above, can be *compensated* for by some other aspect. For instance, if the water were poured from a drinking glass into a long thin test tube, the preoperational child might say that the test tube has more water because the water level is higher or that the drinking glass holds more because it is wider. The child who has mastered the principle of compensation, though, is able to explain that the change in height is offset by the change in width. At this stage, the child can mentally reverse the action. That is, the child can mentally pour the water from test tube into drinking glass and recognize that the amount of water has not changed.

It is also during this stage that students learn to classify and sequence items. Students are able to focus on aspects of items and determine how to group on the basis of similarities. They also are able to reconsider their original groups and reclassify on the basis of other similarities. If you were to go into an elementary classroom during Autumn in the Northern or Mountain states, you might see students gathering leaves to take back into class. Once back in the room, they might be asked to organize them into piles. In the constructivist classroom, they would also be asked to explain the principles upon which they organized their piles. Some might be doing it according to color, or size, or shape, or any number of different possibilities. If asked by the teacher to reorganize their piles, children in this stage should be able to do so according to a different aspect. They could also be asked to sequence these same leaves from largest to smallest or vice versa.

Formal Operations Stage

Sometime during the middle to high school years, most students begin to enter the formal operations stage, though it seems likely that not all students do so, and even those who do probably do not engage in formal operations in all discipline areas. Because of this, it is important for teachers of adolescents to be aware of both the concrete operations and formal operations stages and to provide instruction that can encourage students to move from one into the other. Though some adolescents may never move out of concrete operations (or at least not in your classroom), generally problems present themselves, especially in formal schooling, which cannot be adequately addressed through the use of concrete operations. The disequilibrium created by these problems can be the catalyst that nudges students into the development of formal operational thought structures.

Students at this stage retain all of the structures that they have developed at previous stages. Yet, whereas students in concrete operations tend to be focused on *what is*, children in formal operations can imagine multiple, alternative possible worlds. In this way, the most distinctive feature of this stage is the child's ability to engage in hypothetico-deductive reasoning. According to Woolfolk (1995), students in this stage "can form hypotheses, set up mental experiments to test them, and isolate or control variables in order to complete a valid test of the hypotheses" (p. 40). For instance, presented with information about Mars, its lesser gravitational pull, colder temperatures, and lack of liquid water, the formal operational child could proceed from general assumptions to the specific implications of these assumptions. If asked to imagine creatures who could possibly live on Mars, the formal operational child would likely create creatures that took into account the conditions on Mars, maybe by assuming that creatures would be six times larger, warm-blooded, and with a higher core body temperature to compensate for the lower gravitational forces and colder temperatures. Given the same task, however, the concrete operational child could no doubt draw some fanciful creatures but seldom would provide the connection between the assumptions presented and the specific implications of those assumptions. Middle and secondary school teachers are especially challenged to help students engage in the types of thinking that can facilitate the creation of these mental structures.

SOCIAL CONSTRUCTION OF KNOWLEDGE

Human beings are by their very nature social creatures. At all stages of their cognitive development, children and adolescents seek out the company of others. Through their interactions with others, they test out ideas, come to understandings about themselves and the world, and evaluate the successes of their efforts (see "Social Construction of Knowledge" tasks in *Teacher as Researcher* section). By looking at the sociocultural perspective of learning and depending on your interpretation, Lev Vygotsky either provided an extension or an alternative to Piaget. Whereas Piaget investigated children's cognitive development by looking at individual children, Vygotsky considered children in many different cultures. He noted that Piaget's stages and especially some of the limitations placed upon children in particular stages were not generalizable to all children in all cultures. Vygotsky posited his theory that children's cultures not only influence what they learn but how they learn. According to Woolfolk (1998), "Vygotsky suggested that cognitive development depends much more on interactions with the 'people' in the child's world and the 'tools' that the culture provides to support thinking" (p. 44) than on any solitary quest for knowledge, as Piaget hypothesized. Two aspects of his theory, that of private speech and the zone of proximal development, are especially noteworthy.

In Piaget's research, he noted that children in the preoperational and concrete operations stages often talked to themselves, even when they were in a group. He identified this phenomenon as **egocentric speech** in which children engage in a collective monologue, wherein they speak aloud but aren't communicating with others. He concluded that this is an indication that children at these early cognitive stages are unable to consider the world through anyone's eyes but their own. Vygotsky, seeing the same phenomenon, arrived at different conclusions. He noted that, rather than being indicative of any cognitive limitation, as Piaget had set out, that this **private speech** was often instrumental in helping them to focus on a task and engage in problem-solving activities. Vygotsky believed that children demonstrate their cognitive abilities, rather than limitations, by communicating aloud with themselves, which is useful in guiding their thinking while they develop the cognitive structures to engage this thinking internally.

Though most students are able to make a transition from audible private speech to inner speech by the age of nine, you may still notice students mumbling or talking to themselves. As teachers, being aware of private speech may alert you to times when your students are having special problems that may require your intervention or assistance. You may find yourself more tolerant of children who are talking to themselves, even on a test, and see this not as a disruption but as an important learning strategy. You may also tap into your students' inner speech,

Teacher scaffolding enables students to achieve what they couldn't on their own

asking them to explain aloud what they are doing in working on a particular problem and why. This can provide valuable feedback to you and increase your awareness and your students' **metacognition,** their self-awareness of their cognitive processes, as well as the presence or absence of appropriate strategies for successfully completing activities.

Many students engaging in private speech are attempting to solve problems. In some cases, they are right on the threshold of solving a particular problem on their own, but they just can't quite do it. When your students find themselves in this position, they are said to be in the **Zone of Proximal Development.** Students may not be able to solve a problem on their own but can solve it with a little assistance from someone, peer or adult, more advanced than they. This is what some educators might refer to as a "teachable moment" and is the point at which real learning can take place. At this point, these students need guidance; this guidance is often referred to as **scaffolding,** a concept related to a tutoring situation in which an adult or expert helps someone who is less adult or expert (Bruner, 1992; Wood, Bruner, and Ross, 1976). Just as a scaffold provides workers with stable areas on which they can reach higher than their unassisted grasps would allow, guidance in the form of prompts or cues enables students to reach beyond their unassisted cognitive grasps. This recognition of what children can do with assistance may be an indicator of their true mental functioning and casts a large shadow on some traditional teaching and evaluation strategies. It certainly provides a relatively new twist to the old adage that "two heads are better than one."

PRIOR KNOWLEDGE AND SKILLS

Regardless of how their cognitive development is nurtured, the structures that children and adolescents develop build upon their prior knowledge and the learning skills they bring to new information. One way of thinking about these abilities and the knowledge that students bring with them is to think of them as three types of knowledge: declarative, procedural, and conditional (Anderson, 1983, 1987).

    Declarative knowledge (or "knowing that") is the type of knowledge that students can declare with some sense of certainty. It is "knowing that" hydrogen is the first element on the periodic table or that Mark McGwire hit 70 home runs in 1998. When students know something well enough to state it to another person, they demonstrate their declarative knowledge. **Procedural knowledge** (or "knowing how") requires that students demonstrate their knowledge by acting on something. Students who "know how" to add can be given a sheet of addition problems and be expected to successfully complete it; those who know how to bake can be given the materials and combine them to successfully bake a bundt cake. Finally, students possessing **conditional knowledge** (or "knowing when and why") allows them to demonstrate their abilities to apply both declarative and procedural knowledge in new situations.

Prior Knowledge

How do students learn new information? Those who view teaching as a one-way street from teacher to learner, proponents of the "sage on the stage" metaphor of teaching, believe that information can be transmitted from an authority, such as a teacher or textbook, to a recipient. In this view students are empty vessels waiting for new pieces of information to be poured into them. The various pieces of this new information will be added to existing information and somehow be integrated into a unified set of principles and understandings.

    As we stated earlier, this view of learning does not allow for the learner to be an active maker of knowledge. Cognitive psychology has shown us that learning is more of a two-way street, where knowledge and information is being transported back and forth between two or more "authorities." The teacher or textbook has a certain amount of authority in terms of subject matter while learners also must be considered authorities in terms of their own stores of procedural and declarative knowledge. These types of knowledge represent what most teachers mean when they discuss the prior knowledge of their students. Real learning occurs when students are able to integrate the new information with which they are presented into the existing schemes, the prior knowledge, which they already possess and/or when the existing schemes are reorganized to accept new information (how teachers help students use their prior knowledge within three different whole lesson formats is illustrated in chapter 4).

Students bring a tremendous amount of prior knowledge, often much more than is acknowledged, to every learning situation. It may be fully developed or incomplete, somewhat general or very specific, accurate or misconceived. It also tends to be quite personal and deeply entrenched. And, just because a student brings fully developed, accurate, and specific information to one situation does not mean that that same student will always demonstrate this type of competence in another situation, even one that seems very similar to the teacher. Regardless of the situation, if new information is not integrated with the existing knowledge, learning will be short-term and shallow. Think of your own experiences with trying to cram for an examination. On the other hand, when new information is integrated by the learner, it becomes more fully understood and retained for relatively longer periods of time.

If only learners can integrate new information by constructing and reconstructing their prior knowledge, it would seem to let teachers off the hook for student learning. "If students didn't learn, it's not my fault," a novice teacher might say. "They just didn't participate actively enough." While it's true that learners are ultimately responsible for their own learning, teachers have an important role. Teachers need to provide students with opportunities to recognize what prior knowledge they already possess, expand on their incomplete schema, and confront inaccurate prior knowledge or misconceptions. To fulfill this role, you must be able to do two things: accurately assess student knowledge and identify the learning and problem-solving strategies students currently utilize.

You will need to find ways to assess students' prior knowledge in order to provide students with these opportunities. As teachers attempt to help students recognize what they already know, they have a number of techniques and tools available to them. Many teachers use pre-tests (see chapter 9 for additional information), checklists, and/or informal and formal questioning strategies, in addition to a number of other techniques. What is important to remember about using any of these techniques is that the instrument is only as good as the teacher who listens to or reads the responses. If you ask questions that already have predetermined "right" answers, you increase the likelihood that you will misinterpret what your students already do or do not know. Truly finding out what students know requires that teachers and students listen to one another. An example of how to do this is provided by Langer and Purcell-Gates (1984) who developed

PReP (Pre-Reading Plan), a pre-reading activity designed to help both teachers and students in grades three through twelve become aware of what students already know about a topic.

Pre-existing Learning Skills

It is relatively easy to determine what declarative knowledge students bring to school with them. The same is often true for simple procedural knowledge, such as multiplication or phonics skills, or even more complex procedures, such as graphing an ellipse. If a student can state that an ellipse is a locus of points the sum of the distances of each of which from two fixed points is the same constant, you can determine that this student knows the definition of an ellipse, that she possesses a certain amount of prior declarative knowledge. Just knowing this, however, does not indicate that, given a set of values, she knows the procedure to follow to graph the line. But let's assume that she does, that if she knew that she was supposed to be finding an ellipse she has enough prior declarative and procedural knowledge to be able to do this. These two types of knowing are the basic, prerequisite knowledge that she brings to your math class that will allow her to be successful. What you still do not know, however, is whether she can apply her procedural and declarative knowledge to a unique problem. For instance, would she apply the conditional knowledge that would allow her to recognize that a math problem that asks for the maximum height of a pass being thrown forty-five yards downfield could be solved by utilizing the formula for an ellipse.

In addition to assessing students' prior knowledge, you will also need to find ways to determine what skills students bring that will help them understand their own conditional knowledge. Wade and Reynolds (1989) provide a helpful way to categorize the types of awarenesses that students must possess to become directors of their own learning. They divide them into three categories: **task awareness, strategy awareness,** and **performance awareness.** Simply put, students who possess task awareness can distinguish between relevant and irrelevant information to complete the task. In the previously mentioned math problem, the day of the week or whether the game was played on grass or Astroturf is irrelevant, while the distance downfield *is* relevant. Students who possess strategy awareness know which strategies to apply in order to achieve a specific task or what methods to use in studying a particular subject or topic. These students would not apply the same reading strategies for pleasure reading as they would in reading for a physics test. Finally, students who possess performance awareness know whether or not they are comprehending the materials they are reading. These students will be able to adjust or alter their strategies as the need, in relation to the task, calls for it. You can assess whether students possess these awarenesses and where they may benefit from your intervention.

For most students, growth in learning skills is developmental. In general, younger students have fewer skills and strategies than older ones, and these younger students' skills require lower-level cognitive abilities. As they grow, teachers often assume that their skills grow in relative ways. However, this is not always true. A large number of middle school and secondary students' skills are inefficient (take too much time) and/or ineffective (don't get the job done). With greater demands being placed upon students as a result of new technologies and new relations of workers to the work place, students' abilities to sort and categorize information, discriminate fact from opinion, and then to communicate needed information to others is critical for individual and corporate well-being. Increasing students' self-awareness is one role that teachers can play in preparing students for their futures.

There are a number of approaches to assessing self-awareness. The most effective may be when you actively listen to students as they describe their difficulties in doing an assignment. By listening carefully and posing questions of your students, you may be able to infer the learning skills they are lacking and intervene by teaching them new skills or reminding them of the skills that they already possess but are not using (teaching learning skills and strategies is the topic of chapter 8). Teachers also have access to a great deal of information provided by tests, both standardized and teacher-made. By analyzing students' performances on these tests, you may be able to determine patterns of errors and target those skills that students need to utilize to overcome their errors. Finally, there are a number of existing materials, such as the Learning Style Inventory (Kolb, 1985), which you can use to assess students' preferred modes of learning. Knowing this information may provide you with ways of grouping students for more effective instruction or providing different students with different strategies based on their preferences (different approaches to grouping are taken up in chapter 5).

STUDENTS AND MOTIVATION

We hope that the previous discussion has emphasized how important it is for you to determine the amount and quality of students' prior information and the skills they use to access it. Simply possessing a store of knowledge and a set of learning skills, however, is not sufficient for students to be actively engaged in learning. Students also bring attitudes and inclinations that affect how and when—and if—they learn in the school setting. Active learners must be *willing* to participate and persist at school tasks in order to be successful. In other words, they must be motivated. In the discussion that follows we intend to define motivation, briefly discuss several factors that affect motivation (either inhibiting or enhancing students' motivation), and discuss the implications of motivating students as a way of improving your teaching.

What Is Motivation?

Faced with a school task, some students jump right in and start working, not even waiting for the teacher to finish giving directions. These self-starters are confident in their own abilities and secure in the knowledge that they can handle whatever task they have been handed. Other students lack this confidence and approach academic tasks anxiously, uncertain of their abilities to be successful. Teachers sometimes refer to the self-starters as being "motivated" and to the reluctant learners as "unmotivated." But what accounts for the differences between them? What is meant by motivation?

For educators, **motivation** can be defined as the forces that compel students' movements toward school achievement. Learning to recognize which forces motivate different students in different situations can help teachers plan lessons, relate to students in meaningful ways, and strengthen school-home communication, to name just a few benefits. Part of this recognition, though, is learning that what you, as a teacher, think is motivating and what students think is motivating can be vastly different (see the Garibaldi task under "Motivation" in the *Teacher as Researcher* section). It is also important to remember that what may be motivating for one student could be a "turn off" to another. There is no "one size fits all" approach to motivating students. Ultimately, you will want to help students understand what is motivating to them. Understanding this, students will be more capable of taking control of their own learning process and less likely to feel that school success is something that resides outside of their control.

Factors Affecting Motivation

One major concern for teachers is to determine to what students attribute their successes and failures. That is, do students perceive their successes and failures in school to be due to their own efforts and abilities or to some outside forces over which they have no control? When the former is true, then we conclude that these students perceive their achievement is due to an **internal locus of causality.** The same can be said of students who attribute their failures to a lack of effort. When students are accurate in this assessment, then the internal locus provides them with feedback that can help them achieve success on later assignments. They now know that all they need to do is to try harder, and this effort can provide them with more success in future projects. Making the effort and achieving success will often "motivate" these students to continue to do well on later assignments.

However, when students perceive that success in school is not something that they can attain, they will often be labeled as "unmotivated." If you can determine from where this feeling arises, you are more likely to be able to take steps to help your students overcome these feelings. In many students, this lack of motivation springs from outside themselves. These students are said to have an **external locus of causality.** That is, they attribute success or failure in school to factors over which they have no control, which, in some cases, may have little to do with the particular task they have been assigned. For instance, Nguyen quickly wrote an essay in homeroom one period before he turned it in. He was angry when he received a failing grade and told his friends that it was because the teacher did not like him and that she never liked any of the work he did. In this case, Nguyen denies any personal responsibility and, instead, attributes his failure to a factor, his teacher's preferences, outside his control. If this becomes a pattern, Nguyen may find himself a victim of **learned helplessness.** Students who find themselves in this position make a habit of not trying to succeed. This habitual behavior stems from an attitude that any action taken by the learner will inevitably lead to failure anyway, so why try? The result? A passive learner remains passive, unwilling to

Students with an internal locus of causality attribute success to their efforts

put him or herself at risk (see the Newman task under "Motivation" in the *Teacher as Researcher* section).

One other factor to consider is **engagement,** the emotional involvement of the learner in school tasks. When students are not engaged in an activity, they will go through the motions, maybe even complete the assignment successfully, but they will not place any emphasis on it and are unlikely to learn much. However, when engaged, students are often so involved that they do not notice the passing of time. They will often want to continue an activity long past the time you had planned for it. They may even walk out of class commenting on how quickly the time went. Whether students possess internal or external loci of causality, an engaging activity, one that challenges them in appropriate ways, often one that involves peer interaction, can motivate them in ways that will have them putting near Herculean efforts into a school activity. Some of the most "unmotivated" learners will surprise even themselves.

Implications for Teaching

Developing or finding engaging activities is one of the best ways to motivate students (the chapters in Section III, Exploring Alternatives, describe many such activities). Activities that engage students are ones to which *they* attach meaning.

This is one of the reasons that it is so important to get to know your students—their likes and dislikes, their community, and their culture—as well as you can. If you communicate high expectations and provide activities that are developmentally appropriate and of interest to your students, they will tend to meet those expectations. Though it may be important for some learners that you provide more frequent feedback and extrinsic rewards at first, your ultimate goal for your students is to foster their own self-awareness of their progress and needs, while weaning them from extrinsic rewards and toward an appreciation of the successful completion of a project as its own intrinsic reward.

Activity 1.2

Arrange to tutor a low-achieving, "helpless" student. See if the student tends to attribute lack of success to "inside factors" (not having needed abilities, not working hard enough) or "outside factors" (the test was too hard, luck, or as in the case of Nguyen, perceptions of the teacher). Use your observations of the student at work, plus his/her conversations with the teacher and you as you elaborate on the "inside/outside factors" in a mini-case study. Share your case study with the student's teacher. After reading Alderman's article, describe for the teacher one "link" for helping the student become successful. *Source:* Alderman, M. K. (1990). Motivation for at-risk students. *Educational Leadership, 48* (1), 27–30.

MULTIPLE INTELLIGENCES

When you enter your classroom, you should feel comfortable in the knowledge that students come to you with the capacity to learn. What they learn, how well they learn it, and whether they want to learn what you want to teach them is almost superfluous to this native ability. Not too long ago, however, educators assumed that this native ability, especially that which impacted on school achievement, reflected a single type of learning capacity that was referred to as an intelligence quotient, or IQ. Many of today's educators acknowledge that that view of intelligence is limiting, on both students and teachers, and limited in terms of the forms that education could or should take. Because of this shift in thinking, many of today's scholars acknowledge the benefits of expanding our view of intelligence to include, not one, but many.

Howard Gardner (1983, 1993) coined the term "multiple intelligences" in response to his observations of the implications of empirical research on the brain and human cultures. To his original seven intelligences, Gardner has added an eighth, the naturalist. All represent biological and psychological potentials, which are fulfilled when people have real-world experiences that pertain to them (Figure 1.2). That is, a high potential for musical intelligence is realized by engaging a student in musical training, activities, and performances. Students, as well as all human beings, have strengths and weaknesses in the eight. Within the same classroom, one student may have a high potential in the

---

FIGURE 1.2   GARDNER'S EIGHT INTELLIGENCES

The Intelligences, in Gardner's Words

- *Linguistic intelligence*–the capacity to use language, your native language, and perhaps other languages, to express what's on your mind and to understand other people. Poets really specialize in linguistic intelligence, but any kind of writer, orator, speaker, lawyer, or a person for whom language is an important stock in trade highlights linguistic intelligence.

- *Logical-mathematical intelligence*–the capacity to understand the underlying principles of some kind of a causal system the way a scientist or a logician does; or ability to manipulate numbers, quantities, and operations—the way a mathematician does.

- *Spatial intelligence*–the ability to represent the spatial world internally in your mind—the way a sailor or airplane pilot navigates the large spatial world, or the way a chess player or sculptor represents a more circumscribed spatial world. Spatial intelligence can be used in the arts or in the sciences. If you are spatially intelligent and oriented toward the arts, you are more likely to become a painter or a sculptor or an architect than, say, a musician or a writer. Similarly, certain sciences like anatomy or topology emphasize spatial intelligence.

- *Bodily kinesthetic intelligence*–the capacity to use your whole body or parts of your body—your hand, your fingers, your arms—to solve a problem, make something, or put on some kind of a production. The most evident examples are people in athletics or the performing arts, particularly dance or acting.

- *Musical intelligence*–the capacity to think in music, to be able to hear patterns, recognize them, remember them, and perhaps manipulate them. People who have a strong musical intelligence don't just remember music easily—they can't get it out of their minds, it's so omnipresent. Now, some people will say, "Yes, music is important, but it's a talent, not an intelligence." And I say, "Fine, let's call it a talent." But, then we have to leave the word intelligent out of all discussions of human abilities. You know, Mozart was damned smart!

- *Interpersonal intelligence*–understanding other people. It's an ability we all need, but is at a premium if you are a teacher, clinician, salesperson, or politician. Anybody who deals with other people has to be skilled in the interpersonal sphere.

- *Intrapersonal intelligence*–having an understanding of yourself, of knowing who you are, what you can do, what you want to do, how you react to things, which things to avoid, and which things to gravitate toward. We are drawn to people who have a good understanding of themselves because those people tend not to screw up. They tend to know what they can do. They tend to know what they can't do. And they tend to know where to go if they need help.

FIGURE 1.2   GARDNER'S EIGHT INTELLIGENCES *(CONTINUED)*

- *Naturalist intelligence*–the human ability to discriminate among living things (plants, animals) as well as sensitivity to other features of the natural world (clouds, rock configurations). This ability was clearly of value in our evolutionary past as hunters, gatherers, and farmers; it continues to be central in such roles as botanist or chef. I also speculate that much of our consumer society exploits the naturalist intelligences, which can be mobilized in the discrimination among cars, sneakers, kinds of makeup, and the like. The kind of pattern recognition valued in certain of the sciences may also draw upon naturalist intelligence.

(*Source:* Checkley, K. (1997) The first seven and the eighth: A conversation with Howard Gardner. *Educational Leadership, 55* (1), 12.)

Humans have several intelligences, not just one

bodily-kinesthetic and interpersonal intelligences, and relatively low potential in the linguistic, while another may possess high potential in spatial and low potential in logical-mathematical intelligence. Gardner calls on teachers to value all of these intelligences and to allow students to work on school tasks in different ways to help all students utilize their strengths (see the "Multiple Intelligences" task in the *Teacher as Researcher* section).

By embracing the concept of multiple intelligences, you will be compelled to think about students and your own planning and assessment differently. For instance, if you were reading a play in your seventh grade English class, students could be encouraged to respond in different ways based on their own strengths. Students who possess strong potential in spatial intelligence, for instance, could be allowed to respond to their reading by visualizing the action on stage and designing the sets that could be utilized for putting on the play in the auditorium. Take a look at Figure 1.3 for other possibilities for learning and displaying of learning in Gardner's original seven intelligences (Faggela and Horowitz, 1990).

Encouraging learning and student performances on the basis of different intelligences leads to encouraging assessment through different means as well. Authentic assessment tools must, by definition, parallel the modes of learning (chapter 9 is devoted to a variety of approaches to assessment). In the example above, for instance, the students whose growth in literary response is attributable

---

Activity 1.3

Develop a goal-setting form based on Gardner's multiple intelligences (see and modify the form in the Ellison reference). Fill out the form to establish your own personal goals. After a month, "conference" with yourself about your progress. In front of your colleagues, describe your experience in developing the form and your progress toward the goals. Lead a discussion regarding how the multiple intelligences-based goals procedure might be implemented with students in a hypothetical class. *Source:* Ellison, L. (1992). Using multiple intelligences to set goals. *Educational Leadership, 50* (2), 69–72.

FIGURE 1.3   SEVEN STYLES OF LEARNING

Type	Likes To	Is Good At	Learns Best By
LINGUISTIC LEARNER "The Word Player"	read, write, and tell stories	memorizing names, places dates, and trivia	saying, hearing, and seeing words
LOGICAL/ MATHEMATICAL LEARNER "The Questioner"	do experiments, figure things out, work with numbers,and ask questions	math, reasoning, logic, problem solving, explore patterns, and relationships	categorizing, classifying, working with patterns, and relationships

FIGURE 1.3 SEVEN STYLES OF LEARNING (CONTINUED)			
Type	Likes To	Is Good At	Learns Best By
SPATIAL LEARNER "The Visualizer"	draw, build, design, and create things, daydream, look at pictures/slides, watch movies, and play with machines	imagining things, sensing changes, mazes/puzzles, reading maps and charts	visualizing, dreaming, using the mind's eye, and working with colors/pictures
MUSICAL LEARNER "The Music Lover"	sing, hum tunes, listen to music, play an instrument, and respond to music	picking up sounds, remembering melodies, noticing pitches/rhythms, and keeping time	rhythm, melody, and music
BODILY/KINESTHETIC LEARNER "The Mover"	move around, touch and talk, and use body language	physical activities (sports/dance/acting), and crafts	touching, moving, interacting with space, and processing knowledge through bodily sensations
INTERPERSONAL LEARNER "The Socializer"	have lots of friends, talk to people, and join groups	understanding people, leading others, organizing, communicating, manipulating, and mediating conflicts	sharing, comparing, relating, cooperating, and interviewing
INTRAPERSONAL LEARNER "The Individual"	work alone, and pursue own interests	understanding self, focusing inward on feelings/dreams, following instincts, and pursuing interests/goals	working alone, individualized projects, self-paced instruction, having own space, and being original

(*Source:* Faggella, K., & Horowitz, J., (1990). Different child, different style. *Instructor, 100* (2), 45–54.)

to a demonstration of learning based on their spatial abilities should have their growth measured by a "test" that incorporates spatial dimensions.

COMMUNITY AND CULTURE

To this point we have looked at students and their individuality. We have discussed some of the individual differences that you can expect of your students, in terms of their cognitive developmental levels, the prior knowledge and pre-existing skills each brings to the learning situation, their motivation, and native intellectual abilities. It's also important that you remember that students at all levels are members of groups, communities, and cultures.

As a society, Americans are possibly the most diverse people in the world today. Unlike the populations of other countries, which tend to be relatively homogeneous, Americans, and therefore their schools, are remarkably heterogeneous. The task for teachers is to identify and understand the differences that students possess that can be attributed to their belonging to any of a number of groups based on the culture in which they are nurtured or the community in which they live.

For our purposes here, **culture** can be defined as the features of a group, including the values, beliefs, and norms of behavior, that are inherent in membership in a particular group and which help to distinguish one group from another. On the other hand, a **community** consists of a group membership on the basis of some shared relationship. At times, the line between culture and community can become quite blurred. That is, people's cultures may create a sense of community, such as when recent foreign immigrants settle in areas of the country or a city where others of their culture have settled before. The ethnic neighborhoods—Irish, Jamaican, Slavic, and others—of large metropolitan areas like Chicago and Cleveland are good examples of culture leading to community. At other times, culture is created within communities through the shared efforts of the people who inhabit a particular geographic area. Certain types of folk art, and even rap music, develop through the shared experiences of people based primarily on their proximity, regardless of their ethnic or racial backgrounds.

When students enter school, they already possess attributes of their culture and they already belong to a number of communities, those within the confines of the schools and those that make up the larger world outside the walls of the school. Just as the individual differences that students bring with them will compel teachers to plan for student learning in different ways, so should an awareness of the differences based on students' memberships in different groups, based on culture and/or community, impact the decisions that teachers make. Though the differences are as diverse as the students within any school, we will be limiting our discussion over the next few pages to four groups—based on socioeconomic status (SES), ethnicity, language, and exceptionalities—to which students may well belong. Some of your students may belong to all of these groups; others to only one. Regardless, in order to facilitate students' construction of knowledge, you will need to be aware of the implications of the culture that students bring with them and their membership in school and out-of-school communities.

Socioeconomic Status (SES)

Economic conditions in this country are creating sharp distinctions between the economic haves and have-nots. The range of income between the richest and poorest families is greater now than it has ever been in our history. In addition, this range is also greater than that of any other populous, industrialized country in the world (Hout and Lucas, 1996). During the 1970s, the proportion of children who were poor fluctuated between 15 and 17 percent. But beginning in 1977, poverty rates for children began to rise, so that by 1993, nearly one-quarter (23 percent) of children were poor. More startling, perhaps, is that in 1996, 10 percent of White, non-Hispanic children lived below the poverty line, compared to 40 percent of African-American children and 40 percent of Hispanic children (National Center for Education Statistics 1998). Hodgkinson (1993) estimated that by the year 2000, 5 percent of the nation's poor will be school-aged children. Don't think that this is only an urban problem either. Nearly twice as many poor children live outside of urban areas as inside.

If these figures aren't sobering enough, consider the implications of these figures on the educational atmospheres into which you will be heading (see the Raphael task under "Community and Culture" in the *Teacher as Researcher* section). Overall, children from lower-SES families are more likely to be low achievers than those children from higher-SES families. Certain consequences are predictable. For example, the number one goal in the Goals 2000 initiative was that all children will start school ready to learn. Orlich (1993) believes this goal is unattainable in the near future because of social realities and federal and state fiscal policies. Among the disturbing consequences for poor children are disproportionate absentee and drop-out rates, homelessness, health problems, pregnancy, and suicide. Among the revisions needed in national and state policies, according to Orlich, are the following:

- Extended day care for children of parents who have incomes under the poverty level.
- Breakfast and lunch at school for children of poverty.
- Medical clinics to provide necessary child and adolescent health services.
- Housing policies that create units for poor and single-parent families.
- Class sizes of fourteen to seventeen students in elementary schools. (p. 26)

It is highly likely that you will teach in schools with students from poor families. Though it is difficult for individual teachers to effect a culture of poverty with its inherent low expectations and possible resistance to school culture, there is some positive news on this front. When researchers measured SES in terms of family income or parents' educational levels, the correlation between SES and achievement was relatively weak. However, when a broader definition of SES included parental attitudes toward education, parental aspirations for their children or intellectual activities of the family, then the correlation was stronger (Laosa, 1984). In practical terms, this would seem to indicate that working with

---

Activity 1.4

Teachers who learn about and use out-of-school experiences as a bridge to helping students learn school curricula have students who are more motivated, learn better, and feel more positive about themselves. Read "Learner Experience Strategies in Two Urban School Districts" by Williams and Woods. Identify the strategies used by Baltimore principals and teachers to surface the out-of-school experiences of urban learners. Then determine the extent to which these strengths were used in instructional and other school-related activities. Use or modify these strategies and develop a checklist for use in any classroom, regardless of setting, for recognizing students' out-of-school experiences, interests, talents, and skills that might be utilized later as bridges to connect with daily experiences. *Source:* Williams, B., & Woods, M., (1995). Learner experience strategies in two urban school districts. Philadelphia, PA: Research for Better Schools (ERIC Document Reproduction Services No. ED 390 968).

---

families and their children simultaneously, providing them with visions of a future available through education, could provide the children of poverty with tickets out of their situation, rather than their being condemned to repeat the cycle of poverty (see the Klesius and Griffin tasks under "Community and Culture" in the *Teacher as Researcher* section).

Ethnicity

Just as the economic conditions of students have been changing over the past couple decades, so has the ethnic make-up of this country also been in flux. In 1980, about one out of every five students belonged to a minority group. And, according to estimates from the Bureau of the Census (U.S. Department of Commerce 1997), by the year 2050 nearly two out of every five students will be non-Caucasian. Hispanics will equal all other minorities combined (see Figure 1.4). This ethnic diversity of America's children will mean that the students of the twenty-first century will bring cultures different from those of the majority of their teachers to the school setting. Projecting into the early part of the twenty-first century, many teaching jobs will open up in both urban and rural areas, which means that the teachers who fill these jobs will often deal with students and cultures very different from their own school experiences.

On a community level, parents, educators, and community leaders must sensitize students to the meaning of these demographic changes. Students and teachers alike must foster attitudes that tolerate differences and appreciate the unique contributions of diverse ethnic groups to American culture. As twenty-first century teachers, we hope that you will cultivate the attitude, in yourselves and your students, that all members of society are enriched by a mosaic of traditions and customs.

At the school and classroom level, teachers need knowledge of their students' ethnic backgrounds so they can represent subject matter using familiar topics. Teachers, especially the Caucasian majority, most of whom have been through very traditional K–12 schooling, must also recognize that textbooks, while improving in their efforts to recognize a more multi-cultural, less Euro-centric view of

FIGURE 1.4 POPULATION PROJECTIONS				

U.S. Population by Race and Projections to 2050
(in thousands and percent of totals of all races by year.

Date	White	Black	American Indian, Eskimo, Aleut	Asian and Pacific Islanders	Hispanic Origin
1980	194,713	26,683	1,420	3,729	14,609
	(.81)	(.11)	(.01)	(.02)	(.06)
2000	225,532	35,454	2,402	11,245	31,366
	(.74)	(.12)	(.01)	(.05)	(.10)
2020	254,887	45,075	3,129	19,651	52,652
	(.68)	(.12)	(.01)	(.05)	(.14)
2050	294,615	60,592	4,371	34,352	96,508
	(.60)	(.12)	(.01)	(.07)	(.20)

(*Source:* Adapted from Display No. 12. October, 1997 Resident population—selected characteristics, 1790 to 1996, and projections, 2000 to 2050. *Statistical Abstract of the United States 1997* (117th ed.) U.S. Department of Commerce, Bureau of the Census, 14. Mathematical calculations do not always equal an exact 100 percent.)

American history, do not always tell the whole story of the contributions of different cultures. Both students and teachers can engage in significant learning activities by investigating the "other stories" that naturally spring from school texts. Students who engage in research on their own people's contributions to American society will not only be more motivated but will likely develop skills and understandings that extend far beyond the scope of the assignment. In the process, you'll learn information that will expand your horizons, too.

Language

While not all members of ethnic groups use their native tongue as the primary language of the home, more than 14 million people in the United States live in homes where languages other than English are spoken. In some cities, especially in Southwestern and Western states, nearly 50 percent of the population speak languages other than English in the home. Estimates suggest that between 2 and 4 million limited English proficient (LEP) students attend U.S. schools, a number that is increasing rapidly. Among these language groups, the top one is Spanish, with nearly 73 percent of all LEP students in this country (Hopstock and Bucaro, 1993).

The implications of these figures are numerous. Obviously, American schools will need teachers who can interact with students who have limited English proficiency. Though desirable, it is not realistic to expect that all LEP students will have access to a teacher fluent in their native language. It is reasonable, however, to expect teachers to be flexible in their instructional approaches and assessment practices, while their LEP students grow in their abilities to interact in English. In elementary grades, for instance, allowing students who speak the same home language to pair up and speak in whispers could help them to clarify their ideas or confirm instructions, while providing them with a degree of comfort in a new and strange environment. In secondary schools, oral answers to test questions may provide a fairer assessment of students whose use of conventional prose has not yet caught up to their spoken English. A more complete list of approaches for LEP students is presented in chapter 4 under "Planning in Inclusionary Classrooms".

Teachers are also responsible for communicating with LEP parents and guardians, as well as their children. Like all concerned caregivers, LEP parents want the best educational experiences for their children. However, they may have difficulty initiating and interacting with teachers and other school personnel. Pamela A. Bare (1996), an educator in the San Diego Unified School District, contends that it is up to the school to initiate efforts at opening and maintaining lines of communication with LEP parents. She reports that her district uses multiple approaches to communication. A translation services unit translates school and district documents into various home languages, and elementary schools distribute monthly learning calendars in these primary tongues. The district also provides parent newsletters and training sessions in a variety of home languages. All of these services contribute to the perception of schools as places that welcome the languages their students bring while helping students learn English in a nurturing environment. You'll find websites about LEP students with information helpful to parents, students, and teachers in Figure 1.5.

Exceptionalities

In 1975, the U.S. Congress passed the Education of the Handicapped Act, which proclaimed the right of all children to have a free and appropriate education regardless of any disabilities they might have. A key provision of the act (commonly called PL 94–142) is the mandate for students with significant disabilities to be educated in the **least restrictive environment,** a school learning setting that is substantially the same for all students, including the disabled. In the mid–1970s, many of the most significantly disabled students had not had access to any public education, and many schools responded to the "least restrictive" clause by providing students with their own buildings or classrooms within buildings. This segregation of these students led to challenges by parents, who argued that segregation of students was, by its very nature, restrictive. These parents wanted more efforts on the part of schools to integrate their children into "normal" classrooms. When the courts agreed, schools responded by "mainstreaming" students with exceptionalities from a "special" classroom into certain classrooms with their peers.

Parents, however, again argued that "pulling out" students with disabilities from a special education classroom and sending them to a few selected classes throughout the day, often non-academic ones, was also restrictive. The courts again agreed, and in 1990 Congress passed the **Individuals with Disabilities Education Act (IDEA),** the successor bill to PL 94–142; the concept of **inclusion**

FIGURE 1.5 ON-LINE RESOURCES FOR INFORMATION ABOUT LEP STUDENTS FOR PARENTS, STUDENTS, AND TEACHERS	
Resource	Website
Bilingual Brochures for Parents	http://128.164.90.197/miscpubs/flame/index.htm
Bilingual Families Web Page	http://www.nethelp.no/cindy/biling-fam.html
Dave's ESL Cafe (activities for students)	http://www.pacificnet.net/~sperling/eslcafe.html
Lesson Plans and Resources for ESL, Bilingual, and Foreign Language Teachers	http://www.csun.edu/~hcedu013/eslindex.html
National Clearinghouse for Bilingual Education (NCBE)	http://www.ncbe.gwu.edu/
New York State Bilingual Network (NYSBEN)	http://cela.albany.edu/

replaced that of mainstreaming. In inclusion classrooms, the previous arrangement is reversed. Students begin their days in "regular" classrooms and are "pulled out" for special services only when the school can demonstrate that their efforts to meet the needs of these students have been unsuccessful. These efforts must involve accommodations for students' exceptionalities that often result from co-planning by "regular" and "special education" teachers and may even involve extensive in-class assistance from paid tutors or aides.

Who are these students who increasingly spend large parts of their days in general, heterogeneous classroom settings? Each year the U.S. Secretary of Education is required to submit to Congress a report on the progress being made in the implementation of IDEA. The Eighteenth Annual Report to Congress (U. S. Department of Education 1996) on the implementation of IDEA includes the following highlights:

- 5.4 million children and youths received special education services during the 1994–95 school year, an increase of 3.2 percent over the previous year.
- Learning Disabled (LD) students accounted for more than 50 percent of all students receiving services.
- Students with speech or language impairments, mental retardation, and serious emotional disturbances accounted for an additional 41 percent of all students ages six through twenty-one with disabilities.

- The percentage of African-American students enrolled in special education is generally high in relation to their representation in the general population.
- 95 percent of students with disabilities were served in regular school buildings, with students ages six through eleven most likely to be placed in regular classrooms, demonstrating a trend toward placing children in more inclusive settings.

Learn more by visiting the websites listed in Figure 1.6.

In the lexicon of education, school personnel tend to use three terms to communicate with each other regarding students who are significantly different with regard to mental, physical, or emotional functioning. School-aged children or adolescents who require special education services or some type of related services, such as physical therapy or counseling, are referred to as being **exceptional** (Bullock, 1992). The term **disabled** refers to the functional limitations placed upon a child due to a permanent physical or mental impairment. Finally, the term **handicapped** refers to an individual student's limitation in a specific situation. In some cases, a handicap may be caused by a disability. For instance, a child who cannot speak is handicapped by his disability in a speech class. The same child, though, is

FIGURE 1.6	ON-LINE RESOURCES FOR INFORMATION ABOUT STUDENTS WITH SPECIAL NEEDS AND DEVELOPMENTALLY-APPROPRIATE INSTRUCTION
Resource	Website
Council for Exceptional Children	http://www.cec.sped.org/index.html
Deaf World Web	http://dww.deafworldweb.org/
DO-IT (Disabilities, Opportunities, Internet working, and Technology)	http://www.washington.edu/doit/
Family Village: A Global Community of Disability-Related Resources	http://www.familyvillage.wisc.edu/index.htmlx
International Dyslexia Association	http://www.interdys.org
Scotter's Low Vision Land	http://www.community.net/~byndsght/welcome/
Special Education Resources from the Curry School of Education at the University of Georgia	http://curry.edschool.virginia.edu/go/cise/ose/resources/
Special Education Resources on the Internet (SERI)	http://www.hood.edu/seri/serihome.htm
The National Information Center for Children and Youth with Disabilities	http://www.nichcy.org/

not necessarily limited by his disability when solving math problems or playing basketball.

When you teach in inclusionary classrooms, it will be up to you to impress upon your students that exceptional students are more like them than unlike them. They have the same needs for acceptance, setting and achieving goals, and experiencing the world in their own unique ways. They will also be constructing meaning based on the learning opportunities that you provide them. The meanings they construct will naturally be different from their peers, and what we learn from their efforts and products adds something more to all of our educations.

Activity 1.5

Read a book for adults that portrays the life of a person with a disability (Franklin Delano Roosevelt, Helen Keller, etc.). Script one scene from that book and with others perform it for colleagues in a teacher education class. Further prepare yourself for teaching students in an inclusive setting by reading suggestions in the Fisher, Sax, and Pumpian article. *Source:* Fisher, D., Sax, C. & Pumpian, I. (1996). From intrusion to inclusion: Myths and realities in our schools. *The Reading Teacher, 49* (7), 580–584.

There are additional benefits, however. Working alongside students with disabilities and handicaps can provide "regular" students with opportunities to accept and value the diversity that these exceptional students bring. They also have the opportunity to come to respect and even admire the special abilities and adaptations that many of these students make on a daily basis. For the students with "exceptionalities," the benefits are equally important. One of the most significant is the opportunity to strengthen the social and communication skills that lead these students to integrate more readily into the post-school worlds of work and community.

SCHOOL AND HOME CONNECTIONS

To this point we have been looking at children and adolescents as possessors of native abilities and skills and as members of cultures and communities. We also need to consider them as members of families. As their first and most influential teachers, your students' families will be as varied as the students themselves. You must recognize that families can and should be your greatest ally in your efforts to help your students grow intellectually, socially, and morally. Because of these goals, we want to conclude the chapter by briefly considering the value of connecting with the home, the obstacles you are likely to face, and some guidelines to overcoming these obstacles.

The values attached to home-school ties was accented in 1994 when Congress passed the *Goals 2000—Educate America Act* (see chapter 2 for more discussion on this act and Figure 2.8 in chapter 2 for a listing of all the goals). One of the goals was that by the year 2000 every school will promote partnerships that increase parental involvement. Research findings confirm teachers' observations: when parents are engaged with their children's schoolwork and school activities, the children learn more effectively (U. S. Department of Education, 1987). What type of parental involvement matters most? Steinberg and his associates (1996) believe that common practices such as monitoring and checking homework and encouraging children may well stimulate achievement, especially in the elementary grades. You may be able to assist parents in this task by suggesting websites regarding homework to them. You might begin by using some of the resources named in Figure 1.7. On-line Resources for Tips on Homework, which may prove useful for students across grade levels. However, their research indicates that the involvement that makes the real difference is the type that draws the parent into the school physically—attending school programs, extracurricular activities, and teacher conferences. It may be that when parents take the time to attend a school function, they send a strong message about how important school is to them and, by extension, how important it should be to students. It is not only the child who wins when parents are involved; families benefit, too. When parents or guardians participate in parent-involvement programs, parents' self-images improve, their respect for teachers increases, and their confidence in their ability to help their children with school tasks is enhanced (Burns, 1993). Finally, there are advantages for teachers and schools, as well. One important advantage is that teachers who communicate with families are perceived as better teachers by parents and guardians. These teachers open lines of communication in which they learn valuable information about the child's individual needs and talents, in addition to sharing information that enables these children's families to assist and monitor aspects of their educational program.

Given all of these benefits—for children, families, and schools—then, why don't all parents want to connect with the school, and why don't all teachers open these lines of communication? A number of obstacles to promoting more family involvement exist. From the parents' or guardians' point of view, time and money are often cited as reasons that limit their involvement in their children's schooling. Parents who have to work hard to provide shelter, food, and clothing don't have the time or energy to assist with homework, let alone volunteer for school activi-

FIGURE 1.7 ON-LINE RESOURCES FOR TIPS ON HOMEWORK	
Resource	Website
B. J. Pinchbeck's Homework Helper	http://www.bjpinchbeck.com
Dr. Ah-Clem's Webpages for Students	http://members.tripod.com/%7EDoctorAhClem/writingskills.html
Helping Your Child with Homework	http://www.kidsource.com/kidsource/content/homework.html
Homework Central	http://homeworkcentral.com
Study Web	http://www.studyweb.com
The Kids on the Web: Homework Tools	http://www.zen.org/~brendan/kids-homework.html

ties. Attending conferences during the school day also may be impossible. Parents at the poverty level, those with low-wage jobs or none at all, may be hard-pressed or unable to attend to their children's school-related needs. LEP parents and recent immigrants who do not speak English well or who are unfamiliar with school routines may not respond to teachers' invitations to parent-teacher conferences. In addition, many parents, especially those in lower-SES households, carry their own negative associations with school from their own feelings of inadequacy in school to perceptions of incompetence in dealing with "new" approaches to learning (Potter, 1989).

Not all factors that inhibit parental-school involvement, however, can be laid in the laps of the family. Teachers often do not take the initiative in establishing contacts with the home for many reasons. Some feel that their sense of autonomy will be threatened by parents who are "butting in" to their classroom. Others feel a sense of powerlessness in being able to meet the demands and needs of family problems or strife (Potter, 1989). By choosing not to communicate, these teachers protect themselves from being overwhelmed by situations that they feel they cannot impact. In other cases, some schools unintentionally present an unfriendly or contemptuous atmosphere, created by administration, staff, and faculty, in which parents feel unwelcomed.

Building bonds of trust and communication is difficult, often demanding work; it is also time-consuming. The benefits already cited, though, should encourage you that the time invested in establishing positive, supportive relationships with the home is as important as the time you spend planning lessons and

Teachers take the initiative to build bridges of trust

evaluating student progress (see the "Home and School Connections" tasks in the *Teacher as Researcher* section). As the professional, your reaching out to the families of your students will pay off for all concerned. When you consider how to reach out, though, you must resist approaching all families in the same way. What is often needed is a variety of methods and a repertoire of strategies. Many of these you will learn from colleagues, but for purposes of this discussion we have identified several principles that may guide you in communicating with families:

- Contacts with homes should be non-threatening and respectful.
- Contact the home early in the year to introduce yourself and establish a positive atmosphere.
- Listen to parents and ask questions.
- When calling about a discipline or academic problem, be descriptive (e.g., "Johnny threw paint on seven children this morning.") rather than evaluative (e.g., "Your Johnny is really a rotten kid. Do you know what he did this morning?")
- Communicate effectively, using plain language and avoiding educational jargon.
- Use a variety of contact methods. Some parents will get all they need from a weekly or monthly newsletter, while others may need conferences, phone calls, or notes.
- Provide family involvement ideas and activities.

Activity 1.6

Parent involvement correlates with student achievement. However, conventional parent programs (e.g., newsletters, back-to-school nights) are not always successful with poor and minority families who may have problems with transportation, child care for siblings, feelings of inadequacy because of their own academic shortcomings, difficulties with English, and unavailability during school hours because of work schedules. Drawing on your own creativity and problem-solving abilities, describe a parent-school involvement program that deals with one or more of these problems. Construct a time table for planning, implementing, and evaluating the program in a school neighborhood you first describe.

SUMMARY

In her conversation at the beginning of the chapter, Linda Reyes identified some of the challenges she faced with her first group of students. This chapter has highlighted different challenges to our ingenuity that stem from the multitude of learner characteristics we witness in field experiences, student teaching, and contract teaching. The point that we want to reemphasize is that your teaching practice begins with the consideration of the students whom you will be teaching. Though we talk about students in general terms here, each one of your students will be a unique individual who brings with him or her a variety of talents and skills, knowledge and gaps, feelings and attitudes. All students also bring with them families and communities that have shaped and formed them into the people you will be teaching. Your first task upon entering a classroom is to find out who these people are and what they bring to the teaching-learning transaction. Even before you enter the class, you can plan for and anticipate implications for teaching and learning regarding the general student population with whom you will work. As you study the next chapter, you will identify another set of challenging questions. These center on *what* to teach students. The answers you will consider are almost as involved as the students themselves. But the challenge you will lay out for yourself is to identify curricular content that is appropriate for the students you will come to know. These decisions will be some of the most exciting and important ones you will make, and every one will stem from the knowledge you have gained about the students you are teaching.

REFLECTIONS

After reading each chapter, you will have an opportunity to consider questions upon which to reflect. These provide you another way of trying to construct your own understandings based upon the new information you have just absorbed. In some cases, your instructor may ask you to respond in writing or orally to some of these questions.

1. Linda Reyes (from chapter 1 "Conversation") has decided to give pieces of candy to students who improve their time scores on multiplication tables. Some of her colleagues are critical of this practice, saying it teaches negative lessons about learning. Do you agree or disagree? Draw on what you know about motivation to substantiate your opinion.

2. Concerned about the fourth graders in her class who are below grade-level in reading abilities, Linda consults with Mrs. Karim, her mentoring teacher, about ways to involve students' families in strengthening their reading and understanding abilities. Given what you know about the correlation between socioeconomic status and school achievement, what concrete suggestions might you expect from Mrs. Karim? These suggestions are really "alternatives" for Linda to explore (the E in the IDEAL decision-making model). Test out each of the suggestions/alternatives against the problem Linda has identified. Which ones test-out most favorably?

3. At the middle school in Linda's district, about 25 percent of the students come from homes where the primary language is not English. Thus, they are limited in their ability to read, write, speak, and listen effectively in English . Knowing that the last sentence is a statement of a challenge (that is, Identifying the Challenge in the IDEAL model), further define the challenge. Define, or expand, on the consequences of this challenge as middle school learners move through a typical school day.

4. A first year high school teacher, a friend from college days, and Linda Reyes have phone conversations in which they compare their induction year experiences. A topic of one conversation was parent-school communication. Although they teach at different levels, Linda and her friend have both observed that genuine, two-way communication between school and parents is difficult to develop. Given the latter as a statement of a challenge (identify the challenge), define the challenge by naming common causes and results of the challenge for students, parents, and teachers. Which of the causes and results have your personally observed?

TEACHER AS RESEARCHER

Social Construction of Knowledge

Dillow, K., Flack, M., & Peterman, F. (1994). Cooperative learning and the achievement of female students. *Middle School Journal, 26* (2), 48–51.

The authors note that a number of females entering early adolescence repress what they know and lose their voice in class discussions. Recognizing the learning power that comes through interaction with others, they pose a research question: "Do female students benefit from and achieve at higher levels under certain cooperative learning conditions?" They also provide a rationale for why the research question is an important one. Paraphrase that rationale.

Duis, M. (1996). Using schema theory to teach American history. *Social Education, 60,* 144–146.

Helping students remember and organize what they know before learning new information about a topic is a sound educational practice. But what should teachers do when students have little or no prior experience in which to anchor new content? Duis relates his experience with helping students create appropriate schema for subsequent study of the Construction Period after the U.S. Civil War through group interaction. Summarize Duis' report by (1) repeating the learning/teaching challenge he saw, (2) the "interventions" (learning activities) he used, especially those that engaged students in group work, and (3) the possible results of constructing schema through group effort.

Motivation

Garibaldi, A. M. (1992). Educating and motivating African-American males to succeed. *The Journal of Negro Education, 61* (1), 4–11.

Garibaldi chaired a task force that studied the status of African American males in the New Orleans Public School System. The students' aspirations, a facet of motivation, were compared to the perceptions of their teachers and parents. Reflect on the findings and then consider the fifty recommendations from the task force. In your view, which recommendations address most directly the students' motivation to succeed academically?

Newman, R. S. (1990). Children's help-seeking in the classroom: The role of motivation factors and attributions. *Journal of Educational Psychology, 82,* 71–80.

Opposite the student who has learned the habit of helplessness is the one who actively seeks out help when help is needed. Newman investigated third-, fifth-, and seventh-grade learners who were inclined to seek help. His report describes the methodology of his project in extensive detail. Skim it and then read carefully the "discussion" section. What are the factors of motivation that differentiate help seekers at third and fifth grade versus seventh grade?

Multiple Intelligences

Hoerr, T. R. (1997). Frog ballets and musical fractions. *Educational Leadership, 55,* (1), 43–46.

In grades preschool through sixth, educators at New City School in St. Louis, Missouri, capitalize on multiple intelligences (MI) throughout the curriculum. Use this article as a guided tour of how MI influence curriculum development, student assessment, and faculty collegiality at New City School. As you take the tour, what questions come to mind about helping students learn, documenting student progress, and teachers learning from other teachers?

Glasgow, J. N. & Bush, M. (1996). Students use their multiple intelligences to develop pro-
motional magazines for local businesses. *Journal of Adolescent and Adult Literacy, 39*
(8), 638–649.

Students in Margie Bush's senior English classes in Lima, Ohio, designed and wrote pro-
motional magazines as a way of relating course content and the world of work. In the
process, individual students used their unique strengths in the various intelligences to
learn about marketing services and products. At the conclusion of the project, students
responded to an informal survey regarding their preference for this type of project versus a
traditional research paper. Based on their responses, write a research hypothesis (a statement of expected results) for a formal study of these types of learning activities.

Community and Culture

Raphael, J. (1996). New beginnings for new middle school students. *Educational Leadership,
54* (1), 56–59.

Students at two Tucson, Arizona, elementary schools differ dramatically in wealth and ethnicity. In seventh grade, they meet in the same middle school where their diversities are the
source of potential conflict. School leaders organized a joint curricular project involving the
arts and writing for sixth graders at both schools as a transition to middle school. As you
study the article, (1) identify the purposes of the project and (2) thinking like a researcher,
list three to four types of evidence you'd accept as proof of accomplishing the purposes.

Klesius, J. R. & Griffith, P. L. (1996). Interactive storybook reading for at-risk learners. *The
Reading Teacher, 49* (7), 552–560.

When a culture values literacy, homes transmit that value to their children, and the literacy
of the home, in turn, influences the acquisition of school literacy. The authors describe
"lapreading" as a school activity meant to imitate a common practice in homes where literacy learning is fostered. As serious investigators, the authors did "background reading" on
their subject and built on the findings from previous research. Paraphrase at least three
findings from Klesius and Griffith's background reading.

Home and School Connections

Brand, S. 1996. Making parent involvement a reality: Helping teachers develop partnerships with parents. *Young Children, 51* (2), 76–81.

PITCH (Project Interconnecting Teachers, Children, and Homes) for Literacy is a parent
involvement program that offered a series of workshops to elementary and preschool
teachers and administrators in order to improve home-school relationships. As you read
about PITCH, make a list of four questions about the program's effects on families and
teachers for which you personally would like answers.

Epstein, J. L. 1996. Improving school-family-community partnerships in the middle grades.
Middle School Journal, 28 (2), 43–48.

Assume you have the task of working with other teachers on a committee in your middle
school to strengthen the school's school-family-community partnership program. The committee has asked you to develop a criteria sheet for evaluating the school's present program. Using Epstein's six types of involvement, write general criteria against which to
evaluate the comprehensiveness of any middle school partnership program.

CHAPTER **2**
Analyzing Curriculum

CONVERSATION

The room was his. Leonard Tan took in the whole room in sweeping looks. Floors newly waxed. Bulletin boards bare. Books and supplies in boxes with red marker writing that indicated what was inside: manipulatives, reading corner, science experiments. This is where he wanted to be—where he had been preparing for during the LAST four years. He had just been hired, only four days before the start of school. It had been a long and sometimes frustrating summer, but at least he was here. His own classroom. He took a moment just to scan the room again. Now, it's time to get going, he thought, as he started to unpack.

* * * * * * *

His methods classes had prepared Leonard well for setting up his room. He had done charts and designs of classroom settings and had jotted down notes— what worked and what didn't—from the classes he had visited during his field experiences and student teaching. This was the easy part, he thought, as he glanced at the curriculum guides on his desk. What he didn't know how to do was to set up a year's worth of learning experiences for his students. Sure, he had planned units and delivered lessons in his field work and student teaching, but he had always had someone there to guide him. His cooperating teachers had always known where he was going. He was so busy keeping up with the day-to-day work that he had never thought to ask them *how* they knew. He knew that the curriculum guides would help, and they certainly gave him some information about the kinds of things third graders should know and do. But it didn't give him much of an idea about how he should go about this. What should come first? What LAST? Is there a "magical" sequence? How would he know?

"Hi, Leonard, how's it coming?" Becky Tilles, lead teacher for the third grade, asked as she looked around the room. "The room is looking great."

"Becky, am I glad to see you. I'm getting a little nervous here. The room was the easy part. What do I do with this curriculum guide? The school that I did my student teaching had a much more specific program outlined for teachers there. I thought this guide would be the same way, would tell me more about what I needed to teach and when, but it just gives some objectives that students are expected to work on because they are on next year's proficiency tests. How is that going to help me this year? What kind of things do I do with third graders? You know, I never actually taught third graders in either my field work or student teaching. I did kindergarten, first, fifth, and sixth. I know I need to get to know my kids, and I'm planning on looking at their student folders in the office. But, what do I do then?"

Becky smiled and sat down next to Leonard. "It is pretty overwhelming, isn't it? I think I felt the same way when I came out and got my first classroom. You might be surprised. You probably know a lot more about working with third graders than you think. If you know first grade, then you know what kinds of skills they need and that you helped them develop there. And if you know fifth grade, you know where they will need to go. Well, third graders are in that gap between first and fifth." Becky paused for a minute and laughed. "That probably sounds overly simplistic, huh? It sounds to me like what you probably need is a way to plan. I use a pretty simple way that I learned in my master's work. It's a seven-step process that I've used at each of the five different grade levels I've taught. Why don't you come down to my room and I'll show you?"

DEVELOPING COMPETENCE

1. At this stage in your preservice teaching career, imagine that you could get a teaching job in your desired field at your desired grade level. State what you currently believe students should learn and explain why. What sources inform you that these learning experiences are appropriate for these students at this level?

2. When you hear the terms "Back to Basics" and "Progressive Education" what comes to your mind? After you read the chapter, cite the differences between perennialism, essentialism, and progressivism in terms of how each views the roles of teachers and students.

3. Before reading, identify the purpose(s) that schools serve in today's society. After reading, analyze whether your purpose(s) are more functional or critical?

4. Identify the "lenses" on curriculum, describe the purpose that each lens serves, and explain what kinds of information each provides for a curriculum developer.

5. If you were given a teaching job today, describe how would you go about deciding what students should know and do. After reading the chapter, analyze how using the steps in Hilda Taba's curriculum development model might change how you would decide about what students should know and do.

INTRODUCTION

In the previous chapter, you read about students, identifying the "who" of teaching. This chapter begins to deal with identifying curricular challenges. Curriculum has been defined in many ways. In its narrowest sense it may be defined solely as the content that is taught in a particular subject area. As such, the curriculum for first grade arithmetic may be identified in terms of the particular skills and concepts students learn at that particular level, such as adding and subtracting single digit numbers. In its broadest sense, however, it may be defined in terms of all of the experiences with which students come in contact in the course of their school days and careers. These experiences include both the **manifest curriculum,** sometimes referred to as the **official curriculum**—that is, the knowledge and skills that students are to learn as a result of instruction—and the **hidden curriculum**—that is, the learning that students do as a result of the structure and rules imposed upon them by going to school. We will take up these topics in greater detail within the chapter.

It may be helpful to think of curriculum as the "how," "what," and "why" of teaching. The "how" of teaching takes up the majority of the rest of this book. We begin this chapter by looking briefly at the "why" of teaching; that is, why do teachers and school districts make the choices that they do? Throughout the remainder of the chapter, we will concentrate on the "what" of curriculum planning by making you aware of some of the historical precedents for the types of learning you have experienced as students and the manner in which these precedents may shape the types of learning in which your own students will engage. We finish the chapter by presenting you with a curriculum planning model that you will be able to use as you make your own decisions in planning instruction. Because there are so many possible choices that you could make as you consider the content of your curriculum, it is important that you clearly *identify* what you will teach to your students and reflect on the reasons for your choices.

THE BIG QUESTIONS

Before you can consider how the curriculum should look, it may be helpful to think about some "Big Questions"; the answers to these questions will influence what you teach and how you teach. Consider the following:

- What is knowledge?
- Who decides 'What is knowledge'?
- What is education?
- What is the purpose of schooling?
- How should teaching and learning be conducted?

These are fundamental questions that teachers answer implicitly every day by the nature of how they go about their work. In the course of the thousands of decisions they make on a daily basis, however, many teachers do not necessarily consider their explicit answers to these questions. But answering these questions is important as one considers the "why" aspect of the curriculum. And there are many "why" questions to ask. In fact, in your own schooling experience, you've probably asked the most fundamental of these questions: "Why do we have to know (or do or study or memorize) this?" Your own students will probably ask that same question of you. And you could certainly fall back on the old, argument-ending: "Because I'm your teacher, and I say you do." Or you could ask yourself that same question *before* you actually present information, materials, or activities in class. Why *do* my students need to know this?

The questions that follow represent just a few of the controversies that have been significant in molding the curricula that you experienced in your own K-12 schooling. Regardless of the way in which you or others might answer these questions, there will be someone waiting at the other end of that comment to ask "Why?" Consider:

- What *should* all five-year-olds or ten-year-olds or seventeen-year-olds know?
- Should schools be designed to train students for work or for college?
- Should all children be exposed to the same curriculum or should they be tracked according to their interests or skills or some other factor?
- Why do most high schools offer numerous classes in British and American literature, but few offer Latin American, Asian or African literature separate from a world literature course?
- Who decides what events we read about in history textbooks, and how do they make those decisions?

Let's take a look at the LAST question as an example. Arguably, one of the most significant curricular decisions that school districts make is choosing a textbook. And depending on who responds to this question, there are a number of possible answers. Those answers reflect economic realities and political agendas in our society. They also reflect concerns about infusing national and regional pride in students, as well as social agendas that are designed to provide students with a common historical perspective.

Attempting to answer that question, James Loewen (1995), for instance, places the blame for history textbooks squarely on the heads of publishers. For Loewen, it is an economic issue that drives many of the "why" issues. Noting that history is the most despised course for most high schoolers, he contends that it is because publishers cram their books too full of facts. Why? For several reasons. Among them are: the desire to make all new history texts clones of previous ones; the unwillingness to look at controversy lest they offend someone; and the glossing over of less-than-exemplary behavior on the parts of groups or individuals who were important. Loewen argues that history should be the most interesting of all courses because it's filled with great stories and controversies, but that textbook publishers sanitize the stories to the point where students find nothing interesting in them. They do this because offending a state or region could cost them millions of dollars.

Take those same history textbooks that Loewen talks about, and you have read, and be aware that there are other voices that would join the controversy. A traditionalist, for example, will explain how important it is that all students should be able to share a common historical heritage. That to be well-informed citizens, students must know how the country was built and important events in the struggle to be the great nation we are today. A Marxist, on the other hand, will look at the same textbook and tell you that it is the rich who decide what events should be in texts because they want to tell the stories that justify capitalism and private property. Why? Because it is important that students buy into these principles so that businessmen can sell them shoes and designer clothes and expensive automobiles.

As you go out to take your first teaching job, somebody will have already answered many of these big questions for you. You will not necessarily see or talk with this person. In fact, it is unlikely that it is any one person who has provided the answers. These answers, however, affect what you will be teaching and what your students will be learning. Just because someone else has answered these questions in implicit or explicit ways does not let you off the hook, though. You still need to think about them and about how your answers to them will inform you in what you will be teaching and how you will go about doing this.

In the remainder of this chapter, we will be looking at how these questions have been answered in the past and by whom. At this stage, it is important that you are aware that there is no "right" answer, that each generation answers these questions in a different manner, and that within each generation the answers are seldom easily agreed upon without controversy. You may not even be aware that you have already participated in this controversy. The courses that you took in high school and the material that you studied there grew out of previous generations' efforts to answer these questions.

Activity 2.1

Start by brainstorming some of the "why" questions about your own schooling that come to mind after reading the previous section. Then, take one or more of the "Big Questions" and think about how you would answer them based on your own "why" questions. That is, how do you believe the people who planned the curriculum in the elementary and secondary school(s) you attended answered these questions. What evidence would you point to that would indicate that what you *say* is true, is indeed true? Present your findings and speculations to your peers.

PHILOSOPHIES OF EDUCATION—ATTEMPTS AT ANSWERING THE "BIG QUESTIONS"

What is knowledge? Who decides what we should know? How should we go about teaching and learning important information and skills? These are questions that lie at the heart of schooling. In preliterate societies, however, these were almost non-questions. Knowledge was comprised of the information and skills that one's family, village, or larger society needed to continue to survive and thrive. The body of knowledge would have included the legends, myths, and cultural traditions that bonded people to each other and distinguished one's culture. The skills one might learn would have depended greatly on this culture. That is, a child growing up in a farming culture would have required a different set of skills than a child in a warrior culture. Regardless of the culture into which children were born, their main teachers would have been their parents and the other adults around them. These people would have passed down the body of cultural wisdom and required skills through didactic teaching, demonstration, and practice under the guidance of an expert.

With the rise of civilization, and especially with the explosion of information with which all of us are faced today, the questions of "What is knowledge?" and "Who decides?" are important for us to consider as we look at what type of a curriculum we want to teach. These are fundamental questions that have been food for thought of philosophers throughout the ages. Some of the greatest minds of all time, from Plato to Rousseau to Dewey and others, have attempted to answer these questions and educators have used their answers to inform others of ideal educational aims and curricula. For our purposes here, we want you to be aware of some major theories as they have been applied to education. Three of these major theories are Perennialism, Essentialism, and Progressivism. Proponents of each theory have particular views of knowledge and point to authorities whom they believe have determined what is important knowledge to be learned in schools. Each of these theories has its advocates and critics in contemporary society. And each has had some influence on the instruction that you have received and the kind that you may deliver when you are in charge of your own classroom. And each in its own way, either implicitly or explicitly, is responding, in the very least, to the "what" and "why" of curriculum. Being aware of all three theories will provide you with a foundation to identify what you consider important for your students to study.

Perennialism—Classical Traditions, Great Books, and the Paideia Proposal

Perennial means "continually recurring," and this particular manner of viewing education has continually recurred since the rise of formal schooling, from the Middle Ages to the twentieth century. **Perennialists** look back to the classics and their study as containing some of the shining moments, thoughts, and ideas produced by mankind. The modern university system itself was built on the study of Classical Latin and Greek. Those who favored this approach to education believed that the mental discipline required to study these languages, and to use them to study the great works of philosophy and literature that were written in them, constituted a meaningful learning experience. After all, in the perennialists' way of thinking, if students could apply themselves in the diligent manner required to learn these languages and read these works, they would have gained the benefits of touching the minds of some of the greatest philosophers and writers of all time. To prepare students for the education being offered through the standard curriculum of higher education at the time, Latin grammar schools were chartered in many cities, especially along the East Coast. These preparatory schools would engage students in developing the habits of mind and providing experiences with great works that would enable them to gain a higher education. Their college work would enable these students to deal with the world in thoughtful, moral, and ethical ways.

In theory, these habits of mind and the focus on classical learning informed the educational system of America as it grew in early nationhood. In reality, though, the Latin grammar schools and other early efforts at formal education in America, including English grammar schools and district schools, were decidedly uneven in terms of their delivery of anything that approached a standard curriculum. In fact, throughout much of the nineteenth century there was a great deal of tension between the colleges and the schools that fed them. On the one hand, colleges needed to maintain enrollment to survive; on the other hand, this meant accepting students whom the professors claimed were not prepared for college work. Does

Perennialists believe students should study the classics in order to touch the minds of the greatest writers and philosophers of all time

this sound familiar? Even the most prestigious of our universities, Harvard, in 1894, had to open what amounted to the first remedial writing center in the nation because of the lack of skills that professors were seeing in their entering freshmen (Berlin, 1987).

In response to these concerns, in the latter part of the nineteenth century, Charles Eliot, president of Harvard University, was chosen to lead a group of scholars, called the Committee of Ten, who were looking into finding ways to improve the quality of education in American secondary schools, while providing students with a standard curriculum that would prepare them to succeed in college. This group believed in the perennialist view and looked back to the classics as the best way to prepare students for higher learning, which was still very much an education that relied on the study of works in Latin and Greek. Though relatively few students at the time even went on to college, this college preparatory curriculum has continued greatly to influence curriculum into today, especially in terms of the courses that students take in high school, which in turn influence their education at junior high and elementary school levels.

More recently, those who hold the perennialist view have looked at programs like those advocated by the Great Books Foundation, as well as *The Paideia Proposal* (Adler, 1982), as reflective of their goals for education. Mortimer Adler is the man most closely associated with both of these programs. In the former, developers organized the curriculum according to the Great Books of civilization. In the perennialist view, a great book is one that has stood the test of time. Spanning works of philosophy, social science, literature, and psychology, these books are considered the best that human beings have written, and advocates of Great Books curricula believe that these books are accessible to almost everyone. Reading and discussing these works help students to develop common standards of good taste and moral judgment (see Figure 2.1). Because advocates recognize that many of these works are difficult for younger children and even for many high school students, the Great Books Foundation was founded to promote a curriculum built on shared inquiry and has trained thousands of facilitators over the years. Currently their Junior Great Books program for K–12 students is used in hundreds of school districts, though often this is an elective program. Critics have complained that Great Books advocates, like Adler (Newman, 1998) and Allan Bloom (Casement, 1987), are elitists, favoring mostly white, mostly male, and mostly European writers in their recommended works to the exclusion of other cultures and women. The Great Books Foundation disputes this and has made great strides, especially in the past decade, to avoid such criticisms; a look at the list of works in a sample Junior Great Books reading list (see Figure 2.2) demonstrates that claims of bias are unfounded in their elementary series. These claims may have more foundation at the secondary level (see Figure 2.3).

Adler's (1982) Paideia Proposal was built on the same philosophical underpinnings as the Great Books. Rather than specify a set curriculum of books, however, Adler and his Paideia Group specify a set curriculum for everyone. In the proposal, the group offers specified courses that do not allow for tracking and with virtually no electives throughout twelve years of schooling. They also organize the curriculum into three modes of teaching and learning: acquisition of knowledge, development

---

FIGURE 2.1 PART OF EXPLANATION OF INCLUSION OF WORKS ON JUNIOR GREAT BOOKS READING LIST

Choosing the Great Books Selections
Excerpt from the Junior Great Books Web Page

Every piece of literature requires interpretation to some degree, but not all works lend themselves to extended interpretive analysis. The fact that a work is a "classic" is no guarantee that it can support shared inquiry discussion. It may be beautiful and uplifting—something that every young person should have the opportunity to experience—but if its meaning and intention are transparent to the individual reader, it cannot reward the sustained intellectual work of shared inquiry. For example, not all of Rudyard Kipling's stories in *The Jungle Books* are suited to shared inquiry. Our selections ("Mowgli's Brothers," "Tiger-Tiger!" "Letting in the Jungle," and "The Spring Running") do support interpretive discussion, but the perennial favorite, "Rikki-Tikki-Tavi," does not—despite the fact that all these memorable tales touch upon many of the same themes.

"Rikki-Tikki-Tavi," which tells how a brave young mongoose protects a human household from two menacing cobras, is an inspiring tale of animal heroism and a clear model of devotion and courage. It is a suspenseful, compelling, and satisfying story in which evil is defeated and Rikki's resourcefulness and courage are rewarded. But the motives of the characters are clear; the story's outcome raises no particular questions or problems of understanding in the reader's mind. There is nothing paradoxical or curious about the story that invites further reflection or demands explanation. There are no "whys" to explore.

The Mowgli stories, however, are problematic. Here we are led more deeply into themes of belonging and isolation, and uncertainty about finding one's proper place. The Junior Great Books selections tell how the boy Mowgli grows up a member of the Seeonee wolf pack, only to be cast out by his "brothers" as he approaches adulthood. As we read these stories we wonder why Mowgli ends up belonging neither to the wolf pack nor to the man pack. Because it is not clear why Mowgli must be cast out, both by the wolves whom he loved and by the people of the village (presumably his proper home), the stories present interpretive questions that can be addressed in shared inquiry discussion. By focusing on such questions, students are able to go beyond reading the Mowgli stories merely as adventure. They are able to appreciate Kipling's subtle portrayal of profound human forces and concerns, and to understand and gain insight from the character of Mowgli, who grows up noble and strong despite being isolated from his own kind.

(*Source:* Great Books Foundation Website: www.greatbooks.org. Used with the permission of the Great Books Foundation, Copyright 1999.)

FIGURE 2.2   JUNIOR GREAT BOOKS READING LIST FOR ELEMENTARY SCHOOL

Elementary Reading List (Series 5–1st semester)

CHARLES by Shirley Jackson

GHOST CAT by Donna Hill

TURQUOISE HORSE by Gerald Hausman

MAURICE's ROOM by Paula Fox

BARBIE by Gary Soto

LENNY's RED-LETTER DAY by Bernard Ashley

THE PRINCE AND THE GOOSE GIRL by Elinor Mordaunt

TRAMP by Malcolm Carrick

ALBERIC THE WISE by Norton Juster

PODHU AND ARUWA—African folktale as told by Humphrey Harman

THE INVISIBLE CHILD by Tove Jansson

THE BAT-POET by Randall Jarrell

(*Source:* Great Books Foundation Website: www.greatbooks.org. Used with permission of the Great Books Foundation, Copyright 1999.)

of skills, and enlargement of understanding. Using direct instruction and didactic learning, teachers help students *acquire knowledge* in three areas: literature and the fine arts; mathematics and the natural sciences; and history, geography, and the social sciences. While students are building a body of knowledge in these three areas, they also *develop skills,* such as reading, writing, speaking, measuring, etc.; meanwhile teachers act as coaches as students learn to do something with the knowledge they have acquired. Finally, at the very foundation of the perennialist movement, students are encouraged to *enlarge understanding* of themselves and the world. In this mode, teachers utilize the Socratic method of questioning and discussing in order that students may arrive at deeper understandings of books and the arts to which they are introduced. In these seminars, ideas and values are emphasized and held up to scrutiny by both teachers and students alike.

Perennialists have a clear vision of what schools should be. They mold their curricula around carefully defined sets of learning experiences and materials that treat all students as capable of learning from the greatest works that civilization has to offer. These common experiences will enable students, regardless of their socioeconomic status, gender, or race, to participate on an equal basis in society. Familiarity with this "culture" enables all students to develop accepted standards of truth and virtue.

FIGURE 2.3   INTRODUCTION TO GREAT BOOKS READING LIST FOR HIGH SCHOOL

High School Reading List (Series 1)

WHY WAR? by Sigmund Freud

THE MELIAN DIALOGUE by Thucydides

THE SOCIAL ME by William James

ROTHSCHILD's FIDDLE by Anton Chekhov

CONCERNING THE DIVISION OF LABOR by Adam Smith

CHELKASH by Maxim Gorky

HOW AN ARISTOCRACY MAY BE CREATED BY INDUSTRY by Alexis de Tocqueville

OBSERVATION AND EXPERIMENT by Claude Bernard

EVERYTHING THAT RISES MUST CONVERGE by Flannery O'Connor

AN ESSAY IN AESTHETICAS by Roger Fry

AN OUTPOST OF PROGRESS by Joseph Conrad

ON STUDYING by José Ortega y Gasset

(*Source:* Great Books Foundation Website: www.greatbooks.org. Used with permission of the Great Books Foundation, Copyright 1999.)

Activity 2.2

Form a small group and choose one of the works identified on the Series 5 reading list (Figure 2.2). Read it one time through just for the story aspect. On a second reading, jot down questions you have about the story, the characters, their motivation, etc. Write as many questions as you can. The only requirement is that these questions must be ones that you are not sure how to answer. You may have speculations, possible answers, or theories, but you can honestly say that you do not *know* the answer. Now come back together as a group and begin to ask each other your questions. Referring to the text of the story, attempt to develop a response to each of these questions. Report your experience back to the class with engaging in this Perennialist-inspired "shared inquiry."

Essentialism—The "Back to Basics" Movement

Like the perennialists, those who favor **essentialism** in schools believe that a main purpose of schooling should be to transmit a cultural heritage from one generation to the next. This is done by providing students with knowledgeable teachers who can provide students with instruction in subject matter disciplines. Essentialists, though, distance themselves from perennialists when it comes to the content that should be covered. While perennialists often look to classics in literature

Many Essentialists believe teachers should fill students' heads with the knowledge and information essential for their success

and philosophy as the foundation for their curriculum, essentialists are more likely to be practical, even pragmatic at times. They recognize there are a number of skills and subject areas that are "essential" to students' developing their talents to participate in American society today. Advocates of essentialism in the schools favor instruction in the sciences, history, and the "Three R's" but also recognize the importance of course work in computer science and vocational education. They tend to endorse standardized testing as a way of assuring that students are attaining a level of competence with the information they are supposed to learn. They believe there are "basic" skills all students must possess; they also believe these skills can be tested and their achievement quantified in some manner. Many essentialists favor the "empty vessel" metaphor for education; that is, students come to school as empty buckets, so to speak, and it is the teacher's job to fill these buckets with knowledge. The teacher, in this view, is placed back into a position of authority, responsible for teaching the basic skills and common knowledge that will ensure a literate and well-informed, responsible citizen. One advocate of this philosophy, E. D. Hirsch, has proposed a large, explicit, and integrated body of knowledge that he believes today's students should possess in order to meet this goal of responsible citizenship. Hirsch (1996) takes on both "traditional" and progressive educators as he touts the virtues and successes of schools who have built their curricula upon his core knowledge principles (see the Stringfield et al., website under "Essentialism" in the *Teacher as Researcher* section). In arguing for the need in our schools for children to possess shared knowledge and intellectual "capital" (Figure 2.4), he asserts that those who "possess intellectual capital when they first arrive at school have the mental scaffolding and Velcro to catch what is going on, and they can turn that . . . [into] still more knowledge. But those children . . . [who lack this capital] fall further and further behind. The relentless humiliations they experience continue to deplete their energy and motivation to learn" (p. 20).

Hirsch looks at what research psychologists have noted about learning as a basis of his program. Recognizing the significant effect of prior knowledge on students' abilities to learn, he weaves a convincing case for the essentialist stance that educators must provide students with the prerequisite knowledge that they require so that they can master the later content to which they will be, or at least should be, introduced as a function of their formal education (refer to chapter 1 for an in-depth discussion of the significance of prior knowledge on student learning). He argues against the progressive educators' assertions that children should be educated to acquire a love of learning and critical thinking skills regardless of the content to which they are introduced. He makes a further point that students will develop these critical thinking skills as long as they deal with significantly challenging content but that these skills do not develop in the content void that he claims progressive educators advocate. The Core Knowledge Foundation claims a number of other benefits of this type of philosophy (see Figure 2.5).

Activity 2.3

Go to a library and pick up a copy of one of E. D. Hirsch's *What Every "X"-Year-Old Should Know*. Skim through the book and create a "quiz" to administer to your peers (refer to chapter 9 if you want to practice creating more valid quiz items). Analyze the results and determine on which items your peers did especially well and on which they struggled. Report the results to your class and comment on your opinions on the essential nature of this knowledge.

Progressivism—Teaching Children, Not Subjects

Both perennialists and essentialists align themselves with more traditional approaches to education. Though they disagree on exactly what will be taught and how it will be taught, they agree that there is a body of knowledge out there that students must engage and master. Together they focus on the content that teachers should teach, and both tend to favor teacher-centered classrooms, though to varying degrees. **Progressivists,** however, focus their attention on children first and on the subject matter second. You can see this attention to students for yourself if you consider the *Cardinal Principles of Secondary Education* (Figure 2.6).

FIGURE 2.4   SAMPLE ELEMENTS OF ESSENTIALISM AS PRESENTED IN THE CORE KNOWLEDGE CURRICULUM

Knowledge Builds on Knowledge

We learn new knowledge by building on what we already know. Students in Core Knowledge schools know a lot, because they are offered a coherent sequence of specific knowledge that builds year by year. For example, in sixth grade they should be ready to grasp the law of the conservation of energy because they have been building the knowledge that prepares them for it, as shown in this selection from the physical science strand of the Core Knowledge Sequence:

Kindergarten:

Magnetism, the idea of forces we cannot see. Classify materials according to whether they are attracted to a magnet.

First Grade:

Basic concept of atoms. Names and common examples of the three states of matter. Examine water as an example of changing states of matter in a single substance. Properties of matter: measurement.

Second Grade:

Lodestones: naturally occurring magnets. Magnetic poles: north-seeking and south-seeking poles. Magnetic fields (strongest at the poles). Law of attraction: unlike poles attract, like poles repel.

Fourth Grade:

Atoms: all matter is made up of particles too small to see. Atoms are made up of even smaller particles: protons, neutrons, electrons. Concept of electrical charge: proton has positive charge; electron has negative charge; neutron has no charge. Unlike charges attract, like charges repel (relate to magnetic attraction). Properties of matter: mass, volume, and density. The elements: basic kinds of matter.

Fifth Grade:

Atoms are in constant motion; electrons move around the nucleus in paths called shells (or energy levels). Atoms form molecules and compounds. The Periodic Table: a tool that organizes elements with common properties. Energy transfer: matter changes phase by adding or removing energy. Expansion and contraction. Three ways energy is transferred: conduction, convection, and radiation.

Sixth Grade:

Kinetic and potential energy: types of each. Heat and temperature. Energy is conserved in a system.

(*Source:* Core Knowledge Foundation Website: www.coreknowledge.org. Used with permission of the Core Knowledge Foundation, all rights reserved.)

FIGURE 2.5   CORE KNOWLEDGE FOUNDATION'S LIST OF BENEFITS

Benefits of Core Knowledge

For Students
- Provides a broad base of knowledge and a rich vocabulary
- Motivates students to learn and creates a strong desire to learn more
- Provides the knowledge necessary for higher levels of learning and helps build confidence

For the School
- Provides an academic focus and encourages consistency in instruction
- Provides a plan for coherent, sequenced learning from grade to grade
- Promotes a community of learners—adults and children
- Becomes an effective tool for lesson planning and communication among teachers and with parents
- Guides thoughtful purchases of school resources

For the School District
- Provides a common focus to share knowledge and expertise
- Decreases learning gaps caused by mobility
- Encourages cooperation among schools to provide quality learning experiences for all students
- Provides a strong foundation of knowledge for success in high school and beyond

For Parents and the Community
- Provides a clear outline of what children are expected to learn in school
- Encourages parents to participate in their children's education both at home and in school
- Provides opportunities for community members to help obtain and provide instructional resources

---

(*Source:* Core Knowledge Foundation Website: www.coreknowledge.org. Used with permission of the Core Knowledge Foundation, all rights reserved.)

Written in 1918, it was an early attempt by progressive educators to refocus the aims of education from the college preparatory curriculum presented by the Committee of Ten toward a curriculum that recognized one of the realities of the day—the vast majority of secondary students did not go to college, so why, they asked, should schools prepare them for that?

These progressive educators, almost unarguably beholding to John Dewey and his early work at the University of Chicago, had gained a forum for advancing their ideas. They looked at traditional education and saw a rigid, teacher-dominated setting that forced students to engage in mindless busy work, never capturing students' interests or attending to their concerns. They designed their practices and theories to capitalize on what children wanted to learn. In 1919, the Progressive

---

FIGURE 2.6   CARDINAL PRINCIPLES OF SECONDARY EDUCATION

In 1918, the NEA's Commission on the Reorganization of Secondary Education recommended that the following seven areas of life be addressed as the aims of secondary education.

1. *Health*—encouraged schools to provide health education, physical education as an organized activity, and cooperate with parents and communities in helping students develop life-long healthy habits.

2. *Command of Fundamental Processes*—schools needed to continue to develop students' reading abilities, mathematical reasoning, etc., so that they would be prepared for the challenges of life in complex modern society.

3. *Worthy Home Membership*—students need to develop the personal qualities that will enable them to contribute to and gain benefit from their families and home life.

4. *Vocation*—students need to be prepared to step into a vocation and to have the skills that will enable them to get along with co-workers, while contributing to the needs of society.

5. *Civic Education*—students need to know their rights and responsibilities and develop the qualities that will allow them to contribute as a member of a democratic society and part of the larger world.

6. *Worthy Use of Leisure*—students should be prepared to grow physically, spiritually and psychologically and to enrich themselves in the pursuit of recreational activities.

7. Ethical Character—students must be helped to develop ethical behavior through the use of thoughtful instructional decisions and careful choices of subject matter, as well as through their interactions with their peers and teachers.

(*Source:* Commission on the Reorganization of Secondary Education, 1918.)

Education Association set forth a statement of beliefs. They included the following principles:

- Children should be free to develop naturally.
- Children's interest, promoted through direct experience, provides the best foundation for learning.
- Teachers should act as resources, guiding learning activities.
- Schools and homes should work together in promoting children's development.
- Progressive schools should act as laboratories for pedagogical reform and experiments. (Brown & Finn, 1988)

Teachers who follow progressive principles today would likely use group activities as a way of fostering students' interpersonal skills and preparing them for their adult roles in a democracy. They will allow students to work on projects, possibly providing them with real-world problems to solve or address. During these projects, teachers will provide students with feedback and resources or cues as necessary, gradually trying to place themselves in the background and students in the foregrounds of these learning experiences.

Two educators, John Dewey and William Kilpatrick, exemplified the progressives' positions on teaching methods. Dewey's philosophies still retain their power as ways of thinking about students and schools. A revolutionary in his day, Dewey sought to change the schools as he saw them. He turned his critical eye on all aspects of schooling as it existed in his day. For instance, something as simple as the furniture at which students sat made him question some assumptions about what children and teachers did on a day-to-day basis. He once described for a school supply manufacturer the type of furniture that he wanted for his experimental school; he wanted desks at which students could work. The manufacturer told him that the only types of furniture that they made were ones in which students could listen (Dewey, 1899). His notion that students should actively "work" at learning provides us today with a metaphor for the type of learning in which he believed. He stated that educators should think of schooling in terms of "Explorers and Maps" (Dewey, 1916). As teachers we can give children a map, tell them how to get from point A to point B and show them the most direct route; however, students will learn more if we tell them to get to point B and let them figure out how best to do that. Only if students get to *travel* a route, that is experience their own learning along with all the messiness and even some of the wrong turns they may make, will they truly learn something. After the "traveling," teachers can ask them to draw their own map and tell of their experiences.

While Dewey provided us with philosophical musings, Kilpatrick (1918) provided us with clearly articulated practices that teachers can take into the classroom. His "Project Method" outlines a four-step process (Figure 2.7) that teachers can follow that encourages students to capitalize upon their own interests by "exploring" subject matter in school. He believed that real learning takes place when students are actively engaged in purposeful activities that are self-initiated and self-evaluated.

FIGURE 2.7   KILPATRICK'S PROJECT METHOD

Teachers guide students through four stages of "purposeful" acts:

1. Determining a purpose for learning

2. Planning the project

3. Executing the project

4. Judging the final work

In the first step, students are challenged to find meaningful problems on which they want to work. Once they find a meaningful problem, they need to set about making a plan for how they will be able to solve this problem. They then try out their plan, and they finish by judging the success of their execution. This should sound quite familiar to you as you read this text. In fact, this is simply a slimmed-down version of the IDEAL problem-solving model, the same model we believe provides you with an appropriate way of reflecting on decisions you wish to make in your career choice. This is further testimony, we hope, to the meaningfulness of the project method; if it's appropriate enough for you, we think you'll also find that you can use it effectively with your students.

You can see that there is a vast difference between more traditional educators and their progressive counterparts in the ways in which they see schools operating, both in terms of types of content to be taught and the ways in which this content can be most effectively delivered. The tensions between these two positions have provided education with many of the programs, changes, and conflicts over the past hundred years. Ever since the Committee of Ten pronounced what is worthy of study in high schools, the curriculum has swung back and forth between the traditional (i.e., perennialist and essentialist philosophies) and progressive positions. Today, you will see that most schools have some combination of the two, neither wholly content-oriented nor wholly student-centered.

Activity 2.4

Get together with a group of your classmates and brainstorm a list of the kinds of experiences you have all had in school. Consider courses you've taken, lessons or units that have stood out for you, and activities in which you've engaged. After creating the list, divide a sheet of paper in two and mark one side "Traditional" (e.g., perennialist or essentialist) and the other side "Progressive." Based on your reading here, classify each experience on your list under one of these two broad categories. Transfer these classifications to poster board, transparency, or PowerPoint and share with the class. Be prepared to defend your classifications.

CURRICULUM PLANNING—A PRACTICAL GUIDE

We provided the previous discussion so that you would be aware of some of the ways of thinking that have informed others of the ways that *they* believe one goes about "doing school." As reflective teachers, we are convinced that the more aware that you are of the philosophies that others have identified and the ways in which they've applied these philosophies to working with children in schools, the more consciously you can go about your work. This awareness can also help you to resist one of the major criticisms of educators—that we follow any "fad" that pops up on the horizon. Most of what people call fads are ideas and practices that have appeared before, in some form or another, and that are being recycled through another generation of learners and teachers. Ideally, though, each generation is able to improve upon the practice *because of* knowing the history of the theory or practice. Before proceeding, it may even be helpful for you to reflect on where you see yourself in terms of the philosophy you hold. Are you a perennialist? an essentialist? a progressivist?

Besides looking to a clearly-formed philosophy of education to avoid jumping onto the latest educational bandwagon, you will be well served if you have a system that helps you identify key content as you engage in planning your curriculum. Curriculum planners have numerous models from which they can choose a method that fits their needs. Some of these models are incredibly complex, providing large numbers of decision points and requiring significant amounts of expertise to prove useful. Many of these models, especially the more complex ones, are more appropriate for work as a district curriculum coordinator or on a district-wide committee. For your purposes as a new classroom teacher, we have chosen a model that is almost unarguably the dominant model in use by curriculum designers. Part of the power of this model is its simplicity and the way in which different teachers in different disciplines and grade levels can adapt it to planning instruction in their own classrooms.

Ralph Tyler (1949) is generally credited with developing the technique from which many of the curriculum planning models come. He proposed his model of curriculum development and provided his contemporaries with a four-step process, a recursive one, that was based on the following questions:

1. What educational purposes shall the school seek to attain?
2. What educational experiences can be provided that are likely to attain these purposes?
3. How can these educational experiences be effectively organized?
4. How can we determine whether these purposes are being attained?

While these questions were the ones that he felt should drive any curriculum development, Tyler also realized that any developer needed a great deal of information before doing any meaningful planning. By looking through various "lenses," you can get the information you will need to develop curriculum for your classroom.

"LENSES" ON CURRICULUM

Even those people with the best of eyesight sometimes find themselves in need of something to improve their vision. You may wear polarizing sunglasses to improve your vision on a sunny day or use a magnifying glass for reading fine print on a legal document. Or when you get old like us, you may use reading glasses to read just about anything smaller than the "E" on an eye chart. In each of these cases, it is the lens that helps people to see more clearly, to pick out details that they could not have seen without these aids. When Tyler suggested his curriculum planning model, he also suggested that there were three "lenses" through which you should look *before* you begin planning. Others have added the fourth that you will see below. Each of these lenses can be used to filter out specific information that you need to consider before you identify objectives that you think your students should attain. These lenses are engaged by considering:

- What we know about our students;
- What society wants and needs from its schools;
- What content area experts think students should know and be able to do in the different content areas; and
- What we know about teaching and learning.

A Lens on Students

While Tyler indicated that each of these lenses is equally important, we believe that the first lens through which you need to look is the one that looks at students. With the rise of educational psychology in the latter half of the twentieth century, educators have come to know a great deal about issues important to the cognitive, social, and psychological development of children and adolescents. We touched on a number of these important issues in the first chapter of this book. We want to encourage you to recognize that, no matter what curriculum planning model you may use or how carefully you consider the other lenses, your planning will be in vain if you are not aware of who your students are, what they already know, and what skills they currently possess. That is where all good planning begins.

Educational psychology, though, just provides you with some general principles about children and their development (look back at chapter 1 for a more complete discussion of students). As you look at students, you also need to look at *your* students. As you do this, you may ask the following questions: Who are these people? What do they like? What interests them? What motivates them? As individuals, you will need to ask the same questions. You will also want to observe them carefully. What books is each child reading? What movies does each one like? What music? Is this child from a two-parent home? blended family? And the questions can go on and on. General principles of child development can be a starting point for your curriculum planning, but any successful plan will recognize where each of your students is and try to close the gap between that place and where you want all your students to be at the end of the year.

A Lens on Society

After looking through a lens on students, your planning will benefit by looking at what society needs, wants, and expects from its educational system. You have seen some of that as you read about the different philosophies. Proponents of each philosophy identified needs that they felt must be satisfied for students to become productive members of America in the twenty-first century. These views provide you with points to consider and give you an opportunity to determine where you stand in relation to each philosophy. One source of information for what our society wanted for its students was outlined in national goals as set forth in the *Goals 2000: Educate America Act*, which we will discuss further in a moment.

Here again, however, it also helps to consider different views of society. There are two distinctly different positions that we want to present. These can provide you with two extreme views of society. If you consider these two views to be on opposite ends of a continuum, you will see that there are a number of possible ways of seeing society in between these ends. On the one end is **Functionalism,** a view of society that holds that our society is functioning well on the whole and that schools are necessary to help maintain and improve the "well-oiled machine" of a country in which we all live. In this view, society needs lots of differently skilled people to fulfill different roles. Schools are important institutions for identifying and developing the talents of all children, so that they can take positions in society and contribute their talents and skills. On the other extreme is **Critical Theory** (sometimes called **Conflict Theory**), which is a view that holds that society is run by a dominant culture that wants to maintain the status quo, the way that things are. The dominant culture in society controls much of the money and power, and people in this group use their money and influence to seduce others into accepting the values and norms of a materialistic society, which is what actually keeps them in power. This group controls influential apparatuses, like the media, advertising, and other institutions that sell the "American Dream." They exert their influence even into the schools by dominating school boards, textbook companies, and policy makers who determine what and how students will learn. All of this influence is designed to keep most of society in the same social classes, even while giving the appearance that a person can go from "rags to riches."

Society's Goals—Goals 2000   While all this talk of theories of society may be interesting, you may still be asking yourself: How do I determine what society needs? Here again, some of this work has already been done for you. One source of information to which you can refer is the *Goals 2000: Educate America Act* passed by Congress in 1994. These goals (Figure 2.8) provided schools with some direction in terms of their academic curriculum and their school environment and atmosphere. As ideals to which schools should strive, they presented us with opportunities to assess where we were in relation to these goals and challenged us to close the gap between where we were and where the goals say we wanted to be. Even while all members of society may agree that these are worthy goals, how schools should try to meet these goals may still provoke controversy. The two different views of society, Functionalism and Critical Theory, provide us with further information to consider as we try to determine what society needs from its schools.

Functionalism—Opportunities for All   Those who believe in a functionalist view of society see modern societies as being superior to their predecessors. They also recognize that a modern society is a very complex machine, that there are many different functions people must serve in order to keep the society working smoothly. In order to fill all of these diverse functions, the schools must train and evaluate students based on what they are able to achieve. It is in society's best interest, therefore, that we fill the various jobs we have to offer with the most capable people that we have. Yet we also must recognize that there are many jobs, some

---

FIGURE 2.8   GOALS 2000: EDUCATE AMERICA ACT

National Education Goals
GOALS 2000

By the year 2000,

1. All children in America will start school ready to learn.

2. The high school graduation rate will increase to at least 90 percent.

3. American students will leave grades four, eight, and twelve having demonstrated competency in challenging subject matter including English, mathematics, science, history, and geography; and every school in America will ensure that all students learn to use their minds well, so they may be prepared for responsible citizenship, further learning, and productive employment in our modern economy.

4. The nation's teaching force will have access to programs for the continued improvement of their professional skills and the opportunity to acquire the knowledge and skills needed to instruct and prepare all American students for the next century.

5. U. S. students will be first in the world in science and mathematics achievement.

6. Every adult American will be literate and will possess the knowledge and skills necessary to compete in a global economy and exercise the rights and responsibilities of citizenship.

7. Every school in the United States will be free of drugs, violence, and the unauthorized presence of firearms and alcohol and will offer a disciplined environment conducive to learning.

8. Every school will promote partnerships that will increase parental involvement and participation in promoting the social, emotional, and academic growth of children.

---

of them not so attractive, that must also be filled. If we are to fill all of the positions that we need, we must value each member's contribution to the whole of society. To guarantee that there are people willing to serve all of the functions necessary for our well-being as a society, people must be convinced that they all have had an "equal opportunity" to get the best, most prestigious jobs. Schools, then, must provide equal educational opportunities for all students regardless of their race, gender, socioeconomic class, or any other factor other than their achievement.

In the functionalist view, the **manifest curriculum** (often called the "official curriculum") is one that provides students with the skills and knowledge that they will need to fill the various functions necessary for society to continue working smoothly. That curriculum will be fluid, able to change as society perceives new needs that must be met. In the 1980s, for instance, most schools began to require some type of computer classes for their students because it became apparent that computer skills would be required for students in the future. Regardless of what forms curricula may take, however, students must be evaluated on what they do, not who they are. There is another type of curriculum at work, though. According to functionalists, the **hidden curriculum,** the way students gain the psychological dispositions to enter into the societal mainstream and act as a contributing member, is based on the general principle of equal educational opportunity. This is further broken down into four specific norms that functionalists believe students must believe in, develop, and accept in order to fit smoothly into their places in society after their schooling. These norms are: achievement, independence, universalism, and specificity (Dreeben, 1968).

To proponents of Functionalism, this hidden curriculum acts as a positive force in schools by sending the message that there are norms, ways of behaving that are societally endorsed. Let's take each of these norms in order. You will probably be able to nod your head that, in general at least, these norms were in place at the schools you attended prior to coming to college. **Achievement** means that we base all students' grades or promotion from grade to grade on what they have accomplished, not on their potential or ability or good intentions. Some students have great potential that they never fulfill, and while teachers should certainly try to motivate students to reach their potential, they must base students' evaluations on what they actually produce. You are currently attending college because someone determined, based on some set of objective information, such as high school grades, SAT or ACT scores, and other factors, that you had achieved a level of competence that would enable you to attempt the next level. **Independence** means that all students are held accountable for their work; we encourage students to be responsible for their own work and expect them to turn it in on time in the form that they have been taught. The third norm, **universalism,** means that all of the rules and standards apply to everyone. This is the first part of the fairness issue. In conjunction with universalism, however, is a fourth norm, **specificity.** Specificity allows for legitimate exceptions to universalism. It is important, though, that these legitimate exceptions be applied universally. For instance, many coaches of athletic teams in high schools have a rule that players who miss practice cannot start in the next game. To meet the standard of universalism, coaches must apply that to all of their players, so that even a team's star will not be able to start if he or she misses practice, regardless of whether the game is a meaningless one at the end of a losing season or for the state championship. However, in our society, we also recognize that there are sometimes legitimate differences among reasons for missing practice. The player who has attended a funeral or was not allowed to attend practice because of a religious holiday can be legitimately exempted from the rule. Another player who missed practice because he or she went on a ski trip with neighbors can make no such claim to a legitimate exception.

It is the school's job, then, to prepare students for gaining a place in society. If students are given equal opportunities to succeed, and if they experience these norms throughout their schooling, they will most likely develop the attitudes, both work and personal, that make them contributing members of society. However, functionalists are not blind to the fact that not all people have the same opportunities. Recognizing that ours is not a perfect society, they realize that certain impediments have been placed in the way of many members. What those impediments are and how we should go about remediating them is where even those who agree with functionalist theory take different positions. Simply put, there are three different views—historical, intellectual, and cultural—as to why not all people have enjoyed equal opportunities to succeed.

Those who believe that some members of society have been kept from success through **historical impediments** look at the long history of differential education for minorities in America, including the long-segregated schools of the South and urban centers. They contend that this contradicts the norms of universalism and achievement, and they invoke the norm of specificity in righting these historical wrongs. Advocates of compensatory education believe in programs, such as Head Start and Upward Bound, and justify spending extra money on those groups who have been unfairly stifled by the educational system as a way of helping these minority populations to become fully able to take advantage of the opportunities that are available. Those who see **intellectual impediments** as being the source of some people's inabilities to take full advantage of our free society see the school's main role as being that of a sorting machine. Functionalists in this camp believe that our schools must promote the norms of achievement, responsibility, and universalism while recognizing that no individual or group has a right or expectation of special privilege. The schools must educate all children to their potential, but they must also be realistic in recognizing that not all children are equally capable. Finally, those who ascribe to the **cultural impediments** theory believe that some cultures do not value education in the same way as others. For some individuals, it is not fair that they be expected to engage in a college preparatory curriculum when their families may value work of a different sort. These students then should be engaged in a meaningful and appropriately different education, often of a vocational nature, that allows them to become productive members of society.

Critical Theory—Education of the Disenfranchised   While functionalists look at society as a smoothly-running machine that meets the needs of its members and schools as one of its most important institutions for preparing and "sorting" students according to their accomplishments, critical theorists look at education with a "critical" eye; that is, they often note the contradictions between what educators say they are doing and how the practice of schooling actually plays out within classrooms and in schools. These critical theorists often point out the different opportunities that students have, the different ways teachers go about their business of teaching, and they maintain that these differences are often a function of the socioeconomic status (SES) of the communities in which the schooling takes place.

For those who look at schools in this way, education is as much about *how* schooling takes place as it is about *what* is taught. Just as functionalists do, they also believe that there is a hidden curriculum that operates in schools. But to critical theorists, the hidden curriculum is there so that students will be indoctrinated into their "places" in society. The hidden curriculum includes the ways in which schools operate. These practices, from bell schedules to tracking of students into different curricular opportunities, all provide hidden messages for students. In most schools, for instance, students are not allowed in the school until a bell rings. Another bell rings to announce recess, another for lunch, and so on. According to conflict theorists, this prepares lower-SES students, especially, for working in factories and low-wage jobs where their movements will be controlled by a boss who decides when they can come, go, eat, etc. After a while, students accept these procedures as "the way things are" and no longer even consider them. And to critical theorists this is what makes the hidden curriculum so dangerous and powerful. According to proponents of Critical Theory, it is designed to promote the values of the dominant culture, whose members are highest up on the economic ladder, who have the most to gain from making sure that the status quo is protected or lose if it is not. It's also designed so that the others, the subordinate groups in society, are prepared to accept the "way things are" without wondering how they became that way (refer to the Bigelow article under "Critical Theory" in the *Teacher as Researcher* section).

When critical theorists go into schools they note distinctions in the ways that students and teachers interact. In upper-SES schools, they note that students tend to be more engaged in higher order thinking and inquiry learning activities, that teachers often act as facilitators of learning rather than as authoritarian task masters. These students, by virtue of being born into the "right" families, have access to the latest equipment, the most highly trained teachers, and a curriculum that engages and challenges them. While in the lower-SES schools, students tend to be engaged in more seatwork and work more on the lower levels of the cognitive domain. Teachers in these schools use more teacher-centered models of instruction and tend to be more authoritarian in running their classrooms, requiring strict adherence to teacher-imposed rules. To the conflict theorists, the higher-SES students are being prepared to take their "rightful places" in society. They will be responsible for running corporations and managing people and businesses. Therefore, they must be educated in such a way that they develop problem-solving skills and learn to work together with other people to arrive at consensus on decisions. On the other hand, those students in the lower-SES schools are being prepared for a life of tedium, where the jobs that they will get, many in the service industries and the relatively few manufacturing and factory jobs left, will require them to do repetitive operations, like slinging burgers and putting in the fries, for relatively low pay with little hope of future advancement. These students will work under a manager who will direct them to do certain jobs and they will be expected to follow orders and directions (see the Messner article under "Critical Theory" in the *Teacher as Researcher* section for an activity that exemplifies this phenomenon).

Paolo Freire and Michael Apple are two leading spokespersons for this position. Freire worked with adult literacy in his native Brazil. He noted that the government-sanctioned textbooks that agencies were provided to increase literacy in the countryside often sent hidden messages to the poorer people to whom they were addressed. These picture books tended to show middle and upper class people as responsible and hard-working and the poorer, country folk in the opposite light. He also believed that the books were insulting to the illiterate, using text more appropriate to children than to adults. To combat this condescension, Freire's teachers went into the countryside, lived with the people, and designed materials to meet the needs of individual villages. They built their reading materials on themes that were important to the people, themes of work and family relations that often showed the poor how they were manipulated by wealthy landowners and government officials. Freire (1970) believed that the act of knowing goes from "action to reflection and from reflection upon action to new action" (p. 370). Freire was so successful in educating these people, not only to read but to become aware of their plights as second class citizens, that he was exiled from Brazil as a political enemy.

Similarly, Apple (1991) has seen the same type of behavior in our own American educational system. Like Loewen, who was mentioned earlier in this chapter, Apple has looked closely at textbooks and how they have been regulated from the 1800s to the present. In the late 1800s the textbook adoption process was largely controlled at the state level, which is still true today in a number of states. Apple noted that some of the grass roots, populist movements of the late 1800s and early 1900s brought changes in school texts. These grass roots groups raised objections to the ways in which some issues, especially those that dealt with race, gender, and ethnicity, were presented in books used in schools. On the surface this would appear to be what conflict theorists would want, subordinate groups rising to meet their oppressors. However, what happened, Apple contended, was that the education establishment, especially middle class "experts" and publishing houses, tended to sanitize the struggles of these subordinate groups and offered a type of "official knowledge" that promoted the values and culture of middle and upper class society at the expense of the already disenfranchised.

A Lens on Content

Once you have looked through the lenses of psychology and sociology, you have a third lens to consider, that of subject matter or content. As you have been reading this chapter you may have asked: So, *what* am I going to teach? For many new teachers this is their most important consideration and greatest fear, especially when they go into their classroom to set up for that first year. In this particular text, we will only be addressing this issue in general terms. As a college graduate and new teacher, one of the skills you will have learned is how to research topics of interest and concern to you. You will find that you will be applying your research skills as you look at content. There are many resources out there for you. Some, such as teacher's guides in text books, you are probably aware of, while others, like websites and professionally-developed materials devoted to particular grade levels or content areas, you will encounter as you investigate and explore your profession. For this brief look, we want to begin with some of the major sources of information at which curriculum developers may look, then to some progressively smaller ones. These are all resources of which you should be aware.

Learned Societies   For each content area and every grade level there are learned societies that have helped to set out general content expectations, learning experiences, and, in some cases, very specific content and experiences appropriate for each grade level. We urge you to join one or more of these groups so that you will receive the benefits of their professional journals and state and national meetings and conferences as ways of sharing practices in classrooms and helping to make curricular decisions. Some groups, such as the National Middle School Association (NMSA), focus on content and experiences appropriate for particular ages or grade levels, while others, like the National Council of Teachers of Mathematics (NCTM), address specific content and learning experiences that they consider appropriate in their subject area from grades K–12 (refer to Figure 3 in chapter 11 for a selected listing of various learned societies). The professors who have designed your general methods and/or subject-specific methods courses are aware of these standards and have planned your experiences so that they will be consistent with what these societies are suggesting are appropriate experiences for the students you will be teaching.

State and Local Curricula   As of this writing, there is talk of a national curriculum, but that may be all it is—talk. So, as you prepare for your first teaching assignment, you will probably look to the state and local levels for model curricula or mandated curricula, respectively. Most states have designed model curricula that attempt to provide teachers and students with some common knowledge and experiences in their schooling careers. The state models tend to focus on general goals and may include performance objectives (Figure 2.9). However, these models generally do not specify any particular content, though they may provide examples of possible content or learning experiences as you can also see in Figure 2.9. By not specifying content, one such model curriculum guide in science suggested that the guide "permits the construction of a local science program that is free of redundancy, gaps, and inconsistencies" (Ohio Department of Education, 1994, p. 15). As you notice in the third-grade objectives, the skills students develop—collecting information, describing an episode, and using whole numbers to compare and classify—provide a foundation for the more complex but related performances they will need to demonstrate in tenth grade.

Local school districts use these state models as they plan for their own students. While acknowledging the state model, individual districts are encouraged to take advantage of their own unique resources in devising local curricula. As you probably noticed in Figure 2.9, the examples that the model curriculum developers provide give a great deal of range to the local developers as they determine what equipment they already possess as part of their science program, what expertise local businesses may be willing to provide, and what "problems" for study are available in the area. It is important for students, especially in states where there is proficiency testing of some sort, that they be prepared for state examinations, and districts would be foolish if they did not carefully consider the state models. However, for most schools it is the local curriculum guides that will be of most importance to you. In the best of districts, the objectives and experiences in these guides will be aligned with those of both the learned societies and state models.

A Lens on Teaching and Learning

Since Dewey proposed them in 1902, the previous three lenses have been generally accepted. It wasn't until the mid-1950s to early 1960s, however, that this fourth lens was added (Wiles & Bondi, 1998). Psychology, in general, as we mentioned in the

---

FIGURE 2.9   EXAMPLE OF OHIO STATE MODEL CURRICULUM IN SCIENCE

Science: Ohio's Model Competency-Based Program

Third Grade	Performance Objective
The learner will	decide what information is necessary to make a simple weather report, collect the information, and make the report.
	describe an episode (e.g., storms, rolling and bouncing balls, hatching eggs, falling maplecopters) in terms of its duration and timing.
	use whole number counts and measures to compare and classify familiar objects.

Tenth Grade	Performance Objective
The learner will	identify and discuss structure/function relationships in complex systems (e.g., physiological systems, biotechnical systems, aeronautical systems, energy production and transmission systems, communications systems, transportation systems, waste management systems) with appropriate community and field experts.
	demonstrate skill in the use of interpretation of data from various technologies (e.g., blood pressure apparatus, graphing calculators, high-power microscopy, computer-based interface sensors and software, telescopes, weather instruments, satellite telemetry, Vernier scale instruments, oscilloscopes).

(*Source:* Ohio Department of Education (1994). *Science: Ohio's model competency standards.* Columbus, OH: State Board of Education, pp. 33 & 49).

first lens, provides you with some information about children. Educational psychology, or psychology as it has been applied in school settings, also provides the larger educational community with the information we have today on teaching and learning. Teaching and learning is a very complex act, as you know from your own experiences as a student and as you can probably imagine (and will certainly discover as you continue your training) from the perspective of the teacher. The complexity makes it very difficult to study with great certainty. What works in one school setting with a particular child or group of children may not work in another setting or even with a similar group of children the very next year.

Throughout your teaching career you will need to continue to study teaching, your own teaching as well as others', and the learning that your students are accomplishing, as well as the learning they are not. You will need to do this to add to your professional repertoire of new knowledge, learning experiences and ways of assessing students. What we have chosen to supply you with in the remainder of the book after this chapter are a number of different strategies and ways of thinking about teaching and learning that can provide you with starting points in this career-long development. What we will introduce you to in Figure 2.10 is Hilda Taba's (1962) refinement of Tyler's model of curriculum planning, a simple yet powerful way to proceed with planning for instruction once you have looked through all four of these lenses.

DEVELOPING CURRICULUM

Taba's curriculum planning model is one that a district planning committee might use as they look to reconsider curriculum at a district or school level. As a new teacher, it is likely that you will be handed a guide, sometimes called a "curriculum guide," sometimes a "graded course of study" or a "scope and sequence" handbook. These guides may be very detailed, indicating a particular sequence of instruction as well as the types of materials you are to use. If you have this, you would be wise to follow it as your job may depend upon it. However, depending on the school district, or even the individual school you find yourself within the district, you may have a great deal of freedom to determine the order of activities and even specific outcomes you want your students to demonstrate. If so, this process can help you to plan a nine-week, semester, or year-long curricula for your students.

Just as with Kilpatrick's Project Method described earlier, Taba's curriculum planning model is merely a different application of the IDEAL problem-solving method. The IDEAL model has applications to problem solving in many classroom situations, whereas Taba's model is specific to curriculum planning. Taba's model is well-known to educators. Before we present an example of the model, however, keep a few things in mind. First, Taba's model is a global planning strategy that suggests the major components you will need to consider as you begin the task of

---

FIGURE 2.10   TABA'S CURRICULUM PLANNING MODEL

Regardless of the time for which you intend to plan, following Taba's model you should do the following activities:

1. Diagnose needs (e.g., look through the "lenses").
2. Identify objectives.
3. Select content.
4. Organize content.
5. Select learning experiences.
6. Organize learning experiences.
7. Determine what to evaluate and the means of doing it.

curriculum planning. Second, although Taba's model and the example that follows are presented in a rather linear and step-by-step fashion, it is far more likely that you will move around in the model, considering the inter-relatedness of more than one component at a time. Finally, you are likely to make adaptations and modifications to this model based on the nature of your students, your experience, the guidelines provided in your district's curriculum guide, and the grade level and subject matter you are teaching.

Activity 2.5

After reading the seven-step Taba model of curriculum development and the section that follows, which provides an example of the process, practice using this model yourself. Individually or in a small group, decide upon a grade level and content area. Then make some skeletal plans for a unit of time—a quarter, semester, or year. Put your plan on posterboard or a transparency and share with your classmates. You could also have someone document the process (consider video- or audio-taping your session) and report back to your group the successes, frustrations, and questions you now have.

We think that the best way to proceed from here is to demonstrate how a teacher might go about planning in this way (for a more in-depth look at the whole curriculum planning process, refer to the Sizer book under "Curriculum Development" in the *Teacher as Researcher* section). To do that we'll go back to Leonard Tan and our fictional Midtown school district. Becky, Leonard's mentor, uses the Taba Model to get the "big picture" of the planning steps she will need to consider in much the same way as a cross-country traveler looks at a map of the United States to identify the major highways and cities along the intended route. Like the traveler, who will eventually require more detailed regional maps, Leonard will consider some of the more specific planning strategies for each of Taba's steps, and you will learn about many of these strategies in the chapters that follow.

To simplify things, let's just assume that he'll begin by planning his science curriculum. As we have already indicated, this model is especially useful for long-term, global planning and, while the example we will present is for a first quarter plan, you can use this same process for a semester-long or year-long sequence of instruction. Once you have these global plans committed to paper, though, you will have provided yourself with a general "map" of how you will help your students travel from where they are when they first step into your class to where you want them to go. In chapter 3, then, we will show you how to take these general plans and turn them into the more detailed descriptions that make up unit plans. First, though, let's take a look at what Leonard sees as he looks through the four lenses to diagnose needs.

Diagnose Needs—A Lens on Students

Since this was his first year, Leonard had never met his students before, but he had taught kindergartners, first, fifth, and sixth graders. He certainly figured that this knowledge would come in handy. He knew that, with the younger students, it was hard to keep their attention on units of instruction that lasted much longer than a week, but the older ones sometimes managed to work effectively on three-week units. As he planned, he thought that he might just split the difference for these students, maybe beginning the year with some units of a week or so and building to two-week units. He also recognized that he would need to get to know these students better, find out what they already knew and in what they were interested; so he made a decision that, rather than plan for an entire year, he would just work out a nine-week plan, then adjust the plans to capitalize on these students' strengths and interests.

Diagnose Needs—A Lens on Society

As he thought about the school children and their surrounding community, Leonard knew that this was a formerly thriving city that had hit hard times. He also knew that the former industrial base was no longer in place. Parents wanted to prepare their children for jobs that required critical thinking skills so that they could compete for professional careers and, even though his students were only in third grade, he could set a foundation for them that could help them in their future learning. The parents here believed that education was "the way out" for their children; they had high hopes and placed great expectations on the teachers for preparing their children to become productive and responsible citizens.

Diagnose Needs—A Lens on Content

Leonard felt most comfortable with this particular area. His college coursework had prepared him well. He had used the local school curriculum guides in preparing lessons in his field experiences and in his student teaching semester. The local curriculum for Midtown was very non-directive; it provided some general goals and some specific pupil performance objectives but did not specify with what content he should have students work. Becky, the lead teacher for third grade, had told him that most teachers just developed some new units each year to add to some of the things that they had already done that were successful in the past. The objectives in the local curriculum indicated that the district was more interested in helping students to develop ways of thinking about science and scientific skills, rather than any specific content knowledge.

That worked well for him in terms of what he had studied in college. There, in one of his methods courses, Leonard had used *Benchmarks*, a publication of the American Association for the Advancement of Science (1993). The Association had also stressed ways of thinking. Because of its research base and sections of the book that indicated what children should know and what kinds of misconceptions they might have about science in the third grade, he figured that this would be his best resource to couple with the objectives in the curriculum guide. In looking through *Benchmarks*, he noted that there were a number of different types of content that he could use at this level. He considered what he knew about Midtown and decided that he would focus on "The Living Environment" for this year. This long-term focus would provide him with some direction and make use of the community as his students investigated their neighborhood through scientific methods.

Diagnose Needs—A Lens on Teaching and Learning

Knowing the importance of prior knowledge on students' abilities to learn, Leonard suspected that he would have to build some foundational knowledge for some of his students. He also figured, though, that he needed to use systematic ways of discovering what students already knew before he made too many assumptions. Recalling the domains and criteria (you may want to refer to Figure 11.4 in chapter 11, which shows the different domains and criteria) of the Pathwise Performance Assessment (ETS, 1995) that his college supervisor had used in working with him in student teaching, he remembered that current research supported the notion that teachers tended to be more effective when they used a variety of methods of assessing where students were when they began a year or even a unit. He thought about a number of possible ways of assessing student knowledge and decided that he would use a pre-test of the prerequisite knowledge and skills during the first week. He also knew that he wanted his students to take control of their learning, so he was determined to use a combination of direct instruction, cooperative learning, and guided literacy lessons throughout, beginning with more teacher-directed lessons, as he established routines, and gradually moving toward more student-centered ones.

Identify Objectives

After having looked through the lenses and diagnosed the needs he perceived his science curriculum would be required to meet, he figured he knew just where to go for the second step. The objectives (see chapter 3 for a more detailed discussion), based on the state model curriculum, were already listed in the curriculum guide for the district. Since he didn't need to formulate them himself, it was really a matter of choosing the most appropriate ones. He knew that he wanted his students to "act like scientists" within the general theme he had chosen, so Leonard looked at all of the objectives and chose to concentrate his early efforts on the following:

1. The learner will distinguish between living and non-living things and provide justification for this classification.
2. The learner will use both qualitative and quantitative descriptions to explain the attributes and behaviors of an object or organism.
3. The learner will describe an episode in terms of its duration and timing.

Select Content

Since he had already determined his focus for the year and had identified objectives for this first nine weeks, he could certainly eliminate some possible choices of science topics. However, there were still a lot of topics open to him. He decided just to brainstorm all the things he could come up with that would allow him to take advantage of the school grounds and park across the street. He also wanted to consider all of the possible topics or thematic units that would allow students to do a lot of collecting, classifying, and measuring. Again, he referred to *Benchmarks,* and noted that the authors challenged teachers to "capitalize on the interest that students have in living things while moving them gradually toward ideas that make sense out of nature. Familiarity with the phenomena should precede explanation, and attention to the concrete object should precede abstract theory" (p. 100). Initially, he decided, he would not censor his own brainstorm, so he came up with the following possibilities:

- animals of the park
- plants of the park
- changing seasons
- the unseen world
- states of matter
- pond life
- soil
- rocks and minerals
- air quality
- ecology

As Leonard looked at these, he noticed that some were fairly specific, like plants and animals of the park, while others, like the changing seasons, could (and probably should) be touched upon throughout the year. Looking back to his objectives and forward to some of the activities he had imagined as he was coming up with this list, as well as considering the equipment he had found in the supplies closet, Leonard decided that he wanted to try out plants of the park, pond life, soil, changing seasons, and the unseen world. He also wanted to keep in mind some integrating principles that would help him and the students connect these topics, rather than dealing with them as separate items, so he identified "states of matter" and "ecology" as two integrating principles; he figured he could weave these principles throughout the entire year's science program by connecting the various topics and thematic units to them.

Organize Content

Now that he had decided the content he would use, Leonard had to consider in what order he would have students encounter them. It would be so easy, he thought, if it were history, where he could organize them in chronological order, or even reading, where he could organize them in a developmental sequence, building one topic or skill on top of another. In science, though, he needed to look at these pieces of the program and decide what should go first, then second and so on, and why. Since there didn't appear to be any particular organizing principle, it would be important that he consider the "why?" part carefully. Leonard came up with the following order for the units:

1. Plants of the Park
2. Changing Seasons—Late Summer
3. Soil
4. Pond Life
5. The Unseen World
6. Changing Seasons—Autumn

The "why?" seemed to come to him as he tried manipulating these different units, trying to consider all of the possibilities (You may find the planning matrix introduced in chapter 3 useful for doing this). He wanted to begin in the park, to practice observing and collecting in a place and with things with which students were familiar. By collecting some of the plants at the beginning of the school year, they could begin to look at the park as it appears in late summer. This would lead the children into the second unit; they needed to observe carefully and record their observations of how things looked and felt so that they could compare and contrast later. Leonard also figured, though, that they might want to consider other things besides the plants that they see, things like the insects, geese, and songbirds that gather near the pond, that may "change" along with the seasons. Studying soil would connect the children to the plant world and make a connection to the pond, since they could observe the differences between soil in different parts of the park. Studying the pond in depth would then allow students to focus closely on an ecosystem of great complexity, one with which they may not be as familiar. Their work in the pond could also allow them to collect organisms that they could look at in the next unit—The Unseen World. Finally, in about the ninth week, they could all revisit the park when the Fall colors are nearing their peak and note the changes that the park is undergoing.

Select Learning Experiences

Wow! Leonard sat back for a moment and looked at his nine-week plan. This is pretty good, he thought. This should work. As he looked at the plan, he knew there were a number of different kinds of learning experiences in which his students could engage. He also knew that, as a new teacher, he didn't have a huge file of materials like Becky or the other veteran teachers on staff. He assumed that he would have to plan carefully each day's and each week's lessons in much greater detail (see chapters 3 and 4 for greater descriptions of unit and lesson planning). For now, though, he had some general ideas, and even some specific activities, that he had thought about in the previous step. So, again, he brainstormed, but this time Leonard considered specific ideas for each of the topic areas he had just identified. He also focused his brainstorm on things that the children could actually do or experience. As before, he looked back to the objectives and content but also forward, this time to how he would assess and evaluate student learning. He wanted to be sure that the kinds of knowledge and skills students would develop would also be the knowledge and skills that he tested them on. Leonard wanted to know that every piece of this curriculum puzzle would be aligned with his objectives and appropriate for his students. The content is what the children would discover in the park and within and outside their classroom. The objectives informed him that he would need to work on some specific skills, including classifying, observational skills to denote similarities and differences, and measurement skills. He decided that the experiences that he would select for students would be planned for them to develop these skills. He started with "Plants of the Park" and thought about the following experiences:

- collecting leaves and seeds
- classifying things by shape, size, etc.
- keeping a journal on the different plants
- identifying characteristics of plants

- collecting ferns and grasses
- measuring the sizes of different artifacts
- drawing scale maps of where things are
- listening for and recording sounds of animals and birds

Leonard then went on and followed the same process with each of the other units of content. He realized that some of the skills that his students would begin to develop in this first unit would be ones they would need to use again. He also noticed that some of these skills would allow him to integrate different subject matter into the units, like mathematics in the measuring necessary for both measuring sizes and drawing maps to scale.

Organize Learning Experiences

As he looked at these experiences on his brainstorm, Leonard had to try to figure out which to include and in what order he should put them (Here, again, the planning matrix in chapter 3 could come in handy). Some of the experiences he could organize by using common sense. Obviously before the children could start manipulating, measuring, classifying, or ordering anything, they had to have something to manipulate. Therefore, he needed to plan one of the students' first experiences as a gathering expedition. Then the children could come back and begin to classify what they gathered according to their own categories. He liked this idea since it would not only allow the children a great deal of autonomy, but he could observe how they classified; this would help him gain some insights into each child's developmental level (refer to chapter 1 for the significance of development on student learning). He would probably follow this up with measuring and counting experiences. Throughout the unit, children would be recording their "findings" just like scientists would. The most difficult of the experiences would probably be drawing a map to scale. Leonard wasn't sure that he or the children were ready for this just yet. He kept this in mind as a possible activity, but he also thought that, since they would be revisiting the park in different seasons, he might wait until later in the year to do this. He also thought that he might begin the map drawing on a smaller scale. He realized he needed to think about this more, so he decided not to include that activity as part of this unit. In this way Leonard planned in general ways for each of the units.

Determine What and How to Evaluate

Leonard knew he was near the end now, at least for science. He also knew how important this step was. If he didn't have a clear idea of what he should evaluate and how he was going to do it, then Leonard would never be certain that students were developing the skills that he and they will have worked so hard to attain. As he thought back to his methods courses, he remembered how important it was for students to be assessed in many different ways so that they can take advantage of their strengths. He wanted to do as much authentic assessment (see chapter 9) as he could, systematically collecting data on student performance while they were doing what the objectives called for. However, he also knew that there was still a place for paper-pencil tests, and he would be remiss if he didn't help children to demonstrate what they knew in that form. He remembered, too, that the objectives he had chosen were from next year's proficiency tests and that those would be multiple choice test items; he had to help his students prepare for that type of test item.

He decided that he would try to develop two different "instruments" for measuring each objective. At this point in time, he was just going to do this informally, but Leonard would be sure that these instruments were developed before he started each unit so that he could use these to help him and his students stay on track. For each objective then he was going to develop several items to which students could respond in a paper-pencil test format. Leonard also wanted to do performance assessments, though, of their classifying and observational skills. He decided that he would develop a performance test that students would do in "stations." He envisioned each station in the room having some artifacts at them and students having to respond to specific directions. He wanted them to do this in groups, since that would be the way they would be learning to do many of these skills, and so it would be a group grade. He knew that he could figure out the basic skill stations ahead of time, but he would have to wait to decide what will go in them until after he saw what kinds of things children gathered on their own. . . .

In this way, Leonard would continue to cycle back through the model, planning and more clearly specifying what students would do and how they would do it. This process provides you, as well, with a way to go about developing curriculum within your class, your grade level, your school. The process itself can be very messy sometimes. And while Taba's model appears to be a linear one, proceeding from step one through step seven, we hope that our description of Leonard's process demonstrates that you will often be thinking of step seven when you appear to be focusing on step two. When you get to step seven, you may have to look all the way back to step one because of what you have learned in the process of planning. As you gain experience, the planning gets easier, less time consuming. Be assured, though, that the time you spend at this end will pay off for both you and your students as you work your ways through the school year.

SUMMARY

Being able to develop curriculum plans is one of the most rewarding and intellectually stimulating activities in which teachers engage. As a new teacher, it will be one of the most significant challenges you will identify in your responsibilities as a professional. The process requires teachers to call on vast stores of knowledge, the lenses to which we referred, from a variety of fields and synthesize them into a connected whole. Ideally, curricula that students experience are seamless webs that build upon their prior knowledge and skills and facilitate their developing ever more sophisticated skills and knowledge.

In this chapter you have been introduced to some of these stores of knowledge. Philosophies of education provide teachers with ways of considering their craft and also with ways of going about the practice of teaching. We hope that you will investigate these in greater depth as you consider your own thoughts about the teaching-learning connection. The lenses provide you with things to consider before (and as) you plan; these lenses may also provide you with insight into where others with whom you will work are "coming from" when you seem to have different ideas about what is good for your students. You have also been shown a model of curriculum development that can be used by novices and experts alike. Chapter 2 concludes Section I, Identifying the Challenge. Section II, Defining the Challenge, will provide you with information you can use to further clarify the challenges of teaching your students about important content in meaningful ways. As you continue to read other chapters in this book, you will gain more information about some of the "nuts and bolts" of planning. All of these other topics, however, ultimately must be woven together through the planning process to which you have been introduced here.

REFLECTIONS

1. Look at each of the philosophies of education. Which one would you identify that appears to be more in line with your own thinking? with your professor's? with teachers you have seen in the field? Do you believe that it is important to build your teaching on the basis of a philosophical stance, or is it more important to choose bits and pieces from each philosophy? What do you believe is best for students?

2. Think back on your own schooling experiences. What kinds of procedures, rules, or rituals did you follow that might indicate that a hidden curriculum existed? Was this a good thing for you? for your peers?

3. Look back at the example of Leonard's planning for his nine-week science curriculum. As you look at the lenses he used in diagnosing needs, what sorts of inferences can you make about the lenses on students, society, content and/or teaching, and learning through which Leonard appears to be looking. Is he clearly aligned with a particular philosophy in all cases? Do you think he should be? Support your comments by referring back to the appropriate section of the chapter or from outside reading you may have done.

TEACHER AS RESEARCHER

Curriculum Development

Walker, D. F., & Soltis, J. F. (1997). *Curriculum and aims* (3rd ed.). New York: Teachers College Press.

The authors provide a very readable, though more in-depth, introduction to several of the same subjects addressed in this chapter. In the back of the book are a number of "Cases and Disputes." Choose one of these and present it to the class as a discussion starter. Come up with questions to help your colleagues think like decision-makers: What challenges or issues can you identify (the "I" in IDEAL) in this case? What important questions would you ask of someone in a situation like this as you try to define and clarify (the "D" in IDEAL) the boundaries of this case?

Sizer, T. R. (1992). *Horace's school: Redesigning the American high school.* Boston: Houghton-Mifflin.

Sizer writes a semi-fictional account of teachers engaging in the planning process from the ground up. The process, complete with many of the disagreements that teachers have in planning, is presented in detailed accounts of particular planning sessions. Identify what some of these disagreements are. Talk with class members about some of the plans they designed. Do you think the plans are appropriate responses to the disagreements you've identified (in answering this LAST question you begin to look at the "L" in IDEAL)?

Essentialism

Stringfield, S., Datnow, A., Nunnery, J., & Ross, S. M. (1996). First Year Evaluation of the Implementation of the Core Knowledge Sequence: Qualitative Report [On-line Resource] Available: http://www.coreknowledge.org/CKproto2/about/eval/qual.htm.

This site has results of an on-line study of schools that had previously adopted the Core Knowledge Curriculum. This report presents the preliminary qualitative results. What are the benefits that are cited? Does this convince you that the Core Knowledge Curriculum is an effective way for schools to plan curriculum?

Critical Theory

Bigelow, W. (1990). Inside the classroom: Social vision and critical pedagogy. *Teachers College Record, 91* (3), 437–448.

The author describes the real-world application of Critical Theory in a high school classroom in an urban, lower-SES environment. Bigelow provides activities designed to encourage students in raising critical awareness and his students' sample journal excerpts that demonstrate some success in meeting this objective. Identify some of the problems encountered by both students and teacher in instituting this type of curriculum. Would you suggest that a new teacher try this out?

Messner, M. (1976). Bubblegum and surplus value. *The Insurgent Sociologist, 6* (4), 51–56.

The author describes a classroom "game" that students and instructor can play to demonstrate the ways in which capitalist societies attempt to maintain the status quo. Messner provides a detailed description of the method, rules, and predicted events, as well as a discussion framework for discussing Marxist philosophy. What instructional challenges do history and government teachers face, as identified by Messner? What aspects of the IDEAL decision-making model do students who play the bubblegum game experience (refer to the IDEAL graphic at the beginning of this section and reread the introduction)?

SECTION II

IDEAL

Defining the Challenge

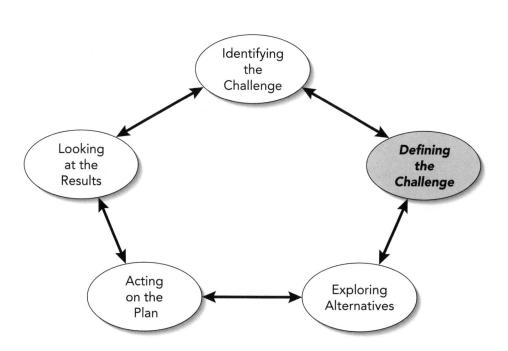

Identifying
the
Challenge

Looking
at the
Results

**Defining
the
Challenge**

Acting
on the
Plan

Exploring
Alternatives

We find that identifying challenges in a general sense is often quite easy. You recognize, for instance, that some of the courses that you are taking in your college career are more difficult than others. Identifying that a course is difficult for you can be quite clear, sometimes painfully and frighteningly so, when you first begin to read the required textbooks or as you prepare for the first test. Defining what it is about the course that is challenging you, however, often requires a great deal of thought. When you engage in the thinking necessary to define your challenge, your intent is to provide yourself with greater clarity about the issues surrounding your difficulty. You may do this by investigating the history of this particular challenge for yourself, or eliminating some possible causes, or classifying this challenge in relation to similar ones that you have had in the past, or a combination of these considerations, or some other way of thinking about the issues that confront you. For example, you may discover that you're having difficulty in a statistics course you are taking. You may recognize that statistics has a good deal of mathematics involved in it and that you've never performed exceptionally well in math. However, you've always found that working with peers has often provided you with some of the support you needed to improve your understanding in previous math classes. You know that some of the people in class have been having difficulty because your instructor has been having lab periods where you've used SPSS statistics packages on personal computers; but you feel comfortable with computers, and those who have complained do not. In fact, that's been the part of class that you've enjoyed the most. . . . And your thinking would continue in this manner. You would be more carefully defining what particular challenge or challenges face you, while you would concurrently be clarifying the resources and skills that you have that will allow you to meet these challenges.

It's often easier to define a challenge in which you are directly involved and for which you may be the only person affected by any plans to remedy the situation. It's a much greater challenge to define carefully the issues that you will address in planning and teaching in schools. Teachers need to analyze many factors as they prepare to teach their students, and no two teachers will necessarily define these problems in the same ways. In the last section, we identified the challenges of teaching in terms of the issues involved in teaching some type of content to the students who are there in front of you. In this section, we will look at how teachers define this content in terms of the students and content that they teach. In chapter 3, the challenges you will need to define are ones of direction and design of student learning. In that chapter, you will build upon the general planning model from chapter 2 by more explicitly sequencing units and writing goals and objectives that provide you and your students with a clear direction for learning. In chapter 4 the challenge you will pose for yourself is clarifying *how* to teach what your students must learn. In that chapter you will be introduced to three different whole lesson models and formats, as well as some other issues to consider as you prepare to teach for student learning.

CHAPTER 3
Constructing Units

CONVERSATION

During the previous school year, Mike Ball (an eight-year veteran and newly-appointed chair of the English department at Spinner High School) was a valued mentor to James Nygun, who was beginning his first year teaching. On a sunny morning in mid-August, Mike and James met at a local golf course to enjoy a round or two of golf.

"Hi James! It's good to see you!" greeted Mike as the two teachers approached the first tee. "You're looking tan and fit! Have you enjoyed your summer vacation?"

"It's been great Mike," replied James. "But to be honest I'm really looking forward to getting back to the classroom. I miss the kids, and I'm excited to try some new things. I'm really looking forward to getting a head start on planning for the school year. To be quite honest, there were times last year when I felt that I was staying barely ahead of my students."

"I know what you mean James," responded Mike as he prepared to tee off from the first hole. "Curriculum planning can be quite challenging. I remember my first year teaching. I had never read most of the stories and books that are listed in our district's curriculum guide, so I spent my first year reading *and* planning to teach!"

"Yeah, that pretty much describes my first year," chimed James. "But now that I have a much better *feel* for the subject matter, I'm actually looking forward to the challenge of planning for instruction."

Swish! Mike hits a perfect shot off the first tee!

"I'll show you some strategies that I have used to help me organize and sequence instruction," grins Mike as he watches his golf ball bounce down the fairway. "When we get to the clubhouse I'll sketch a planning matrix that I use to keep me focused. Loser buys lunch!"

"Great," smiles James as he selects a three wood from his golf bag. "At least if I lose the game I'll come out a winner as far as the challenge of planning for instruction is concerned!"

DEVELOPING COMPETENCE

1. Distinguish between courses, units, and lessons as portions of instruction.
2. Distinguish between instructional goals and learner objectives.

3. Use curriculum guides to identify instructional units for your teaching area of interest.

4. Explain the important contributions of Benjamin Bloom, Robert Gagné, and Jerome Bruner in planning for instruction in the cognitive domain.

5. Create a planning matrix for an instructional unit.

6. Write lesson objectives and behavioral objectives for the three domains of knowledge.

INTRODUCTION

When people in the general population think of teaching, they tend to think of those things that teachers do when they conduct classes. They may remember someone like Mrs. Santori demonstrating through whole-class instruction when to use a semicolon. Or maybe it's when someone like Ms. Rachter began a chemistry class on gases by breathing helium and beginning her introduction in a high and squeaky voice. Or maybe even when someone like Mr. Ball captivated his class with a dramatic reading of the carnage of ancient Roman gladiatorial games. Or maybe . . . you can fill in your own names and events. Just as with "stage productions," before any of these "classroom performances" take place, there is a great deal that teachers do behind the scenes to prepare.

When teachers contemplate their teaching, especially at the start of a new school year, they often begin by thinking of time. What will happen in the space of a year? a semester? a grading period? What should my students know at the end of the school year that they don't know now at the beginning? How will I know what to teach on a day-to-day basis? Planning for instruction is a complex and ongoing process. Although teachers may go about the process in slightly different ways, there are some general principles that effective teachers use in planning for instruction. This chapter will provide you with ways of thinking about the subject matter or curriculum that you will teach and strategies for organizing and sequencing subject matter in a logical and systematic manner. Thinking back on Taba's Curricular Planning Model that was introduced in chapter 2, we will consider what Taba refers to as "identifying objectives, and selecting and organizing content."

COURSES, UNITS, AND LESSONS

When teachers talk to each other about subject matter or curriculum their conversation usually revolves around segments of the curriculum—more specifically **courses, units,** and **lessons.** Figure 3.1 illustrates the relationship between these segments of the curriculum. In terms of time consumed and the amount of curriculum content to be taught, a **course** is the longest and the most extensive. In junior high and high school, a course is usually a semester or a whole year in length. Biology, algebra, or English composition are typical high school courses. In elementary and middle school, it is more common to refer to courses as "sub-

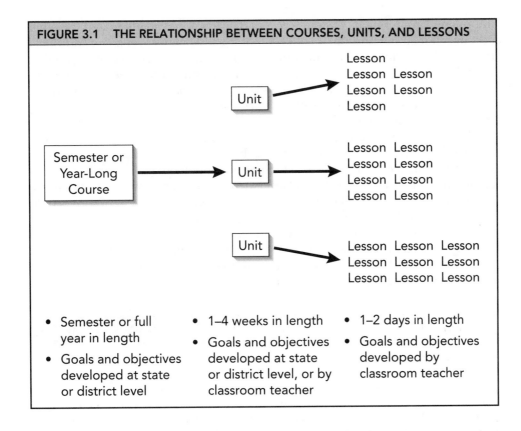

FIGURE 3.1   THE RELATIONSHIP BETWEEN COURSES, UNITS, AND LESSONS

- Semester or full year in length
- Goals and objectives developed at state or district level

- 1–4 weeks in length
- Goals and objectives developed at state or district level, or by classroom teacher

- 1–2 days in length
- Goals and objectives developed by classroom teacher

jects." Language arts, mathematics, and science are typical elementary and middle school subjects, and they are usually scheduled for an entire school year. Some subjects at these levels, such as health, music, and art may be scheduled several times a week over an entire year or semester, or they may be blocked for a period of time (e.g., three weeks of art, three of music, etc.) and rotated throughout a year or semester. Whatever their configuration, these courses (or subjects) provide the systemic organization under which most schools conduct their teaching and learning interactions. The "chunking" of content into courses is the initial step in identifying what you will be teaching your students. The determination of the specific skills and knowledge that comprise the courses you will teach is made at the state or district level where teams of subject matter and instructional experts develop subject level and grade level **curriculum guides.** Sometimes these guides are called a **graded course of study.** A curriculum guide provides teachers with a broad map of the subject matter and skills they are expected to teach in a particular course or subject. You have a professional obligation to follow your district's curriculum guides, thus ensuring the continuity of instruction within and between grade levels. You will want to compare your curriculum guides with other sources to ensure a comprehensive coverage of the subject matter and skills. In particular, manuals for standardized tests are an important consideration. Although school districts adopt standardized tests that best match their curriculum, it is likely that the tests may cover some additional material. Furthermore, you will want to coordinate the sequence of instruction with the test administration dates, if it has not already been done for you in the curriculum guide. Standards published by professional teaching organizations, textbooks, and student interest inventories are other sources that may provide information for course-level planning.

Planning for a semester, much less an entire school year, would be a formidable task for even the most experienced teacher because this involves too much of the curriculum at one time. Instead, teachers identify more manageable segments of the curriculum. These shorter and less extensive segments of the curriculum are called **units.** A **unit** is a relatively small and manageable segment of the curriculum. Units of instruction that vary in length from one to four weeks are generally pretty reasonable time periods for planning. Ultimately, the length of time for a unit depends on the complexity of the subject matter, the nature of your students, the amount of time on a daily or weekly basis that is scheduled for the course, and your own planning experience and skills.

Activity 3.1

Examine curriculum guides for the grade level and subject that you are interested in teaching and note the organizational structure and content of the guides. School districts in your area should have copies of curriculum guides that you can examine. In addition, your campus library may have copies of guides or subscribe to the Kraus Curriculum Library. Make a list of some possible units that are suggested by the guides and estimate the instructional time (number of weeks) you think would be needed to teach the units.

Considering what must be taught over several weeks is certainly a much more reasonable amount of planning; but, you must still consider what happens on a day-to-day basis. Those daily classroom activities are the smallest segment of instruction, and they are called **lessons.** Sometimes a lesson can be completed in one class session and other times a lesson extends over several days. It is often what teachers do in those individual lessons that constitute what the public perceives as teaching. For now, we are going to concentrate on the challenge of planning the larger units of instruction, and lessons and lesson planning will be addressed in more detail in chapter 4.

Although curriculum guides are an essential resource for identifying the subject matter you will teach, you are still likely to find yourself asking questions like these: How do I go about translating the information in a curriculum guide to the day-to-day business that takes place in my classroom? How do I ensure that teaching and learning is done in such a manner that my students arrive at the destination point at that end the school year? As you will see in the next section, this is done by considering the **instructional goals** and **learner objectives** that are the very essence of the teaching and learning process.

INSTRUCTIONAL GOALS AND LEARNER OBJECTIVES

Instructional goals and **learner objectives** are both statements that describe what you expect to happen in your classroom. The terms *goal* and *objective* are rather similar in meaning. In fact, most dictionaries and thesauruses use these terms interchangeably. Sometimes the terms *goal* and *objective* are confusing for beginning teachers, because veteran teachers, textbook authors, college professors, and other educators may use the terms interchangeably. We have chosen to be very explicit in our definition and will be consistent throughout the text. The distinction between the two terms is made when we clarify them with the adjectives *instructional* and *learner*. An **instructional goal** is a statement that identifies the *teacher's* intent or purpose of instruction. Instructional goals are the foundation of what *you* expect to happen on a day-to-day and week-to-week basis in the classroom. In contrast, a **learner objective** is a statement that identifies in very clear and explicit terms exactly what the *learner* will know or be able to do as an outcome of instruction. So throughout the text, when we talk about instructional goals we will be focusing on teachers, and when we use the term learner objective we will be shifting our focus to students.

Table 3.1 compares several instructional goals and related learner objectives that Mrs. Allen has identified for her seventh grade middle school students. Notice that the learner objectives flow naturally from the instructional goals. That is, the instructional goal helps Mrs. Allen to focus on where her students should be heading, and the learner objective identifies the skills or knowledge that her students will need to demonstrate to show that they have arrived at the goal. Let's take a closer look at how Mrs. Allen uses instructional goals to create learner objectives.

The first instructional goal in Table 3.1 happens to be for mathematics, and Mrs. Allen identified the goal directly from her district's curriculum guide. The purpose of the instructional goal is to help students acquire the skills to interpret

TABLE 3.1   A COMPARISON OF INSTRUCTIONAL GOALS AND RELATED LEARNER OBJECTIVES

Instructional Goal		Learner Objective
To foster students ability to interpret and create tables and graphs.	⇒	The student will be able to interpret tables and graphs.
To promote the appreciation and value of historical and contemporary literature.	⇒	The student will read the following literary genre: novel, short story, poetry, drama, biography, myths, and folk literature
To introduce the concepts of vertebrates and invertebrates.	⇒	The student will list the differences between vertebrates and invertebrates.

and create various tables and graphs. The related learner objective changes the focus from what Mrs. Allen wants to achieve to what her students will actually do to demonstrate that they are moving toward or have already grasped the goal. It is likely that Mrs. Allen will provide examples and work through a number of practice exercises with her students to help them develop their skills. Note that the difference in wording between the instructional goal and the learner objective may appear to be subtle, but it is an important difference.

The second instructional goal in Table 3.1 is from the district's language arts curriculum guide. The instructional goal is to promote students' appreciation of the different kinds of literature. Before Mrs. Allen can find out if her students either appreciate or value these works, the learner objective of reading a variety of genres must be identified as a natural and meaningful extension of the instructional goal. In doing this, Mrs. Allen has many decisions to make from the different methods or activities that she can use to the different types of stories she may assign or suggest. Because the goal involves both appreciation and valuing, it is possible that some students may never appreciate reading Jonathon Edwards' "Sinners in the Hands of an Angry God," but they may still value it for what it says about the austerity of Puritan life in Colonial America.

Goals and objectives can be identified for courses, units, and lessons, and you will draw upon the inter-relatedness between learner objectives at the course, unit, and lesson level to make instructional decisions about teaching and learning. At the course level, goals and objectives are very broad statements that are typically established at the state or district level. Because course goals and objectives are very broad statements, they are not practical for day-to-day planning. Most likely, you will begin your instructional planning at the unit level. In fact, unit level planning is a very effective way to ensure that the various segments of the curriculum are solidly linked. From the vantage point of units, or the "middle" segment of the curriculum, you can easily keep course and lesson objectives in view. Consequently, an important task you will face at the beginning of each year is to identify the unit objectives that will be the essence of the course or subject you teach. Some curriculum guides may identify unit goals and objectives and others may not, leaving those decisions to you or to a team of teachers in your school. Instructional goals at the lesson level are the most specific,

---

FIGURE 3.2   INTERNET SITES ABOUT INSTRUCTIONAL GOALS AND LEARNER OBJECTIVES

- **Developing Educational Standards**
  http://putwest.boces.org/standards.html

- **Understanding Objectives**
  http://edweb.sdsu.edu/courses/EDTEC540/objectives/ObjectivesHome.html

- **Writing Behavioral Objectives**
  http://www.valdosta.edu/~whuitt/psy702/plan/behobj.html

- **How to Write Behavioral Objectives**
  http://members.spree.com/teach2prime/objectives.htm

and you will be in complete charge of identifying and writing them. Figure 3.2 identifies some Internet sites where you can learn more about instructional goals and learner objectives. As you can see in the figure, several of the websites use the term "behavioral objectives." Behavioral objectives are quite similar to learner objectives, and you will read more about behavioral objectives in the last section of this chapter.

LEARNER OBJECTIVES AND THE DOMAINS OF KNOWLEDGE

Once the learner objectives are identified, it is important to consider the type or **domain of knowledge** that will be the main focus of instruction. Three domains of knowledge are commonly used by educators, and these domains can be used to classify both unit and lesson objectives. Table 3.2 presents examples of learner objectives classified according to the three domains. Note that the learner objectives from the **cognitive domain** deal with what the student knows, or comprehends.

TABLE 3.2   LEARNER OBJECTIVES FROM THE COGNITIVE, AFFECTIVE, AND PSYCHOMOTOR DOMAINS

Learner Objectives from the Cognitive Domain	Learner Objectives from the Affective Domain	Learner Objectives from from the Psychomotor Domain
The student will use the dictionary to determine the meaning and/or spelling of words.	The student will value cultural differences.	The student will perform a tumbling routine.
The student will read, construct, and interpret charts, tables, and graphs.	The student will appreciate reading poetry for enjoyment.	The student will use American Sign Language to communicate a simple message.
The student will write business and friendly letters.	The student will choose to follow classroom rules.	The student will construct an equilateral triangle using a straightedge and compass.
The student will read myths, legends, folk tales, and fables.	The student will choose to recycle.	The student will demonstrate the procedure for a fire drill.
The student will use observation and instruments to predict weather changes.	The student will consider the opinions of others in making personal decisions.	The student will maneuver within a computer program using a keyboard or mouse.

This domain is primarily concerned with the intellectual skills and knowledge that are the mainstay of the typical classroom subjects. For example, the cognitive learner objective of using the dictionary to determine meanings and/or spellings of words could be explicitly taught in a unit on dictionary use.

In contrast, objectives from the **affective domain** concern the feelings, attitudes, and values of the learner. Generally these will reflect affective goals that you may wish to instill in your students, rather than feelings, attitudes, and values that they may currently possess. For instance, students with little exposure to other cultures or people different from themselves are unlikely to come to school with much understanding of the differences between themselves and their peers from a different culture. They may think that certain rituals or behaviors common to the other culture are "weird." Given these thoughts, it is also unlikely that these students will *value* their peers' differences. It may then become your goal to increase *knowledge* about other cultures, a cognitive objective, so students will begin to *value* the differences, the affective objective. In this way cognitive and affective objectives work in an integrated manner to further student learning. Working in the affective domain is often "muddier" than the cognitive. It is very clear when or if a student can use a dictionary to determine the meaning of a word. It is not nearly so clear whether a student truly values cultural differences. Affective objectives are seldom the main focus of instruction; rather, they are often considered an indirect outcome of instruction.

Finally, objectives from the **psychomotor domain** may simply require a physical skill or manipulation, such as executing a tumbling routine. Or, psychomotor objectives may involve a combination of physical skill and mental thought such as using a computer mouse or keyboard. In this case, the student must have both the manual dexterity and eye-hand coordination to manipulate a mouse and the underlying understanding of the purpose and use for a particular computer program.

Some learner objectives do not fit neatly into one domain. Consider the following objective for a health education class: "The student will demonstrate CPR." This objective would be considered a **combination objective** because it clearly crosses all three domains. To demonstrate CPR the student must have an understanding of the circulatory system (cognitive domain), execute chest compressions (psychomotor domain), and value the need to know first aid skills (affective domain). As a health education teacher you would need to decide which aspects of CPR should be taught first and how to integrate the various components of the objective. Figure 3.3 lists many good websites where you can learn more about the domains of knowledge.

Activity 3.2

For a subject or grade level of interest to you, compile a list of instructional goals or learner objectives from curriculum guides, professional standards, textbooks, or other sources. Classify the goals and objectives according to domains of knowledge. If the goals or objectives seem to fit into a combination of two or more domains, consider if one domain is more predominant than another.

FIGURE 3.3   INFORMATIONAL SOURCES ABOUT THE DOMAINS OF LEARNING

- **The Cognitive Domain Websites**
  http://www.it.utk.edu/~jklittle/edsmrt521/cognitive.html
  http://www.valdosta.peachnet.edu/~whuitt/psy702/cogsys/bloom.html

- **The Affective Domain Websites**
  http://www.it.utk.edu/~jklittle/edsmrt521/affective.html
  http://www.valdosta.peachnet.edu/~whuitt/psy702/affsys/affdom.html

- **The Psychomotor Domain Websites**
  http://www.it.utk.edu/~jklittle/edsmrt521/psychomotor.html

- **The Three Domains of Learning Websites**
  http://websites.ntl.com/~james.atherton/learning/bloomtax.htm
  http://www.usd.edu/admin/vpaa/assessment/taxonomies.html
  http://home.regent.edu/loulz/taxomomyvb.html#return4

The domain of knowledge is an important consideration because the nature of the learner objectives will have an impact on many of the instructional decisions you will make. For example, objectives from the cognitive domain may be taught and assessed in a different manner than those from the affective domain and psychomotor domains.

LEARNER OBJECTIVES AND GAGNÉ'S FIVE CATEGORIES OF LEARNING OUTCOMES

Another approach to classifying learner objectives was suggested by learning theorist Robert Gagné who identified five categories of learning outcomes (Gagné 1965; Gagné, Briggs, and Wager 1992). Table 3.3 compares the five categories with the domains of knowledge and provides examples of a corresponding learner objective. Note that Gagné's first three learning categories, **verbal information, intellectual skills,** and **cognitive strategies** are actually components of the cognitive domain. Gagné's **attitudes** and **motor skills** are equivalent to the affective and psychomotor domains respectively.

One reason that Gagné's classification system is noteworthy is that it considers the cognitive domain in considerable detail. This is particularly useful for most teachers because the majority of their learner objectives are likely to come from the cognitive domain. This added detail may prove especially helpful because the greater detail compels you to consider more carefully the particular cognitive skills that your students must use. This may also help you to overcome a tendency that some teachers have of focusing on verbal information (memorization of terms, names, dates, etc.) instead of higher level intellectual skills and cognitive strategies.

Let's examine Gagné's cognitive categories of learning in more detail. According to Gagné, **verbal information** describes factual knowledge or labels. Verbal information is often important for everyday living. For example, knowing that a flashing red traffic light means "stop" is an essential piece of verbal

TABLE 3.3   GAGNÉ'S FIVE CATEGORIES OF LEARNING OUTCOMES

Gagné's Category of Learning Outcome	Domain of Knowledge	Learner Objectives
Verbal Information	Cognitive	The student will name the presidents of the United States.
Intellectual Skills	Cognitive	The student will rewrite fractions in lowest terms.
Cognitive Strategies	Cognitive	The student will use an outline to organize class notes.
Attitudes	Affective	The student will choose to eat a balanced diet.
Motor Skills	Psychomotor	The student will use a potter's wheel to form a clay bowl.

information. In addition, verbal information is foundational to the more complex intellectual skills. Although your students will arrive at school with considerable amounts of verbal information, you will need to assure that they have *mastered* the necessary verbal information before they can go on to more complex tasks.

Imagine that your fifth-grade mathematics students are learning about graphs and tables, and at some point during instruction, your students will "commit to memory" the following pieces of verbal information:

A bar graph uses parallel bars of varying lengths to illustrate comparative amounts.

A pie chart is circular in shape with wedges or 'slices' that illustrate parts of a whole.

A time line uses a zigzag or curved line to show trends over a period of time.

It is unlikely that you and your students would have to spend much time simply memorizing this verbal information. In other words, you are not likely to make the verbal information the *focus* of instruction. Through discussion and example, your students would master these concepts in a natural way as they *interpret* and *construct* their own tables and graphs. These are more complex cognitive tasks that Gagné considers intellectual skills. Simply put, **intellectual skills** involve learning *how* to do something. These skills are the basis of most school learning.

Now, assume that you are teaching a high school history class that is studying the Viet Nam war. Eventually, your students will be able to compare and contrast the social, economic, and political conditions that led to United States involvement in and eventual withdrawal from the war. But before they do that they will have to memorize names, dates, places, and other facts, or verbal information. In this case there may be a day or two of instruction that is devoted to the verbal information, and you may even give a vocabulary test to assess your students' progress. Without the requisite verbal information it will be difficult for your students to move on to the intellectual skill of considering the complex issues surrounding the war. Admittedly, memorizing vocabulary words and other related verbal information can be challenging. To help your students master this task, you will probably instruct your students in a study method they can use to organize the verbal information for later recall. In other words, your students are learning a **cognitive strategy,** an aspect of the cognitive domain that refers to the students' abilities to think and learn. Cognitive strategies are special kinds of intellectual skills, and they will be discussed in more detail in chapter 7.

Activity 3.3

Use the list of goals and objectives that you identified in Activity 3.2 and reclassify them according to Gagné's five categories of learning. Compare your results with that of a classmate. Did you classify the goals and objectives in the same manner? How does Gagné's greater specificity within the cognitive domain effect your classifications?

LEARNER OBJECTIVES FROM THE COGNITIVE DOMAIN

For the majority of teachers, most of the teaching and learning decisions they will make center on the cognitive domain. Not surprising, learning theorists and curriculum specialists have written extensively about teaching considerations in this domain. Three educators whose writings are considered particularly noteworthy are Benjamin Bloom, Jerome Bruner, and of course, Robert Gagné.

Benjamin Bloom's Taxonomy of Educational Objectives

The *Taxonomy of Educational Objectives, The Classification of Educational Goals, Handbook I: Cognitive Domain* was published in 1956, and it is considered to be one of the most influential educational works of the past fifty years. It is a standard reference in curriculum development and teacher education, and it would be rather unlikely to come across an educator who has not heard of the taxonomy. Benjamin Bloom, an examiner at the University of Chicago, was the editor of the handbook and for this reason the taxonomy is most commonly referred to as *Bloom's Taxonomy*. In fact, the work represents the contributions of over two dozen educators who contributed to the development of the taxonomy over a five-year time period. The idea for the taxonomy was generated by a group of college and university examiners who felt that a common frame of reference would help them share ideas and materials related to testing.

In addition to focusing attention on testing, the taxonomy served another purpose. It also helped educators change their focus from the teacher's actions in the classroom (instructional goals) to what the learner knows or does (learner objectives), and it emphasized the need for clearly stated learner outcomes. The taxonomy contains six major levels of learning and a number of sub-categories within each major level. The major levels and examples of learner objectives are listed in Table 3.4.

TABLE 3.4   BLOOM'S *TAXONOMY OF EDUCATIONAL OBJECTIVES*

Level of Learning	Definition	Learner Objective
Knowledge	*Memorization*–Remembering or recalling previously learned information	The student will name the Great Lakes. The student will define the term 'photosynthesis.'
Comprehension	*Understanding*–Grasping the meaning of learned information	The student will explain the process of evaporation. The student will summarize the plot of a short story.
Application	*Using*–Using learned information in new situations	The student will solve two-digit addition problems that require regrouping. The student will use a question mark to end an interrogative sentence.
Analysis	*Taking apart*–Breaking down learned information into its component parts so that its organizational structure may be understood	The student will outline the main points in a written passage. The student will distinguish between the economic, political, and social antecedents to the Civil War.
Synthesis	*Putting together*–Putting learned information together to form a whole	The student will create a model of a simple closed electrical circuit. The student will design a personal World Wide Web home page.
Evaluation	*Judging*–Use criteria or standards to make a judgement	The student will rate a written composition on elements of grammar, organization, and style. The student will justify their position on an ethical issue.

Note that the levels of learning are arranged in a hierarchy with knowledge and comprehension levels considered less complex mental tasks than synthesis and evaluation. At the **knowledge** level students merely recall information from memory, and at the **comprehension** level they can restate or translate information in his or her own words. At the **application** level, the learners use information in a new situation. At the **analysis** level, they break down material into its component parts and see the relationships between the parts. In contrast, the learner combines elements or parts in such a way to create a new structure at the **synthesis** level. At the **evaluation** level, students use criteria and standards to make an assessment. The following example illustrates how the levels are integrated within a learning task.

In her language arts class, Martha is learning about the aspects of fictional writing. Martha can name the major elements of a story such as characters, plot, setting, and point of view (knowledge), and she can summarize in her own words the plot of *A Wrinkle in Time,* a story that her class has read and discussed together (comprehension). Martha has selected a new book from the library that she will read on her own and report about to the class. She will use what she has learned about fictional writing to identify the elements of the new book she is reading (application). Martha will note the unique qualities of the characters and the major events of the plot (analysis). By considering the nature of the characters and the events of the story, Martha will begin to formulate an idea of how the story will conclude (synthesis). Finally, in writing her book review, Martha will consider why she would or would not recommend the story to other students (evaluation). As you can see, a seemingly simple question like, "Would you recommend this book to someone else your age?" involves a number of complex mental operations. As a teacher, it is important for you to be aware of these operations as you plan student activities.

Over the years, *Bloom's Taxonomy* has received both praise and criticism. Suffice to say that the taxonomy is one tool that helps teachers consider the complexity of learning tasks by promoting the distinction between lower level cognitive skills such as memorization and more complex mental processes. An excellent and comprehensive review entitled *Bloom's Taxonomy: A Forty-Year Retrospective* was published in 1994 by the National Society for the Study of Education (Anderson and Sosniak, 1994).

Jerome Bruner's Structure of Subject Matter

In 1959 a conference of educators, scientists, and other scholars was held in Woods Hole, Massachusetts. The conference was sponsored by the National Academy of Sciences, and its primary purpose was to consider new educational methods, particularly in the area of science. Chaired by Harvard psychologist Jerome Bruner, the committee considered many issues related to curriculum design. The *Process of Education,* published by Bruner in 1960, was a direct outcome of the conference, and it outlined an ideology of education that is still endorsed today. One of the hallmarks of the book was the consideration of the structure of subject matter. Bruner and his colleagues concluded that subject matter is composed of **concepts, facts,** and **generalizations.** This structure is a vital

{222222

consideration in teaching because it provides learners with a framework for organizing the information they already know and managing the new information they will subsequently encounter. Table 3.5 displays some examples of concepts, facts, and generalizations related to a mathematics unit on tables and graphs.

Concepts are categories of common objects or ideas. "Pie chart" is a **concrete concept** because it has certain observable physical characteristics and attributes. Rather than referring to a pie chart as "a circle with wedge-shaped slices", however, we use the term or concept "pie chart." In contrast, the concept "order" is considered an **abstract concept** because it cannot be defined based on physical or observable characteristics. Instead, abstract concepts rely on verbal definitions for their meaning. **Facts** are statements about concepts, and they come to us through direct observation or from trustworthy sources such as first hand accounts, dictionaries, and encyclopedias. Facts are very small pieces of subject matter. Although they are important pieces of information, by themselves they may be of little value to the learner. In contrast, **generalizations** are broad statements of fundamental principles and ideas that give structure and context to subject matter. Generalizations integrate facts and concepts, and in doing so, facilitate memory and transfer of learning to new situations.

Notice the interrelatedness of these three components for Sarah, a fourth grader, who is learning about different kinds of tables and graphs in her math class. For a class project, Sarah has recorded various weather-related information including the daily temperature and rainfall, and she would like to construct a graph to display the data she has collected. Sarah recognizes that tables and graphs are valuable tools for organizing numerical information and displaying comparative values, trends, and relationships (generalization). She knows that the specific type of table or graph she will construct depends on the type of data she has collected (general-

TABLE 3.5 FACTS, CONCEPTS, AND GENERALIZATIONS FOR A MATHEMATICS UNIT ON TABLES AND GRAPHS

Concepts	Facts	Generalizations
Bar chart Pie chart Vertical Horizontal Order Large Small	The individual segments of a pie chart are called 'wedges.' The bars on a bar chart can be displayed vertically or horizontally. The bars on a bar chart are usually ordered from largest to smallest.	Bar charts and pie graphs aid in the understanding of statistical relationships by presenting numerical data in a visual representation. Bar charts and pie graphs clarify the comparison of values, trends, and relationships that may not otherwise be apparent. The choice of a particular table or chart should be based on the type of data and the information to be communicated.

ization). Because her part of the project deals only with the average rainfall in various regions over the course of the year (fact), she considers her options. She could use a bar chart or pie chart (concepts) but settles on a bar chart, remembering that the bars can be displayed vertically or horizontally (fact). In this case she will display them horizontally, maybe drawing water lines in buckets, so her classmates can get a sense of how much more it rains in some months than others.

By building your units upon a foundation of concepts, it is easier to determine the factual material needed to build these concepts and to identify the relationships, or generalizations, among them. This process not only allows you to emphasize the most important facts as they relate to particular concepts, but it also informs you as to which aspects of text material can be de-emphasized or even ignored. These are important considerations as you consider how your students will best spend their class time and how you will properly evaluate them.

Robert Gagné's Verbal Information and Intellectual Skills

Gagné, a psychologist at Princeton University at the time, was a participant in the 1959 Woods Hole conference. He was particularly interested in the *process* of learning and has continued to write about this topic extensively. Among a number of topics, Gagné considered the complexity of learning in the cognitive domain. Specifically, Gagné identified three categories of verbal information and five categories of intellectual skills, and these components are illustrated in Table 3.6.

Note that although Gagné distinguished between learning labels, learning facts, and learning organized knowledge, these three aspects of **verbal information** are comparatively simple learning tasks. The learner is merely recalling information from rote memory. Some educators refer to this type of learning as subject matter knowledge or *declarative knowledge*. Gagné differentiated between verbal information and more complex learning tasks in which the learner is compelled to demonstrate various skills and abilities. At the lowest intellectual skill level, the learner is simply able to **discriminate** similarities and differences between objects. As skill levels develop, the learner is able to identify **concepts** based on concrete or defined characteristics. Finally, the learner is able to apply **simple rules** in a consistent manner and combine rules to **solve problems** that are more complex. Intellectual skills are sometimes called *procedural knowledge,* or knowledge of how to learn. The following example illustrates how verbal information and intellectual skills are integrated within a learning task.

Consider the situation in which Ben, an eight-year-old boy, sees an advertisement for a toy that he would like to have. Ben notes the price of the toy, counts the money in his piggy bank, estimates the amount of money he still needs to purchase the toy, and then approaches his parents with a plan to complete some household chores to earn the additional money. Estimating the amount of money needed to purchase the toy and devising a plan to earn the money is an example of problem solving. To reach this level of cognitive maturity, Ben learned considerable verbal information and other intellectual skills. When Ben was a toddler, his parents were careful not to leave small objects such as buttons or coins lying about on the table because Ben was liable to mistake these round objects for a tasty treat and inevitably, they would wind up in his

TABLE 3.6   GAGNÉ'S HIERARCHY OF LEARNER OBJECTIVES

Verbal Information	Definition	Examples
Learning Labels	Naming objects	The mathematical symbol π is called 'pi'. Recalling that the sphere on which a map of the earth is depicted is called a 'globe.'
Learning Facts	Stating certainties about people, objects, or events	Albert Einstein formulated the theory of relativity. Deciduous trees lose their leaves once a year. The stock market crashed on October 29, 1929.
Learning Organized Knowledge	Larger bodies of interconnected facts	The functions of the major organs and systems of the human body. The characteristics of the nine planets in our solar system.

Intellectual Skills	Definition	Examples
Discrimination	Noticing similarities and differences of objects	Recognizing that Dachshunds, Collies, and Dalmatians are dogs. Recognizing that a cat and a dog are different types of animals.
Concrete Concepts	Identifying tangible objects by identifying observable attributes	Selecting the red M & Ms from a dish of candy. Sorting blocks by shape.
Defined Concepts	Identifying abstract objects by providing verbal definitions	Demonstrating an understanding that sugar sweetens the taste of a beverage when adding it to iced tea. Displaying an awareness of the concept 'safety' by wearing a seatbelt when driving a car.
Simple Rules	Responding to a problem in a consistent and predictable manner	Forming plurals by adding 's,' 'es,' or 'ies' to the end of a word. Multiplying the price of an item by a certain percentage to calculate sales tax.
Problem Solving	Combining simple rules to solve a complex problem	Solving a complex algebraic equation. Debugging a computer program.

mouth. As Ben's intellectual skills developed, he was able to discriminate between buttons, coins, and *edible* objects. In fact, presented with a handful of coins and buttons, Ben could select the coins by noting the differences in size and shape between the coins and the buttons. Eventually he could sort coins into piles of copper-colored pennies and silver-colored dimes, nickels, and quarters (discrimination). By the time Ben started school, he could select pennies from a handful of coins (concrete concept) and state the name of the coins (learning labels). When Ben went to the store with his mother or father, he usually asked for a quarter to put in the gumball machine. Ben had learned that money can be used to purchase things (defined concept) and that the cost of a gumball is a quarter (learning facts). At eight, Ben has learned that a dime, although smaller, has more value than a nickel or penny and that two nickels or ten pennies have the same value as a dime (learning organized facts). Finally, he can count the coins in his piggy bank (simple rules), and estimate the additional money he needs and devise a plan to earn the money (problem solving).

Bloom, Bruner, and Gagné Compared

As you begin to consider the day-to-day endeavor of teaching and learning, these three theorists provide you with a means to examine learner objectives in the cognitive domain. Although they describe somewhat different approaches, Bloom, Bruner, and Gagné are similar in that they distinguished between less complex rote-level learning (knowledge and comprehension, verbal learning, and facts) from more complex learning. Furthermore, they acknowledge that simple learning tasks, albeit foundational, are rarely the desired outcome of instruction. The distinction between the theorists is that Bruner considered the subject matter or **declarative knowledge,** while Bloom and Gagné considered the process of learning or **procedural knowledge.** In other words, Bruner examined *what* subject matter the learner should know and Bloom and Gagné addressed *how* the learner will *use* the subject matter. We will re-visit Bloom, Bruner, and Gagné in the last section of this chapter as we suggest an approach for identifying learner objectives at the lesson level.

LEARNER OBJECTIVES FROM THE AFFECTIVE AND PSYCHOMOTOR DOMAIN

In the previous sections, learner tasks from the cognitive domain were examined in considerable detail. For most teachers, the majority of their teaching will focus on learner objectives in this domain. Some teachers may focus their instructional decisions in other domains. For example, education course-work for physical education focuses almost exclusively on the psychomotor domain. Nearly all teachers have objectives that fall into the affective domain, and many of these fall under the general category of classroom management. We all want students who choose to follow rules and cooperate with others. Most of us also want students who develop a love for or appreciation of learning, works of literature, scientific discovery, and so on. David Krathwohl (1956) developed a taxonomy for classifying learner objectives in the affective domain, and the taxonomy is summarized in Table 3.7.

TABLE 3.7   KRATHWOHL'S TAXONOMY OF THE AFFECTIVE DOMAIN

Level of Affect	Definition	Learner Objective
Receiving	*Taking in*—being aware of events, sensations, or other phenomena	The student recognizes cultural differences. The student listens to a variety of musical genres.
Responding	*Active awareness*—doing something with or about an event, sensation, or phenomena	The student follows classroom rules. The student reads for recreation.
Valuing	*Accepting*—recognizing or supporting the worth of a thing, phenomena, or behavior	The student acknowledges the opinions of others. The student recognizes the importance of saving money.
Organization	*Create*—develop a set of values	The student develops a plan to save money for college. The student follows safe driving practices.
Characterization	*Integration*—act consistently in accordance to one's values	The student makes moral decisions based on a personal code of ethics. The student sets personal goals based on a philosophy of life.

The lowest level of this taxonomy is called receiving. At this level the learner merely listens to or is aware of a particular communication such as when children listen as the school rules are recited in class. The highest level of the taxonomy is called characterization by value. Children who choose to follow the rules because they believe in the inherent value of adhering to school policies are operating at the highest level of the hierarchy.

Influenced by Bloom's and Krathwohl's work in the cognitive and affective domains respectively, Anita Harrow (1972) developed a taxonomy for classifying learner objectives in the psychomotor domain. Harrow identified six classification levels, each with corresponding sub-levels. The six general levels of the taxonomy are listed in Table 3.8.

The lowest level of the taxonomy is called reflex movements and involves involuntary movements such as when children *automatically* close their eyes when splashed with water. In contrast, choreographing an ice-skating routine to music is an example of the highest level of the psychomotor domain. This level is called

TABLE 3.8   HARROW'S TAXONOMY OF PSYCHOMOTOR OBJECTIVES

Level of Movement	Definition	Learner Objective
Reflex Movements	Involuntary movements in response to a stimulus that are functional at birth.	Learner objectives cannot be written for involuntary movements.
Basic-Fundamental Movements	Simple movement patterns that form the basis for more complex movements.	The student will hop on one foot. The student will grip a pencil.
Perceptual Abilities	Abilities such as visual and auditory discrimination, eye-hand coordination that occur as a response to perceptual information.	The student will follow a set of verbal instructions. The student will catch a ball.
Physical Abilities	Abilities such as endurance, strength, and flexibility which are the foundation for the development of skilled movements.	The student will perform a backwards somersault. The student will decrease resting heart rate following fifteen minutes of speed walking.
Skilled Movements	Complex movements such as sports, dancing, and recreational skills.	The student will swim 100 meters using the breaststroke. The student will use sandpaper to smooth a piece of wood.
Non-discursive Communication	Expressive and interpretive movements that are used to communicate feelings such as facial expressions and body language.	The student will move to the rhythm of music.

non-discursive communication, and movements at this level consist of expressive and interpretive skills. The majority of students do not require instruction in physical skills. However, preschool children learning how to grip a pencil or use scissors and older students in physical education and shop classes, of course, do need skilled instruction in order to become proficient. It's important for you to recognize that physical behaviors are the basis of some tasks in most subject classes throughout the grades. A student whose eyes cannot track a line of print will have difficulty learning to read; one whose eye-hand coordination is not developed may have difficulty with word processing on a keyboard.

DEVELOPING INSTRUCTIONAL UNITS

We have just spent a good deal of attention considering the domains of knowledge, especially the cognitive domain. As a teacher, it is important that you are able to classify objectives because it can affect your ability to make important decisions. For instance, if you were to brainstorm all of the possible objectives you would like your students to accomplish, your ability to classify them may lead you to discover that you are focusing too much on knowledge level or verbal information objectives. Noticing this, you would be able to reconsider some of these objectives, or maybe even the structure of the subject matter itself, to more effectively challenge your students to work on higher-order thinking skills. In addition to classifying unit objectives according to the domain of knowledge, there are a number of other unit-level planning decisions that you may need to consider. Figure 3.4 summarizes these decisions, and in the paragraphs that follow we will list and discuss these decisions in a sequential manner. In reality, however, you will more likely consider these decisions concurrently.

Focus and Sequence of Instruction

Perhaps one of the initial tasks in developing units is to establish the **focus of instruction.** Typically, the focus of instruction is a skill, topic, or theme. These

---

FIGURE 3.4 INSTRUCTIONAL DECISIONS RELATED TO UNIT LEVEL PLANNING

Question	Decision	Considerations
What is the aim of the unit?	*Focus*	• Topic • Skill • Theme
In what order should the instructional material be taught?	*Sequence*	• Chronological • Developmental • Thematic
How detailed should instruction be?	*Depth*	• Available time • Importance of subject matter • Students' prior knowledge
How much subject matter should be covered?	*Breadth*	• Available time • Importance of subject matter • Students' prior knowledge

may run through the entire course or may be identified for specific units. For example, the focus of an elective English course may be the topic of "Great Books," while another course might be based on the theme "Coming of Age." At the unit level, a three-week unit in a high school biology class might be the topic "photosynthesis." A middle school language arts class might engage the skill of letter writing. Likewise, an instructional unit in a fifth-grade math class might be the skill "adding fractions." In elementary grades, the various subjects are often integrated around particular themes. For example, a first-grade interdisciplinary unit might have the theme "My Neighborhood," which could be used as the focus for math, reading, social studies, or virtually any subject. Examples and ideas of instructional units may be found in curriculum guides, professional development workshops and publications, and simply through talking with teachers in your school district.

In addition to focus, another important consideration is the **sequence** of the units. In other words, what topics and skills should be taught the first few weeks of the school year, what should be taught next, and so on. In some school districts, the sequence of instruction may be determined by district-level curriculum experts. In other school districts, teams of teachers determine the sequence of instruction for the subjects or grade-levels they teach. And still in other school districts, these types of planning decisions are left up to individual teachers. Some teachers base the sequence of instruction on the textbook they use for the subjects or courses they teach. Text publishers tend to sequence their books on one of three guiding principals: (1) *chronological order*—history textbooks, (2) *developmental or hierarchical*—math, reading, language arts, computer, and other skill-based textbooks, or (3) *thematic or topic-based*—science or social studies textbooks. Although textbooks can be a valuable reference for considering the sequence of instruction, you should never completely abdicate your decision-making expertise to a textbook publisher. Ultimately, you have the professional responsibility to consider the learning characteristics of your students while making curricular decisions, such as adding, deleting, and rearranging textbook material as necessary to meet your objectives. Another important factor you will want to consider in sequencing units is the date that district or state-level standardized tests will be administered. In many states, students are required to pass proficiency tests prior to receiving a diploma. A well-planned instructional unit serves little purpose if students are tested before they have an opportunity to learn the subject matter or skills.

Depth and Breadth of Coverage

A temptation for novice and veteran teachers alike is to include too much material in a unit. The danger, of course, is that in "covering the waterfront," no substantial content is learned. The issue here is **depth** versus **breadth.** You will have to decide how many topics to take up in a unit (breadth) and how much detail to include (depth). These decisions are based on a number of factors: How much time is available for instruction? In addition to the length of the class and the number of school days, what other factors such as all-school testing days, holidays, and school functions must be considered? How important is the subject matter for a particular group of students? Does the unit lay the groundwork for subsequent learning, or is the unit more for enrichment purposes? Given their mental development and schema (prior knowledge and knowledge structures), how ready are students for the unit? These and other questions will likely cross your mind as you plan your units. Your answers to these questions will help you determine whether you need to cover a particular topic, skill, or concept somewhat broadly or in much greater detail.

USING A PLANNING CALENDAR TO IDENTIFY INSTRUCTIONAL UNITS

Now, let's look at how Ms. Jones, a middle school social studies teacher, approaches her beginning-of-the-year planning. In the district where Ms. Jones teaches, the school year is 180 days or 36 weeks long. At the start of the school year, Ms. Jones has identified approximately nineteen unit-level objectives for the school year. By considering the focus, sequence, and depth and breadth of the units, Ms. Jones can begin to map out a rough plan for the school year. She can estimate which units are likely to be shorter (one or two weeks) and which will take longer (three or more weeks). With a calendar in hand, Ms. Jones tentatively marks off the weeks, labeling the units as she goes. Figure 3.5 illustrates Ms. Jones's planning calendar for the first three months of the school year. Although Ms. Jones will make changes and modifications to her planning calendar as the school year proceeds, this long-range planning technique gives her some assurance that her students will have the opportunity to learn all of the unit objectives during the school year.

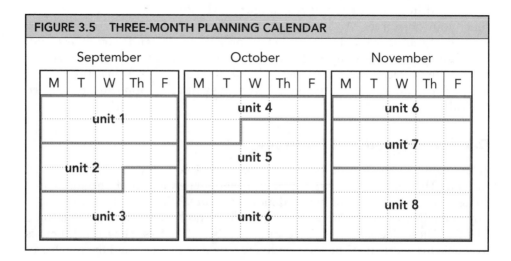

FIGURE 3.5   THREE-MONTH PLANNING CALENDAR

September					October					November				
M	T	W	Th	F	M	T	W	Th	F	M	T	W	Th	F

September: unit 1, unit 2, unit 3

October: unit 4, unit 5, unit 6

November: unit 6, unit 7, unit 8

USING A PLANNING MATRIX TO IDENTIFY LESSON OBJECTIVES

In Figure 3.5 you saw how a planning calendar can be used to approximate the amount of time required for instructional units during the school year. Once the units are mapped out, you can begin to plan at the lesson level. Lesson planning is the most detailed type of instructional planning you will undertake, and many of the subsequent chapters in this text address the various facets of lesson planning in considerable detail.

At the heart of lesson planning are the lesson objectives, the building blocks of teaching and learning. Perhaps the most important instructional decision you will make will involve identifying the appropriate lesson objectives. If you overlook key objectives at the lesson level, then the likelihood that your students will successfully achieve the related unit objective may be compromised.

Through their previous years of experience with both the subject matter and type of students, experienced teachers may be able to skillfully and intuitively generate lesson objectives. Like a skilled architect who readily knows the building materials and tools to select to complete a particular project, experienced teachers may be able to construct a unit somewhat naturally without referring to a blueprint at each and every step. Of course even the master architect must refer to a blueprint when the building task is new or particularly complex. Likewise, both the beginning teacher and the apprentice architect need to approach their tasks with a systematic plan in hand. For both, the results of omitting a foundational *building block* can be equally disastrous.

A number of excellent references illustrate methods for identifying lesson objectives. For example, Thomas R. Guskey (1997) suggests that teachers construct a table of specifications to identify learner objectives within a unit. Jerrold E. Kemp, Gary R. Morrison, and Steven M. Ross (1994) advocate the use of a task analysis as a method for determining the content in an instructional unit. Robert M. Gagné, Leslie J. Briggs, and Walter W. Wager (1992) promote the use of several different types of task analyses and a scope and sequence matrix. Finally, a very well-known reference by Walter Dick and Lou M. Carey (1996) presents numerous methods including a hierarchical analysis and a cluster analysis. Although they use slightly different approaches, each of these educators suggest systematic methods for identifying lesson objectives. As you gain more experience, you may want to consult these references, adapting these prescribed methods or discovering your own approach to suit the needs of the learning task at hand. Unfortunately, these methods can appear complex and over-whelming for the beginning teacher. We advocate a much simpler approach for identifying lesson objectives. Our approach is a modification of a planning matrix suggested by Lou M. Carey (1994) in *Measuring and Evaluating School Learning*. Although the focus of Carey's text is on assessment and test construction, it has an excellent chapter on analyzing unit objectives and is well-suited for beginning teachers.

Using a planning matrix to identify lesson objectives from the cognitive domain is especially appealing. A matrix is simple to develop, it can be easily modified and adapted for use with different grade levels and subjects, and it integrates declarative knowledge and procedural knowledge almost instantly. Look at the generic planning matrix in Figure 3.6. Note that the rows along the left side of the matrix are labeled declarative knowledge, or the subject matter to be learned. At the unit level, subject matter consists of a number of sub-topics or, what Bruner would call *concepts*. The columns along the top of the matrix are labeled procedural knowledge, or the process of knowing. Both Bloom and Gagné differentiated between simple and complex learning. Note that the complexity of the learning process increases as you move across the matrix from left to right. Although four rows and four columns are displayed in this particular matrix, the actual number of rows and column is left strictly up to you since you will best know the complexity of the subject matter (the number of rows) and learning process (the number of columns).

Now, let's examine the planning matrix in Figure 3.7 that Ms. Williams is creating for her fifth-grade mathematics unit on tables and graphs. Ms. Williams has written the unit objective at the top of the matrix and has chosen specific row and column headings. Based on the amount of time allotted for the unit and information in the district's curriculum guide for mathematics, Ms. Williams has identified three major sub-topics or concepts for the unit (bar chart, pie chart, and time line.) A similar matrix created for junior high school students might include several additional sub-topics such as scatter plots and flow charts.

Next, Ms. Williams considered the complexity of the learning processes, and she decided on three columns for her planning matrix. Ms. Williams recognized there were a number of new terms, vocabulary words, and definitions that students would need to *know* before they would be able to interpret and construct tables and graphs. Recalling that Bloom, Bruner, and Gagné acknowledged that the rote learning of factual information is an important but not a very complex learning task, Ms. Williams created a column called "recall factual information" in

FIGURE 3.6 GENERIC PLANNING MATRIX				
Procedural Knowledge / Declarative Knowledge	Lowest level learning process	Lower level learning process	Higher level learning process	Highest level learning process
Sub-topic or concept				
Sub-topic or concept				
Sub-topic or concept				
Sub-topic or concept				

FIGURE 3.7	MS. WILLIAMS' PLANNING MATRIX		
	Recall Factual Information	Interpret Examples	Construct Examples
Bar Chart			
Pie Chart			
Time Line			

the left column of her planning matrix. Once her students have mastered the new terminology, however, they will begin to use this information to interpret various examples of tables and graphs that she will provide. Thus, the middle column in the planning matrix is labeled "interpreting examples." This column represents moderately complex learning tasks. Finally, the third column of the matrix, "constructing examples," is the most complex task in Ms. Williams' planning matrix. At this learning level, the students will synthesize the information and skills they have previously learned to solve the problem of creating a table or graph for *real* data they actually collect. A similar matrix for junior high students might include an additional column called "evaluate examples," which would likely follow "interpret examples" in the planning matrix. The purpose of this task would be for students to evaluate the quality of tables and graphs. Are they constructed correctly? proportionally? convey information properly?

Finally, Ms. Williams is ready to complete her planning matrix by writing the corresponding lesson objectives in each of the boxes or cells of the matrix. Her partially completed matrix is illustrated in Figure 3.8. By writing lesson objectives that integrate the appropriate declarative and procedural knowledge, Ms. Williams is confident that she has identified the necessary "building blocks" for the unit.

Some Additional Notes on Creating and Using Planning Matrices

A planning matrix can be a valuable tool for helping you identify the set of lesson objectives that, in combination, identify the knowledge and skills of an instructional unit. It should be noted, however, that a planning matrix is a fairly individual creation. Given the same unit objective, it is not likely that two teachers would produce exactly the same matrix. In constructing the matrix, each teacher would need to consider a number of factors such as the characteristics of their students, students' prior knowledge, the amount of time allotted the unit, and the emphasis given in the district's curriculum guide. A planning matrix should be considered a *working* document, and teachers should revise and modify as needed.

In addition, the *emphasis* of instruction may not be on each and every learner objective in the planning matrix. For example, Ms. Williams' students are not

Unit Objective: The students will interpret and construct various types of charts and tables.

	Recall Factual Information	Interpret Examples	Construct Examples
Bar Chart	The learner will recall that... – the base of a bar chart is called the horizontal axis. – the side of a bar chart is called the vertical axis. – bars can be arranged vertically or horizontally. – the length of the bar indicates the value of the category. – in a vertical bar chart, the scale of the chart is listed along the vertical axis and the categories are listed along the horizontal axis. – in a horizontal bar chart, the categories are listed along the vertical axis and the scale is listed along the horizontal axis.	The learner will... – identify the category of information depicted on the horizontal axis of various bar charts in newspapers, textbooks, and other sources. – identify the scales of measurement displayed on various bar charts in newspapers, textbooks, and other sources. – make interpretive, comparative, and predictive statements about information depicted in bar charts located in newspapers, textbooks, and other sources.	The learner will... – collect weather-related information and construct a bar chart to illustrate the data.
Pie Chart	The learner will recall that...	The learner will...	The learner will...
Time Line	The learner will recall that...	The learner will...	The learner will...

likely to be engaged in a lesson that merely focuses on memorizing various facts about tables and graphs (the far left column of the matrix). Rather, Ms. Williams is more likely to integrate facts and verbal information as students learn to interpret examples of simple tables and graphs.

As instruction proceeds, Ms. Williams will note which students may be struggling with the more complex lesson objectives. This may be an indication that they need assistance as they move from lower to higher level tasks. Perhaps Ms. Williams will need to focus more instruction on the foundational concepts and skills or modify her matrix to include an additional intermediate learning level. Or, it could be that Ms. Williams may have incorrectly assumed a level of prior knowledge or may have inadvertently omitted key objectives from the matrix. In any event, a careful scrutiny of the objectives within the matrix may provide Ms. Williams with some valuable insight about her students' learning patterns.

Finally, Ms. Williams can use the matrix to consider the sequence of instruction. For example, she may decide to devote the first days of instruction to column charts alone, choosing to focus instruction on the lesson objectives *across* the first row of the matrix. Or, Ms. Williams could initiate instruction by comparing and contrasting the various charts and graphs, teaching *down* the columns of the matrix.

Activity 3.4

Select a unit level objective for a subject and grade level of interest to you and create a planning matrix. Begin by identifying the sub-topics or concepts along the rows of the matrix. Then, identify learning processes or procedural knowledge across the columns of the matrix. Complete the matrix by writing the learner objectives that are suggested by each cell.

WRITING BEHAVIORAL OBJECTIVES

Earlier in this chapter we differentiated between course objectives, unit objectives, and lesson objectives. There is one other type of learner objective that we have not talked about yet. It is called a **behavioral objective.** A behavioral objective is a more explicit and precise variation of a lesson objective. Like a lesson objective, a behavioral objective is a very specific statement that identifies what a student will know or be able to do as a result of instruction. In contrast, a behavioral objective has some additional information. Compare the lesson and behavioral objectives in Table 3.9.

TABLE 3.9   A RELATED LESSON AND BEHAVIORAL OBJECTIVE

Lesson Objective	Behavioral Objective
The students *construct* a **bar graph.**	Given temperature and rainfall weather data, the students will *construct* **bar graphs** that are labeled with the unit of measurement.

TABLE 3.10   A RELATED LESSON AND BEHAVIORAL OBJECTIVE

Lesson Objective	Behavioral Objectives
The student will *identify* the **differences between various charts and graphs.**	From memory, the student will *list* at least three **differences between a bar chart and time line.** OR The student will *list* at least three differences between a bar chart and time line.

Notice that the behavioral objective is an elaboration of the learner objective. In fact, the lesson objective is actually imbedded within the behavioral objective; however, there are two important distinctions. First, the behavioral objective begins with a phrase that states the circumstances under which the behavior will be observed. This initial phrase is called the **conditions.** Second, the behavioral objective includes a phrase that identifies the **criteria** that will be used to determine satisfactory performance. It is the inclusion of conditions and criteria that distinguishes behavioral objectives from lesson objectives. There are occasions, however, when the conditions and criteria are not as obvious. Consider the lesson objective in Table 3.10 above.

The intent here is that students will recall from memory the differences between a bar chart and a time line. Other than their memory, the students do not need any specific information or materials to list the differences. Of course if this is a written assignment, the students are likely to need a pencil and some paper. Pencils, pens, paper, and other similar items are merely routine instructional materials and are not unique conditions for this objective. Some teachers consider the condition *"from memory"* to be somewhat superfluous, and choose to omit it. The performance criteria is that students will be expected to list *"at least three differences."* In this example, the criteria is embedded within the objective.

There are other times when specific criteria are not necessary. Consider Table 3.11. In this example it is simply understood that a time line must be labeled *correctly*.

TABLE 3.11   A RELATED LESSON AND BEHAVIORAL OBJECTIVE

Lesson Objective	Behavioral Objective
The student will *identify* the **horizontal and vertical axis of a time line.**	Given a drawing of a time line, the student will *label* **the horizontal and vertical axis.**

LESSON OBJECTIVES AND BEHAVIORAL OBJECTIVES COMPARED

As you have noticed, lesson objectives and behavioral objectives are quite similar in how they are written. Although professional educators may vary slightly in the way they write lesson and behavioral objectives, all will agree that writing clear and precise statements of learning outcomes is an important skill. The distinction between lesson objectives and behavioral objectives tends to be in how they are used. Many teachers use lesson objectives to plan for *instruction*, and they use behavioral objectives to plan for *assessment*. In Chapter 4, "Constructing Lessons," you will see how teachers consider the lesson objectives in their day-to-day planning. In Chapter 9, "Planning Assessment Strategies," you will learn how teachers use lesson or behavioral objectives to plan for tests and other assessments.

SUMMARY

In this chapter, you have seen how teachers begin to go about the challenge of planning for day-to-day instruction by identifying the instructional goals and learner objectives that are the essence of the teaching and learning process. Classifying objectives and goals according to the domain of knowledge is an important step in the planning process, and three renown educational theorists—Benjamin Bloom, Robert Gagné, and Jerome Bruner—are noted for their theories about learning in the cognitive domain. Although goals and objectives can be identified for various segments of the curriculum, we advocated that unit level planning involves a "chunk" of the curriculum that is both reasonable and manageable. We presented two specific tools—a planning calendar and a planning matrix—that can facilitate planning at the unit level. In the next chapter, you will examine the challenge of planning instruction at the lesson level.

Just as cross-country travelers need a detailed map in order to safely and successfully arrive at their final destination at the appointed time, so will you need a systematic plan with which to navigate your students across the school year. With deliberate and forward planning, you can be assured that your students will arrive at the end of the school year with the knowledge and skills necessary for the next step in their learning journey.

REFLECTIONS

1. A few days after the discussion about curriculum planning with his department chair, James Nygun sat down with his planning calendar, the district curriculum guide, and the list of English competencies that his students will encounter on the district's proficiency test. After identifying the various instructional units for the year and sketching out a draft of his planning calendar, it seems obvious to James that he was a few weeks *short* on instructional time. What factors would you suggest James consider as he reconciles the difference between the amount of instructional material and the number of weeks in the school year?

2. To hold the interest of her tenth-grade math students, Cynthia Romanowski plans to develop some instructional units that focus on the interests of her students. For example, because the local professional baseball team has made it into the playoffs for several years, most everyone in the school is an avid baseball fan. Cynthia *knows* that there are

all sorts of baseball related statistics that will have her students eager to study the laws of probability. How can Cynthia capitalize on her students' interests, and at the same time ensure that she covers the material in her district's curriculum guide?

3. At the completion of a unit on tables and graphs, Ms. Williams considers both the successes and difficulties her fifth-grade students have experienced. She reflects upon the planning matrix she created and examines the list of learner objectives that were the focus of the unit. How might she use her insights to revise the matrix and objectives? Why might she want to modify the matrix and objectives directly *after* the unit is completed?

TEACHER AS RESEARCHER

The Domains of Knowledge

Ivie, S. D. (1993). Never to bloom again. *Contemporary Education, 64* (2), 104–107.

Hwang, B. & Hestad, M. (1993). Let's bloom. *Contemporary Education, 64* (2), 108–111.

The authors of these two articles provide two very different perspectives with regard to *Bloom's Taxonomy.* In the first article, professor Ivie contends that the taxonomy suggests a narrow approach for categorizing thinking, and he cites a number of examples to illustrate its misuse. In contrast, professors Hwang and Hestad support the importance and usefulness of the taxonomy. Read both articles and decide which authors present the most convincing argument.

Martin, B. L. (1989, August). A checklist for designing instruction in the affective domain. *Educational Technology,* 7–15.

Instruction in the affective domain is important but challenging. The author describes a five-step model for designing instruction in the affective domain and provides a detailed checklist that summarizes the key aspects of the model. Skim the entire article and read carefully the "needs assessment" section. What are the three areas that the author suggests should be considered in identifying affective objectives? Why are each of these areas important?

Planning for Instructional Units

Gronlund, N. E. (1991). *How to write and use instructional objectives: Part II Writing instructional objectives in various areas* (pp. 29–63). New York: MacMillan Publishing Company.

Differentiating instructional objectives according to the cognitive, affective, and psychomotor domain is a classification system that educators have used for some time. In a series of short chapters, Gronlund suggests a slightly different classification system. Skim through the chapters and identify the four types of learning outcomes. In what ways does this approach differ from the traditional three-domain system?

Guskey, T. R. (1997). Outlining learning goals and objectives. In *Implementing mastery learning* (pp. 28–51). Belmont, CA: Wadsworth Publishing Company.

Guskey describes and illustrates a process for developing a table of specifications, the purpose of which is to outline unit level goals and objectives. Compare and contrast the table of specifications to the unit planning matrix by selecting a unit level instructional goal of interest to you and using both methods. In what ways are both methods similar? How do they differ? Which do you prefer?

CHAPTER 4

Constructing Lessons

CONVERSATION

Sally Westerly almost flew into school on Monday morning. As a first-year teacher at Midtown Middle School, she was usually excited about coming to school. After all, this is what she had hoped for. Today, however, she was even more energized than usual. Over the weekend, she had planned her first cooperative learning lesson and was eager to try it out. She couldn't wait until her students arrived. The kids would have so much fun and learn so much that they would probably vote her Teacher of the Year. No, maybe Teacher of their Lives. This was going to be a great day, she thought . . .

At 3:00, Maria Rosada, team leader for Sally's students, found Sally slumped over her desk. The room smelled of disaster, desks askew, paper scattered all over the floor. Maria knocked at the open door, and Sally looked up, the frustration and disappointment etched on her face. Sally opened her arms wide in a gesture toward the room, began to say something, then stopped.

"So, what happened to you today?" Maria asked.

"It was awful," Sally sighed. "I thought I had it all set up. I thought up this really great project that students could do in groups. I had all the materials with me. I spent all weekend cutting out pictures from magazines so the kids would have what they needed. I even let 'em choose their groups so they would be extra motivated to do the project, and they wouldn't have to worry about not wanting to work with someone. I did everything, and then—This!"

"By everything, Sally, what do you mean?"

"Well, like I said, all the materials. I even had the directions for the project written down. I told them they could work with their friends. I even had a group reward for the group that got done the quickest . . ."

"So, what exactly went wrong? Why don't you tell me a little more?"

"Well, they were acting like spastic fireflies. They were all over the room. Some students were taking things from other groups. Others wouldn't even share materials in their own groups. It was just a mess. I'll tell you what, I don't think I'll ever do this again."

"I don't think you need to go that far. It sounds like you did a lot of things right. It certainly sounds like you prepared them for the content task. And it also sounds like you can identify the challenge you're going to have the next time."

"That's for sure. If I ever do this again, I need to find a way to make sure they know what I expect as far as behavior is concerned."

"That's a good place to start," Maria said as she smiled. "Now, why don't you use me as a sounding board. See if you can clarify more precisely what the problems were and what seem to be their causes. . . ."

DEVELOPING COMPETENCE

1. React to a veteran teacher who tells you he never writes detailed lesson plans and thinks that doing so, even for novice educators, is a waste of time.

2. As you reflect on lessons you have experienced as a student, what activities typically happen at the beginning, middle, and end of the lesson? Compare your experiences with the three main phases of a lesson plan as described in this chapter.

3. Study the examples of a Direct Instruction Lesson Plan and then name specific actions by the teachers that actually "direct" student learning.

4. Identify the types of student learning best served by the Guided Literacy Lesson Plan.

5. Choose one of the Cooperative Learning Plans to analyze. How do the subject matter and social skills activities reinforce *both* subject matter and social skills objectives?

6. As a beginning (or experienced) teacher, which of the adaptations for modifying lessons for students with special needs would you feel most comfortable trying out?

INTRODUCTION

Of all the decisions that teachers make, choices about lesson plans are the most visible. Teaching from lesson plans fills the "space" of each school day. Students and other teachers, as well as guests and supervisors, regularly see and experience first hand the results of teachers' skillful lesson planning. You have just seen how instructional goals and learner objectives frame the planning of courses, units, and lessons (see chapter 3). You will now see how teachers further define the challenge of moving goals and objectives from the lesson plan book into the "nuts and bolts" of appropriate lesson plan formats. As you study this chapter and begin to write your own lesson plans, you may wish to "surf" through other teachers' plans (see Figure 4.1). Be ready to deal with the fact that their terminology will not always match ours. Be critical as well as appreciative of what you find. No doubt you'll find plans that are real gems and you'll download them for your files. Others will have to be modified before they meet your high standards for solid instruction.

FIGURE 4.1 ON-LINE RESOURCES FOR LESSON PLANS	
Resource	Website
AskERIC Lesson Plans	http://askeric.org/Virtual/Lessons/
Busy Teachers' Website K–12	http://www.ceismc.gatech.edu/busyt/homepg.htm
Education Planet	http://www.educationplanet.com/lessonplanet/
Teachers Helping Teachers	http://www.pacificnet.net/~mandel/
Teachnet.Com	http://www.teachnet.com/lesson.html
World School	http://www.wvaworldschool.org/
WWW4teachers	http://www.4teachers.org/premier/

WHY PLAN?

Do you plan out your day in advance? Maybe you think through the next day's schedule before you go to bed at night. Or perhaps you actually write out a plan for your day the first thing in the morning. Sometimes the plan just sits in your head, while other times you write it out on paper or in a datebook. Whatever way you do it, you take steps to assure yourself that your day will be both busy and productive, that everything you do will help move you toward important goals. In a similar way, teachers plan lessons so that class time is used well and students develop the skills and knowledge that they have so carefully identified and defined.

We define a **lesson plan** as a detailed arrangement of action steps, activities, and resources developed by the teacher to help students achieve desired lesson objectives. It is consistent with the unit objectives and usually lasts for one to several days. The importance of planning lessons can't be overstated. There are specific reasons you need to develop the skills of lesson planning. Some of the more important are that they:

- Chart a course for you and your students to follow in developing the attitudes, skills, and subject matter that you have identified in your lesson objectives. While planning, you must be aware of your students' abilities, interests, and needs, as well as the content they have already encountered, are to master now, and will address in the future.

- Assure that you and your students will make valuable use of the instructional time within every school day. Well-planned lessons decrease the possibility that you will have "dead air" time, especially at the beginning and end of class.

- Require you to identify the instructional resources you will use. Planning enables you to be confident that the materials, equipment, and the assistance of media specialists, parent volunteers, and aides are in place when you present your lesson, so that you decrease the likelihood of something going wrong.

- Prompt you to consider how to assess your students' learning. As you make decisions about the activities that are the heart of your lesson plans, you become more fully aware of what you really want students to learn and how they are to learn it. This will compel you to think about how you are going to assess students in a way that is consistent with your decisions about the "what" and "how" of your students' learning (chapter 9 takes a look at a host of approaches to assessment).

Novice and Experienced Planners

Basically, both novice and experienced teachers prepare lesson plans as intrapersonal communications. They talk to themselves and in the process clarify lesson purposes, actions, and assessments. They then use the resulting plan to guide classroom interactions. What differs sometimes is the amount of lesson plan *writing* that novice and experienced teachers actually do.

During your field experiences, you may observe teachers teaching lessons without the benefit of detailed lesson plans, or in some cases no written lesson plan at all. These veteran teachers' excellent lessons appear to happen spontaneously. In fact, what seems natural and unrehearsed is the product of careful planning, albeit informal and done in quiet moments during planning periods at school, at home, or in the car on the way to an event. In their decision-making, they have considered many variables: different students' achievement levels, what they want students to learn, students' schema, the time available, resources, etc. Although experienced teachers may not write formal lesson plans, they are experts at visualizing upcoming instruction. Shulman (1987) refers to this process as "representation," in which the teacher mentally thinks through the array of analogies, metaphors, examples, demonstrations, and simulations that help bridge the gaps between teachers' understandings and students' minds and experiences. We believe that you and other novice teachers must actually write lesson plans in order to learn and practice the basics of sound instructional design. And to help you progress from written plans to unwritten, visualized plans, we suggest that you and all teachers in training write lesson scripts; these scripts, similar to the work of playwrights, allow you to create "mental motion pictures" that capture the actual complexities of teaching a lesson (Section IV includes one such lesson script).

While lesson plans are very important, especially for the novice, it is equally important that you not blast your way through a lesson just because "that's what the plan said." You may modify or even abandon your original plan in response to students' needs or "the teachable moment." Master teachers know that in the midst of a planned lesson, a spontaneous comment by a student—even though it may seem to be off target—may spark considerable interest and curiosity among class members. These teachers recognize the potential for learning in such situations. They are flexible enough to postpone the planned lesson in order to take advantage of these exciting learning and teaching times. Also, these experts have systematic ways of checking their students for understanding. If students aren't comprehending the lesson, master teachers are able to provide other examples than the ones they've already used or reteach an earlier skill that it seems students need to have reinforced before they are ready to move on. In either case, they recognize that the lesson plan provides them with a place to start and, ideally, a road map for the day, but that the plan is only going to work if students are successful in developing the skills or knowledge identified in the plan.

LESSON PLAN FRAMEWORK

When teaching individual lessons, especially during the internship or student teaching periods, you are expected to provide your cooperating teacher with detailed lesson plans that reveal your ability to plan for effective instruction. We recognize that each field experience or pre-service teaching assignment may require a different form of lesson plan. We also know, however, that the elements that follow are components of all good plans. The six components we present here are consistent with PRAXIS III, a system of performance assessment for beginning and continuing teachers, produced by ETS (Dwyer, 1994). As of this writing, several states are actively considering adopting PRAXIS III as a way of assessing the actual classroom performance of teachers. In some of these states, teachers will be granted a beginning teaching certificate or license based, in part, on their observed ability to plan, deliver, and assess instruction that incorporates the components.

They are generic enough to allow the planning of different lesson plan formats, three of which are described in this chapter. The six components that you need to keep in mind are summarized in Figure 4.2 and described in greater detail below.

FIGURE 4.2   ESSENTIAL COMPONENTS OF A LESSON PLAN FRAMEWORK

1. Lesson Objectives
   Pinpoint outcomes of learning. Must be appropriate to specific learners.

2. Student Grouping
   Have students work individually, as partners, or as a class, depending on purpose and content.

3. Instructional Methods and Strategies
   Determine specific lesson plan format and teaching and learning strategies.

4. Activities
   Brainstorm possibilities. Then identify actions that align with lesson objectives.

5. Instructional Resources
   Choose those that add learning power to activities.

6. Assessment/Evaluation
   Collect and act on evidence of student achievement throughout the lesson.

Lesson Objectives

As you define the challenges of teaching specific content to a unique group of learners, lesson objectives provide you with the direction that you will require as you plan for student learning. As you saw in chapter 3, whether you are writing learner objectives or specifying them more precisely in terms of behavioral objectives, it is the description of what students will do—in the cognitive, affective, or psychomotor domains—with the content you have chosen for them that constitutes the direction of their learning and your planning. The more clearly you specify these learner outcomes, the more likely you will be to help students meet the goals you have set for them.

Activity 4.1

Imagine that you have your own classroom of students and you are working on some content within your area of specialization (e.g., reading at the elementary level, middle school science, etc.). Identify one or two learner objectives as you learned to do in chapter 3. Be sure to recall the domains of learning as presented in that chapter; they will help you pinpoint what you want students to learn. Imagine that you are asked to explain the appropriateness of these objectives by your cooperating teacher or a PRAXIS examiner. Display the objectives and your rationale regarding the appropriateness of these objectives for the specific group of learners in the class you will be teaching.

Student Grouping

Another consideration you must address is how you will organize students for the activities you will plan. You have numerous options available. Students work by themselves when reading for personal enjoyment, writing to express an opinion, or drilling for mastery in math facts. They work as partners or in groups of two or more to discover information, solve problems, and learn how to be processors and communicators of information. Finally, they work in whole-class settings when the purposes are to distribute information in an efficient way, elicit and exchange a broad range of opinion and attitudes, and administer examinations.

Here you explicitly state how students will be grouped for instruction. You may also indicate how this grouping arrangement will change because of the different activities in which students will engage during class. In addition, you should also be able to offer a rationale, if asked, for the appropriateness of these grouping arrangements. You should be able to explain why, for instance, a whole group format would be effective for presenting new information to your particular students for some specific content. For most lesson plans, you will devise a combination of whole class, small group, and individual work.

Instructional Methods and Strategies

Specific instructional methods and strategies, often validated by educational research and described in professional journals, make up many of the systematic plans that you will consciously adapt and monitor as you seek to improve student learning. These tools come in two forms: those that you retain control over—the teaching strategies—and those that you teach to students—learning strategies. **Teaching strategies,** largely teacher-centered methods, are a series of steps that teachers follow in directing students' actions so that they acquire cognitive, affective, and psychomotor behaviors. For instance, if you wanted to begin a lesson by helping students call to mind and organize what they already know about a topic, you might choose the brainstorming strategy (brainstorming and other strategies are taken up in detail in chapter 7). On the other hand, **learning strategies,** although initially taught and monitored by you, are largely student-centered. Used by individuals or groups, these strategies are meant to help students in self-study to meet the cognitive, affective, or psychomotor objectives you have set for them (see chapter 8 for examples). When students need a learning strategy to accomplish independently what the teacher has assigned, the teacher takes the opportunity to model the strategy for students and engage them in the practice of it. Only after providing the tools that students need can you expect that they will be able to independently complete your assignments.

For this component of the lesson plan, you should explicitly name the methods and strategies you will be using. You should name the particular lesson plan format you will be using, as well as any specific strategies you might "plug into" the format. For example, in the Guided Literacy Lesson Plan described in this chapter, you might plug in a metaphor making strategy as a way of capturing students' attention and building on their prior knowledge during the set induction phase. At this point in time, don't worry if this portion of the plan seems a bit shallow to you. This is one place where you will see your own growth as you pick up methods and strategies and as you gain more experience and encounter more of the professional literature. As you gain teaching experience and read the professional literature, your depth of knowledge will increase. Learning the names of specific strategies will help you sort through them and make conscious selections from an ever-growing repertoire.

Activities

Think of activities as actions planned by the teacher to help students develop the learnings stipulated by the lesson objective. As such, they are a means to an end. As you plan, you should first define what it is students should learn. That critical decision becomes a guide to further decision-making regarding which of several possible activities you might include in your lesson. Activities fall on a continuum regarding who holds center stage, the teacher or the students. They are seldom exclusively teacher- or student-centered but are somewhere in between. For example, when a visitor to your classroom observes you reviewing yesterday's math homework, you will be in the center of the activities, calling on students, directing attention to key steps in a process, giving directions, or administering an oral test. On the other hand, during another portion of the same class period, students may be the center of attention as they engage in research projects and cooperative learning groups while you play a supporting role as resource person or facilitator.

In this particular component, you will need to name the activities you will use to meet the lesson objectives you have identified. At this point in the framework, you can think in terms of three phases of lesson activities. For each phase, you will approximate the time needed for completion and provide enough details so that an experienced teacher could visualize your plan and actually teach from it. The beginning phase is referred to as set induction, the second is interactions, and the third closure. Literally, **set induction** means to bring about a mental frame of mind that prepares students for further learning activities. This is accomplished by helping students call up and clarify pertinent information previously learned. New subject matter and learning processes are introduced and connections to old knowledge and processes are established. During the **interactions** phase, students are actively engaged in learning new subject matter and processes. Their minds are actively "in gear" as they meet new information in text and other materials. Mental or social processes are learned and practiced when students work independently and with each other and the teacher. In the third phase, **closure,** subject matter knowledge and processes of learning, either mental or social, are reinforced, extended, and evaluated. Some of the activities in different phases will be semi-structured teaching and learning strategies while others will be more free-form. Again, though, you should be prepared to justify the appropriateness of these activities based on learner characteristics and curricular demands.

Martha Shemanski considered these factors as she contemplated the design of a unit on Australia for her second graders. Her mind raced as she brainstormed all the possibilities. She could have a boomerang throwing contest for her students. Or she could organize a "trip to the outback" in the field behind the school. Or she could have students construct native animals out of papier-maché. But in the midst of her excitement over these fun-filled projects, she thought to ask herself a critical question: "What is it that I *really* want my students to *learn*?"

Classroom projects can be fun. Speakers can be entertaining, and field trips can be a welcome break in routine. Like Martha, you will want to fashion activities that are fun and appeal to a variety of interests whenever you can. As a first priority, however, keep in mind Martha's realization that activities must be chosen so that they align themselves with your lesson objectives and are appropriate for the students in the class. They are a means to an end, not the end themselves.

Instructional Resources

The sage who came up with "a picture is worth a thousand words" understood the power of visual aids in communicating ideas. Today's teachers are not limited to photos and posters, of course, to enhance classroom activities and students' learning. You can purchase instructional resources that allow students to interact with graphic images and "real-time" action sequences with real-world sound tracks. With computer programs you can create resources that are custom-made to enhance curricular topics. New technologies come on the market constantly and the opportunities you'll have to clarify and expand on content area concepts will be virtually unlimited (chapter 6 deals with the ever-changing scene of technology in education).

Amidst the excitement of the electronic age, however, we need to offer a cautionary note in our definition of instructional resources. We define **instructional resources** as tangible, instructional tools used to aid in the process of instruction and learning. In other words, resources are chosen because they add "learning power" to activities. Showing films or permitting students to play computer games during class time because their topics are vaguely associated with a current topic or because we need to keep students occupied on a Friday afternoon fail to meet this criterion. In fact, instructional resources don't have to be fancy at all. They can be as common and ordinary as the textbooks that students have, the board which is in the room, or a large piece of butcher paper on which students will write. Recently, one of our student teachers was extracting DNA as an experiment in a high school biology class; the lab book described some fairly exotic chemicals that students should use. Her main resources: onion slices, dish soap, house salt, and meat tenderizer.

We also remind you that teachers need to choose activities that are aligned with lesson objectives. We want to further impress upon you that instructional resources must also be aligned in such a way that they support what you have chosen to do. LaShaun Hill, a high school government teacher, followed that advice when he constructed a computer slide show in conjunction with the following lesson behavior: *The student will differentiate among the legislative, executive, and judicial functions at the local, state, and federal levels of government.* LaShaun drew and sequenced slides that first defined and illustrated the functions of the three branches. He then superimposed the function slides on the levels of government slides, thus leading his students to see the two overlapping areas of relationship. Recognizing that resources, regardless of their sophistication, do not in and of themselves teach, LaShaun wisely chose teaching methods that allowed him to directly instruct students in the different functions of the government. He also used his questioning techniques to draw out students' understanding. He was aware of how his materials would help him clarify this information for his students, but he also knew that his skillful use of his own tools, in the form of questioning strategies, would allow him to deliver this content and assess his students' understanding of it throughout the lesson.

For this component, you will need to identify all of the instructional resources you and your students will need to engage in the lesson. It is helpful to make such a list because it will ensure that you will not forget something that is crucial to your lesson. It also may help to remind you of things you will need to reserve, like a VCR from the media center, or provide, like the household items mentioned above. Be prepared to explain how the resources are aligned with lesson activities and how they contribute to the development of the lesson objectives.

Assessment/Evaluation

Although we are familiar with assessment which occurs at the end of a lesson in the form of a quiz or test, in a larger sense **assessment** is the ongoing gathering of evidence about students' achievement. As such, it is a continuous process throughout a lesson. Before a lesson even begins, teachers seek to find out what students already know about the new topic. They may do this informally through skillful questioning that gets at students' schema or more formally through printed questionnaires and inventories. Gathering this information assists teachers as they make decisions about where to begin instruction and how to fashion it. Assessment done while teaching a lesson or unit gives teachers immediate feedback about students' progress toward desired learning outcomes. Experienced teachers use this information to make "mid-flight" corrections in their lesson plans. Direct teacher observation and questions that require all students to respond simultaneously may provide the evidence on which they base decisions about going back to reteach a needed concept, going forward with the lesson, or seeking out even more information before deciding which way to go. Sometimes teachers choose not to assess students' progress at the end of a lesson, preferring to wait, instead, for the end of the entire unit. Whether it occurs at the end of a lesson or of a unit, after-instruction assessment serves the purpose of gauging the achievement of individuals as well as the whole class (see chapter 9 for assessment and assessment strategies and chapter 10 for evaluating student achievement).

As a reflective teacher, there are many important questions you will want to ask yourself. To what extent were my lesson objectives met? Will portions of the lesson need to be retaught? Just when and how do I plan to look for evidence of my students' learning of the objectives (e.g., assessment)? When and how do I use my professional judgment to determine if students' growth is adequate (evaluation), given the variables of students' prior knowledge and other characteristics, sufficiency of learning resources, and, yes, even the quality of my instruction?

For this portion of the plan, you should be able to do two things. First, identify what method(s) you will use to gather information about student performance related to your stated objective(s) during or immediately following the lesson that you teach; this is referred to as **formative assessment.** This is the information you would use to determine whether you should proceed with your sequence of instruction as you had planned it. Second, identity what methods you will use to determine the extent to which students have developed the lesson behavior(s) by the end of your unit; this is known as **summative assessment.** This is the type of information you will probably use to determine a grade and may come in the form of a test, paper, project, performance, etc. Be prepared to justify the method and the timing of your assessment and evaluation.

Activity 4.2

Obtain a teacher's edition of a subject matter textbook. Find a plan of a lesson and analyze it according to the six elements of the lesson plan framework presented in this chapter. As you analyze, consider the following questions: Are all the elements present (even if they don't use the same terms)? Has the order of presentation been changed? Are the results of these changes positive or negative? Would you be able to teach from this plan? Write a summary of your analysis and present it orally to members of your class.

THREE WHOLE LESSON MODELS AND PLANS

Among the many lesson plan models that have found their way into the professional literature are the three we have chosen to include in this text. For each we begin by describing the model, that is its research base, the views of its key proponents, and times of best use. We then present an overview of the lesson plan, a purposeful scheme for action that emanates from the model. Finally, we offer detailed examples of the plan. Common to all are the essential lesson plan components and the three phases of lesson development: set induction, interaction, and closure. What distinguishes the plans are the steps in each phase. Elementary and secondary school examples of each lesson plan, together with the steps that make up each phase, are presented in outline form in the next sections of this chapter. A variety of teacher-asked questions and grouping arrangements (chapter 5), instructional resources (chapter 6), teaching and learning strategies (chapters 7 and 8), and assessment strategies (chapter 9) will be presented in Section III of this text.

Many of the lessons delivered in schools have the basic features of one of these lesson formats: the Direct Instruction Lesson Plan, the Guided Literacy Lesson Plan, or the Cooperative Learning Lesson Plan. We want you to recognize, however, that there is no one plan that can or should be used exclusively; that's why we are offering you choices. As we stated previously, though, your choices need to be made on the basis of your lesson objectives, the content with which you are dealing, and your knowledge of your students and their needs. Teachers must know several different lesson plans in order to accommodate these different student characteristics, lesson objectives, and overall instructional intentions. By experiencing and experimenting with all three of the plans, you will become more confident about modifying them to better accommodate your learners' needs.

Direct Instruction Lesson Plan

The **Direct Instruction Lesson Plan** is a form of teacher guidance characterized by a high degree of structure and teacher control. It is sometimes called explicit instruction because the action in each step unfolds in a very deliberate fashion and is fully and clearly expressed by the teacher (Rosenshine, 1987). The elements in Madeline Hunter's lesson design for effective instruction are similar to those described in this section as well (Hunter, 1994). Of the three lesson plans described in this chapter, the teacher's presence in the classroom is most prominent in the direct instruction lesson plan. That does not mean, however, that only the teacher's voice is heard. In opposition to the "teacher as teller" role, where the instructor lectures and has one-way recitations with just a few students, the teacher of a direct instruction lesson plan works hard to engage students' minds and encourages their active involvement in a variety of ways.

The genesis of the direct instruction is the teacher effectiveness research of the 1970s and 1980s. Rosenshine (1983) reports that seven studies conducted in that period looked at groups of students in different schools and the teachers who taught them. In each study, students were pretested in the areas of math and reading and then, after instruction, tested again. As the teachers taught, researchers observed their teaching methods. They recorded the amount of time teachers spent presenting new material and the time students were given for practice. Researchers also recorded the number and type of teacher questions, the nature of feedback, and the directions given for practice, among other areas of interest. After instruction was finished, the researchers compared the students' performance on both the pretest and the posttest. By pulling together data from the most successful classes in all the studies, Rosenshine identified the methods that teachers used in the high achievement classes. He discovered a general pattern of effective instruction and the functions of that pattern (Figure 4.3).

The Direct Instruction Lesson Plan is often acknowledged as a useful planning tool for teaching math and reading skills, factual knowledge, such as that found in science (Rosenshine, 1987) and the physical abilities in the psychomotor domain (consider the place of direct instruction in teaching beginning reading as you study the Direct Instruction item in the *Teacher as Researcher* section of this chapter). It is efficient in conveying information in a short period of time. Moreover, it has been suggested as appropriate for teaching the cognitive abilities employed in comprehension and general learning strategies (Pressley & Woloshyn, 1995). Both the lower and higher order thinking abilities identified by Bloom (1956) are the foundation of these learning strategies described in chapter 8 along with two strategies for teaching them—Think-Aloud, which parallels the steps in direct instruction, and Reciprocal Teaching.

Authors of instructional methods books have rearranged and modified Rosenshine's effective instruction functions (Burden & Byrd, 1994; Joyce & Weil, 1996; Pasch, et al. 1995). We, too, have reformed his work, packaging two steps in each of the three lesson phases (see Outline of Direct Instruction Plan in Figure 4.4). As you gain experience, it is our hope that you, in turn, will profit from modifying the Direct Instruction format by collapsing, blending, and shaping the phases and steps presented here to better meet the needs of your students and the content

---

FIGURE 4.3   ROSENSHINE'S FINDINGS ON EFFECTIVE TEACHING

Research on Effective Teaching

The effective teacher:

1. Reviews the previous day's work (and reteaches if necessary).

2. Presents new content/skills.

3. Initiates initial student practice.

4. Provides feedback and correction (again, reteaches if necessary).

5. Supervises students' independent practice.

6. Conducts weekly and monthly reviews.

FIGURE 4.4   OUTLINE OF THE DIRECT INSTRUCTION LESSON PLAN

1. Lesson Objectives

2. Student Grouping

3. Instructional Methods and Strategies

4. Instructional Activities

   Set Induction Phase
   - Review previously learned material, skills
   - State the objectives for the lesson

   Interaction Phase
   - Present new information and/or skill
   - Organize group practice

   Closure Phase
   - Supervise independent practice
   - Assess mastery of content and process

5. Instructional Resources

6. Assessment/Evaluation
   - Check students' mastery throughout the lesson (formative)
   - Check mastery at end of lesson or related lessons (summative)

---

objectives you have identified for them. As you try this for the first couple of times, however, it will probably be more appropriate that you do each step as described and in the order presented.

Set Induction Phase   In this phase, you need to make certain that students have mastered the material taught previously (e.g., "Let's name the parts of a cell as we learned them yesterday") or remind them of a need that they displayed earlier (e.g., "The last time we studied maps, we found that we had some difficulty interpreting degrees of latitude and longitude"). During this portion of the phase, activities may include students' brainstorming their associations of the topic from the previous day, correcting each other's homework, or reviewing notes. Although this step is typically short in relation to the others, you must take the time necessary to reteach forgotten or poorly understood information or underdeveloped skills that students will need to be successful on the day's tasks.

Once you have reviewed previous material, you have created a pathway to new material. Students' minds are alert to pertinent information or the need for new skills; they have a focus for learning. You can then explain, in general, the nature of the new material and what, specifically, students should know or be able to do at the end of the lesson (see lesson objectives, chapter 3). Whether the new material is cognitive content or strategies, or physical skills, you should present the learner objective(s) in language that students can comprehend. For example, a high school symphony director may appropriately talk to his orchestra students about developing their ability "to distinguish among polyphonic compositions," while an upper elementary school music teacher might tell her general music students that she wants them to "find out how rock-and-roll and heavy metal music are different."

Interaction Phase   During this phase, you will present new material using a variety of learning resources and approaches. If your intent is for students to learn cognitive content material, you may choose guided observation, oral explanation, and/or graphic examples, all accompanied by discussion, as your methods. If, however, your intent is for students to learn cognitive strategies, you will most likely model the processes in small steps, which helps students gain access to a strategy for learning new material. Teachers often demonstrate the physical skills in gym, art, and shop courses. They do this by taking on the roles, first, of expert modelers of the skill and then, during student practice, of coaches. During this phase teachers will often debrief, or direct questions to all students to check individual and group understanding of content and skill during, as well as at the end, of the presentation.

After presenting the new information or skill, you will provide a teacher-led practice session aimed at helping students develop the behavior(s) stated in your lesson plan. However, group practice varies depending on the nature of the material. For lower-level cognitive information, you may work with a whole class, a small group, or partners and ask a large number of questions or prompts, respond to students and correct errors, and even reteach, if necessary. When the focus is a cognitive strategy or physical skill, students may initially practice with partners who take turns observing and coaching each other until they consistently achieve a high degree of accurate responses. As is true in presenting information, debriefing is an important part of group practice. Effective teachers frequently assess whether *all* students understand the ideas being taught or whether they are developing the skills in a cognitive or psychomotor strategy. The information that teachers obtain through such debriefing gives them insights into the gaps in student thinking and actions. By engaging in frequent, systematic debriefings, you will more likely provide students with substantive feedback and more helpful and timely corrections.

Closure Phase   With teacher presentation and group practice complete, you will conclude your direct instruction lessons with the assignment of independent practice. You will continue to supervise students as they work at their seats, in study carrels, or at a computer. Activities may range from solving story problems in math, to writing vocabulary terms on a word puzzle, to butting a soccer ball with their heads, to perfecting the steps in the PORPE strategy for studying for a test (see chapter 8). Debriefing is a critical feature of independent practice just as it was in presentation and group practice. As you learned in chapter 1, metacognition is the ability to think about one's own thinking. Debriefing fosters this skill and provides students with checkpoints to monitor and evaluate their own learning. As you consider the information that debriefing may yield, you may decide that students need additional explanations and reteaching or that they have sufficiently mastered the material and that it is time for them to apply the information in some other context.

Finally, you will need to assess your students' mastery of content information and processes. While you have been doing this throughout the lesson by way of informal debriefings, a more formal formative or summative assessment can and should also occur soon after the day's instruction. You may check students' actual performances through tests and assignments, lab assignments, oral presentations, short writings, and answers to teachers' questions that document their knowledge of subject matter, physical skills and/or study-related processes. At specific points in time, you may also ask consciously reflective questions such as, "How did the PORPE test-taking strategy we learned last week work for you in yesterday's test?" Reflective questions will help determine how effectively students transfer and apply their learnings to school tasks.

Activity 4.3

Write a classroom scenario in which student needs and curriculum demands lead the teacher to choose the Direct Instruction Lesson Plan format. Develop the lesson plan. Remember to include systematic formative assessments throughout and then again at the end of the lesson.

Example Plans–Direct Instruction

Elementary Grades Model

SUBJECT   Science   *GRADE* 4
TOPIC   Water routes

1. *Lesson Objective*
   Students will trace the route of water through the hydrologic cycle.

2. *Student Grouping*
   Whole class, then pairs, then individual seat work

3. *Instructional Methods and Strategies*
   Direct Instruction model; teacher-led review; Reciprocal Teaching; teacher-created learning station

4. *Instructional Activities*[1]

   I.   Set Induction Phase

      A. Teacher conducts a review ("Yesterday we discussed the ways in which the Great Lakes have become polluted.") using a map of the Great

---

[1]In all of the "Instructional Activities" sections that follow, the words in parentheses are the ones that a teacher might say to fulfill the requirements of that particular portion of the lesson plan. While your lesson plans will probably not contain these sentences and phrases, you may find it helpful to jot your transitions down so that you will have them available when necessary. Even as veteran teachers, we find, especially when we teach new materials, that providing ourselves with notes like these can help us make smoother connections from one part of a lesson to another.

Lakes showing the bordering states; shows illustrations of different types and sources of pollution. (9 mins.)

B. Teacher connects review to new lesson ("Now that we remember the types and sources of pollution, it's time to learn how pollution gets into the waters of the Great Lakes.") and states objectives ("When we finish this lesson, you will be able to explain the pathways of waters on Earth, called the hydrologic cycle. If we know how these pathways work, we'll see how pollution follows the same pathways to enter the Great Lakes and harm them."). (1 min.)

II. Interaction Phase

A. Teacher presents and explains hydrologic cycle. (10 mins.)

1. Using a large poster of the hydrologic cycle (see Figure 4.5), teacher points to the poster while orally explaining the path ("The rain falls on the land and either runs off the surface back into the Lakes through streams and creeks, or soaks into the ground . . .").

2. Students predict the next location on the path based on directional lines on the poster.

3. Teacher checks students' developing knowledge through oral questioning ("If the rain fell right here [pointing to poster], where would it have to go next?" "Where is the water on this surface [pointing to poster] going to end up?").

B. Group practice (30 mins.)

1. Student pairs work with two desk copies of the hydrologic cycle,

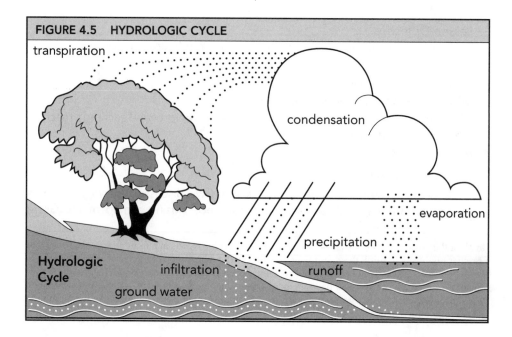

FIGURE 4.5   HYDROLOGIC CYCLE

one labeled and one unlabeled. Students use reciprocal teaching strategy and alternate as "coach" while the other points and orally identifies in sequence the location of the hydrologic locations.

2. Teacher circulates, observing students' progress, providing feedback as necessary, and determining when pairs are ready for the next step.

III. Closure Phase

A. Independent practice–During a learning stations period, students take turns at flannel boards where they place objects, such as trees and clouds, directional lines, and labels to recreate the hydrologic cycle. (15 mins.)

B. Assessment–The teacher debriefs by asking questions, correcting, and/or praising students for their mastery of material. (8 mins.)

5. *Instructional Resources*
Illustrated map of the Great Lakes (Great Lakes National Program Office 1990); large poster of hydrologic cycle; worksheets of both labeled and unlabeled hydrologic cycle for each student; flannel board with necessary attachments.

6. *Assessment/Evaluation*

A. Formative–During both the interaction and closure phases, the teacher observes students and asks oral questions of individuals, partner groups, and the whole class.

B. Summative–In two days, all students will independently draw, from memory, a picture of the hydrologic cycle. Criterion is a faithful reproduction of the cycle, including all major points and labels. Spelling will not count at this stage.

Secondary Grades Model

SUBJECT   Government   *GRADE* 9
TOPIC   Learning strategy for distinguishing major and minor ideas in social studies texts

1. *Lesson Objective*
Students will outline content area text material using the Idea Line learning strategy.

2. *Student Grouping*
Whole class, group practice in pairs, independent learning

3. *Instructional Methods and Strategies*
Direct Instructional model; modeling of Idea Line learning strategy

4. *Instructional Activities*

I. Set Induction Phase

A. Teacher reviews observed problem in learning ("Tomorrow we'll start our new unit on branches of government. We'll read a chapter in the civics text and discuss the important ideas. First, though, I have noticed that some of you have had difficulty deciding which ideas in a chapter are major and which ideas are minor. To help you understand these differences, I'm going to teach you a learning strategy called Idea Line."). (2 mins.)

    B. State objectives ("After today's lesson, you'll know a strategy to help you study more efficiently. Idea Line has five steps, and you're going to know them so well that you could actually teach them to someone else. You'll be able to use this method to study the next chapter."). (1 min.)

II. Interaction Phase

    A. Presentation (15 mins.)

        1. Students copy the five steps of Idea Line [see a full description of Idea Line learning strategy in chapter 8] in the Learning Strategies section of their notebooks.

        2. Using text material previously covered, teacher models the five steps by talking out loud the thought processes of each step.

        3. Teacher debriefs students by asking questions ("What are the steps in Idea Line?" "How does using the Idea Line strategy help you learn?" "At what points in your study would using the Idea Line be a good idea?").

    B. Group Practice (20 mins.)

        1. In pairs, students use a second piece of familiar material to practice the five steps. They work through the steps together, discussing the rationale for their order and how their minds work to process the information.

        2. Teacher observes pairs and asks questions that focus attention on identification, sequence, and completion of steps.

        3. At the conclusion, students are asked additional debriefing questions ("Which steps were easiest/hardest for you? Why?" "At which steps did you find yourself bogging down?").

III. Closure Phase

    A. Independent practice–Using yet another piece of familiar material, students work independently in practicing the five steps. (15 mins.)

    B. Assessment/Evaluation (2 mins.)

        1. The teacher supervises, stopping to help students by redirecting their attention, assisting in the identification of obstacles, and encouraging efforts.

        2. A new text assignment is given and students are directed to apply the newly-learned strategy ("We will now start to read the chapter on 'The Branches of Government.' Use the Idea Line learning strategy to make this material yours. Tomorrow we will discuss what you've read as well as how the strategy worked for you.").

5. *Instructional Resources*

   Three short parts of chapters in textbook; board for writing out steps; student notebooks.

6. *Assessment/Evaluation*

   A. Formative–Students answer questions orally and respond in their Learning Strategies notebooks to prompts such as, "The hardest step for me was ___." or "The next time I use this strategy I want to remember ___."

   B. Summative–The next day, students orally report to each other and the teacher their experiences in applying the strategy. Teacher will continue to observe and gather data on students' improved abilities to distinguish between major and minor ideas in text material.

Guided Literacy Lesson Plan

Have you ever had writer's block? Most of us have had the frustrating experience of trying to write an essay or research paper and encountering a brick wall in front of us. We stare at our paper or word processor for what seems like hours, but nothing comes. Ideas vanish. To break out of our writer's block, we enlist the aid of a friend. We talk to our friend about the ideas we've gathered from sources, share our point of view, listen to our friend repeat what we've said and attempt to answer questions. Slowly but surely, the block is lifted, and, even though the task of writing is still difficult, we find words and sentences to express our meaning. We're back in business.

The underpinnings of the **Guided Literacy Lesson Plan** are insights from cognitive psychology and its more recent manifestations in constructivism (see chapter 1). This theory recognizes that students learn most deeply when they make knowledge, rather than passively receive it. In the Direct Instruction model, your role was to deliver information and skills to students in an efficient manner. In Guided Literacy, rather than delivering information to students, your role is to help students connect old and new knowledge, making it their own by shaping and reshaping new understandings into personal pictures or representations of concepts and generalizations. To do this, students must possess strategies for constructing knowledge. Thus, an additional role you have is teaching the strategies that permit independent and lifelong learning (A full treatment of a number of learning strategies will be found in chapter 8).

Just as tools are important to the construction of a building, so too are tools important to teachers, as they instruct students, and to students, as they build their own knowledge structures. In the Guided Literacy Lesson Plan, these tools are the language abilities of reading, writing, speaking, and listening. In some colleges of education, a separate course is often devoted to teaching future teachers how they can help students learn from language activities in their subject matter courses. Such courses use textbooks with titles like *Content Reading and Literacy* (Alvermann & Phelps, 1998) or *Teaching and Reading in the Content Areas: Developing Content Literacy for All Students* (Cooter & Flynt, 1996).

Scholars commonly use the word "literacy" these days to refer to the unique knowledge and skills associated with various fields. That is, you may hear people speak of mathematical literacy, computer literacy, or job literacy. In this text, we use the term, however, in its original context, that of language knowledge and skill. Specifically, the Guided Literacy Lesson Plan incorporates teaching and learning strategies and other activities involving the language processes of reading, writing, speaking, and listening. We know that language and thinking are related, and that the act of writing, for example, clarifies and shapes our thoughts (see the Winograd and Higgins items under "Guided Literacy" in the *Teacher as Researcher* section regarding writing and school math). When teaching involves students with two language abilities, reading and speaking, for instance, the potential for learning in all curricular areas is much greater than when reading and speaking are done separately. Consider this example: A teacher engages students in a role-playing activity in which the students think and speak on their feet and, after listening carefully, respond orally. Subsequently, these students read a newspaper article, which refers to the topic of the role-play. The chances of students comprehending the reading at a high level are much improved because of the oral activity that preceded it. The social nature of the role-play helped, too; it triggered intellectual and emotional engagement and was inherently motivating for the majority of students.

When we couple insights from cognitive psychology with the language abilities of reading, writing, speaking, and listening, we put in place a potent mechanism for teaching and learning. Driven by at least one lesson objective, the Guided Literacy Lesson Plan allows students to acquire facts, concepts, and generalizations in content areas and to process these acquisitions through the use of higher order thinking strategies. Teachers who choose the Guided Literacy Lesson Plan are opting to teach students "what and how," the what of subject matter and the how of learning to process subject matter independently (see Figure 4.6).

You will notice that the same three general phases apply to this plan as they do to the other two. You will also note that within those phases you will engage in some very different activities for very different purposes. Here, again, you will note that there is a step-by-step procedure that we offer you, and we encourage you to follow it as written until you understand the power of this particular format. Then we certainly encourage you to modify as appropriate for the content or students.

Set Induction Phase In the Guided Literacy Lesson Plan, this phase begins with your using teaching strategies and other student-centered activities designed to introduce students and their prior experiences to the subject matter named in the lesson behavior. You need to establish an anticipatory frame of mind by helping students recall pertinent facts, develop vocabulary concepts, and recognize purposes for study. If necessary, you may need to correct misconceptions regarding the subject matter, fill in gaps in subject knowledge, and model learning strategies in preparation for the next phase. The instructional purposes for this phase include helping students do the following:

- Activate and organize prior knowledge.

FIGURE 4.6   OUTLINE OF GUIDED LITERACY LESSON PLAN

1. Lesson Objectives

2. Student Grouping

3. Instructional Methods and Strategies

4. Instructional Activities

   Set Induction Phase
   - Introduce subject matter
   - Establish anticipatory frame of mind

   Interaction Phase
   - Guide recognition of important ideas
   - Develop concepts and generalizations
   - Monitor use of learning strategies

   Closure Phase
   - Reinforce subject matter and processes
   - Help students organize and extend thinking

5. Instructional Resources

6. Assessment/Evaluation
   - Raise questions of students throughout the lesson (formative)
   - Administer quiz at end of lesson (summative)

- Connect old and new knowledge.
- Develop new concepts and generalizations.
- Master a learning and problem solving strategy needed for studying the content.
- Form purposes for learning.

Interaction Phase   During this phase, you aid students in processing subject matter from one or more sources of information. While this is often text material, there are many types of "texts," including computer programs, guest speakers, videos, educational television programs, field trips, and CD-ROMs with which students can interact. In a variety of whole class, small group, and individual work settings, you will help students meet, engage, and make subject matter personally their own. To help students do this, teachers:

- guide students' observations or recognition of important facts and ideas;
- encourage students to further develop concepts (key vocabulary) and generalizations;
- monitor students' applications of learning strategies during independent study.

Closure Phase Finally, during this phase, you will return to appropriate teaching strategies and student-centered activities to bring the lesson to a conclusion. At this point, you will reinforce subject matter knowledge and mental processes named in the lesson objective. At the same time, students organize information, elaborate on the information, and extend their thinking in order to make all their learning deeper and more meaningful.

Activity 4.4

Using a chapter from a subject matter textbook or a book, story, or video a class might use, design a Guided Literacy Lesson Plan for a class of students you profile. Highlight on the lesson plan all references to reading, writing, speaking, and listening. In an endnote, explain how one or two of these language processes may help students comprehend the subject matter referred to in lesson objectives.

Example Plans–Guided Literacy

Elementary Grades Model

Subject   Science   *Grade 3*
Topic   Endangered and Extinct species

1. *Lesson Objectives*
   Students will define "endangered" and "extinct" species.
   Students will list reasons that animals become endangered or extinct.
   Students will apply steps in the Fact Card learning strategy.

2. *Student Grouping*
   Whole class, then small groups or pairs, then individuals

3. *Instructional Methods and Strategies*
   Concept Attainment strategy, Fact Card learning strategy, picture viewing, computer use, reading, writing, talking, listening

4. *Instructional Activities* (2-day lesson plan)
   I. Set Induction Phase [talking, listening] (20 min.)
       A. Teachers show students pictures of animals that are extinct, such as dinosaurs, and endangered, such as panda bears.
       B. Teacher uses a Concept Attainment strategy (see chapter 7 for a full description) to help students develop definitions for "endangered" and "extinct" and provides examples and non-examples of each.
       C. Students hypothesize about "reasons" for endangerment and extinction.
   II. Interaction Phase [listening, talking] (30+ min.)
       A. Students watch "Threatened." Film presents examples of endangered animals and discusses plans for protection. Teacher introduces film ("Let's watch to see if they cover some of the things that we guessed about.").

    B. Teacher and students review reasons covered in the film compared to the class's hypotheses.

    C. Teacher introduces Fact Card learning strategy to students ("We will do Fact Cards so that we can write summary sentences about things we learn.").

    D. Teacher models steps of how to write paraphrased facts on cards.

  III. Closure Phase [talking, listening, writing] (40+ min.)

    A. Students each receive several four-by-six cards, then do research using their fact cards for a specific endangered animal of their choice. Possible sources may include a trade book, magazine, website, or appropriate CD-ROM, such as Compton's Encyclopedia.

    B. In small groups or pairs, students apply "Ecology Treks" on the computer. Students "travel" through various climate zones, meeting simulated challenges on the way, and record on the Fact Card if "their" endangered animal will survive in the simulated climates encountered.

    C. Individually, students write three to four summary sentences from the Fact Card on their animal and how it will best survive.

5. *Instructional Resources*
   Pictures of endangered and extinct animals; IBM PC with color graphics card, sound board, and hard drive; "Threatened" videodisc (Barr Media Group 1992); "Ecology Treks" (1993) computer program.

6. *Assessment/Evaluation*

    A. Formative—Throughout the three phases, the teacher will observe students and pose questions to the whole class, small groups, and individuals ("Can someone tell me the difference between 'extinct' and 'endangered'?" "Why do some animals become endangered?" "Tell me the steps, in order, for using a Fact Card"). Students will turn in Fact Cards and they will be observed for completeness.

    B. Summative—At the end of the second day, students' summary sentences will be collected and graded. At the end of the week, students will take a multiple-choice or short answer quiz on the concepts of extinction and endangerment and why some animals are endangered.

Secondary Grades Example

SUBJECT   Basic English   *GRADE* 10
TOPIC   William Faulkner's "Barn Burning"

1. *Lesson Objectives*
   Students will define setting.
   Students will relate the concept of setting to theme.
   Students will interpret the theme of "coming of age."
   Students will employ a learning strategy for reading about setting.

2. *Student Grouping*
   Students will begin the lesson as a whole class. They will break into small groups briefly, come back as a whole class, and finish with individual work.

3. *Instructional Methods and Strategies*
   Guided Literacy model; teacher-led review; Reading for Setting learning strategy; Teacher modeling (Think-Aloud strategy); Reciprocal Reading teaching strategy (chosen for basic-track students to provide a model of interpretive reading)

4. *Instructional Activities* (two to three day lesson)

   I. Set Induction Phase [talking, listening, writing]

      A. Teacher-led review of a recently covered story in terms of setting ("Where did the story take place?" "How did the character's physical location affect the outcome?" "Describe the house that he lived in." "In what ways is the description important in understanding the character's personality?") (5–7 mins.)

      B. Teacher engages students in defining "setting." Students discuss and then write definition in notebook. (3–4 mins.)

      C. Teacher models Reading for Setting learning strategy ("Okay, now I know that the man is standing in a dark room, and it's about 1950, and he's cold. I'm beginning to wonder about . . ."). (4–5 mins.)

   II. Interaction Phase [listening, talking, reading] 2 days

      A. Students watch the film, *Barn Burning* (40 min.). Teacher-led, brief class discussion follows, centering on setting and plot of the story (coming of age).

      B. Students and teacher read teacher-selected sections of the story aloud, taking turns with reading (Reciprocal Reading teaching strategy).

      C. Class discusses differences between film and story, pointing out similarities between the two in terms of setting.

      D. Students break into groups to address specific questions relating to setting ("How is Abner's personality created by where he lives and works?" "How is Sarty's self-concept related to his 'home'?" "Where is Sarty when he finds out that his father lied to him? What, specifically, does he see, hear, and smell at that point?" "Does the ending of the film seem more violent to you than the text's ending? Why?" "Why is seeing a scene different for some people than reading it?").

      E. Students come back together as a class and discuss their answers to these questions.

      F. Teacher explains theme of "coming of age," inducing a class definition and drawing out examples. Class and teacher discuss Sarty's "coming of age."

   III. Closure Phase [writing] 1+ day

A. Students respond to various questions throughout lesson, as well as summarize their discussions after group work.

B. Students are assigned an essay for which the writing topics focus on "coming of age" and setting. They are encouraged to develop a strong sense of setting in their essays. Students are allowed to choose from topics, such as:

1. Pretend that you face the dilemma of Sarty Snopes. Write your own ending to the story when you've decided how you would handle the "old fierce pull of blood" that Sarty deals with.

2. Explain what "coming of age" means to you. When did yours start? How was the outcome affected by where you were at the time? In what ways were your experiences and Sarty's the same?

5. *Instructional Resources*
Class copies of "Barn Burning" by William Faulkner; a television and a VCR unit; *William Faulkner's Barn Burning* (Learning in Focus 1980).

6. *Assessment/Evaluation*

A. In the set induction phase, the teacher provides a list of processes in the Reading for Setting learning strategy and asks students for a show of hands to determine which students recognize a complete and accurate list. Throughout whole class and group discussions, the teacher listens to responses to questions to determine which students see connections between setting and theme.

B. After the closure phase, the teacher reads the students' essays and notes the number and quality of setting/theme connections that they make. After reading, the teacher interviews individual students regarding statements in their essays ("What thought processes did you use to arrive at this conclusion about setting?").

Cooperative Learning Lesson Plan

It is reported that the late Vince Lombardi, legendary coach of the Green Bay Packers, once said that winning was the only thing that mattered in the game of football. Indeed, the desire to be "number one" is a preoccupation in most Western cultures. It can be observed, not only in the sports arena, but also in education where we often observe fierce competition for the top grades and the highest scholastic honors. While often used as the mantra of competitors, what often gets lost in his message is that Lombardi first had to build a team, a group of people who shared some common goals and understandings. Those team members often had to set aside personal achievements for the good of the group; in essence, they had to cooperate with each other and their coach. It was only after molding this team that Lombardi competed against other teams.

Some educational scholars have looked at the effects of competition in the classroom and have found them wanting, both philosophically and educationally. When students compete with each other, they tend to protect what they know and do not readily admit their curiosities and questions; as a result, they limit their communications with others and, ultimately, their knowledge stores to what they already know or can discover on their own.

Some very prominent critics maintain that competition impedes the academic learning we want for all students, while it indirectly teaches the negative values of selfishness and intolerance. In its place they advocate a classroom environment and educational practices which use cooperative learning as one of a number of ways of prompting student learning (see the "Cooperative Learning" items in the *Teacher as Researcher* section). In contrast to competition, a **Cooperative Learning Lesson Plan** venture puts all students on equal footing, encourages interpersonal interaction and communication, promotes active construction of knowledge, and fosters the social skills needed for effective intragroup relationships. If this is not enough of a reason for fostering social skills, look in any large newspaper's classified section and you will see the business sector clamoring for highly-qualified workers who can work in a team atmosphere. Therefore, when you want to teach academic content and social skills in conjunction with each other, cooperative learning is the lesson plan framework to use.

One other concern about cooperative groups that critics often raise is that the brightest students are held back by the group activities. Most experimental studies of cooperative learning reveal that equal benefits accrue for high, average, and low achievers in comparison to their counterparts in control groups (Slavin, 1995). A further benefit appears to be that relations between students of different races may be affected positively. Clark (1991) reported that, when African-American and Caucasian students work cooperatively on class assignments and in extracurricular activities, interracial friendships are enhanced. Even if friendships do not form within these groups, students gain skills that they can use beyond the classroom. Again, if we go back to the business world, one of the leading reasons that people lose their jobs is that they cannot get along with co-workers. It would seem, then, that we have an obligation as teachers to prepare our students for the cognitive and social demands of work places in the twenty-first century.

There is a solid body of research evidence that supports the idea that the social skills practiced in cooperative groups are associated with heightened achievement. Slavin (1995) reported on ninety-nine studies that evaluated forms of cooperative learning in which groups of elementary or secondary students worked together to learn. Sixty-three (64 percent) of these experimental-control comparisons significantly favored cooperative learning. Only five (5 percent) significantly favored control groups. The studies do not show conclusive evidence, however, on how much—or to what degree—achievement is influenced by cooperation. Furthermore, on the basis of current research, it can be concluded that cooperative learning produces higher academic achievement than competitive and individual learning efforts (Johnson, Johnson, & Smith, 1995). One possible explanation for this is the cognitive elaboration theory (Wittrock, 1978). Wittrock theorized that, in order to retain information and relate it to prior knowledge, the learner must restructure or elaborate on the material. In cooperative learning groups, elaboration occurs when members explain and defend propositions. Whether group academic achievement transfers to individual achievement, however, seems to rely on whether group learning includes an emphasis on individual accountability, group discussion, attention to group outcomes, and higher-order tasks.

In addition to the association between cooperative learning and achievement, students involved in cooperative learning can profit in a number of other ways. Studies suggest that students also grow affectively, motivationally, socially, and cognitively. In cooperative learning, students are encouraged to support each other, to prize collective achievement as well as personal achievement, and to build the abilities needed for effective team membership. As a result, students have greater self-pride and confidence. Cooperative group members work toward individual and group goals. Every student's individual labors contribute to group success, and in reverse fashion, meeting group goals encourages individuals to strive harder. All members learn that success is the result of effort, not luck (for a reminder of internal and external loci of causality, see chapter 1). Growth in interpersonal and team collaboration is a life-long endeavor, but it is enhanced in a deliberate way through cooperative learning activities. Students learn how to get along with each other by sharing, turn-taking, assisting, talking, and caring about feelings. When problems in the group arise, such as members not sharing the work load equally, students can hold group meetings to discuss the problems and work to resolve them. Academic achievement increases in cooperative learning ventures because, as students talk and problem-solve together, they elaborate on their understandings, clarify meanings, and promote the use of critical thinking competencies.

There are many different reasons and purposes for which you might choose to use the cooperative learning format. Sometimes teachers put students into groups for purposes of skill instruction, discussion, review, and/or accomplishing specific tasks, such as conducting a lab experiment, constructing a physical model, or writing the script of a scene they will later perform. Usually in these instances, the task is emphasized and the social skills are assumed or ignored. Although group work is the activity in these instances, it does not qualify as cooperative learning. Johnson, Johnson, and Smith (1991) have compared traditional learning groups and cooperative learning groups and we present their summary of differences in Figure 4.7.

To the differences that Johnson et al. present, we add one more. The cooperative learning groups we advocate are designed to accomplish the twin goals of content and social skills learning. In the example lesson plans that follow this discussion, you should notice how both types of learning are introduced and then intertwined as lesson activities unfold.

The nature of the academic learning differs by the cooperative learning strategy the teacher uses. Slavin and his associates advocate a number of Student Team Learning Methods. Strategies in this category tend to yield achievement of lower-level cognitive skills over the short term. Other methods of cooperative learning, including Group Investigation and Learning Together, comprise a second category. They promote higher levels of cognitive functioning over the long term. A full description of selected strategies will be found in chapter 7.

FIGURE 4.7 WHAT IS THE DIFFERENCE?	
Cooperative Learning Groups	Traditional Learning Groups
Positive Interdependence	No Interdependence
Individual Accountability	No Individual Accountability
Heterogeneous Membership Encouraged	Homogeneous Membership
Shared Leadership	One Appointed Leader
Task and Relationships Emphasized	Only Task Emphasized
Social Skills Taught Directly	Social Skills Assumed or Ignored
Teacher Monitors Groups and Intervenes	Teacher Ignores Groups
Group Processing	No Group Processing

(*Source: Active learning: cooperation in the college classroom*, Johnson, D. W., Johnson, R. T., & Smith, K. A. (1991). *Interaction Book Company*. Excerpt from p. 3:3, Table 3.1: "What Is the Difference?")

As you become familiar with these strategies, you and your colleagues will no doubt find yourselves adapting them to your own circumstances. However, it is good to note that strategies that generate higher academic achievement and improved social interactions always include group goals, such as team rewards, and also provisions for individual accountability. That is to say that when group members see equal opportunities for success, they become interested in promoting the achievement of their classmates as they concurrently see how their single achievements contribute to important group outcomes.

We present below two cooperative learning lesson plans that focus on the teaching of specific content and do so in a context of social learning. In each, the content to be learned is explored through tasks and assignments typically used in a subject matter class: report-writing, surveys, experiments, end-of-chapter questions, text or reference book study, or problem-solving activities. At the same time, explorations are enhanced by student interaction and collaboration. When you wish to simultaneously teach toward academic and social objectives, you will want to design a cooperative learning plan, modifying it based on class experiences and personal inclinations. Each of the sample lessons here follows the three-phase format used earlier in our discussions of the Guided Literacy and Direct Instruction plans (see Figure 4.8).

Set Induction Phase Early in this phase, you announce the subject matter named in the lesson objectives and tell students how you will be assessing their development of the skills and/or knowledge on which they will work within the group. You may also need to activate students' background knowledge regarding the subject matter and focus attention on the specific subject matter lesson objective. If prerequisite knowledge is shallow, erroneous, or absent, choose a teaching strategy to establish accurate facts, concepts, and generalizations associated with the topic in students' minds (see chapter 7 for teaching strategies).

FIGURE 4.8   OUTLINE OF COOPERATIVE LEARNING LESSON PLAN

1. Lesson Objectives

2. Student Grouping

3. Instructional Methods and Strategies

4. Instructional Activities

   Set Induction Phase
   - Focus student attention on subject matter objectives
   - Focus student attention on social skill objectives
   - Explain group procedures and expectations

   Interaction Phase
   - Form groups to learn subject matter and social skills
   - Monitor learning of content and social skills

   Closure Phase
   - Assist students in reviewing subject matter achievement
   - Debrief students on application of social skills

5. Instructional Resources

6. Assessment/Evaluation
   - Keep records of social skill use during group work (formative)
   - Collect evidence of subject matter mastery at end of lesson (summative)

After helping students to become aware of the content goals, introduce and discuss the social skills of interpersonal cooperation and small group functioning in which students will engage. Elicit student responses about the need for the particular social skill for working well in a group. Then facilitate students' descriptions of what the skill will "look like" and "sound like" if group members are indeed practicing it.

Once they are aware of both content and social skills objectives, you should then explain in detail how cooperative groups will function. Announce how many students will be in a group, the bases on which they'll be assigned, the roles students will play (if necessary), and assessment of groups and their individual members on both subject matter and social skills lesson objectives. As students become more familiar with cooperative groups, you may want to involve them in shaping lesson objectives. As you strive to move students toward greater independence, teach them how to develop and then use a **rubric,** a scoring device that assigns points or values to a continuum of performance levels consistent with the lesson objectives. Rubrics can help students self-monitor the subject matter goals in their particular groups. When you are sure that students know the rules of participation, give them a signal to begin working.

Interaction Phase   During this phase, you will be able to determine the clarity of your directions and planning as you watch students work. Ideally, heterogeneous student groups will work together to learn subject matter that comes from one or more sources, such as a text, CD-ROM, guest speaker, educational television program, or illustrated lecture. As students actively interact with the material, they simultaneously apply the skills of social interaction introduced during the set induction.

While students are actively engaged, instead of overtly directing students' actions, you act as a "guide on the side," monitoring students' learning of subject matter and group processing skills. For the most part you should not intervene, preferring to let students work out issues on their own by turning their attention inward toward other group members rather than toward you as the authority (the Cooperative Learning strategies in chapter 7 are good for helping students use each other as resources). You should, however, monitor and supervise students in systematic ways regarding their development and attainment of the social skill; you may use anecdotal records, a checklist, or some other form that allows you to gather data on students' performance of the social skill.

Closure Phase   After the group work is over, provide students with a signal to re-form as a whole class. At this point, you need to follow up on your earlier announcement of how you are assessing their attainment of the subject matter objective. That may involve collecting a paper or a completed project from groups, or it may involve a group or individual quiz, either the same day or some day following the activity. However you do it, though, it is important that students receive relatively quick feedback on their achievement of the content objectives.

At this point, you will also provide some type of systematic follow up in debriefing students on their practice of the social skill. Use open-ended sentences (e.g., "We did a good job of practicing _____ by doing ____, _____, and ____.") or prompts that encourage a commitment from students (e.g., "Next time we work in groups, we can do an even better job of _____ by doing . . .."). It is often motivating for students to hear your positive comments about their developing behaviors. Initially, evaluation sessions are teacher-led, but the teacher gradually "fades" into a position of interested observer as students learn both how to assess and evaluate individual and group progress. The teacher retains responsibility for recording individual scores of academic achievement and making decisions regarding moving to a new lesson, assigning course grades, and consulting about promotions and placements in special classes. When the school's arrangement for reporting to parents includes a provision for social learning, it is again the teacher's job to indicate progress on this dimension. In addition, when group goals have been met, class or school recognition or rewards can be given. Sometimes these are certificates inscribed with group members' names; more often, they take the form of high verbal praise and congratulations.

> **Activity 4.5**
>
> Design a Cooperative Learning Lesson Plan. Assume you are sharing your plan on a world-wide website. For teachers who access the website, write a short description of the social/collaborative needs of your learners. Then, in a note, explain how your plan (a) addresses these needs and (b) simultaneously promotes the cognitive lesson objectives.

Example Plans–Cooperative Learning

Elementary Grades Model

SUBJECT   Math   GRADE 4

TOPIC   Large Numbers

1. *Lesson Objectives*
   Students will order large numbers using sequential place value (cognitive objective).
   Students will accurately read and write long numbers in word form (cognitive objective).
   Students will work cooperatively in a group by encouraging others (social skills objective).

2. *Student Gouping*
   Whole class, study groups, expert groups, then whole class to finish

3. *Instructional Methods and Strategies*
   Cooperative Learning model; teacher explanation; Group Question strategy; teacher-led class discussion; Jigsaw cooperative learning strategy (see chapter 7)

4. *Instructional Activities*

   I.   Set Induction Phase (15 min.)

        A. Focusing students on subject matter objectives
           Discuss the importance of place value in understanding and reading large numbers. Give examples by lining up the numbers in columns:

$$4,567,391$$
$$1,448,459$$
$$567,439$$
$$9,995$$

        Review how to read the numbers aloud and how to write them. Do several examples with the students on the board. Correct common mistakes, such as disorganization in digit placement and reading the million, thousand, and hundreds places in order.

        B. Focusing students on social skills objective
           Lead class discussion on the need for the social skill of encouragement ("Have you ever worked in a group where you didn't feel like you were

a part of the group? How did that feel?"). Then, lead discussion to describe encouraging behaviors ("I'm going to write down what you tell me about encouragement. First, I want you to think about what it sounds like when your other group members are encouraging each other. What kinds of things will they say or would you say? . . . Now, what does it look like when people are encouraging each other?").

C. Explaining group procedures and expectations

Explain how the students will be organized into study groups ("I will assign each of you a number from one to five. You will go to the area of the room that corresponds to your number"). Explain the jigsaw procedure. Keep it simple; jigsaw seems confusing at first ("After you form groups, I will come around and assign you a letter of the alphabet from A to E. In a couple minutes we're going to form new groups according to the letter you receive and you can share with your new group what you have learned"). Review the procedures of group work and ask that students observe themselves and each other as they maintain a positive attitude in the group by encouraging each other. When students understand their subject matter objectives, social skill objectives, and procedures for working in groups, give the signal to have them form their groups.

II. Interaction Phase (20 min.)

A. Student Behavior

1. Students break into their expert groups according to the country that they were assigned (e.g., all number ones will work together on the United States, all number twos will work together on China, etc.). Within these expert groups, each student must become the expert on reading and writing a large number (population) correctly. Students will use the Internet, an atlas, or encyclopedias to find the population of their countries. The number should be relatively current, but need not be the most recent source; the important thing is that they find and agree on a large number to work with. As a group, they are to master how to say the number correctly, how to write it numerically, and how to write it in words. Each student should write this information on a three-by-five card.

2. Rearrange students back into their study groups. Using their cards, students should "teach" their numbers to the study group. They should read their numbers aloud and show how it looks written numerically.

3. On large place value charts, have the study groups order the countries from smallest to largest based on population. Remind students to take care to line the digits according to place value. Next, have them write the numbers in words on paper. Present the charts to the class.

B. Teacher Behavior

While students are engaged, you should be moving around the room monitoring group interactions, especially as they relate to the social skill. For early efforts, it is a good idea to jot down on a piece of paper many of the examples of what you see and hear in terms of encouraging behaviors.

  III. Closure Phase (10 min.)

  A. Processing subject matter
  Review the large place value chart for accuracy. Randomly choose a member from each of the groups to read the number as written. Discuss any errors ("Why did they happen? What is the correct way to write that number?").

  B. Processing social skills
  Ask all group members to write out the sentence on the board and fill in the blanks with specific descriptions of how their group met the social skills objective [My group members did a good job of encouraging each other by ___, ___, and ___.]. Allow group members about 2 minutes to share their responses, then ask for members of each group to share how their specific group encouraged other members. Finally, share your own anecdotal records with the entire class.

5. *Instructional Resources*
Place value charts; research materials such as an atlas or Internet browser

6. *Assessment/Evaluation*

  A. Formative Assessment–The teacher keeps anecdotal records of social skills during group work. In addition to the anecdotes, however, he/she also monitors students' conversations within groups. The place value chart will provide some information on groups' development of subject matter objectives.

  B. Summative Assessment–At the end of the week, students will individually take a quiz on large numbers. Individual performance will be charted and bonus points will be given to all members of every study group averaging 90 percent correct on the quiz.

Secondary Grades Model

SUBJECT   Geography   *GRADE* 10
TOPIC   United States

1. *Lesson Objectives*
Students will collect facts about features of a specific geographical area of the U.S. Students will construct a relief map.
Students will share responsibility for tasks necessary to complete the project.

2. *Student Grouping*
Whole class, Think-Pair-Share partners, back to whole class, then to cooperative groups, and back to whole class for presentations

3. *Instructional Methods and Strategies*
Cooperative Learning model; teacher-led class discussion; Think-Pair-Share strategy; Group Question strategy; Group Investigation learning strategy

4. *Instructional Activities*

I. Set induction phase (20 min.)

A. Focusing students on subject matter objectives

1. After introducing a unit about United States geography, use the Think-Pair-Share strategy to have students brainstorm a list of questions about areas of curiosity that have geographical significance.

2. Bring the class back together as a whole. Compile a list of questions from those offered in the pairs. Sort these into related categories; for example, questions that ponder the impact of oceans could be put into a "Hawaii/California" category; desert questions could be put into a "Southwest United States" category; and mountain questions could be put into a "Rocky Mountain" category.

3. Announce objectives ("Today we will be gathering information to see if we can answer some of these questions. We will also begin a project of constructing a relief map that your group will design based on some of the information you discover.")

B. Focusing students on social skill objective
Lead class discussion on the need for the social skill of sharing responsibility ("Have you ever worked in a group where one group member did all the work? How did that feel?"). Then, lead discussion to describe sharing behaviors ("I'm going to write down what you tell me about sharing responsibility. First, I want you to think about what it sounds like when your other group members are sharing equally in the responsibilities of completing a project. What kinds of conversations will be taking place in those groups? . . . Now, what does it *look like* when people are sharing the responsibility for completing an assignment?").

C. Explaining group procedures and expectations
Explain how the students will be organized into groups ("I have prepared a list of groups and group members on the board. These groups have been formed on the basis of different skills that each individual has demonstrated on earlier projects. Each group, for instance, has some skilled artists, strong researchers, etc."). Then describe the time frame and other expectations for working with materials, including any necessary safety concerns for use of the construction materials, if appropriate. Review the procedures of group work and ask that students observe themselves and each other as they attempt to complete the task by equally sharing responsibility for the variety of things that will need to be done. When students understand their subject matter objectives, social skill objectives and procedures for working in groups, give the signal to have them form their groups.

II. Interaction Phase (one to two days)

A. Student Behaviors

1. Using the Internet, an atlas, or other appropriate research materials, have groups research the geographical area assigned to them. They should use the group of related questions as their guide.

2. Groups create a relief map detailing the geography of the area, including neighboring states, water sources, mountain areas, lands converted to forests, and so on. Students may work on a wood base and use whatever materials available; these may include Plaster of Paris, paints, or sand.

3. Groups prepare a presentation for the class on their geographical area. Each student is required to have a part in the presentation.

4. Each team appoints a representative who will meet briefly with a central coordinating committee. This committee will decide upon the order and organization of presentations.

B. Teacher Behavior

While students are engaged, you should be moving around the room monitoring group interactions, especially as they relate to the social skill. Depending on your knowledge of your class, you may also want to monitor the use of materials. This skill is one that should probably not be introduced until the class has had some practice in working in cooperative groups and they have established positive attitudes and relationships in other efforts. It is still a good idea to jot down examples of what you see and hear in terms of sharing responsibility.

III. Closure Phase (one day)

A. Processing the subject matter objectives

Students share their presentations with the class. Each group should specifically answer the questions compiled by the class and explain its relief maps. After the presentations, as a class, students and teacher can assess what they learned about the varying geography within the United States.

B. Processing the social skill objective

Ask students to fill out a pie chart individually. Have them divide the pie into appropriate pieces that indicate the amount of work different individuals, including themselves, did in completing the project. They should also explain their chart by making specific comments about how the group shared the workload and how important decisions were made within their group.

5. *Instructional Resources*

Research materials such as an atlas, Internet browser, or United States relief map; provide appropriate art materials, including a base for each group, paints, clay, or plaster, etc.

6. *Assessment/Evaluation*

A. Formative Assessment—The teacher keeps anecdotal records of social skills observed during group work. In addition to the anecdotes, however, the teacher also monitors students' conversations within the group. Observing the progress of the relief maps will provide some information on groups' development of subject matter objectives.

B. Summative Assessment–The most immediate assessment of the subject matter objectives will be based upon the accuracy of the group's relief map and the accuracy and quality of the class presentation. Within a week, students will take a quiz on geographical highlights of the United States. The pie chart will provide student perceptions on shared responsibility within the group.

PLANNING IN INCLUSIONARY CLASSROOMS

The chances are good that some of the faces in your first classroom will be students with disabilities. In chapter 1, we reported the history of mainstreaming and the more recent emphasis on inclusionary classrooms. In these classrooms, the look of education is different from what many of us have experienced. Their classroom teachers are discovering how to maintain high goals while adapting the amount or complexity of material, the pace of instruction, and instructional approaches to the individual needs and abilities of their students.

We encourage you to consider ideas for adapting instruction when you have one or a limited number of special needs students in your regular education class. Applying these ideas can start a process that results in advantages for the whole class (an elaboration of this point will be found in the Katims and Harris item under "Guided Literacy" in the *Teacher as Researcher* section). When you begin to adapt your objectives, resources, strategies, and activities for a special needs youngster in your class, you will find, as countless other teachers have, that extending modifications to non-disabled students often results in improved achievement for them, too. Aligning instructional practices with the *actual* abilities of students brings them success, and with success, they will have greater confidence in their abilities to learn. That, in turn, improves students' engagement, or the persistence to task that comes from an inner sense that learning is good for its own sake.

Activity 4.6

Observe instruction in an inclusionary classroom. Identify the characteristics of the special education students and others who, for one reason or another, have difficulty learning. Then identify (the "I" in the IDEAL model) the approach to co-teaching the two teachers are using and any lesson adaptations. After that, clarify (the "D" in the IDEAL model) the reasons why they have chosen this approach. Finally, reflect (which in the IDEAL model is synonymous with the "L," Look at the Results) on the approach and adaptations. Which students are benefiting? Speculate on the reasons.

The adaptations shown in Figure 4.9 are based on work by Deschenes, Ebeling, and Sprague (1994). We have modified their nine types of adaptations and added others. We urge you to see the presence of special needs students in your class as a challenge to your creativity as a professional educator. Mix and match these modifications on a day to day basis, choosing specific combinations to fit your students' specific needs, your goals and objectives for the entire class, and the resources at hand.

FIGURE 4.9   ADAPTING CURRICULUM AND INSTRUCTION IN INCLUSIVE CLASSROOMS

1. Size
   Adapt the number of items that the learner is expected to learn or complete. Example: Reduce the number of items on a math exercise sheet from fifteen to five.

2. Time
   Adapt the time allotted and allowed for learning, task completion, or testing. Example: When writing an in-class summary of a class discussion, allow the student to complete it out of class or during the succeeding class period.

3. Level of Support
   Increase the amount of personal assistance with a specific learner. Example: Arrange for an upper-grade "helper" who will tutor in an area of need or supervise homework.

4. Input
   Adapt the way instruction is delivered to the learner. Example: Present a wall chart with magnetized parts to help visual learners and those who need to manipulate objects.

5. Difficulty
   Adapt the skill level, problem type, or the rules on how the learner may approach the work. Example: On a computer program that assesses mastery of syllabication rules, use a criterion of 85 percent rather than 95 percent.

6. Output
   Adapt how the student can respond to instruction. Example: Instead of answering questions in writing, allow verbal responses.

7. Participation
   Adapt the extent to which a learner is actively involved in the task. Example: Instead of physically acting out the action of a play, have a student sit and whisper forgotten lines to actors during rehearsal.

8. Alternate Goals
   Adapt the goals or outcome expectations while using the same materials. Example: On a blank treble clef staff, have a student place and name notes while others apply knowledge by recording a simple musical phrase.

9. Substitute Curriculum
   Provide different instruction and materials to meet a student's individual goals. Example: While the rest are reading the next section on types of bone fracture, one reads an article in braille on general injury prevention.

There is one group of students who are disabled because of language difficulties. The term that is usually applied to the group is limited English proficiency (LEP). As we pointed out in chapter 1, the size of this group is increasing dramatically, and the challenge of instructing them most often rests with regular classroom teachers. Some LEP students speak English but cannot read or write it. Some know their native language well but are illiterate in all the English language arts, while others are illiterate in both their native language and English. Their lack of ability in English is influenced, moreover, by their capacity to learn, interest in academics, and level of parental support, characteristics which hold for their non-LEP peers as well.

Amidst this diversity, classroom teachers can address the needs of LEP students while attending to the rest of the class. The suggestions that follow derive from the experience of many teachers who have LEP students in their classrooms.

- Make learning visual. Whenever possible, use drawings, objects, and demonstrations to help LEP students as well as their English proficient classmates access relevant prior knowledge and construct new understandings. Even stick figures and rough sketches drawn on the board can illustrate relative size and magnitude, sequence, cause and effect, and other relationships.

- Build vocabulary functionally. Some direct vocabulary instruction, involving word structure and phonics, is helpful in establishing sight and sound of words, as well as the meanings of important subject matter terms. However, repeated use of new terms in conversations where students share, request, and question information of interest to them is the key to a large vocabulary.

- Maintain personal journals. Have students record what they learned, what they were confused about, or what they'd like to know on a daily basis. The level of their English proficiency will be revealed by their word choice, phrase and sentence structure, and grammatical awareness. Your private response to journal entries each week will complement progress in English and open up opportunities to strengthen subject matter knowledge.

- Establish peer tutoring arrangements. The learning of both LEP and English proficient students is enhanced through tutoring. For example, a student who is still learning English may be a strong math student who can assist an English speaking classmate with a mathematics assignment.

- Use grouping structures flexibly. Mix and match whole-class, small group, and individual work to promote achievement. For example, introduce the two or three major concepts of your lesson to the whole class. As you witness students catching on, establish small groups for follow-up and reinforcement while you work with LEP groups and individuals for additional instruction and clarification. Recall what you've learned in this chapter about cooperative learning groups. Other material on methods of classroom grouping is in chapter 5.

- Foster an encouraging atmosphere. Orally and in writing, have students tell stories and describe the customs of their homes. By your patient and helpful example, let all students know that we learn from each other. In the process, LEP students' hesitancy and mistakes in language are accepted as necessary for growth.

- Show interest in LEP students' cultures. Learn as much as possible from community resources, the Internet, and computer programs. By sharing what you're learning about them, you open lines of communication with students and earn their trust.

In the final analysis, helping LEP students with English and subject-related skills requires a cluster of teaching attitudes and skills. As Canney et al. (1999) see it, effective teachers are patient, persistent, and respectful of students' culture. They know how to adjust the curriculum while maintaining high standards, and they find ways to involve LEP students in the life of the class.

SUMMARY

Professionally trained teachers know how to make decisions about what students need to know. They also know how to make a related set of decisions regarding how to teach. Committing these decisions to paper is the act of constructing lessons. The finest experienced teachers we know consciously plan their lessons in advance of teaching. Although they may not write down all their decisions in a formal lesson plan, they can easily describe orally the cognitive, affective, and/or psychomotor behaviors they want their students to develop and the instructional activities they'll employ to guide student growth in these behaviors. They can readily visualize the sequence of instruction within the constraints of class time. They see how students will work individually, in groups, and as a class. They plan for the resources they and students will need, and in their minds they review the possibilities for assessing students' growth toward lesson objectives both during and after teaching.

Our hope is that eventually you will be known as an excellent, as well as an experienced, teacher. To attain that distinction, we believe that you need at this point in your career the guidance of your course instructor, the information in this chapter, and practice in choosing and then writing out in considerable detail lesson plans for a variety of learning outcomes.

To that end, we have described three lesson plans together with actual elementary and secondary level examples of each. The Direct Instruction Lesson Plan, marked by a high degree of structure and teacher control, follows a sequence of teacher presentation, group and individual practice, and assessment. It's best suited for mastering low-level cognitive skills, segmented factual information, learner strategies, and/or psychomotor skills. The Guided Literacy Lesson Plan helps students apply their language abilities for the purpose of constructing information while learning the strategies needed to independently study subject matter at the higher levels of thinking. And the Cooperative Learning Lesson Plan is based on the recognition that both social and academic learnings are important, that both can be learned in conjunction with each other, and that academic learning can be enhanced in a social, that is to say cooperative, setting.

Increasingly we are seeing inclusionary classrooms at all grade levels where one or two teachers meet a classroom of special and regular education students. We have presented suggestions for adapting your lessons for special needs students, including those with limited English proficiency. Adapting lesson plan activities often has a positive co-benefit: It helps regularly functioning as well as special needs students work toward instructional objectives.

In these last two chapters, our aim has been to investigate the part of teacher decision-making called Defining the Challenge. We have expanded on the perennial and challenging questions of how to give direction to instruction and how to frame it in terms of unit and lesson planning. We assume that you are now ready to explore alternative approaches to planning and teaching and to address the central challenges with which you will be faced as an educator.

REFLECTIONS

1. Look back at the opening conversation. Imagine that you are Sally and try to identify any other issues she may not have seen and clarify what she may have inadvertently done to undermine the success of her lesson. If you were she, which of the lesson models would you use? On what assumptions are you basing your choice? Explain.

2. You know that the IDEAL decision-making model used in this book defines the "I," Identify the Challenge, and "D," Define the Challenge phases as having two aspects: the who (students) and the what (subject matter to be learned). Keeping that in mind, find a well-detailed lesson plan written by a teacher (good sources are unit and lesson plan databases on the Internet or commercially-available lesson plan databases purchased by a university library). Identify and define the challenge, that is the students (grade level, other named characteristics) and the content (unit or lesson topic, lesson objectives, and/or major facts, concepts, and generalizations). Reflect on and then answer these questions: What additional information do you wish for? Based on what you *do* know, are the objectives appropriate for the named students?

3. Choose one of the example lesson plans in this chapter to act out, either in front of role-playing, fellow students or mentally in your head. As you act on this plan (the "A" in the IDEAL model), what additional information can you add to the plan? That is, what questions, directions, comments do you see? What other actions, resources, or assessments do you visualize?

4. As you observe a practice teaching episode by a class member or an actual teaching episode on a field experience visit, infer the lesson behavior from the activities of the class period. Share the inference with the teacher. How accurate was your inference? Reflect on the observation, your inference, and your conversation with the teacher. What have you learned that you will carry into your teaching?

TEACHER AS RESEARCHER

Direct Instruction

Foorman, B. R. (1995). Research on "The Great Debate": Code-oriented versus whole language approaches to reading instruction. *School Psychology Review, 24* (3), 376–392.

Which is the better way to teach beginning reading? By using direct (explicit) instruction to help students see the relationships between letters and sounds? Or by using students' own oral language and their own stories as a meaningful context in which to teach words? Foorman summarizes the research on both sides of the debate. What is her conclusion and what suggestions for teaching new readers do you think she'd make?

Guided Literacy

Winograd, K., & Higgins, K. M. (1995). Writing, reading, and talking mathematics: One interdisciplinary possibility. *The Reading Teacher, 48* (4), 310–317.

The writers observed elementary math students identify and write their own real-to-life "story problems and solutions." In the social setting of their classroom, students also talked with and listened to each other as they wrote and read each others' mathematical formulations. However, on the basis of further observations, the writers raised an hypothesis regarding the sufficiency of engaging students as problem writers and solvers when the goal is promoting students' mathematics learning. What is their hypothesis? Describe a mini-research project for testing their hypothesis.

Katims, D. S., & Harris, S. (1997). Improving the reading comprehension of middle school students in inclusive classrooms. *Journal of Adolescent and Adult Literacy, 41* (2), 116–123.

The purpose of the reported study was to increase the comprehension of both general and special education students in inclusive seventh grade reading classes. Describe (a) the characteristics of the students who took part in the actual study; (b) the materials, instructional procedures, and tests used in both the experimental and control classes; (c) the overall results for both groups; and (d) possible implications for teaching.

Cooperative Learning

Klemp, R. M., Hon, J. E., & Shorr, A. A. (1993, January). Cooperative literacy in the middle school: An example of a learning strategy based approach. *Middle School Journal*, 19–27.

The instructional problems teachers encounter in day to day teaching are the bases of classroom research questions. Think of yourself as a teacher-researcher who has read and studied the Fact Storm activity and is now ready to try it with actual students. List at least three instructional problems you may encounter as you visualize yourself implementing the activity.

Gillies, R. M., & Ashman, A. F. (1996). Teaching collaborative skills to primary school children in classroom-based work groups. *Learning and Instruction, 6* (3), 187–200.

The sixth grade students in this study were divided into two kinds of groups. In the first, members were trained in ways of cooperating with each other. In the second, members were not trained but rather told to help each other. Identify the outcomes of the study in terms of social and academic learning for both groups. What ideas from this chapter do you associate with these outcomes?

SECTION III

IDEAL

Exploring Alternatives

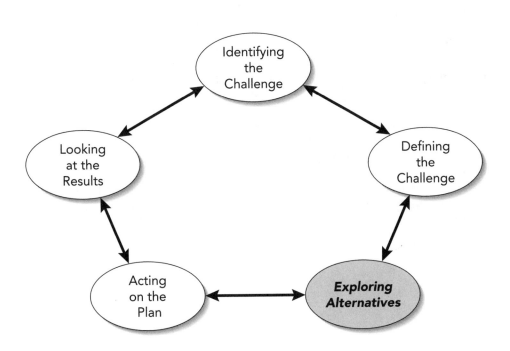

If you're anything like us, each new day begins with so many possibilities. There are things that you want to do, things you have to do, and things you'd rather avoid but may do anyway. You may find yourself mentally going through this list of possibilities as you take a morning jog or walk. You may actually write them down on a list while sitting at the kitchen table after you start your coffee. As you begin to make the decisions about what to do with your day, you may think of several alternative plans. You could do a load of laundry in the morning while you read that chapter in Plato's *Republic* before you go to the store for groceries. Or you could get the shopping out of the way early before the market gets crowded and do your laundry and reading in the evening. However you go about it, considering all the possible things that you need to do in a day provides you with a way to organize your time so that you can be productive.

When teachers approach their planning, they do the same type of thinking. They explicitly apply this same method to considering their planning and teaching responsibilities. In a general sense, by providing themselves with several ways that they can accomplish all that needs to be done in a day, teachers determine which of these possible plans can make the most effective use of their time. Specific to their planning for instruction, though, effective teachers consider all the alternative methods that they know to help students achieve to their highest potentials. They consider all of the "tools" they have available to them and which ones they can use to help students build their understandings of the bodies of knowledge that comprise school learning.

The chapters in this section will provide you with some of these same tools that you can begin to store in your own teaching repertoire. Remember that, as someone new to the teaching field, you cannot be expected to have available to you the same number of alternative ways of reaching students. The topics in these chapters, however, will give you a start. In chapter 5, you will be introduced to various tools of the profession, things like questioning strategies and ways of grouping students. Chapter 6 will provide you with a number of ideas to consider as you choose instructional resources to support student learning and your teaching of content and skills. Chapter 7 focuses on teaching strategies that can help you accomplish specific instructional purposes. Chapter 8 describes learning and problem-solving strategies that you can teach to your students to help them successfully meet learning goals, both yours and theirs. And chapter 9 explores ways of measuring and assessing student achievement. Taken as a whole, developing competence in all of these areas will provide you with a foundation upon which you can make sound instructional decisions as you make plans for student learning.

CHAPTER 5

Tools of the Profession

CONVERSATION

Raheela Khamfur sat in her classroom. The day had just ended, and she was taking these few moments to reflect on what had taken place in her physics class that day. Students had been having a lot of trouble with solving problems of acceleration using the vectors that had been introduced in the text book. Many of the problems dealt with airplanes, so she was trying to explore alternative ways of getting them on a little more familiar ground. That's it, she thought. Ground is what they understand, and the hills that surrounded the schools gave her all sorts of ideas about how to help them to understand better the various forces that acted with and against moving bodies as they accelerated.

Now, how best to teach this? She had tried today to introduce this concept in a whole-class format with students being individually accountable for working on the problems. Some students were getting it, but too many were not. She'd have to change some things. She had a pretty good idea which students were getting it and they'd passed in their work, so she could go over that tonight and form them into groups. An alternative approach popped into her head. She could possibly split them up into pairs, one student who had the concept with one who didn't. She suspected, though, that there would not be enough "got it" students to go around, so she could use a small group arrangement as a backup plan.

Though she wanted to use small group work as an activity, she still felt more comfortable re-introducing this concept to the whole group in a teacher-led discussion. If she were going to do this again, though, she would have to be much more aware of the types of questions she asked and the order in which she presented them. These students, especially those who appeared really lost, were going to need to be led in small steps toward the objective. She knew that a lot of her students were running in P.E. these past couple weeks, preparing for the two-mile run. She had heard a number of them talking about how hard it was to run up Donner Hill about a half-mile into their training runs. This seemed like it could be a really good place for her to start the lesson.

She thought about the variety of questions she might ask and tried to visualize her fifth-period class, many of whom were coming straight from running. How might they respond if she started class by casually asking, "So, how was it running Donner Hill today?" She suspected that an open-ended question like this might surprise them but would probably lead to a number of students responding. That could be a real positive; it would get them interested. She could almost hear William in the back saying, "It really sucked." Most things "sucked," according to William. Actually, that might not be such a bad thing to hear, she thought. She could follow that up with a question like, "What made it suck?" He was almost sure to say something about how hard it is to run up the hill. That could lead to her asking a couple other questions that would get them to see how the gravity vector has to be taken into account when you work with these kinds of problems.

She continued to imagine her class for a little while longer and actually jotted down some of the types and levels of questions that she wanted to make sure she would ask. She knew that it wouldn't necessarily go as she imagined it, but she found that this kind of preparation helped her mentally prepare herself for the next day's lesson. Besides, before she finalized any plans, she wanted to look at their work tonight. She began to pack up her briefcase while she continued to think about tomorrow's lesson. A feeling of satisfaction came over her. She didn't have to use the first grouping pattern that came to her; she knew and had tried out several. Similarly, she had developed skill in asking a host of question-types; she could sort through them until she found the one that fit the subject and her kids. How had her mentor put it? Professional teachers are always adding to their "bag of tools"?

Though she knew that it wouldn't necessarily go as she imagined it, choosing from alternative "tools" now during lesson preparation gave her a sense of confidence. Come what may tomorrow, she had the flexibility of making changes in mid-course. "Exploring her alternatives" today had been one smart move.

DEVELOPING COMPETENCE

1. In the Conversation above, Raheela could have asked, "What is the gravity vector?" a lower level question, or "Under what circumstances does the gravity vector affect our movements?" a higher level question. What different instructional purposes would be served by asking these two questions? What purposes are accomplished by asking convergent and divergent questions?

2. As students, we sometimes answer a question in class and feel bad about the response or lack of response we receive. Describe responses that teachers can make that avoid hurt feelings and, more positively, direct further learning.

3. Outside of class, college students sometimes commiserate with each other over a vaguely-worded assignment. "What does she really want us to do? Frankly, I don't have a clue!" Giving focused and clearly-stated assignments is a vitally important competence. What pointers will you keep in mind as you explain your expectations for an assignment? your directions for participating in group activities?

4. When teachers have the option of arranging classroom furniture and resources the way they want, they influence the atmosphere in which teaching and learning takes place. Picture different room arrangements and defend them based on the student behaviors you desire.

5. You've probably been in teacher-arranged small groups that were fun and productive. Most likely you've also been in small groups that were a disaster—frustrating and non-productive. Analyze different grouping arrangements with regard to the conditions that promote positive results. What cautions about grouping are worth remembering?

INTRODUCTION

All professions have their tools. And by their tools we know the professions. Carpenters have drills and saws, hammers and tape measures. Plumbers carry pipe wrenches. Musicians may carry music stands and their instruments in leather gig bags. You can see many of these people and guess their profession just by the tools you see them carry. The teaching profession has its "tools," also, though most of these tools are not obvious to the eye. In fact, most of the tools that teachers possess are intellectual ones.

The most effective teachers you've known possess a great number of these intellectual tools and are very sophisticated in using them. Instructional tools like effective questioning techniques, effective student grouping, and creating a wonderful classroom atmosphere, when used properly, are signs of great teachers as surely as pipe wrenches are signs of plumbers. Remember that Socrates gained his reputation as an outstanding teacher not because of colorful slide presentations or music and light shows, but because he mastered the art of using the question to stimulate thought in his students. In this chapter, you will be introduced to, and encouraged to practice with, some of these tools of the profession, just like apprentice plumbers would use the same tools as their mentors.

QUESTIONING

First of all, we should point out that, when we speak of questions and questioning, we are considering all of the ways in which teachers attempt to prompt their students to respond. In other words, not all teacher "questions" will be worded in such a way that they end in a question mark. Sometimes teacher questions are worded in more of a directive nature requiring the student to complete a task, such as, "Find the picture that . . ." or "Name a category of animal which . . ." Although most of the examples that follow are in the form of a question (like Jeopardy), your questions might be in more of a directive nature, yet still be well-worded and effective. Ultimately, you will know whether your "questions," regardless of their forms, are effective by seeing if students are able to respond in ways that you anticipated. If they do, then you're probably doing fine; if not, then you will need to identify the problems they are having and determine what steps you can take to help them understand how it is that you want them to respond.

Lower- and Higher-Level Questions

Good questioning is the building block of most thought-provoking lessons at any grade level. It is a *SKILL* that you can learn. And to teach effectively, you must learn how to use questions and to develop questioning skills that provide students with cues and hints but still allow them to construct their own understandings of the content on which they are working or the processes they are using. One way to begin to think about questions is in terms of lower and higher levels. To do that you can think back on the previous chapters' discussions on Bloom's Taxonomy. In the taxonomy, you will often see the first three levels—knowledge, comprehension, and application—considered as lower-level skills and the other three—analysis, synthesis, and evaluation—as higher-level skills. Figure 5.1 shows the types of questions that might be asked at each of the levels.

FIGURE 5.1   LOWER- AND HIGHER-LEVEL QUESTIONS AND BLOOM'S TAXONOMY

Lower Level Questions

1. *Knowledge*–to recall facts, repeat information

   What year did the Civil War begin?

   What is the length of the radius of the given circle?

2. *Comprehension*–to show an understanding of material

   What do the words "civil war" mean?

   How do you find the area of the circle?

3. *Application*–to apply to a real-life situation

   Can you name another country that had or is having a civil war?

   What is the area of the top of a table whose circumference is 50 cm?

Higher Level Questions

4. *Analysis*–to show advanced comprehension, understand relationships

   How were the battles of Bull Run and Gettysburg similar? How were they different?

   How would you prove that the tangent to a circle is perpendicular to a radius of the circle?

5. *Synthesis*–to bring ideas together to draw conclusions

   What characteristics are shared by all civil wars?

   What factors led up to the American Civil War?

   How is the constant pi (π) derived?

6. *Evaluation*–to judge, examine, weigh

   How do you think a civil war could be prevented?

   What method do you think is the most efficient way to solve this problem and why?

Learning how to ask lower-level questions is important in helping you determine students' basic recall and understandings of concepts as you have taught them. By carefully wording your questions so that students respond as you anticipate, you will be able to determine whether students are meeting the lower-level objectives of lessons prior to moving on to more challenging tasks. This is especially important for you to consider when the lower-level objective provides the foundation for the later skills that you want students to develop or knowledge that you want them to acquire. For example, if you wanted students to apply their knowledge of area to find the total area of a surface, they would first have to recall what the word "area" means. Otherwise, you would be speaking what would amount to a foreign language to them. To be able to work with information, students must possess or have access to that information. And, that is where your skillful use of lower-level questioning will provide you with the feedback that you need to adjust your teaching so that students can benefit.

Activity 5.1

Read a short story, a myth or a fairy tale (we often use children's stories with our pre-service teachers) and formulate a series of questions based on Bloom's Taxonomy that you might ask of students in a classroom. Be sure to ask at least one question at each of the levels. If possible, have students who are at an appropriate age-level for the story read the story, and have a discussion using your questions. Or have your peers read the story and lead the discussion with them. Did the readers respond as you anticipated they would? Why or why not? Would you change any questions? Explain. Report on the experience to your class.

Ultimately, though, we want to have our students at all levels of schooling, from pre-kindergarten through twelfth grade, to think critically about the world around them, the information they have acquired, and the skills they are developing. This is where higher-level questions come in. Analysis questions ask students to dissect or break apart a concept. Questions that ask a student to compare or contrast typically fall in the analysis category. Synthesis questions ask students to draw conclusions after looking at a collection of facts or ideas. And evaluation questions ask students to judge the value or worth of something based upon a set of criteria. While you may rightly expect that the lower-level questions that you ask of students can and should be answered quickly, asking any of these higher-level questions will require that students take time to reflect before they may be able to produce an answer. In order to be certain that students have enough time to reflect, after asking a higher-level question you will want to make use of "wait time" (which will be discussed later in the chapter) in a very conscious manner.

Convergent and Divergent Questions

When forming questions, not only should you consider the level of thinking skills that students will be required to use in answering, but you should also consider the types and/or amounts of responses your question will prompt from your students.

Well-worded **convergent questions** have one answer or a limited number of acceptable answers. For example, "Who is the president of the United States?" has only one acceptable response at any given time. A question like, "What are the three notes that comprise a C major chord?" has more than one correct response, but the number is limited. The term "limited" is somewhat relative, though, depending upon the topic under consideration. At one time in your schooling experience, you may have been required to memorize the words most commonly signaling a prepositional phrase. Depending on the source you used, you may have had to memorize fifty-six individual words. When your teacher asked, "What are the prepositional phrase signal words?" you were limited to fifty-six. What distinguishes a convergent question of this type from a divergent one is that the teacher can anticipate every one of the correct responses.

Divergent questions, on the other hand, are ones that present the possibilities of being answered in many different ways. Although often there will still be correct and incorrect answers, students have more freedom in responding to "free think" the answer to a divergent question. The "open-endedness" of these questions encourage students to consider many possibilities. And that is where a major distinction lies. As a teacher, if you asked, "What are the responsibilities of the president of the United States?" you will probably be able to anticipate many of the responses that students will likely make. Indeed, you certainly should be able to anticipate some of these. However, asking these types of questions often lead teachers and students to have their own "ah-ha" insights, thinking about possibilities that they had never considered before.

For instance, if we build on the previous example about prepositions, while asking students to name the signal word for a prepositional phrase is convergent, asking them to give an example of a prepositional phrase in a sentence is divergent. Students have an infinite number of possibilities that you will not be able to anticipate in all of their forms. And with a question like this, you will certainly find correct and incorrect answers. You will have to weigh each example based upon your knowledge of what can and cannot be a prepositional phrase. You would know, for example, that just because a student uses one of the signal words doesn't mean that the phrase is a prepositional one. For instance, the word "like" is a signal word but not in, "I like school." On the other hand, one student might say: "The sentence, 'Due to circumstances beyond my control, I cannot do this activity,' has two prepositional phrases. One begins with the signal word 'beyond,' and one begins with 'due to,' which we didn't study."

One last point to make. Don't make the assumption that a convergent question is always going to be a lower-level one and that a divergent one will be higher-level. You can create both convergent and divergent questions at both ends of the knowledge-evaluation continuum. The divergent question on prepositions that you just read is a low-level divergent question that asks students to *apply* their understanding of prepositional phrases and signal words to provide examples. Similarly, the convergent questions above were low-level, calling for simple recall of information.

To create high-level divergent questions, you would need to ask students to analyze, synthesize, or evaluate something. For instance, you might prompt students by saying, "Convince someone that a college education is worth it." There are many ways to convince and there are many definitions of "worth it" that students have available to them as they try to do this, and all students' opinions can be accepted as individually valid as long as they respond to the prompt. The open-endedness of these types of responses can be very liberating for students and encourage them to respond more readily. On the other hand, higher-level convergent questions by definition must be more limited in scope of response, yet still work on the upper three levels of the taxonomy. For example, if you placed students in a mock trial situation, you will eventually ask them: "Based on the evidence you've just heard, is the suspect innocent or guilty?" To respond to this, students will have to analyze all of the arguments they have just heard, and evaluate the credibility of the witnesses. In the end, though, there are only two possible responses that they can make (see the Small article under "Questioning" in *Teacher as Researcher* section for examples of convergent and divergent questions).

Activity 5.2

Choose a unit topic from your curricular area of specialty and a specific grade level. For your unit, write several examples of each of the following:

- Lower-level divergent questions
- Higher-level convergent questions
- Lower-level convergent questions
- Higher-level divergent questions

Planning Questions

Can a successful lesson be made up entirely of one type of question? The sentence you've just read is a rhetorical question that we placed at the beginning of this section in order to prompt you to think about the topic. We planned to start this section with a question so that you would think about the previous information you've just read about questions. By now, we hope that you might even be thinking about what type of question this is. We also hope that you answered "no." Whether they are divergent or convergent, lower-level or higher-level questions, it's unlikely that you will be successful in your use of questioning if you rely only on one type of question throughout. As you've already read, different types of questions allow you to discover different types of understandings that students have about the topics that you and they are studying. While expert teachers are quite adept in their questioning skills, able to adapt the types and levels of questions in the midst of a dynamic conversation to best meet the learning needs of their students, as a new teacher you will be well served by determining some major questions you want to ask and planning the order in which you want to ask them. This type of planning will help you avoid the "rookie" mistakes of asking too many lower-level, convergent questions or higher-level, divergent questions for which students are not yet prepared.

Let's consider some examples here. If the intent of a teacher were to generate student interest that enters them into a discussion at the beginning of class, would she be able to do so by asking questions like, "What color is the sky?" and "How many fingers am I holding up?" At best, these call for one-word answers and certainly are not discussion-worthy. Her decision to use low-level, divergent questions would not meet her stated intention. As you already know, discussions are best generated by divergent questions. However, opening a class lesson with a divergent question like, "When looking at the equation of a line, how would you determine whether the slope is ascending or descending?" might require too much reflection and organization of thought for your students to respond without first reviewing some newly-learned concepts or having the students begin to respond to some lower-level type of questions first to simply get "warmed up." In this case, one or two students might be able to answer the question, but the majority of your students would not have the mental framework set that will allow them to benefit from the answers.

When to Use Lower- and Higher-Level Questions

Use lower-level questions, both convergent and divergent, when you want to focus students at the beginning of a lesson by having them recall what they learned previously or when you want to see what they already know from past experience. Try to reserve lower-level, convergent questions for situations appropriate for quick recall. Lower-level, convergent questions are also helpful to use when you want to quiz orally as many students as possible to determine if they are being attentive or if they understood the basic concepts of a lesson. By planning these questions into specific points in your lesson, such as at the end or at a mid-point before you move onto another concept that hinges on the understanding of a first concept, you will be able to ensure that your students are ready for the next learning activity.

On the other hand, you will want to use higher-level questions when you want to encourage discussion or you want to stimulate student thinking. Often, though not always, more students will be able to participate in this type of discussion if they are led to these types of thinking. For example, one mistake that inexperienced English teachers often make is to open their questioning of a story the students have recently read by asking "What is the theme of this story?" This is an appropriate question for stimulating students to think about the story, and it could certainly lead to discussion if students are willing to share their different opinions as to the theme. By beginning discussion in this way, however, students who are less convinced of their understanding or the validity of their opinions will be less likely to participate, and discussion often ends up being limited to the teacher and a couple of students. Had the teacher begun with lower-level questions, students would be more able to participate early in the discussion, experience success in their participation, and be more likely to risk their opinions at the analysis, synthesis, and evaluation levels.

Higher-level questions are also very effective to use when you want to have students solve multiple-step problems and/or organize their problem-solving logically. Sometimes students are able to formulate their responses to a higher-level question orally and they should be encouraged to do so, but if your students are not able to mentally retain multiple logical steps in their minds, they may need paper and pencil (or computers) to help organize their thoughts and formulate their responses before sharing them. The metacognitive aspect of having students analyze their own problem-solving techniques and sharing these with the class has a further benefit, too. When explaining their own methods to the class, other students will be encouraged to evaluate whether a particular method might work for them. The discussions, both class-wide and among individuals, will be part of an atmosphere of a culture of thinking that you will have created through the types of questions you ask.

Pinnacle Questions

Let's apply this information about designing questions to finding out whether students are meeting your objectives. After determining the objectives of the lesson, you will want to design questions that will lead your students to respond in ways that will help you determine whether they have met these objectives. We will call these questions the **pinnacle questions** of your lesson; that is, your students must answer this question or these questions in order to demonstrate that they understand the concept, skill, or attitude you are teaching. In some cases this may mean that your main lesson goal is a higher-level one. To reach that goal, however, your lesson plan may imply that there are one or two lower-level objectives that students must meet in order to demonstrate the higher-order skill. This may require your asking several lower-level convergent or divergent questions, as well as a higher-level divergent one. So, after designing all of the questions, organize them so that the students are already focused when they hear the divergent, higher-level question, the pinnacle question that will allow them to demonstrate whether they have developed or are developing the skill that you want them to focus on. It is possible that your students may struggle with pinnacle questions when you first introduce them. This is fine since the question serves as a motivator, and if the students can answer the question immediately, then maybe you really do not have anything to teach that day. Plan to repeat the pinnacle question(s) in various forms and at various times during the lesson and definitely at the end of the lesson when you are summarizing what students have learned.

For example, if your lesson objective is: "Students will describe the differences between Donatello's 'David' and Michaelangelo's 'David.'" Then the pinnacle question could be: "What are the differences between Donatello's 'David' and Michaelangelo's 'David'?" However, you do not necessarily want to begin a lesson with this question unless your students come into your classroom focused and with the previous knowledge that they already needed to answer the question. Besides, if your students can answer this question in the first five minutes of the lesson, then your lesson objective has been met and your lesson is complete (and you haven't planned very well)! Rather than begin with the question, then, you will still want to focus students on the topic and may actually hint at what the lesson's objective is at the beginning of the lesson. You could do this by stating, "Today we are going to determine what the differences are between two significant pieces of sculpture that, initially, may seem quite similar." Making such a statement helps your students know what the goals of the lessons are. This type of statement can prepare them for where you will be going, creating the scaffolding for your questioning.

Assuming that they have already studied both sculptors, you may want to begin your questioning with low-level, convergent questions that help all students to focus on the topic at hand. You could show a model or picture of Donatello's sculpture and might begin by asking:

What is the name of the sculptor of this piece?

What is the piece called?

What are some words you would use to describe Donatello's style in this piece?

You could then ask the same questions while showing the Michaelangelo model. After this, you may ask one more question: "What are the similarities among the two sculptures?" Once you and the students have established that you share the same background knowledge needed to complete the lesson task and you have focused their thinking at the analytical level that they will need, then they will be better able to tackle the pinnacle question. Students should provide numerous responses to your pinnacle question. At this point you will need to take in these responses and help students to determine the acceptability or unacceptability of their answers. Before making this judgment, however, listen carefully to what they say. After all, you've asked a divergent question and, though you may have some very specific answers that you anticipate students both will and should make, you also may find yourself delightfully surprised by the type of response and the thinking that has gone into it. Use these responses as teachable moments, to help students both value the responses of themselves and their peers and to clarify their thinking and thinking processes.

Avoiding "Bad" Questions

We have discussed the content of good questions and the reasons why you should plan and organize your questions, but there are some traps into which many new teachers often find themselves falling. Poorly worded questions or the illogical organization of questions will frustrate both you and your students. Figure 5.2 shows three reminders you will want to consider as you write and plan questions to use in your lessons. As you write your own questions, use these as a checklist to determine whether you have probably created "good" questions. In the discussion that follows, we will present negative examples of each of these mistakes and then demonstrate how to rewrite them to avoid the problem.

Imagine that you are in an art class, and the teacher shows you a picture that you think looks like the finger-paintings of a seriously disturbed psychopath. She waits for dramatic effect while you take this in then says: "Why is this piece of art

---

FIGURE 5.2   TIPS TO AVOID BAD QUESTIONS

- Avoid "leading" questions.
- Phrase your questions in a positive manner whenever possible.
- Be sure that the wording cues students to the type of information for which you are looking.

good?" This is what those in the legal profession would call a "leading" question. The teacher is implying by the wording of the question that she believes the piece is a good piece, and that you should, too. But this does not match your opinion. This certainly will shut you, and probably many of your peers, out of any discussion that the teacher had intended to encourage. Teachers who encourage discussion would want to be certain that every student in the class could voice his or her opinion, even if it differs from their own. More importantly, these teachers want to help students to develop their own ways of coming to understand art or literature or history. Depending on your intention, you could ask a similar question in a couple of ways that would better meet your goals. If you want to have students evaluate the piece against some of the criteria that you have been studying, you might ask, "Why would some critics consider this piece to be a masterpiece?" If, however, you were more intent on having students develop their own standards, you might ask: "How many of you like this piece? Why? How many of you do not? Why not?" Either of these last two questions would allow students to participate in honest and varied ways, while not stifling some who hold a different opinion.

A second problem comes in when teachers word questions in negative ways. How many times have you really wanted to show your lack of knowledge or inability to do something? Not often, we would guess. The teacher who asks: "Who doesn't know who Michaelangelo is?" puts students in a very difficult position. Because of its wording, students who respond to this question admit to ignorance. That is, students would be admitting to ignorance *if* they were confident enough to admit that they do not know the answer. The other problem with this type of question is that, if no one raises their hands, the teacher erroneously believes that all students have the required knowledge they need. Better alternative questions might be: "By a show of hands, how many have heard of Michaelangelo?" or "Who can tell me or remind me who Michaelangelo is?" Both of these wordings allow students to demonstrate what they *do* know, rather than what they don't. It will also give you a better "read" on whether you need to build students' background knowledge or not.

Now, imagine that you are in an art class, and the teacher holds up a statue and says: "What do you see in this sculpture?" The primary problem with this question is that the teacher is not clearly specifying what it is she wants from the students. Does she really want to know what the students see with their eyes when they look at the sculpture? Or does she, instead, want the students to describe how they feel when they look at the sculpture or to describe how it is similar to something they already know? You can assume that a teacher asking this type of question knows that it is divergent, that students will respond in many ways, but she may have some specific ways in which she anticipated that they would respond. If she was looking for the emotional impact of this piece on students and a student responds with, "A man posing," the teacher will realize that the question is not getting at the information she wants. In oral questioning, this is not a lost cause because she can adjust her question by rephrasing it, which we will discuss in more detail later. But what happens when the question is asked on a test? A badly worded question may creep into the written tests of even the most veteran teachers. Unfortunately, the teacher does not realize it until she is grading the tests and finds that a good portion of the students do not respond in the manner intended. This is why it's important to provide cues to the ways in which you want students to respond. The more precise the wording of the question, the more likely you will get from students the information for which you are looking. Better ways of asking this question might be: "When you look at the sculpture, describe how it makes you feel," or "When you look at the sculpture, tell me who it reminds you of."

As you think about constructing good questions, there are many things to consider. Should my question be high-level or low-level, convergent or divergent? Have I written them clearly? Are they organized logically? While you could go a little crazy thinking about all of the possibilities, the two most important questions to ask yourself would be: Are my questions written in such a way that I will know if students are developing the skills or acquiring the knowledge I've planned in my objective?; and Are my questions worded in a way that they will meet the purpose of the discussion? Figure 5.3 provides you with a few other tips you may find helpful as you design, organize, and plan to use questions as one of your professional skills. Figure 5.4 contains websites that can give you other examples of types of questions and ways to develop them.

FIGURE 5.3 TIPS ON QUESTIONING

1. Begin the lesson with lower-level or higher-level convergent questions about what students learned previously in order to focus them.

2. Be certain that you write, **in advance,** at least two or three higher-level divergent questions toward the beginning of the new content to encourage students to think about the day's new learning. Be careful about the wording of these questions, especially in your early days of teaching. Students who do not reply appropriately to your question and who are being cooperative with you should act as a signal that you need to reword the question.

3. After writing your questions, analyze them to determine if they fall into the appropriate categories for your needs. Remember to use a variety of types of questions.

4. Use lower-level convergent or divergent questions during a lesson to assess that students are being attentive or at the end of a lesson to evaluate quickly as many students as possible on their understanding of lower-level objectives.

5. If you are assigning questions from an accompanying textbook, evaluate the questions according to the four question-types. Is there a fair distribution of questions? Are there more than just lower-level questions in order to challenge your students? Are the questions ordered so that the students begin with lower-level convergent questions and then move to higher-level and more divergent questions?

FIGURE 5.4 ON-LINE RESOURCES ON QUESTIONING FOR TEACHERS AND STUDENTS	
Resource	Website
A Questioning Toolkit	http://www.fno.org/nov97/toolkit
Questioning and Understanding to Improve Learning and Thinking (QUILT)	http://www.ed.gov/pubs/ triedandtrue/quest

Wait-Time

After determining the questions you will ask and planning their order, the main thing left to do is to ask them of your students. It may be a little unsettling, though, if you think you've prepared well-worded questions in a logical progression, but students don't respond quickly and accurately. One factor that you should consider that can increase the chance that your students will respond to your questions is to be aware of the amount of time it may take for students to formulate and consider their responses. In other words, you need to wait for a bit of time. **Wait-time** is a term used to describe three to five seconds of silent waiting by a teacher who has just asked a question in order to provide enough time for the students to think about and respond to the question. As you think about your questions, you will also need to think about how much time students might need. Students will usually need more wait-time when responding to higher-level questions than they will for lower-level questions, but this may not always be true. As a decision maker, it will be up to you to develop the patience you need to wait for students. That couple seconds of silence is sometimes uncomfortable for a new teacher, but planning in wait-time will pay dividends in more and better student participation.

If you were in a class studying *Othello*, and the teacher were to ask: "How did Othello react to the rumor regarding Desdemona?" what often happens is that one or two students tend to have answers to all the teacher's questions and always try to answer them immediately. By waiting, even if you have to consciously count five seconds silently to yourself, you will give other students the time they need to process a question before they respond. Research gathered on teachers who were trained to use wait-time revealed that the number of responses from less-able students increased, the length of student responses increased, the number of student-to-student interactions increased, and the number of student questions increased (Rowe, 1974). Don't think, though, that if a little wait-time is good, a lot must be better. Wait-time of three to five seconds is generally sufficient. Some experts (Goodwin, 1983) contend that students perceive wait-time of more than twenty to thirty seconds as punishing.

One last note about wait-time. We have just described the time that you wait *after* asking a question but *before* students respond. But what can you do after that student answers? A teacher who quietly waits *after a student responds* to a question can also be effective in encouraging student participation. This technique is called

wait-time II. Wait-time II gives other students in the classroom an opportunity to respond to the first student's response. By being consciously aware of its importance and systematically applying wait-time to encourage students to respond to questions, you will place more of the responsibility of carrying a discussion on students and less of it on yourself.

Responding to Students

Okay, so now you've asked your well-worded and organized question and you've waited for students to respond. Once they answer, though, they are going to be looking to you to provide them with some feedback on what they've just said. Even if you've mastered the questioning steps mentioned above, you need to determine how you are going to respond to students' correct answers in a manner that will keep their brainwaves going, as well as how you are going to respond to incorrect answers. No matter how wonderful the questions are that you prepare or how well you can anticipate their probable responses, no lesson with real students follows a script that will allow you to know ahead of time how you will respond. Because of that, you will need to acquire and practice some techniques (see Figure 5.5) that you can apply to any discussion.

After the teacher asks a question, the students can do one of three things: They can respond in some way by providing the information that they believe the teacher wants; they can ask a question; or they can give no response at all (Goodwin, 1983). If a student chooses to respond and does so correctly (that is, with the information that you are seeking), you will want to reinforce the student by positively acknowl-

---

FIGURE 5.5   FIVE WAYS OF RESPONDING TO STUDENT ANSWERS

After students answer a question, you can:

1. *Reinforce their response* by acknowledging, either verbally or nonverbally, that the answer is correct.

2. *Probe the answer further* by asking another question that allows the student to clarify or expand upon their original answer.

3. *Adjust/refocus the student response* by first indicating that the answer may have been on the right track but then asking a new question that clarifies the information that you want.

4. *Redirect the response* by asking another student to respond to the previous student's answer.

5. *Rephrase the question* when the student response indicates that either the student did not understand the question or the question was poorly worded.

(*Source:* Goodwin, S. S., et al. (1983). Effective classroom questioning. (ERIC Document Reproduction Services No. ED 285 497).

edging that the answer is correct. Reinforcement can be verbal, such as, "O.K." or "You're on the right track." It can also be nonverbal, such as a nod or a smile. You may want to use reinforcement to affirm a correct answer. You can even reinforce a student's effort to respond by saying something like, "That was a great try." By encouraging a student who is not apt to respond, but who has just done so, even if he is wrong, you will be more likely to see him willing to try to participate in the future.

One of the most demanding uses of responding is following up a student's response by asking probing questions. To do this, you will need to ask another question that makes students clarify, analyze, or extend their responses. A teacher in a literature class might engage in an exchange like the following:

> Teacher: What sorts of things does Don Quixote do that make you question his sanity?
>
> Student: Well, for one, he thinks that windmills are giants.
>
> Teacher: He does, doesn't he? And how does Sancho react to this?

In the conversation at the beginning of this chapter, you saw that Raheela learned to plan her questions. While we have encouraged you to do the same, and indeed the original question about Don Quixote's sanity may have been one of the pinnacle questions for this teacher's lesson, there is no way that you can plan for probing questions. To follow up on student responses in this manner, you will need to know your students and your content well, and you will need to listen carefully to what each student says so that you can probe their responses appropriately. This will take time and practice, but it will certainly help students to go beyond their initial thoughts and encourage them to anticipate these kinds of questions in later discussions and writing assignments.

A teacher helps a student adjust or refocus when the student's response was on the right track, but is not exactly what the teacher wanted. The teacher can ask another question that helps guide the student to a more accurate response. The adjust/refocus technique differs from the probe technique in that the probe technique guides the student to the next concept or to some conclusion where the adjust/refocus technique tries to help a student clarify her understanding of the topic at hand. In that same literature class, you might hear the following:

> Teacher: What sorts of things does Don Quixote do that make you question his sanity?
>
> Student: I thought that Sancho Panza was pretty crazy, too.
>
> Teacher: You did, huh? Hold onto that thought for a while because that's an important aspect we might want to follow. For now, though, let's concentrate on Quixote. What sort of things did *he* do that some might find crazy?

In this case, the student obviously responded to the "crazy" idea, and the teacher decided to accept that response while refocusing this student on Quixote rather than Sancho. Notice also that this teacher has combined reinforcing the student, by showing how much merit this particular idea could have, then refocusing his attention to the question under consideration.

When a teacher asks another student to respond to the answer that a previous student has given, she is using the redirect strategy. This technique is especially effective in encouraging more students to participate and fostering a class discussion atmosphere (such as the "volleying" we will discuss shortly). You can also use this technique when you want to encourage students to help each other refine their thinking. One further way of using this strategy is, if one student has given an incorrect answer and you don't want to say, "No, that's wrong," you can ask another student to "help out" their peer. Back to our literature class, if a teacher were redirecting you might hear:

Teacher: Why did Quixote call Aldonza "Dulcinea"? [pause for wait-time] What do you think, Jenny?

Student: Because he liked her.

Teacher: Do you agree that this was the reason? [pause] What about you, Clarence?

One final technique is rephrasing. This is the one that teachers use when they realize that the first question asked gets either no response or appears to be misunderstood by most of the class. The teacher must then re-ask the question, but she needs to rephrase it in a manner that the students will better understand what information she is seeking. For example:

Teacher: How crazy is Quixote?

Student: Very crazy?

Teacher: O.K., I guess that was a bad question. Let me try again. What sorts of things does Don Quixote do that make you think that he may be crazy?

If we look back to the earlier pinnacle question and make the assumption that the teacher wants students to focus on the examples that hint at Quixote's sanity, you can see that the first question will not indicate to students that that is the information the teacher wants to uncover. It would only be by coincidence that a student would be able to guess that when she asks that question, she is really looking for something else. Here again, this is a good reason to plan out your important questions. But for those times when you are facilitating students' discussions and you find that they are not giving the information you want, take the time to listen to their answers and change the wording of the question to specify more precisely what you want.

In short, a teacher can respond to students who answer correctly by reinforcing or probing. Students who are headed in the right direction can be encouraged by adjusting/refocusing or redirecting. Finally, a teacher who does not receive an answer to a question or does not receive the answer she was expecting can rephrase the question. Practicing these skills in simulations and with peers or students will provide you with some experience in the "thinking on your feet" that is required to use these effectively.

Activity 5.3

Take one higher-level, divergent question you wrote in the last exercise (or write a new one), and imagine that this question is a pinnacle question of a lesson you are teaching. Try to anticipate how students might answer in a "real" classroom and how you would respond to their answers. Write the script of a possible dialogue with your question as the first line of the script. Use at least three of the techniques of responding. Share your scripts with classmates.

Volleying

When you play tennis, one of the objects of the game is to keep a consistent volley of the ball between the players. Each time the ball is passed from one player to another is considered a volley. When you first begin to play tennis, the number of volleys you can make until someone misses is usually small. However, as you and your partners and opponents gain more skill, you can keep a steady number of volleys going before play stops. Keeping classroom dialogue "in play" is similar to keeping a tennis ball in play. In order to monitor the volley of classroom dialogue in a class, the teacher needs to visualize the "play" in which students are engaged. Imagine that you, as the teacher are holding a tennis ball and when you ask a question, you "serve" the ball. When a student answers, he returns the ball.

In most classrooms, the dialogue "ball" constantly gets returned to the teacher (see Figure 5.6). This type of volley would look like the following:

Teacher: Name a mammal.

Student 1: A tiger.

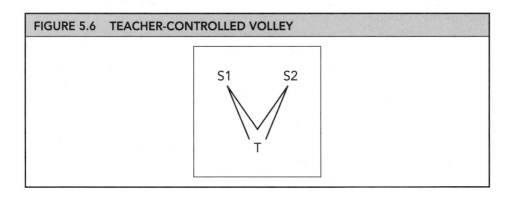

FIGURE 5.6   TEACHER-CONTROLLED VOLLEY

Teacher: Good. Now, someone else, name an amphibian.

Student 2: A lizard.

Teacher: Right. Now, name ...

In this example, the dialogue ball always returns to the teacher. This type of dialogue is not going to produce a stimulating classroom discussion if it continues in the same manner for two reasons. First, the teacher is only asking convergent, lower-level questions. Therefore, the students can only respond in simple, one-word answers. Second, the teacher always receives the volley back to herself by reinforcing a student's answer then asking more of the same type of questions.

In order to produce a more interesting classroom volley, the teacher could have conducted the dialogue as follows:

Teacher: Name a mammal.

Student 1: A tiger.

Teacher: Chrystal, is he right?

Student 2: Yes.

Teacher: Why?

Student 2: Because a tiger is warm-blooded.

Teacher: *(Smiles, nods, and waits. Another hand goes up. Teacher points to Student 3.)*

Student 3: And because the tiger has fur.

Student 4: No way, mammals don't always have to have fur . . . .

This teacher was able to create more classroom dialogue and more volley by having the first student justify her answer, creating a higher-level question, and by allowing wait-time to create the opportunity for other students to respond and discuss the first student's response. The graphic representation of the above discussion is in Figure 5.7 (The curved line that swings towards, but does not reach, the teacher indicates that the teacher intervened, but used non-verbal cues to mediate the dialogue.).

As you can see, there is much more to formulating, organizing, and asking questions in a classroom than it may appear. Good, experienced teachers make it seem so easy, but most novice teachers need to realize that good questioning takes practice. That practice includes learning ways to wait for students to form their answers, as well as responding once they have answered. It also involves being aware of the "flow" of the conversation. Teaching and encouraging students to volley the dialogue ball among themselves will provide them with a rich classroom atmosphere that encourages them to think, analyze their thoughts, and support their peers in their own thinking efforts.

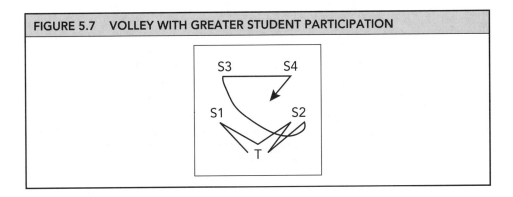

FIGURE 5.7   VOLLEY WITH GREATER STUDENT PARTICIPATION

CLARITY OF DIRECTIONS

Ultimately, all teachers need to assign tasks for their students to complete. When a teacher is able to communicate clearly the expectations of a particular assignment to the students, then students are able to complete assignments accurately, and neither teachers nor students become frustrated. However, if a teacher is disorganized or unclear in describing her expectations to students and/or in communicating the goals of an assignment, both student and teacher frustration can run high.

In order to avoid this type of frustration, it is important that you plan any activity as thoroughly as you can. Try to visualize the entire process in which students will need to engage to complete your assignment. If, for instance, you are planning to take your class on a field trip to a park and you would like your students to collect items such as leaves and flowers, imagine the entire field trip step-by-step in your mind and try to anticipate any possible trouble points. Details are important to your students. What mode of transportation will they take to get there? If they are taking a bus, will you be assigning seats? How will they carry the specimens they collect? The more specific you can be with your expectations, the more your students will rise to meet them. If you intentionally choose to give your students some latitude in their decisions, make this clear, as well. For instance, in the example of the park field trip, if it does not matter to you whether they find flowers or leaves, then make this point clear to your students.

Whenever possible, have your directions in written form as well as delivering them orally. Having the directions written down, whether on a handout or on the board or other prominent place within your room, also protects you from the student who claims that you never mentioned that one very important directive that he did not do. One simple way to make certain that the students understand your directions is to ask a student (or several) to repeat the directions back to you. If there is any confusion among the students about the directions, you will discover it when they repeat them back to you.

One important class management tip for teachers using smaller group formats is always to remember to give the directions for a smaller group activity *before* the students break into their groups. A common mistake that most novice teachers who are committed to the Cooperative Learning strategy make is that they deliver the directions for the group activity in a whole-class format, but once the students get into their groups, they find out they need to clarify a direction for students. The teacher has only two options for clarifying the issue to the entire class: she may either try to get the attention of all the students and regain whole-class control or she may go from group to group delivering the new information. Since it is much more difficult to regain the attention of everyone in the class, especially in a timely, efficient manner, it is better if you are clear in your directions before splitting students into groups and having them get involved in the activity. To avoid the situation entirely, prepare and deliver your directions, both verbally and in writing, then ask the students if there are any questions. Provide sufficient wait-time before sending the students into their groups.

In addition to the specific words you use, your level of voice control can also be a very effective professional tool that can be used to clarify directions by conveying the importance of certain statements. When you are trying to cue your students into an important detail, saying it a little louder sends a message that this is important. By raising the volume of your voice, it also sends a signal to students who have been daydreaming that they'd better listen up. Finally, repetition can also be an important tool. Students will quickly cue in to listening carefully to assignments or directions that you repeat two or more times.

Clearly-worded directions, like carefully-worded questions, will make it more likely that students will know what you expect of them. Knowing your expectations, most students will rise to the challenge. By trying to visualize what the students will go through in meeting these expectation, you can provide yourself with a visual map that will help you to decide what important details to include, and what confusing or minor points you can exclude, in providing students with directions for completing assignments or participating in activities.

NONVERBAL TOOLS

To this point, we've talked mainly about the things that teachers *say* in classrooms that help students to participate in the activities designed to help them to learn. When you think of teaching, the verbal abilities of teachers you admire may have been some of the most memorable aspects in their classes. You may be able to remember specific, thought-provoking, lively discussions that you experienced in favorite teachers' classes. As you think back on these while reading the previous section, you may have come to realize their skillful use of these verbal tools. But teaching is more than talking, and the "tools" that teachers have available to them go beyond their abilities to use words.

In this section, we are going to look at the tools that teachers use to enhance student learning but that have nothing to do with their verbal skills. We are going to stretch the term "nonverbal" here just a bit. When you think of nonverbal, you may think about our first topic, body language. But teachers also send messages about learning when they set up their classrooms. So, we will also look at how teachers create a classroom atmosphere by manipulating the physical environment.

Body Language

A teacher's body language can speak volumes to a student. Perceptive students can sense how a teacher feels about the students or about a topic by where they stand or how "open" or "tight" they may seem. You have seen some of these techniques (see Figure 5.8) used by good teachers all your academic life but never recognized them as professional tools that you can acquire by looking for them among your mentors and practicing them yourselves.

Teachers who use dynamic classroom body language often share many techniques with quality stage actors. One of the most important is maintaining eye contact with your students. If, initially, you are feeling nervous about meeting the gaze of your students, practicing setting your eyes upon an area just above the heads of the students in the back row. Eventually, as you feel more comfortable, you will begin to move your eyes about the room as you speak. When only one section of your class seems to be attentive, even the most veteran teachers fall into the habit of mostly addressing those students. Take care to catch yourself if you are doing this and force yourself to move your eyes about the class.

Maintaining good eye contact conveys to your students that you are interested in them. Another body language technique that conveys that interest is your classroom movement. A dynamic teacher moves about the room and walks within arms' length of the students within the first few rows. This can be difficult to do if you need to carry a heavy text book around with you, but it is important to move toward the students for at least a portion of the class. Be careful, however, not to pace from side-to-side or move so much that your movement becomes distracting. Moving too little can also be a problem. A teacher who stays behind a lectern for most of a class is perceived by the students as having a barrier between the teacher and the students. If you need to use a resource that is at the front of the classroom and requires that you turn your back to the students, such as a chalkboard, be certain not to completely turn your back to the class, but keep a shoulder turned toward your students.

When your students are involved in cooperative learning, you will find yourself moving somewhat differently. In this case, you should circulate about the room in order to be certain that your students are on task and to act as a resource should they have questions. Sitting at the teacher's desk doing paperwork while students are completing group work conveys the impression that the activity is not very important, and that the teacher's paperwork is more important than the students' learning. Circulating around the room also helps you to maintain classroom control and to quickly intervene with students who need to redirect their attention.

FIGURE 5.8 TIPS ON USING BODY LANGUAGE IN CLASS

- Maintain eye contact
- Move appropriately among students
- Maintain a connection with students by avoiding barriers
- Provide positive, nonverbal reinforcers (smile, lean forward, etc.)

When conducting a class discussion be aware of your body language as a student is contributing to the discussion. Are you nodding in agreement? Are you maintaining eye contact with the student? Are you moving or leaning toward the student who is speaking? All of these nonverbal cues can encourage students to engage in more extended bits of discussion. Be aware, though, that sometimes moving toward a student can interfere with some communication. For instance, if the student who is speaking is sitting directly in front of you, that student may be prone to speak quietly to you instead of speaking up so that the entire class can hear. Nodding and maintaining eye contact, yet gradually moving away from the student will encourage the student to speak up so that he may be heard by the entire class. You might want to try this before you interrupt and ask him to speak up.

Physical Environment of the Classroom

How a teacher arranges the physical setting of her classroom can affect the behavior, attention, movement, and sometimes even the learning of students. "External characteristics" of the learning environment include the physical arrangement of the furniture, the availability of resources, and the length of the class session (Chapin, 1996). Often, a teacher may not have control over some of these factors. Sometimes desks cannot be rearranged or there is no place to store student resources. Some teachers "travel" during the school day and teach in various classrooms throughout the day. In these cases, control over the physical environment of the classroom is limited. As a new teacher, you may find yourself with a "classroom on a cart." If this is true for you, try to negotiate with the teachers whose room you share for some space, board and storage, and about how the room will be arranged.

Obviously, traveling will limit your ability to design a room as you want it. When, however, you are able to create the physical environment, there are some classroom arrangement techniques about which you should be aware that can influence the students' classroom behavior. For instance, a teacher typically has control over the seating arrangement of a classroom. Arranging seats so that students are not distracted by friends or others can be an effective tool. Furthermore, if your students will be working in pre-arranged groups, then seating them by the groups will enable them to begin working quickly and with a minimum of movement when asked to begin group work. Teachers that conduct class discussion frequently may wish to arrange the student desks in a circle or semi-circle. A teacher can ask students in a larger lecture hall or a smaller group of students who are scattered about a classroom to move into the first few rows of the classroom in order to help the students hear you, participate, and maintain their attention. As with the other tools that we have mentioned, you have many options available to you when doing something as seemingly simple as arranging seats. The implications of this, however, can be great. You send messages about the types of learning activities in which students will engage and the kinds of learning that you value by the way in which you arrange and rearrange your room for the various activities in which students participate.

Throughout the year, you will use many different resources within the activities you design for students. When these activities involve using specific resources, you will need to think about where you should store them within your classroom and how students should gain access to them. In order to facilitate the proper pacing of a lesson, for instance, you would want to be sure to place any resources—such as computers, calculators, lab equipment, maps, etc.—in an area where you and students can easily use these tools. Also, consider the best manner for distributing the resources or getting the students to them. Should one member per group or row obtain enough for the other classmates? Or should each student take responsibility for getting his/her materials when they are needed? If your students are using classroom computers, how should the students get to the computers, who should have computer control, and when?

There is no one "right" way to set up a classroom. You would be wise to look at how other teachers set up their rooms and ask them why they do it as they do. As you take on the responsibility of your own classroom, you will probably want to experiment with a number of different ways of arranging the physical environment. See what works best and under what conditions. At all times, think about what messages you might be sending and what purposes you hope to meet by arranging your room as you do. And remember that a well-arranged and properly-stocked room is a resource that will help you teach and students learn (the importance of students' physical comfort is referred to in the Morine-Dershimer article under "Physical Environment of the Classroom" in the *Teacher as Researcher* section).

Activity 5.4

Use graph paper or a computer program and draw a diagram of your ideal classroom. Diagram and label the student desks, and the teacher's desk, and the classroom resources, such as computers, bookshelves, etc. Consider any special areas you would like to have, such as a reading corner or learning centers. Consider the following questions: What messages are you trying to convey about the teaching and learning that take place in this room? Are your student desks in rows, a semi-circle, or some other configuration? Are they structured for group work? Will the teacher desk be a barrier between the teacher and students? Can the students easily reconfigure themselves for other grouping formats such as pairs or larger groups?

Share these with your classmates. Consider making a resource book of the different designs that you all created.

STUDENT GROUPING

The last professional tool that we want to introduce to you deals with the manner in which you will choose to group your students. This tool has received increased attention over the years as the role expectations of teachers have evolved. Teachers need not hold center stage all the time. Student groups, when carefully planned and managed, can lead to socially constructed meanings that are frequently more interesting, relevant, and lasting than those produced by teacher-controlled whole group sessions. Teachers are becoming much more aware that, because students bring different skills and "gifts" to class, different ways of arranging students serve to meet students' strengths while helping them to develop a variety of skills, both academic and social. In order to accomplish instructional goals, teachers should consider how best to group students in the class in order to attain their goals. When a teacher thoughtfully groups students based on the objectives of a lesson, the student grouping aspect of lesson planning adds a dimension to the class and increases students' motivation and enhances their active participation.

Very generally speaking, students can be grouped either heterogeneously or homogeneously. **Heterogeneous grouping** involves grouping students in such a way that the group represents a range of student characteristics. **Homogeneous grouping,** on the other hand, involves grouping students in such a way that each student within a particular group has some specific academic or social characteristic in common. For instance, placing students in groups based on an academic ability, like their reading level, would be considered homogeneous grouping. This type of grouping is commonly called **tracking** and is very controversial in the education community. Some feel that instruction is better tailored to needs when students are tracked. Others believe that it lowers the esteem of lower achievers and does not prepare higher achievers to work with people of all abilities. In addition to the esteem concerns, low-ability students often end up doing more rote work, like worksheets, which tends to keep them in the low-ability groups (the Shields study under "Student Grouping" in the *Teacher as Researcher* section presents one view of this debate). Groups that are heterogeneously grouped by ability will have at least one lower-achieving, average-achieving, and higher-achieving student in each group.

Grouping students heterogeneously by ability is the basis for cooperative learning (see chapter 4 for more discussion of cooperative learning), an educational concept championed by Slavin (1989) in which heterogeneously-grouped students are given a goal to achieve and each student within the group has an integral role in completing the task. For instance, in a cooperative learning experience in which cooperative groups must design a city park within a given budget, one member of the four-member group might act as the treasurer who must determine that the park is within budget. Another student may draw the design of the park. A third student might be charged with determining that the park meets safety needs and logistical considerations, and a fourth student may be required to present the park plan to the class. In a cooperative group, the students work together in a democratic manner and all students must rely on each other for the completion of the activity (a counterpoint to cooperative grouping is provided in the Marlow article under "Student Grouping" in the *Teacher as Researcher* section).

Alternative Criteria for Grouping Students

There are many people, including a great number of parents and teachers, who believe that grouping by ability makes a great deal of sense for both teachers and students. Most studies (Good & Marshall, 1984; Slavin 1987, 1990), however, have demonstrated that, while high-performing students benefit slightly, lower-ability students suffer numerous problems, including the ones we've stated above. As a new teacher, you need to be aware that there are other ways in which you may group students. Flood et al. (1992) suggest the following nine grouping alternatives listed in Figure 5.9. These alternatives provide you with criteria, other than general ability, which you can use to organize or reorganize students. You may be able to adapt and modify these in other ways to create even more alternatives for grouping students that you will have at your disposal. What will be important to you as you decide which, if any, of these criteria are helpful is knowing your students, the learning goal you have set for them, and then determining which of these methods might help them best reach those goals.

Other non-ability factors that you can consider are demographic ones, such as gender and age. In regards to gender, there has been recent attention on whether it is beneficial to separate girls into their own single-gender course sections, particularly in the areas of science and mathematics and typically at the junior high and high school level. The rationale for doing this, some believe, is to provide the girls in these separate sections the non-competitive, collaborative learning environment they need in order to succeed in these traditionally male-dominated subject areas.

One recent trend that has, in fact, resurfaced is the multi-age classroom. This classroom is a self-contained primary classroom that contains students of various ages. For instance, a multi-age classroom could have students of both grades two and three in it. The advantages of this grouping arrangement appear to be that teacher and students often are able to remain in a classroom together for two or more consecutive years, eliminating the need to determine a student's special needs or interests (both advantages and disadvantages are discussed in the Viadero article referred to under "Student Grouping" in the *Teacher as Researcher* section). Also, these classrooms tend to create a family atmosphere within the school, a collaborative rather than competitive spirit among the students, and allow a teacher flexibility with the curriculum. The demand on a teacher's time preparing so many diverse learning experiences appears to be the primary disadvantage. Also, some parents fear that their younger children may feel intimidated by the size and/or skill level of the older classmates (Schaeffer & Hook, 1996; Viadero, 1996).

One last type of grouping involves "cyber" groups. The World Wide Web provides some wonderful resources for teachers who would like to group their classes to exchange data or have a cultural exchange with students at another geographical location including another state or nation. A website (www.stolaf.edu/network/iecc.) hosted at St. Olaf College in Minnesota accepts e-mail postings from teachers who are looking for a classroom with which to collaborate for either a classroom exchange or a curricular-related project. Through distance learning, the same sort of classroom exchanges can occur with e-mail partner exchanges following the collaboration. Technology will increasingly make geographical class exchanges or student-to-student e-mail exchanges a possibility.

As you can see, there are many criteria you can use to group students. Having all of these alternatives, as well as the ones you develop yourself, available to you presents you with many ways of helping students to become better learners. Regardless of the criteria that you choose, though, you need to think carefully

---

FIGURE 5.9   CRITERIA FOR GROUPING STUDENTS

1. *Skills Development*–When some or all students need to acquire a certain skill, such as outlining a paragraph or averaging a series of numbers, a teacher can group students based on which students need the skills instruction. This allows you to target the skill, not the general ability.

2. *Similar Interests*–You can group students once in awhile based on a similar interest all the students in a group may have (e.g., all students interested in researching mammals would collect in one group, amphibians in another, etc.).

3. *Quality of Academic Skills/Work Habits*–After learning more about students' individual strengths and weaknesses, you may group in order to scatter students with a particular skill or work habit among other students so that the student can model the skills or habits to others.

4. *Knowledge of Content*–You may wish to place students with similar content knowledge together to pool their knowledge or scatter them depending on the goals of the task.

5. *Knowledge of Strategies*–Similar to previous, you may scatter students who have a talent in some strategy, such as logical argumentation or problem-solving techniques, about the room so that the other students can learn by watching their classmates.

6. *Task/Activity Criterion*–Tasks that you require may influence your grouping (e.g., a mock newspaper using a word processing package should have students with a familiarity with the graphical functions or with a knowledge of layout format scattered among all the groups).

7. *Social Reasons*–Group your students based on their social skills, separating leaders, talkers, etc., into different groups, to help facilitate the completion of certain tasks.

8. *Random*–Sometimes the easiest and possibly most equitable way to form student groups is simply to have students "count off." Besides having students "count off," you can use other random methods of grouping (e.g., month of birth; favorite color).

9. *Student Choice*–Sometimes teachers may allow students to choose their own groups. Be careful not to use this method as the sole method of grouping. As the teacher, you need to remember your obligation to develop all the skills of your students, including the social ones and those related to their skills and knowledge.

(*Source:* Flood, J., Lapp, D., Flood, S., & Nagel, G. (1992). Am I allowed to group? Using flexible patterns for flexible instruction. *The Reading Teacher, 45* (8), 608–616.)

about how a particular arrangement will best serve the needs of your students in meeting their goals, rather than what is easiest for you to do.

Methods of Grouping Students

In addition to the criteria that you consider for organizing groups, Flood et al. (1992) also note that teachers have a great range of choices for the sizes of groups. The authors list six possible group formats, which are shown in Figure 5.10. The dyads, or pairs, format is especially helpful when the students need to work on a skill that may be intimidating to work on individually, such as a science lab experiment or a computer project. Half-class formats are especially helpful to create a competitive environment, such as a chapter review game. Remember that the size of the group should be dependent on the purpose and intents you hold for students. Be aware that as the size of the group gets larger, the amount of time to participate available to all group members will diminish. The positive aspect of larger groups, though, is that there are more ideas and talents that people can share. You will want to provide students with many different grouping arrangements so that you and they can take advantage of the learning that they can gain from others, while recognizing that students still need to be accountable for their own learning.

Other Grouping Considerations

As you think about the criteria you will use and the sizes of your groups, you may also want to consider two other factors—leadership and group materials. Within the groups, Flood et al. (1992) cite three possible categories of leadership: teacher-led, student-led, and cooperative. The teacher-led group would most likely occur in a whole class group format, but may also occur in smaller group formats, such as a half-class or even a small group, as in the case of elementary grade reading groups. For instance, if you organized students based on the "skills development" criterion, you may move among several different groups, providing students with meaningful activities to help them develop the skills and reinforcement or corrective feedback on their efforts. In a student-led group, students may be assigned or

---

FIGURE 5.10   POSSIBLE GROUPING ARRANGEMENTS

1. Individuals

2. Dyads (or pairs)

3. Small Groups (three to four)

4. Large Groups (seven to ten)

5. Half Class

6. Whole Class

(*Source:* Flood, et al., 1992.)

may self-select to manage the group process. This is different from a cooperative grouping, where roles and tasks tend to be distributed evenly and the leadership style should be democratic, with all students in the group taking the responsibility for providing leadership.

One last consideration that you will want to make as you think about grouping students is the materials you will provide them. The group material may fall into one of four categories: same material, different levels of material with a similar theme or topic, different themes within a topic, and different topics (Flood, et. al., 1992). As a teacher assigning tasks to groups, you may assign the same task, or same material, to each group. However, depending on the criteria you used to assign groups, you may find you will need to vary the readability of material for some groups or to provide the same material but in the students' native language. Further, you may wish to have the entire class study a certain topic, but each group may study a different theme, such as the situation in which the entire class is studying modes of transportation, but each group takes a different mode to study and then reports back to the class. Finally, having each group study a different topic may be appropriate when students are grouped by their interests and you allow them to choose a topic aligned with their interests.

Activity 5.5

One of the questions on the Praxis III Instruction Profile inquires about the teacher's grouping arrangement for the lesson to be taught and the basis upon which the grouping has been made. Within your subject area and/or grade level, create examples of activities that you could assign to the following group formats:

- Random pairs studying themes within a topic
- Student-led (based on work habits) small groups
- Interest-based groups studying different themes within a topic
- Teacher-led half class groups

Share these with other students working in the same grade level or with similar content areas.

Whichever group format you choose for your students, it is important to remember to vary the formats. Follow a few days of whole class format by a smaller group activity. Likewise, a course of study consisting of entirely smaller group work can become tedious for students. After a couple days of group work, it may be helpful and a good productive activity to have a whole class debriefing session or to review a skill or have a discussion. As you think about student grouping, you may want to refer to Figure 5.11, which contains websites about the topic. The Kidsource sites contain articles about some student grouping issues, while the Best of Bonk site contains suggestions and activities to improve the cooperative learning experience in your classroom.

FIGURE 5.11 ONLINE ARTICLES AND ACTIVITIES ON STUDENT GROUPING	
Resource	Website
Best of Bonk on the Web– Cooperative Learning Handouts	http://www.indiana.edu/ ~bobweb/ co_hand.html
Reese, D. (1998, May). Mixed-age grouping: What does research say and how can parents use this information?	http://www.kidsource.com/ kidsource/content4/ mixed.age.group.pn
Tomlinson, C. A. (1995, October). Differentiating instruction for advanced learners in the mixed-ability middle school classroom.	http://www.kidsource.com/ kidsource/content/ diff_instruction

SUMMARY

As a teacher you will have at your disposal a number of inexpensive, intangible tools—"tricks of the trade" so to speak—that can help you keep students attentive and stimulated. These tools may be verbal, such as questioning techniques and giving clear directions, or nonverbal, such as using body language, arranging the physical environment of a classroom, or using student grouping techniques. In the work that you will do at home or in your office as you plan for instruction and in your classroom as you deliver it, you will have all of these tools to choose from. You can become technically proficient at their uses in individual settings, and we trust that that is part of what you are doing in the class for which you are reading this book. But only through practice and reflecting on the successes you have and changes you would make to lessons, units, and courses will you become able to combine the use of these tools so that you say just the right thing and make just the right movement or grouping decision in class day after day. That is what sets teachers who are artists apart from those who are technically proficient. They explore their alternatives and skillfully choose those that paint bright and exciting educational scenes. The remaining chapters in this section have the same goal: to enlarge your palette of alternative instructional resources, plus teaching, learning, and assessment strategies.

REFLECTIONS

1. Remember Raheela Khamfur in the conversation at the beginning of this chapter? Her physics students were working on problems of acceleration. Some of the students were getting the hang of the notion but many were not. Have an imaginary talk with Raheela about grouping for the purpose of building concepts. Offer some alternative grouping arrangements she might try along with pitfalls to avoid.
2. In their lesson preparation, experienced teachers think up and rehearse a variety of questions to ask in upcoming classes. They ask a variety of questions that challenge and prompt student thought. In a college or field experience class, notice the variety of questions asked. Reflect on their effectiveness in terms of what you've read in this chapter.

3. Call to mind a classroom you've observed lately. What atmosphere was created by the way the desks were arranged and material was placed within the room? In what ways was the physical environment helpful or harmful to the purposes of the teacher and the physical and mental climate for the students?

TEACHER AS RESEARCHER

Questioning

Small, R. C. (1992). Connecting students and literature: What do teachers do and why do they do it? In N. J. Karolides (Ed.), *Reader response in the classroom: Evoking and interpreting meaning in literature* (pp. 1–20). New York: Longman.

Small contrasts the teaching of a poem by two seventh grade teachers, one traditionally oriented and one reader-response oriented. Transcripts of the class discussion demonstrate two very different choices of types of questions, as well as different methods of responding to students and patterns of student-teacher response *volleys*. After reading chapter 5 and this article, identify the number of divergent and convergent questions used by each teacher, the volley patterns, and the different methods used in responding to student answers.

Physical Environment of the Classroom

Morine-Dershimer, G. (1977, April). *What's in a plan? Stated and unstated plans for lessons.* Paper presented at the Annual Meeting of the American Educational Research Association, New York, New York. (ERIC Document Reproduction Service No. ED 139 739).

In this paper, the researcher studies the differences in planning procedures between teachers. She divides the teachers into those with high average students scores and those with low average student scores. Then she provides the teachers with reading and math curriculum and asks them to adapt the materials for their class. Among the results, Morine-Dershimer finds that the teachers with the low average students scores were more likely to be "inattentive to the appropriateness or comfort of (the) physical arrangements of their pupils". What do you think would be the reason for this result? What effect, if any, do you think knowing about the grades of a student or class has on a teacher's behavior? (Read about the Pygmalion Effect.)

Student Grouping

Marlow, E. (1996, September). Cooperative learning versus competition: Which is better? *Journal of Instructional Psychology, 23,* 204–9.

Marlow writes a convincing argument stating that, with all the recent emphasis on cooperative learning, classrooms should contain healthy competition as well as healthy cooperation. He recommends guidelines for planning competitive events and raises questions about both competitive and cooperative classroom behavior. After reading the questions, how might you collect data to answer one or more of these questions in your own classroom one day?

Shields, C. M. (1996). To group or not to group academically talented or gifted students? *Educational Administration Quarterly, 32,* 295–323.

In this study, Shields compares the performance and attitudes of eighty-three academically talented or gifted fifth graders in homogeneously grouped classes with gifted fifth grade students in heterogeneous classes. At the beginning of the year, there were no differences in performance and attitudes between the groups. At the end of the year, the students who were homogeneously grouped scored better in academic self-concept, independent development, self-acceptance, degree to which teachers reinforce student self-concept, and peer relations. After reading the article, what criticisms would educators who are in favor of heterogeneous grouping have regarding this study? Based on the results presented in the study, if this study were repeated with homogeneously and heterogeneously academically challenged students, do you think that the homogeneously grouped students would have more positive attitudes at the end of the year? Why or why not?

Viadero, D. (1996). Mixed bag. *Teacher Magazine, 9* (1), 20–23.

This article cites many research studies, pro and con, of multi-age classrooms. Overall, however, the article emphasizes the positive results of selected studies. List the positive as well as the negative effects on the multi-age classroom students as stated throughout the article. Which list is longer? Add your own opinions about the positive and negative effects to each list. Which list contains the items that will most likely influence your opinion regarding the multi-age classroom?

CHAPTER **6**

Integrating Instructional Resources and Technology

CONVERSATION

Sally Fortner, a first-year earth science teacher, was practically bursting as she strode into school Monday morning. She was going to begin a unit on rocks and minerals within the next week and had been trying to figure out how to excite and inform her students about the different types of rocks. She just happened to flip on Saturday morning TV and surfed through the channels until she found "Bill Nye, the Science Guy" preparing a laboratory volcano. She decided to click on the record button and was really glad she had. For the next half hour, Bill showed volcanic explosions, island formations, magma, and tectonic plates. Many of these concepts were in the text material and some even had pictures, but the show made them come alive. She knew this would be fun for her students, and she wanted to share her good fortune with her mentor, Tracy Cameron.

"Tracy, I have got the coolest video," she said, holding the tape out to be admired. "This is a Bill Nye show that will work great in my next unit. I think I'll show it right away so that students will get excited about the topic. In combination with that new CD-ROM we have on the rock cycle, students will really have a lot of fun with this unit. What do you think?"

"I think I'm glad that you're this excited about your unit," Tracy said, finishing the word "unit" in that way that Sally had learned meant that Tracy had more to say.

"Okay, I know that there's a 'but' in there somewhere," Sally replied. "Help me out. What am I missing here?"

"I suppose there is a 'but.' I'm not trying to dampen your enthusiasm, and it sounds like you've gathered some good and possibly appropriate resources for your unit . . ."

"But . . ." Sally chimed in as Tracy said the word.

"But," Tracy repeated. "I'm concerned that you've mentioned that these resources will be 'fun' but not what they will do as far as helping students to develop the knowledge and skills you want them to have. I'm concerned that you may be letting your resources determine your objectives for the unit, rather than choosing resources that support and supplement your goals and objectives. Why don't we sit down and take a look at the Course of Study and your own goals and objectives and see if and where these resources can be used."

"I thought you might say something like that, so I sketched out a plan. How about if we meet at lunch, and I'll show you my plans and where I thought these might fit in?"

DEVELOPING COMPETENCE

1. Think about how you learn best—through sight, sound, touch, or a combination of these. Explain how the modification of Dale's Cone, a concept introduced in this chapter, can help teachers better meet learners' needs.

2. Consider the ways in which your own teachers have presented information to you in large and small groups. After reading, analyze the methods described in this chapter for their advantages and possible drawbacks in the classrooms in which you have observed or attended.

3. Before reading, list all of the ways in which you've used technological resources (e.g., computer software, televisions) in your own schooling career. After finishing, list any additional ways in which technology could be used. Compare your lists. If you see differences, how do you account for those differences? If the lists are the same, what do you think that says about your teachers' uses of resources?

4. Think back on your own experiences with instructional software in school experiences and describe what software you've used and under what circumstances. After reading the chapter, explain what impact understanding the various categories of instructional software can have on your planning and teaching. Can you see uses for both lower-level and higher-level instructional software in the content you intend to teach?

5. Think about the instructional technology you already know about and with which you feel most comfortable. After reading, list the three pieces of instructional technology (hardware or software) mentioned within this chapter with which you are least familiar. How might you become more familiar with these resources, either directly or indirectly? Where in your current learning environment might you find an example of one or two of the items you listed?

INTRODUCTION

In chapter 5, we discussed the psychological and cognitive tools that a teacher uses in the classroom. In chapter 6, we will deal with the tangible tools of the trade. In many of the learning situations you design, you will choose to use audio and/or visual material to assist your students in trying to comprehend the concepts, skills, or values you wish them to learn. However, throughout their careers, teachers are increasingly being challenged by newer and more advanced equipment for use in their lessons. One of your challenges will be to decide *when*, *what*, and *how* to use instructional resources to support your own instruction.

In meeting this challenge, one of your first concerns may be acquiring the skills needed to produce the teaching aids or to operate the equipment you will have available to you. While this is important information, this chapter is not meant to be a "how to" chapter; so much of that kind of information is specific to the particular equipment you have available to you in your school or at home. Instead, we will discuss many of the types of resources that are available to today's teachers and, more importantly, how to select the proper resources and to apply them in the classroom in appropriate ways.

What is an instructional resource? The term is difficult to define and becomes increasingly more difficult as technology has broadened our options. Consider, for example, the content of Shores' 1960 book, *Instructional Materials: An Introduction for Teachers*. The three basic categories of materials for teachers at that time according to the book were books, pictures and objects, and audio-visual developments, which included equipment such as the opaque projector, the filmstrip projector, recordings and films, and radio and television. Since 1960, the appearance of the personal computer and the integration of other advances in technology have widened the options for teachers. Your choices of instructional resources now include CD-ROMs, DVDs, document cameras, and, certainly, the Internet. For our sake, we will consider an **instructional resource** to be any tangible tool developed or used by a teacher to support or enhance the instructional process.

TIMELESS WISDOM

Even though the resources themselves have evolved over the years, some of the theories regarding how students benefit from good resources remain constant. Before you can choose the best resource from all of those possible or available for a particular lesson, you, as the conscientious decision-maker, need to understand the theoretical implications behind the choices you make. Your decisions will, either overtly or covertly, display your beliefs about how students learn and may even uncover some hints about how you best learn as well.

Modalities

In every classroom every day, students use combinations of their senses of seeing, hearing, and moving and touching. Which of these senses—seeing, hearing or moving and touching—does a student prefer to use when taking in new information? Barbe and Milone (1980) studied elementary children and placed them into three different categories based on their preferred ways of learning. These categories were called **modalities,** and students were identified as visual learners, auditory learners, or kinesthetic learners.

Students who prefer to learn through seeing are **visual learners.** They learn well by watching demonstrations and reading text. These students need to take notes which aid in studying the material; sometimes simply taking the notes, without necessarily going back and studying, assists these students in remembering material. These students are also capable of visualizing three-dimensional figures from two-dimensional diagrams and benefit from such teaching techniques as semantic mapping (for further discussion of this method, see chapter 7).

Those students who prefer to learn through their sense of hearing are **audi-tory learners.** They learn well through teacher lecture or from studying in study groups with other students. They may be less apt to take large amounts of notes since they are able to retain the information from simply hearing it through discussion and lecture. Students who are adept at auditory learning also remember large amounts of information by using auditory repetition. These students think in sounds and find details less important than generalizations (Barbe & Milone, 1980).

The third category, those that prefer to learn through the sense of touch, are considered **kinesthetic learners.** Kinesthetic learners learn by doing or becoming directly involved in an activity. These learners remember best what was done and not necessarily what was seen or talked about. When placed in new situations, these students like to try things out and to manipulate items (Barbe & Milone, 1980). These students might be the first volunteers to try a particularly difficult dance step or to demonstrate a physics experiment using pulleys and levers.

According to Barbe and Milone (1980), "approximately 30 percent of elementary school-age children have a visual modality strength, 25 percent have an auditory strength, and 15 percent are kinesthetically oriented. The remaining 30 percent have mixed modality strength" (p. 45). In choosing resources that support your lesson objectives, then, learning experiences that involve as many of the three categories as possible will most effectively reach the majority of students. Also, for a student who may learn from more than one modality, a lesson offering various modalities may reinforce the material for students who are then able to draw conceptual conclusions of their own.

Activity 6.1

Write a journal entry about a learning experience that was very significant to you. It does not have to be an experience that took place in a traditional school setting. Write down the details of the experience. Then, write down what resources, if any, were present during the experience. Were they visual, auditory, kinesthetic, or a combination? To what level did you get actively involved? What does this analysis tell you about your own learning style? Write a short description of your learning style and then ask a friend or family member to describe your learning style. Do the two match? If there are some discrepancies, what do you believe is responsible for the differences?

Let's see how this knowledge might be applied in a basic addition lesson. To teach to those who learn best through auditory instruction, Mrs. Minor tells the class, "I have two apples and a friend gives me three more. . . ." The auditory learners in the class can focus in on these instructions and use their strength to begin to develop the concept. If all students learned this way, Mrs. Minor's entire lesson could be spoken and delivered efficiently. However, in order to teach those who learn best through visual means, while she is talking Mrs. Minor uses large, colorful apple cutouts which adhere to a flannel board. Not only does this provide visual learners with the cues that they need, but for those students who learn best through mixed modalities, auditory-visual cues can cement an understanding that the single modality might not. Finally, after instructing in a whole class grouping, Mrs. Minor gives students some type of counters to represent apples, and she asks them to calculate using these manipulatives. Although this is just a simple example, you can teach to multiple modalities at many levels in nearly every content area (refer to the Hyerle article under "Modalities" in the *Teacher as Researcher* section for an activity related to this concept).

DALE'S CONE

While the study of modality strengths is fairly general, other theorists are a bit more specific about the types of activities a student experiences in the classroom. Edgar Dale (1969) formulated a pyramid of experience loosely based on the three modalities. Dale organized the classroom experiences a student may have along a continuum from direct, purposeful experiences (learning by doing) to experiences that involve more abstract thinking processes. At the most concrete level, students experience the actual activity that is to be learned, such as taking a trip or making a piece of artwork. If it is not possible for students to experience these tasks first-hand, then the teacher needs to create what Dale refers to as a "contrived experience," one that simulates the real experience. If a true simulation is impossible, then you, as the teacher, need to design other learning experiences that will help the students to understand the concepts, skills, or values related to the real experience. Figure 6.1 provides an elaborated version of Dale's Cone.

For instance, let's say you are teaching students about the battle of Gettysburg. Ultimately, the truest learning experience would be for the students to travel back to Civil War-era Pennsylvania and to see the actual battle in action. Since, time travel is not a field trip that can be approved by the principal's office yet, the next best experience would be to have the students travel to Pennsylvania to see a reenactment. This can be a pricey trip, so now you are challenged to determine how to help your students "feel" as though they were actually there, but without leaving the school building and probably not leaving your classroom. The simplest method for you to choose is to simply have the students read the account from their textbooks. However, Dale would tell you that the less your students are involved in active doing, the more they need to use their abstract thoughts. Therefore, the higher your students' classroom experience appears on the pyramid, the further away they will find themselves from the actual experience and the more they will need to use abstract reasoning to learn about the battle. Few students, especially younger ones, have well-developed abstract thinking skills. The lower on the pyramid an experience appears, the more your students will be able to use their concrete thinking to meet your objectives. The middle range of the pyramid provides some suggestions for your lesson plan that are more exciting than silent reading yet less expensive than a bus trip to Gettysburg.

So, does this mean students should never have to read any textbooks any longer? Well, obviously no. Your simulated classroom experience can be supplemented by a homework reading or writing assignment or followed-up by a videotape. First of all, although abstract thought is more difficult than concrete, your students need to be encouraged to think abstractly in order to be good problem-

FIGURE 6.1   THE CONE OF EXPERIENCE

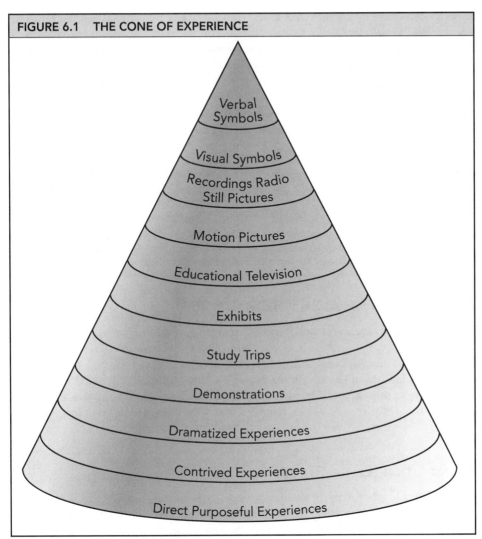

(*Source:* Dale, E. (1969). Audiovisual Methods in Teaching. (3rd ed.) Holt, Rinehart, and Winston, Inc. 107. Used with permission.)

solvers. Secondly, these higher-end pyramid activities combined with the lower-end ones can reinforce what students have already learned and assist them in filling in gaps in their knowledge and understandings. As a general rule, create a lower-end activity to maximize the percentage of learning and then supplement it with higher-end activities to help students enhance their thinking, reasoning, and creativity.

Take, for example, the simple single-digit addition example mentioned earlier. If Mrs. Minor's objective were that her students should add two single-digit numbers together with 90 percent accuracy, the simplest lesson plan would involve a demonstration at the chalkboard followed by practice. However, this experience would be categorized at the middle of the pyramid (refer back to Figure 6.1) and would involve more abstraction on the parts of students than if they were to test the problems and answers themselves through the use of manipulatives. We are aware that as you begin your careers, a relatively small number of the experiences you choose to support your lessons will fall into the higher categories of the pyramid. However, as you accumulate successful lesson plans in your file cabinet and come to understand the types of experiences on which students are most successful, your ability to design and choose resources that provide students with more significant learning experiences will grow.

Activity 6.2

Think of a concept that you may find yourself teaching to your future students. Now, referring to Dale's Cone of Experience, construct a lesson experience for each of Dale's levels in which the students would acquire the understanding of that concept. Which of the possible lessons you designed would you prefer to implement? Why?

CHOOSING THE RIGHT RESOURCES

Dale's Cone provides you with one source of information as you consider the many choices available to you as you select the right resources to support your lesson goals. You will need to think about your lesson objectives, lesson format, and the availability of the resource, as well as how students will use the resource. Since the most important of these is your lesson objective and format, we will discuss possible resources based on whether you will likely use them in large-group, small-group, constructivist, or independent learning experiences.

Presentation (Large-Group)

Nearly every teacher experiences the need to present information to a large group of students, in many cases an entire class. In the past, the resources most frequently used for this purpose have been the overhead projector and/or the chalkboard. Certainly, these are still in use. They can be very effective in presenting information to a whole class of students in an efficient manner, and we are assuming that you have had experience with these resources as students and possibly in a college class or field experience. Today, and in the future, teachers have a few more alternatives to explore as they make decisions regarding resources to support student learning. While we cannot see the future, the following discussion will present some media that you are likely to find in your schools if not your individual classrooms. Inspired use of these tools can lead to more effective learning for your students.

Presentation Software   Classrooms are increasingly being equipped with computers that may have some type of presentation software installed. This presentation software, like Microsoft's PowerPoint™, can act as a high-tech slide projector. The instructor develops a number of slides instead of transparencies or opaque visuals. These "slides" can then be shown by activating the "slideshow." The entire class can view the images on the computer monitor with the assistance of an LCD (liquid crystal display) monitor, which is placed on top of an overhead projector and projected onto a screen, or by linking the computer to television monitors in the classroom. You may not find that the *information* changes much in making the transition from transparencies to presentation software, but the *effects* can be dramatically different. You can integrate color and graphics with text to present information in ways that reinforce your lesson objectives in memorable ways for students. You can also present a more efficient and "professional" presentation, no longer needing to shuffle among transparencies and adjust each one on the overhead projector.

Dry-erase Boards   In many classrooms, the traditional chalkboard is being replaced by a new type of board. The dry-erase board uses markers on a slick, white surface. The pen marks can be erased with a soft eraser. Dry-erase boards are particularly useful in rooms that contain a large amount of highly technical equipment, such as computers, because the dry-erase boards do not produce as much "dust" as chalkboards, a condition that can be hazardous to delicate equipment. Dry-erase boards are also useful for creating diagrams and graphs with different colors. Although colored chalk is available for use with chalkboards, these colors are sometimes difficult to see, especially on older boards; however, the contrast of the colored pen marks against the white background of the dry-erase board makes their graphic appear more striking.

Document Cameras   These first two pieces of equipment discussed above are simply new twists on traditional teacher resources; most of you will already have enough experience on computers to quickly learn how to use presentation software and have no trouble adjusting to dry-erase boards. A newer piece of equipment, which is becoming increasingly more available, is the document camera (also called a "doc camera") which acts somewhat like an overhead projector. Teachers place presentation materials on a flat bed while a camera, suspended from an arm approximately one to two feet overhead, transfers the image to a classroom monitor, such as a television. The doc camera has been used primarily in televised lesson classrooms (like distance learning classrooms), since it can send an image to a distant classroom more clearly and sharply than teachers can send the image of a large chalkboard and the writing on it.

Although it may feel like using an overhead, some aspects are different. For instance, since images are being transmitted by a camera, the teacher's hand can be seen manipulating the visuals. Rather than needing to use special equipment, teachers may use typical markers and sheets of paper when writing. The doc camera also offers a number of advantages over traditional overhead projectors. For instance, teachers can display pictures from a book or graphs from a newspaper simply by placing them within the doc camera's field of vision, instead of first transferring them into transparency form. Also, some doc cameras have a back-light feature that projects a soft light from the flat bed. This allows teachers to display already-produced transparencies or even transparent visuals as small as a slide.

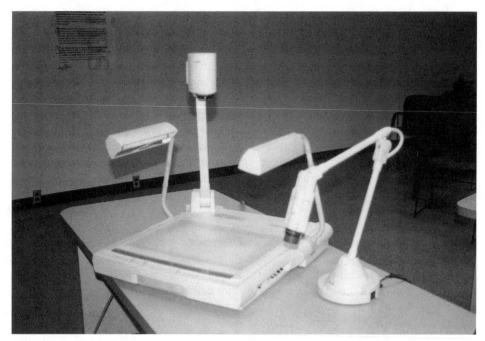

A Document Camera

Smartboards™   A piece of presentation equipment even newer than the doc camera is the Smartboard™. The Smartboard™ can act as a television monitor, a touch-sensitive computer monitor, and a writing tablet. For instance, the Smartboard™ can display any visuals shown from a linked doc camera, or it can display a video tape played from a linked VCR. Not only this, but the Smartboard™ can act as a computer monitor, displaying the screen of a linked computer. Since the Smartboard™ is touch-sensitive, any computer commands that would normally be enacted by mouse control can, instead, be enacted by tapping on and even dragging a finger over the Smartboard™. Therefore, an instructor can "double tap" an icon on the screen to upload an application, such as a World Wide Web navigator. Once the Web page is loaded, the instructor can "tap" on any link and the appropriate page will load. This incredible feature reduces the amount of time teachers must spend behind the visual barrier of the computer stand and places the instructor dynamically between the students and the visual. The finger-touch commands also apply to other application software, such as presentation soft-ware, so that the instructor merely needs to tap the screen in order to move to the next slide. Finally, the Smartboard™ contains a pen tray. Each pen is actually a "stylus," which does not contain ink, but the location of the pen in the tray indi-cates the color of the "ink" it produces. At any time, an instructor can pick up a pen and write on the screen. The writing will superimpose itself on any computer page, so that an instructor may, in effect, circle a Web hyperlink or even write a new term on a slide show page. The Smartboard™ also comes with software that produces a full-screen white page for merely jotting notes. These notes can then be

An Instructor Writing on a Smartboard™

saved to the computer's hard drive or even sent to the printer if one is attached. To see a picture of a Smartboard™ and to read about services that the company provides to teachers, you can visit the company's websites listed in Figure 6.2.

Standards for Effectively Using Visuals   Regardless of the manner in which you present visual information to large groups of students, there are some basic characteristics that all visuals should possess. You need to be certain that all presentation materials, whether shown to large or small groups, are legible, accurate, and relatively uncluttered. Projected visuals, especially, should be kept simple with little extra material on them. Each visual should contain no more than one main topic and its underlying points, written in phrases and each denoted with a "bullet" listed beneath. When using a chalkboard or writing by hand on any projector, remember to keep your notes legible and orderly. Items that no longer pertain to the discussion and/or have been copied by students should be removed or erased, so that students are not distracted from the points under discussion.

   You will also need to consider environmental factors in the classroom that may inhibit students from obtaining a clear view of visuals. Windows on the side of a room may produce a glare on a board or monitor. An overhead projector that is not aligned directly in front of a screen may produce a trapezoidal image (rather than a rectangular image), an effect known as "keystoning." The size of the lettering you use should be appropriately large; the general rule of thumb is to have the minimum letter height be at least 1/4 of an inch for each eight feet of distance the viewer will be from the material. In other words, if students will be 24 feet from the screen, your lettering should be approximately 3/4-inches high. To add emphasis or to visually separate concepts for your students, you can use color in creating the visual. Even at a chalkboard, colored chalk can be useful in highlighting key words or emphasizing the difference between two graphics. Besides, visual learners will always appreciate and benefit from your addition of color.

Finally, though we have been talking about a number of the newer resources that you may find available to you in your own classroom, you should not discount the impact of yourself as an instructional resource. More than any visual you will produce and display over your career, the one thing your students will remember about your class is your presentation style and interest in your subject. As we mentioned in chapter 5, you should try to keep any visual barriers, such as podiums or computer stands, between you and your students at a minimum. Students will probably maintain more interest in a lecture, or other type of primarily auditory presentation, if you face your students, speak clearly and directly to them, are animated or appropriately dramatic, and are able to manipulate your visuals while maintaining your students' attention.

Social Learning (Small-Group)

As you read in chapters 4 and 5, cooperative learning provides important learning opportunities in many classrooms, especially heterogeneously-grouped classrooms. In these activities, students are most effective when they fulfill specific roles within their groups so that each individual has specific tasks to complete. Effective teachers, therefore, are conscious of the importance that certain resources play in assisting students in successfully completing their tasks.

When engaging in cooperative learning activities, you should provide students with the materials necessary to complete tasks that allow them to acquire knowledge and develop specific skills, both cognitive and social. These materials may be as low-tech as a sheet for the group members to have that contains focus questions or topics. Using some of the same computer skills that you have developed in presenting large group visuals, you could design the sheet with the focus questions, or some type of large-group visual to which all group members could refer and which would serve as an aid in keeping students attending to the task at hand. You don't necessarily have to use all of the technology available just because it is there. You must decide on the appropriateness of the resource for the task at hand.

Word Processing Equipment   As teachers in the twenty-first century, you will have many choices of resources to consider as you try to match your use of instructional technology to your lesson objectives. For instance, many cooperative groups require the role of a recorder. Besides using the typical tools of pen and paper to capture the product of the group, in the high-tech classroom students can use word processing equipment to do this. In some classrooms, you may have computers that can be brought to the group or the group can gather around the computer. If portability is an issue and laptops are too costly a solution, you may be able to use other types of lower-grade word processing units, whose files can then be transferred into a word processing file on a computer. Some less expensive units will hold nearly eight pages of text and only show users approximately three lines at a time. Others not only allow users to see the entire text through a generic word processing file, but also permit them to scribble notes on the screen with a stylus. These notes are then translated into word processing text by the computer. Furthermore, after the file is completed, the file can be "beamed" to a computer with a word processing package. This feature not only allows the teacher and/or the groups to quickly link their products together, but also allows the students to display their results to the entire class, assuming that the receiving computer is linked to an LCD monitor or television.

Semantic Mapping Software   Another technical tool that cooperative groups may find helpful is semantic mapping software (see chapter 7 for a full discussion). Students can use semantic maps to help them organize their brainstorming ideas. Semantic mapping software allows students to create their semantic maps on the computer and to save and print the maps when needed. Also, the software can take a semantic map and convert it to an outline, which could be an important feature for students who need to convert their ideas into a more formal composition.

Simulation Software   One type of instructional tool, simulation software, has often been overlooked as a cooperative learning resource. Using simulation software, students encounter situations that can require them to engage in collaborative problem-solving. Oregon Trail™ is one simulation software that has gained tremendous popularity in the schools. In this environment, students travel the Oregon Trail with a wagon of five people and work to complete the trip with all members healthy and alive. Other types of simulation software simulate the development and construction of cities, the lives, and challenges of colonies of ants, and the evolutions of planets. The goal of the software in most cases is to help users better analyze problem situations and improve their decision-making skills. Using simulation software in cooperative groups encourages those solutions to be made through group consensus—a skill needed in the modern workplace. Working on the software in groups may also improve the motivation of individual members to complete the experience instead of becoming dismayed after a few poorly-made decisions. In general, all students in the group can benefit from the discussion generated by the random problem situations that occur and from the lesson of the group dynamics that may emerge from the group. More about the use of simulation software and other types of instructional software will be presented later in the chapter.

The Internet   Another often-overlooked cooperative learning tool is the Internet. Besides having each group use the World Wide Web as a research tool, your students can use e-mail to collaborate with students from all over the world. Several websites provide a method to find other classes from around the country and around the globe that may be interested in the same lesson objectives as you and your class. Using e-mail, your class and your e-mail partners can exchange data that can later be compared, or they can share their cultural lives and rituals with each other. Your class may also offer to collect the contributions of all the classes and publish them in print or on-line. Figure 6.2 provides two websites that can get you started on one of these projects (see the Harris article under "Cooperative Learning" in the *Teacher as Researcher* section for an activity on tele-collaborative projects).

Other Technological Options   Besides preparing a print or on-line report, you may require each group to make a presentation to the class. Obviously, your students could use all the resources that we discussed in the large-group presentation portion. You can encourage your students to produce visuals for the presentation in which main points are highlighted and displayed appropriately, and in which their presented materials meet some set of standards as described above. Students can be taught to convert word-processed files into to presentation slides. If time is at a premium, overhead transparencies and large posters could suffice. As with consensus-building skills, students' abilities to communicate and present themselves and their work will be valued in the workplace, and your efforts to develop these skills will benefit your students in ways that they cannot yet imagine (see the Bennett and Diener article under "Cooperative Learning" in the *Teacher as Researcher* section for an activity related to cooperative learning with technology.)

Technology and Inquiry Learning

When students engage in meaningful inquiry within the classroom, they become actively involved in their learning and create an understanding of those things they see, hear, and experience. These lessons often stem from student activities which include collecting data, analyzing the data, making and testing conjectures

FIGURE 6.2 ON-LINE RESOURCES FOR TEACHING AND TECHNOLOGY	
RESOURCE	WEBSITE
Smart Technologies' Home Page	http://www.smarttech.com
Smart Technologies' Teacher Newsletter	http://www.smarttech.com/ leaders
On-line Class: K-12 Teaching Units Delivered in Collaborative Internet Classrooms	http://www.onlineclass.com
International E-mail Exchange Connection	http://www.stolaf.edu/ network/iecc

drawing conclusions, etc. Therefore, due to the "hands-on" nature of these lessons, a teacher employing inquiry teaching methods must carefully consider the resources necessary for a successful lesson.

Inquiry lessons, wonderful as they are for students, generally take a great deal of teacher planning, both in designing the lesson and acquiring the resources necessary to engage in the activities. Whether the lesson is a biology lesson in which the students analyze leaves, a history lesson in which they draw conclusions from city records, or a math lesson in which they collect and analyze data regarding the probability of selecting a particular item, teachers' preparations consume a good deal of time. In preparing for these kinds of lessons, you may have to acquire certain items, arrange fact-finding trips, collect and assemble materials or manipulatives, and maybe even construct teacher-created tables or guiding questions. And, although it is a benefit to the students to organize data themselves in whatever manner they find most efficient, you should also be prepared to guide your students by assisting them in their efforts to find additional materials they may request or need.

The high-tech resources available for these kinds of learning activities are increasing as technological potential within classrooms increases. Students can use a computer loaded with a number of application packages, such as word processing, database, spreadsheet, paint tools, and presentation software as they record and present their findings. Many schools make certain that most of their computers contain a "works" package, which provides a sampling of those applications packages mentioned above. Portability may be an issue for any technology used in inquiry activities. With the use of devices such as the ones described in the social learning section above, students can record and analyze their thoughts or data in the woods, at the library, down the hall, or sitting on the classroom floor. Students can also share their files with others in their cooperative groups and send their final, collaborative works to the teacher's computer via e-mail or "beaming." Students may present their findings by using many of the techniques and resources described earlier in large group visuals. Given the right software packages, students are also able to use computer technology to present their findings in more authentic formats, such as newspapers, brochures, manuals, and World Wide Web sites.

Technology and Independent Learning

When most people think of independent learning, they may flash back to their own school days and think of sitting at a desk completing worksheets or reading textbooks in solitude. This type of bookwork or paperwork is a common image of independent learning. However, these types of work do not necessarily have to bring with them the tedious drudgery that many of us remember. To avoid these negative experiences, you should be aware of important characteristics about the books or work that you choose to assign to your students. In addition, you should be aware of other types of resources, aside from books, that are available for use in independent learning situations.

Evaluating Textbooks   Sometimes teachers have opportunities to voice their opinions regarding the use of a particular textbook; in other cases, books have already been selected by other teachers or committees. Obviously, you are more likely to be satisfied with preparing and assigning independent work if you have been able to choose your own textbook. Even if you were on the textbook committee, though, it is possible that your choice of a book may not be the one that the committee finally agreed upon. As a new teacher, you will most likely be told what books are currently used for a particular course. As you look at books and as you assign student work in them, there are a number of factors that affect how information is presented and organized that you should consider. By being aware of principles that you can use in choosing a text and making your students aware of ways in which information is organized and presented in the books they are using, you and your students are more likely to benefit from the assigned independent work.

Activity 6.3

Interview a public school teacher, preferably one from your grade level/subject area, about the textbook selection process at that school/district. How are textbooks chosen? Who is involved? How often are textbooks replaced? Do the teachers have any input in the selection and, if so, how much weight does the teachers' opinions carry? What other supplemental resources are available to teachers and others in the building (e.g., software, hardware, scissors, paper, etc.)? How much money a year is available for these supplemental resources?

As you look at texts, consider some of the following qualities and questions that you may want to ask for each:

- General layout–Textbooks should have a sense of order to them. Students need to be able to find the information they need, and textbooks should provide hints and cues for helping them to do this. Ask yourself what is the organizing principle for the book? How are chapters sequenced? What type of introductory comments or follow-up exercises are presented in each chapter? Is there a glossary? An index? Are there features in each chapter that highlight important words or topics for students?

- Visual aids–Remember that some students are linear thinkers and can easily read text and retain what they have read. Other students think more holistically and need to picture the whole concept before being able to retain details. Textbooks that begin chapters with key points, use color to denote similar concepts, or place the contents of the chapters in an uncluttered, well-ordered manner help holistic learners grasp the concepts being discussed. Consider the quantity and placement of pictures, graphs, and others visuals in the text. Ask yourself is there a sufficient amount of pictures to allow visual, holistic learners to obtain or confirm a mental picture of the concepts in the reading? Are there too many pictures? Do the tables and graphs add to the written material or do they provide a way to reinforce information already read?

- Readability–Students must have text materials that they can read on their own, especially in an independent learning assignment. Many scholars have developed readability formulas over time to assist instructors in determining the grade level of a document. One readability formula Fry developed produces a grade level from a graph after entering the number of syllables or the number of sentences contained in several 100-word passages. Other readability formulas also exist. One simple way to test the readability of a passage is to type it into a word processing package that will produce a readability figure on it. Whatever readability method you choose, the empirical figure should be only one piece of evidence in determining whether the text is suitable for a particular age group. Ask yourself is the language level of the text suitable for your intended readers? Does this text require prior knowledge that your students already possess? Are important terms defined and explained?

Activity 6.4

Take a book from your curricular area and evaluate it based on the criteria described above. What are the strengths of your book? If you were asked to teach from the book, would you have to compensate for some weaknesses? If so, how would you do this?

Other Resources   Besides using textbooks to engage students in independent study, other resources exist as well. **Programmed learners** are instructional materials that lead the student through predetermined content and intermittently test students on what they just studied by presenting a number of related questions, instructing the students to produce an answer, and then having the students check their own answers. Programmed learners, especially in the form of printed materials, were very popular in the 1970s when the philosophy of many schools was that allowing students to progress at their own speed was most beneficial for the students. Students completed kits or packets and charted their progress as they moved to the next level or next stage. With the introduction of the computer in the classroom, text- or kit-based programmed learners have been replaced with self-paced software programs such as tutorials which will be discussed more fully later in this chapter. Also, resources such as **flash cards,** cards that contain a question on one side and the answer on the other, provide alternatives to text-based learning and are motivational for the student since the cards provide immediate feedback as students flip through them. Although not many book-based programmed learners exist any longer, the idea remains alive and can be found in the form of many web-based courses. The number and availability of these courses is increasing for high school as well as college students.

Even if your students are not interested in web-based courses yet, they will inevitably be interested in the World Wide Web for a host of other purposes, however. Through the use of any of several search engines, students can find a wealth of information on any topic. Many pages have been created on the Web that have information on anything from the Civil War to Shakespeare's works. However, there are also many pages on the Web that contain material that may be too mature for your students or that may contradict the moral beliefs of students' parents. Therefore, it is important that schools have a policy on their books known as an **Acceptable Use Policy.** Also known as an AUP, the policy typically states that the school will only encourage the use of the Internet for academic reasons, and that the school may reserve the right to access a student's e-mail files. Parents can choose to grant or not grant permission for their children to access the Internet in school by signing an AUP. Teachers interested in providing Internet accessibility for their students should inquire of the school administrators what the expectations are for student use and what repercussions may result should a student violate an expectation. You can find an example of an AUP by going on-line to http://www.erehwon.com/k12aup.

Activity 6.5

Increasingly, some teachers at both the high school and college level are beginning to develop courses that can be taken using the World Wide Web. Find one of these courses by using a search engine or by going to one of the following:

http://www.cyberschool.k12.or.us
http://www.utexas.edu/world/lecture

Has the instructor used good decision-making in his/her course design? Do you think the instructor has appropriate and clearly stated course objectives? Are appropriate teacher tools used for each activity? To what level of Dale's Cone does the instructor take the students? Would you be interested in being a student in this class? Report your analysis to your classmates.

THE USE OF INSTRUCTIONAL SOFTWARE

Up to this point, the computer software we have discussed has primarily fallen into the category of application software—that is, software that has loose parameters and allows users to create files of their choosing. Word processing software, spreadsheets, database shells, and draw packages are some examples of application packages. We have also briefly discussed the use of the World Wide Web, which is viewed through the use of a Web browser.

However, the software market is flooded with thousands of pieces of instructional software from which teachers and students may choose. These software packages vary greatly based on subject matter, student ability level, student motivation factors, and the software-maker's goals for students. In the section that follows, we will look at several categories of instructional software and later analyze them based on their perceived strengths.

Categories of Instructional Software

Generally, if a piece of student-used software does not fit within the category of application software, then it most likely falls under one of the following five categories. Some instructional software packages may possess traits that fall under more than one of the categories. For instance, a piece of software may be considered a tutorial as well as a drill and practice type of software.

Tutorials   Tutorial software teaches a concept to users. Users either read text on the screen related to a topic of interest or listen to commentary through computer speakers. An example of a tutorial software package is one that allows students to choose a battle of the Revolutionary War and then presents information on that battle through sound, words, and pictures. Typically, users are able to repeat a section for review and can progress at their own speeds. At one time, the image of this use of computers was one that produced fear in the hearts of many educators when computers first arrived in the classroom; many teachers feared that their jobs would be eliminated, and students would simply do all their learning at computer terminals. However, as a teacher, you still have a very important function in integrating the use of this technology into your classroom. When selecting a tutorial program to supplement a course or unit, you should remember to evaluate the readability and/or listening comprehension level of the software and to judge whether it is suitable for its intended users. You will want to apply many of the same standards for choosing a textbook as were named earlier.

Drill and Practice   Drill-and-practice software, in short, is a high-tech stack of flash cards. The software presents a question to the user, waits for a response, and then provides immediate positive or negative feedback. For example, a software package that presents a word in English asks the user to type the French translation of the word and then responds, "Bon!" or "Ce n'est bon!" During the late 1970s and early 1980s, drill-and-practice software was the most frequently occurring type of software found in schools, followed closely by tutorial software; by some estimates, 90 percent of the software in the schools during that time was drill and practice. This was primarily due to the fact that both are very easy for amateur programmers to write. Thousands of teachers who had purchased home computers and had time during the summer wrote programs that fell into one of these first two categories of software.

Databases   Database packages contain large amounts of information, typically all pertaining to one main topic, that may be searched or sorted based on the needs of different users. For example, using a software package that contains facts on the nutritional values of many foods, users can search for the calorie and fat content of a particular fast food meal, sort a list of vegetables according to content of beta carotene, or find whether there is a fruit that is a good source of fiber. There are database programs that contain a wealth of information on countries of the world, the works of various authors, and historical events. Some of the most popular types of databases in many homes and schools are encyclopedias on CD-ROM. As with a text encyclopedia, students can easily search for topics. However, in addition to finding and printing pertinent information on a topic, the CD-ROM version may provide sounds bites and colored pictures that students can download as well as links to closely-related topics that students can access with the click of a button.

Simulations As introduced earlier, simulation software presents a situation in which users must make decisions and adjust their "play" according to the consequences of those decisions. The software "simulates" an environment in which users encounter problem-solving situations so that they can learn from the outcomes of their decisions. These packages are relatively inexpensive ways for students to vicariously experience situations that could be costly or dangerous to experience in reality. Examples of simulation software packages on the market include ones that simulate your first days as a new, elected member of Congress, the planning and development of a planet or city, the workings of ant colonies, and even a frog dissection.

Games/Problem-Solving These software packages present users with problem-solving situations and often some type of win/lose scenario. Users may be motivated by and rewarded with points for having solved a problem or puzzle. One type of problem-solving software may have users solve a specified number of math problems within a certain amount of time, or "shoot down" the words that are not verbs, or place patterned tiles on a game board so that a predetermined set of conditions apply. The range of problem-solving software that exists varies greatly and is primarily dependent on the instructional goals and the user level of the software.

Evaluating Instructional Software

With so much commercially-produced instructional software on the market, teachers need to be aware of how best to choose these packages for their classroom and how to apply them when they are available. Even a high-quality instructional software package can be used ineffectively in a learning situation if you have not considered your students' needs or if you do not establish the purpose of using the software within your unit of study.

As we discussed in chapter 3, classifying student activities in terms of Bloom's Taxonomy can act as a way for you to monitor your own teaching, making certain that students are engaged in meaningful and thought-provoking learning experiences. To do this, teachers should plan activities in their classrooms that address all the levels of the Taxonomy, but should take extra care to be certain that students are engaged in upper level activities as these are often neglected in the classroom. There is no one best way to have students work on these different levels.

However, you can use the different types of software we've just discussed at a variety of taxonomic levels. You must be aware, though, of the possibilities and limitations of each type. Let's apply Bloom's Taxonomy to the categories of software discussed above. For your quick review, Bloom's six levels are summarized below (see Figure 6.3).

Some packages are best suited to working on lower-level cognitive objectives. For instance, the goals of tutorial software are to instruct users in a number of concepts and the facts associated with those. Typically, users are not engaged in any activities that encourage application or analysis/synthesis skills. Therefore, tutorial software in its purest form is most appropriate when your goal is for students to work on the lower-level cognitive skills of knowledge and comprehension. Similarly, the goal of drill-and-practice software is to reinforce the quick recall of basic facts and information. Therefore, drill-and-practice packages would also be appropriate when working on lower-level cognitive skills. While these packages can be very useful for the purposes for which they are designed, it is important that you are aware of their general focus on lower-level objectives. Believing that students were working on critical thinking because each one has to engage in working on his or her own through the package would lead to mismatching your objectives with what the software is capable of accomplishing.

Some packages, though, are very effective at working on higher-order thinking skills. The strength of a good database package, for instance, lies in its ability to enable users to organize and sort the data so that students may draw conclusions from the wealth of information provided. Therefore, database software enables users to apply higher-level thought processes, such as analysis and evaluation. You should remember that a database by itself typically does not entice students to use it; it lacks the "bells and whistles" of other software packages like games and even simulations. Producing an effective lesson requires that you provide students with interesting problems to solve for which the information in the database is essential. Once students have become accustomed to solving teacher-set problems, you can challenge them to set their own problems or to set problems for their classmates.

In their purest form, simulations appeal to users' abilities to judge, examine, and weigh information as they arrive at decisions, just as the highest levels of

---

FIGURE 6.3   BLOOM'S TAXONOMY OF COGNITIVE OBJECTIVES

Level 1–Basic Knowledge–to recall facts, repeat information

Level 2–Comprehension–to show an understanding of material

Level 3–Application–to apply to a real-life situation

Level 4–Analysis–to show advanced comprehension, understand relationships

Level 5–Synthesis–to bring ideas together

Level 6–Evaluation–to judge, examine, weigh

Bloom's Taxonomy prescribe. While using the software, students are constantly analyzing situations, drawing conclusions based on previous experiences, and making judgments as to the courses of action they may take. These higher-level cognitive tasks enable students to use lower-level skills to build an information base. That is, they experience and must retain some terminology or basic concepts regarding the environment they are in, but the simulation also encourages students to focus their attention on using higher-level cognitive processes.

Game/problem-solving software varies widely in its goals. With arcade-type "blaster" software, students' retention of basic facts may be reinforced. Others, such as computerized chess games, encourage students to use higher-level thought processes. Because of this wide range of possibilities, it is not always simple to categorize the types of objectives that could be developed or reinforced through the use of games. If you are considering adding these packages to a classroom library, you will need to consider each game-type of software individually and evaluate each based on your desired learner outcomes.

Although you will try to encourage higher-level thinking from your students, that is not to say that you should never use drill-and-practice or tutorial software in your classroom use. There are times when you may need to provide experiences for a class or for a select group of students in which they review or reinforce basic skills or knowledge. For such specific purposes, these types of software can be both appealing and time efficient. On the other hand, students who are exposed to drill and practice or tutorial software only are not challenged to develop their higher-level thinking skills through the use of technology. Studies show that in the past urban schools were more likely to use drill-and-practice software than suburban schools, whose students were more likely to be exposed to application and higher-level software (Marshall, 1990). Being aware of this, if you have a choice in the selection and use of instructional technology in your classroom, you should consider what level of thinking skills you are trying to address and select your software accordingly.

We have been discussing commercially-developed software to this point, but what we haven't yet discussed is how you can use application software packages. Indeed, even a spreadsheet or word processing package can be used to create an effective learning experience. For instance, chemistry students can place their lab data onto a spreadsheet and analyze the results. Language arts students may create a newspaper from the Medieval era by using a desktop-publishing package. Also, students might place the details of lives of several United States presidents into a database so that they might be later organized and sorted. As in the use of commercially-produced databases, you will need to prepare a lesson and provide students with directions and examples that will enable them to meet the objectives of the lesson. The lesson ideas are endless; they can be implemented on any computer that contains a simple works package and they can all address higher-level thinking processes. Even with a very low software budget, you can still provide higher-level thinking experiences using application packages that most computers already have.

Finally, when using a commercially-produced software program within a unit of study, you should take care to integrate the software within the context of the unit and not simply use the software as a "free" day in the computer lab. The software you use must have some instructional purpose that is connected with the unit you are teaching and the skills you are helping your students to develop. You should prepare students for this purpose by explaining the expectations of the lesson. You may also need to prepare and distribute items such as guiding questions or directions for observations or recording data. After the computer experience, you should have students draw conclusions from their experiences by assigning follow-up activities such as student reports, a discussion, or some other culminating activity (see the Caftori article under "Instructional Software" in the *Teacher as Researcher* section for some cautionary advice on the use of software in classrooms). The Pep Registry of Educational Software Publishers provides a website (available http://www.microweb.com/pepsite/software/publishers) that has a registry of software publishers, as well as software reviews and information regarding the evaluation of software.

TELEVISION AND OTHER TEACHING TOOLS

Although they have received a great deal of attention in the past few years, computers are not the only technological resources available to teachers. Tape recorders, CD players, even filmstrip and 16-mm film projectors are used everyday in many schools. Yet, of all these, television and videotapes continue to be the most popular resources for teachers and students. The challenge for you is to make sure that rolling out a VCR and monitor is valuable in terms of student learning and not just a pastime.

Years ago, a television in the classroom was primarily used when a teacher tuned in to an instructional program that was being aired by a local station, such as a public television station. Nowadays, most teachers use the television along with a VCR to play a recording of an instructional program on an appropriate day and time. Many public television stations offer schools contracts and programming schedules so that schools may create a videotape library of instructional programs. Schools and academic departments may also build their videotape libraries by purchasing videocassettes through distributors and catalogs. Of course, you should always preview a videotape before showing it to a class and should lead the class in introductory and summarizing activities. You should also be aware that you may record and show a recording of a video production, but only under the guidelines of the Fair Use Clause, which is described in depth later in the chapter.

Millions of televisions have been installed in classrooms across the nation through a program known as Channel One. Channel One provides schools with televisions in every classroom; in exchange, each school agrees to show a fifteen minute news program aimed at school children. However, the news program also contains a few commercials, also aimed at school children. For this reason, Channel One is controversial and may not be welcomed by all schools. One advantage of having the Channel One televisions in the classroom is that once your students have seen the fifteen minute news segment, you may use the television for whatever purpose you choose. Therefore, schools may use the televisions to broadcast student-produced programming from a school's television studio, and you may simply wheel a videocassette player or computer up to the television in order to show a videotape or a slide show to a class.

Although most schools do not have the luxury of having a television studio, many are increasingly adding a video camera or two to their library of resources. Teachers can use these video cameras in the classroom to record student presentations or even to place the cameras in the hands of students and enable them to create their own works. Once on videotape, video can be digitized and transferred to computer files and even burned onto CD-ROMs for long-term storage.

While television and computer technology has provided experiences for students that they may never have otherwise had, this technology can also be misused and abused by teachers who forget the nature of demanding students in this technology-laden world. It is one thing for you to show a videotape within the context of a unit or lesson; it is another to show videotapes once a week or more in order to avoid classroom disruptions or the planning of more creative lessons. While at home, students today often have a wide selection of television channels, a home library of videotapes, and any resource imaginable via the World Wide Web. A student who attends your class everyday only to watch a videotape will quickly rationalize that he could have stayed home and had the same experience. You need to choose carefully the times you assemble a full class of students just to present a "talking head," be it on a television screen or live (in terms of a "lecture"). You have a professional obligation to be certain that you use technology wisely and only when its use can enhance the learning experiences of students. You need to make use of your opportunities to capitalize on the social environment of the classroom and create learning experiences that engage students through activity and the discussion of ideas. Technology, television in particular, can support those efforts by providing students with some common experiences, but their real learning will come after the viewing and will be a result of well-chosen post-viewing activities.

COMMUNITY-BASED LEARNING EXPERIENCES

Besides capitalizing on the social environment of the classroom, you can capitalize on the resources available within your local and global societies. It may be appropriate within certain courses or lessons to introduce students to a location in your community or to a significant person. These resources are often overlooked, but members of the community can make valuable contributions to your classroom and provide students with memorable experiences.

Bringing speakers into the classroom is a wonderful way for you to break up the routines of the classroom by adding a fresh perspective to a classroom discussion. Before you contact a speaker, though, check with your school administrators about procedures for bringing in an outside resource. In some schools, there may be a speaker fund from which you can provide a small honorarium as appreciation. You also need to prepare both students and speaker prior to the speaking engagement. For instance, you may encourage or help students prepare questions before the speaker arrives. Whether the speaker is compensated or not, you should certainly make a reminder call before the engagement and send a note of appreciation afterwards.

Connecting to the Global Community

With the increased availability of distance learning technology in schools, some speakers may be available to speak via microphones and monitors or e-mail. The advantage of using this technology to bring in speakers is that students may have the opportunity to converse with a speaker that they may not have been able to speak with otherwise. Having your class e-mail guest experts makes the experience convenient for the experts since they can respond to your students at a time when it fits their schedule and you can assemble all your students' questions into one e-mail. If your school has video-conferencing technology, your class may be able to "visit" a location or a person through a live video link up. The Pacific Bell Videoconferencing website (available http://www.kn.pacbell.com/vidconf) is dedicated to providing teachers with locations that offer "virtual field trips." The site contains tips to ensure that your visit is a successful one.

If the speaker is in high demand, some distance learning technology may enable multiple classroom sites at different schools to simultaneously participate in a live presentation. Speakers presenting via distance learning technology should be reminded to encourage students at all sites to ask questions and should pose questions to all participants so that no group of students feels like passive observers. Also, sometimes the speaker may need a few extra minutes of debriefing about and "practice" with the equipment, depending on the ease of use, before the students arrive so that no student time is wasted while the speaker is becoming acquainted with the equipment.

Increasingly teachers find themselves in distance learning classrooms as instructors. In rural areas, for instance, low school enrollments may inhibit schools from offering some upper-level courses or some electives. However, through the technology of distance learning, three or four classrooms can be technologically linked so that all students may share one teacher. In larger schools, distance learning technology enables students to experience college level coursework and may allow teachers in these schools to team teach with teachers from a distant school.

If you find yourself in a distance learning situation, you need to understand that, although recent technology has made the technology relatively "transparent," you will need to make some modifications to your teaching style. Prior to teaching a lesson, you need to become familiar with the equipment in the classroom. You will need to adjust to things like wearing a portable microphone or using the appropriate resource technology (such as using a document camera instead of an overhead). On the day of the lesson, you should be aware of your attire, since sharp plaid prints and other "busy" fabrics can often distract students at the other site. While delivering lessons, you should make a conscious

Video-Conferencing Session

effort to include students at the other sites through questioning and activities. Also, you should try to address most comments to the camera capturing the image, rather than to the monitor displaying a picture of the students. In team teaching, all team members should be aware of each other as resources and be certain to share time in appropriate ways. One other adjustment comes in evaluating student learning. You should consider using alternative forms of evaluation whenever you can substitute for a paper and pencil test. When an in-class test is deemed necessary, you should consider asking that a proctor be present in the far site room or that, at the very least, students seal their tests in envelopes on air and sign the seal.

Field Trips

One of the most popular community resources for students during the past decades has been the field trip. However, many schools are shying away from this activity due to liability and transportation cost issues. If you wish to take your class on a field trip, you should be certain to confirm the procedures and policies regarding the trip with your school administrators. All students who attend the trip should have a signed permission slip from home. Although the permission slip does not necessarily release the school from any legal liability, it is still important that parents or guardians provide evidence that they are aware that their child is participating in the school event. As with other ways of supporting instruction, field trips can be memorable experiences, but they must

Example of Distance-Learning Classroom Facility

be integrated into the unit plan. In order to do this, you should be certain that students are informed of expectations for both learning objectives and behaviors.

CURRICULUM-BASED RESOURCES

If you are preparing to teach in a certain discipline, then you may find yourself using resources specific to that content area. For instance, science teachers need to use lab equipment such as Bunsen burners and magnifying glasses, and math teachers need to demonstrate the use of calculators. Teachers in all areas who attempt to create authentic learning experiences will find themselves acquiring content-specific resources. For example, an authentic social studies learning experience may require that students use commercially-produced maps. In all of these examples, you will need to build an awareness of the kinds of resources within particular content areas and at specific grade levels that are available to you and supportive of your students' learning.

As you acquire many of these resources unique to your lessons and content area, you should remember a few things. Be aware of the budget that the school may provide for purchasing these items and become knowledgeable in the use of the resource. You should feel comfortable demonstrating its use safely and competently to your students. Also, you will probably need to determine how to store the resources securely (particularly with expensive calculators or potentially dangerous science equipment) so as to protect students from harm and protect the school from financial loss, as well as yourself from possible legal liability. These are important items for you to discuss with veteran colleagues and administrators.

CREATING RESOURCES

Sometimes, after you have looked through every catalog, library, and resource closet in your school, you still may not find the resources you need. At this point, you can find the scissors, paper and glue, and create the item from scratch. Walk through any school in America and you will see teacher-created materials tacked on file cabinets or hanging on classroom walls. Whether any particular resource that you develop lasts will depend upon two primary qualities: its form and its function.

You can enhance the form, or "design," of a resource by remembering a few basic design principles. When using color, be certain to use contrasting colors, especially on images or words that students may need to read from a distance. For instance, yellow lettering on a white background is not as effective as navy lettering. If you outline the yellow letters with a black line, however, you provide the necessary contrast for students to see the letters. Remember to keep the designs simple and avoid clutter that may produce too much "noise" and distract students from the message you are trying to convey. Finally, keep a sense of balance in the piece. Balance may be "formal." For instance, you may want to have a symmetrical design, in which all the objects are balanced on each side. Often, though, viewers find it more interesting if the piece has "informal" balance; that is, the size and shapes of objects are varied and well-distributed, and the resource has a relatively small amount of white space. For instance, a poem mounted onto a board that seems to have too much "white space" in the bottom right-hand corner may have the balance corrected informally by placing two small, identical designs that relate to the poem in the bottom right-hand corner.

In terms of its function, though, creating resources that may be long-lived will depend entirely on your creativity. You will need to find ways to create boards, posters, etc., that rely on timeless elements, rather than current events. For each of your units, you will have certain concepts that you will be trying to help students develop. You can tie these concepts to images and text that you can use for a number of years. For instance, if you were to develop a poster for a group of ninth graders on the elements of a story, you may want to give examples from a short story that has been a traditional part of their eighth grade curriculum, rather than using a TV situation comedy. The short story will likely be there long after the TV show has ended its run. But that is not to say that you should not develop current events resources. These can be both appropriate and supportive of learning. Students in social studies classes, for example, could enjoy a community events bulletin board or one devoted to recent congressional hearings. Even in doing this kind of resource, though, you can provide yourself with elements that you can use over again. When cutting out letters, for instance, you can use a title like "News of the Day" for a longer period of time than "1997's News." Thinking about the form and function of your resources can help you to create useful resources that reinforce or extend students' learning without your "reinventing the wheel" every time you teach a concept or unit.

PLANNING TO USE RESOURCES

Whatever resources you choose for a lesson, it is very important that you integrate them carefully within a lesson. It is helpful to plan for how your resources will be used within your lesson and to write these uses into your lesson plan so that you don't forget when or how you planned to use the item. When using a commercially-produced resource such as a videotape or an instructional software package, you should always preview it to determine if it is suitable for student use and, if it is suitable, to determine what kinds of introductory remarks you should offer prior to students experiencing the resource. Figure 6.4 shows an example of a form that teachers may use to evaluate an instructional software package.

Good teachers not only choose their resources well, but they also plan for the worst, especially in dealing with technologically-based resources. Remember Murphy's Law ("If something can go wrong, it will."). Speakers may get lost or ill, overhead projector bulbs may burn out, computer programs may crash, and Web sites may be temporarily inaccessible. Students will not always be patient as you try to correct problems. Though stressful, these situations provide you with wonderful opportunities to demonstrate your careful planning and effective decision-making skills as you choose an appropriate alternative way to deliver the lesson.

TEACHER PRODUCTIVITY RESOURCES

All of the resources we have discussed to this point are meant to assist you while you teach. However, there are a number of resources you can use to make lesson planning and student evaluation quicker and more organized. Years ago, teachers were provided with a lesson plan calendar book, a grade book, and a typewriter. But with the introduction of technology into schools, you now have a greater selection of resources to make your job easier.

When evaluating students in the past, teachers primarily used paper-and-pencil assessments such as quizzes and written tests. Today, creative teachers may experiment with assessment alternatives that are more authentic and, therefore, more reflective of real work and life skills (see chapter 9 for a more detailed discussion of authentic assessment). Often technology plays a role in these assessments since technological tools are increasingly becoming a part of every adult's work and home life. Technology has even helped teachers ensure fair testing conditions by enabling them to develop test banks (databases of test questions) from which they create original tests, alternate forms of a test to discourage cheating, and make-up tests.

Test bank software programs like the one described above are available for teachers to purchase for as little as fifty dollars. The software market is filled with other programs designed to make a teacher's out-of-class work easier and

---

FIGURE 6.4   INSTRUCTIONAL SOFTWARE PACKAGE EVALUATION FORM

Instructional Software Package Evaluation Form

Title of Software _____

Publisher/Source _____

Intended Age/Grade of Audience _____

Other Available Information (cost, production date, one piece of a package, etc.) _____

_____

_____

Category (check) _____ *Database*

_____ *Tutorial*

_____ *Drill and Practice*

_____ *Interactive Game*

_____ *Simulation*

_____ *Application*

Rating the software: For each item below, circle one number (1=low, 5=high).
Elaborate on rating by writing descriptive comments.

1. **Consistency with Research/Best Practice**
    (constructivism, higher order thinking, etc.)

    1   2   3   4   5

    COMMENTS _____

    _____

2. **Learning Value**
    (information, skills, strategies, etc. considered to be very important in the teaching and learning of the content area, etc.)

    1   2   3   4   5

    COMMENTS _____

    _____

3. **Entertainment Value**
    (animation, "bells and whistles" are on a par with contemporary commercial games and enhance rather than overwhelm valued learnings)

    1   2   3   4   5

    COMMENTS _____

    _____

4. **Graphics/Sound**
    (technically well done, clear, consistently high quality throughout)

    1   2   3   4   5

    COMMENTS _____

    _____

5. **Ease of Use**
    (directions are simple and direct; response time is short and program moves quickly, etc.)

    1   2   3   4   5

    COMMENTS _____

    _____

6. **Support Materials**
    (suggestions to teacher for curriculum integration, classroom management, e.g. grouping, troubleshooting, etc.)

    1   2   3   4   5

    COMMENTS _____

    _____

faster. You can find grade book programs that calculate each student's average and letter grade. In addition, you can find software packages that create a cross-word puzzle after you enter a list of words, a word search, a seating chart which rearranges students randomly and helps you keep track of student participation, and electronic portfolios of students' works.

Besides purchasing software to make your class preparation easier, you can use the World Wide Web to find free resources such as actual lesson plans. Some sites even have resources like "math questions of the day" or synopses of works of literature that can save you a tremendous amount of preparation and library time (refer to chapter 11 for a listing of learned society websites that can link you to some of these resources).

COPYRIGHT LAWS

We could devote an entire chapter of this text to all the material regarding copyright law and a teacher's use of instructional resources. Because technology has enabled everyone to copy and distribute writings and works of art so easily, publishers are also able to more easily discover a violation. So, we all should be aware of the guidelines and be careful to work within them.

The short version of copyright laws is this: No source is to be copied without the permission of the author. You should always get permission from the author or publisher to copy a written work or copy a video to be used in class. The technology that may tempt a teacher to violate a copyright law is the same technology that makes it very easy to obtain permission. Simply e-mail or word process a letter to the publisher stating the material you wish to use, the number of copies, and the purpose of the copy (that is, for educational reasons, not for profit).

The courts understand that the job of teaching often requires you to find a resource that would be ideal for tomorrow's lesson or requires that you go "back to the books" to find a new, creative idea because you never expected that the students would not grasp today's lesson. Therefore, in gathering materials to support instruction, teachers are granted protection under the Fair Use Clause. The Fair Use Clause states that you may copy a resource "in the heat of a creative moment" and use it for an upcoming class. The item must be brief, spontaneous, and meet the test of cumulative effect. Let's take each of these characteristics separately. For purposes of copyright, the definition of **brevity** is shown in Figure 6.5. As you can see, it provides you with a good deal of leeway in terms of the amount of material that falls under this definition. **Spontaneity** simply means that the use could not have been foreseen. For instance, you may have just stumbled upon a story or just heard a song on the radio that fits within your current unit. **Cumulative effect** means that the multiple copying should only be for one course and should not be a frequent event (Fischer, Schimmel, & Kelly, 1995).

As for videotapes, the law allows educational institutions to tape copyrighted television programs, but they may only keep the tape for forty-five days, at which point the tape must be erased or destroyed. If you are interested in keeping a copy of the tape after the forty-five-day period, then midway through the time period,

FIGURE 6.5   DEFINITION OF BREVITY
1. Complete poem, if it is less than 250 words and printed on not more than two pages.
2. An excerpt from a longer poem, if it is not more than 250 words.
3. A complete article, story, or essay if it is less than 2500 words.
4. An excerpt from a prose work, if it is less than 1000 words or 10 percent of the work, whichever is less.
5. One chart, diagram, cartoon, or picture per book or periodical.

you should contact the publisher to obtain permission to keep the copy (Fischer, Schimmel, & Kelly, 1995).

Copyright protection does not only apply to video and text materials; software is also copyrighted and carries with it strict authorized use regulations. As a general rule, only one piece of software may be loaded on one computer. It is illegal for you to buy one software package and load that same software on a classroom set of five computers. In order to legally run one software package on several machines, the teacher must either obtain a site license from the software distributor, which often charges a rate based on the number of computers on which the software will be loaded, or the teacher must initially purchase a lab pack from the distributor. Given the prices of some software packages for computers, it is sometimes tempting to ignore the legal requirements, but remember that you are also a role model in terms of the ethical choices you make.

ALWAYS STAY CURRENT

As we mentioned at the beginning of the chapter, instructional resources have come a long way since 1960. This development has not yet plateaued; you need to realize that you and your students will benefit from emerging technologies if you stay current. Though we cannot say with certainty whether the schools in which you teach will have access to the resources we have mentioned already or the innovations we will identify, some of the technological developments educators have to look forward to will be exciting and have the potential for transforming classrooms.

In the near future, teachers can expect expanded Internet capabilities in their classrooms. Currently, developers are working on expanding Internet bandwidth, which will be capable of handling the real-time transmission of sound and moving images. As a consequence, students at a computer (or LCD panel) in a classroom will be able to "dial up" a scientist, musician, etc., and converse with the expert in real, synchronous time.

Synchronous learning, or learning that occurs in real time, will give students opportunities to have their questions immediately answered by a teacher or fellow student. These types of learning experiences will increasingly become available regardless of the participants' geographic location. With expanded bandwidth and other technological advances, students may be able to remain at home (or in a hospital or other remote site) and still participate in a classroom discussion through computer technology. **Asynchronous learning,** learning that occurs through messages and notes that are available to students at their convenience, is also becoming increasingly available. As we mentioned earlier, courses offered via the World Wide Web are growing in number and offer learning opportunities for students and adults who cannot attend a traditional class during traditional school hours. As discussed earlier in Community-Based Learning, even those students who attend school classrooms may find themselves experiencing synchronous and even asynchronous learning advancements if the classroom is linked to another site through cameras or if the students of the class use the Internet to obtain class readings or to continue a class discussion with the instructor or other classmates.

Television may increasingly become a resource in the classroom, particularly if schools become partners in the plan to make most video resources available "on demand." Video-on-demand is a plan to allow home, business, and school television users to "order" a videotape to be played at a location and time specified by the user. With this program, teachers could select classroom videos from a wide array of choices, have them available at class time, and have the use charged to the appropriate account.

Finally, the advancements that have taken place in the field of **virtual reality,** that is, any program that simulates another environment, will, no doubt, increasingly make their way into the classroom. Currently, students have primarily experienced virtual reality though arcade-like games at home or in malls. Gradually, however, teachers can expect to be able to take their students on virtual trips to ancient Egypt, the Louvre Museum in Paris, or even the moon without leaving their classrooms. Students may experience these "field trips" either by visiting them on the Internet (with technology similar to visiting a Web site) or by wearing goggles or sitting in rooms that project an image within the student's entire sight range, including peripheral sight. This technology will not eliminate the need for teachers, but only increase the need for teachers with good lesson-planning and decision-making skills (see the Scheffler and Logan article under "Staying Current" in the *Teacher as Researcher* section). Figure 6.6 contains two websites, one on reinventing schools and one on technology tips for teachers; they offer readings on where technology is going and ideas about how to manage it in your classroom.

FIGURE 6.6 MORE ON-LINE RESOURCES FOR TEACHING AND TECHNOLOGY	
Resource	Website
Reinventing Schools: The Technology is Now	http://www.nap.edu/readingroom/books/ techgap/welcome.html
Tammy's Technology Tips for Teachers	http://www.essdack.org/tips

SUMMARY

Much has been written over the years about how resources affect students. Students take in new information through the senses of sight, sound, and/or touch, although some may prefer one over the others. In addition, students differ in their capacity to deal with abstractions. Dale's cone of abstract to concrete experiences reminds teachers to match students' levels of thought development to appropriate learning activities.

Whether using a large-group presentation style, cooperative learning, constructivist teaching, or independent learning experiences with students, resources can enrich a lesson and increase student attention. Technology, including computers, has transformed much of what teachers do in the classroom over the years.

Instructional software is widely available to teachers, but not every piece is appropriate for every situation. Tutorials and drill-and-practice software is best suited for lower-level thinking activities, while simulations and databases encourage higher-order thought processing. Application software is also a readily available, inexpensive tool for supporting higher-level learning activities.

Within classrooms, television, most often paired with video tape players, is used and has become more prominent because of the Channel One program. Resources from outside the classroom include speakers and field trips. Technology can link students and community resources together through distance learning. Teachers who find themselves delivering lessons through distance learning should remember to prepare by practicing and to consciously include students at distant sites.

Teachers should preview all commercially-produced resources and abide by all copyright regulations when bringing an outside resource into class. There are many tools, electronic and otherwise, for teachers to purchase, which can make the clerical aspects of the job easier. Regardless of the choices teachers make, those who intend to keep the attention of their students over many years should always remember to keep abreast of new developments in classroom resources. These are considerations that you will want to keep in the forefront of your thoughts as you read chapters 7 and 8 and consider the ways in which technology can be used to enhance your use of specific teaching strategies and students' learning strategies.

REFLECTIONS

1. Now that you have been given some general guidelines for using a variety of resources for large and small group presentations and individualized learning, look back at Sally's "dilemma" in the conversation at the beginning of this chapter. Imagine that you are Tracy, and consider some questions you might ask Sally to help her "explore the alternatives" she has available as she tries to engage students in her rock unit. As you consider these alternatives, see if you can identify some learning objectives that would be appropriate for students and could guide the use of the alternatives you have chosen.

2. You were just given the advice to "stay current." Think about your goals for your own teaching career and your own comfort level with technology. How will you attempt to stay current in the field of technology? Consider writing an action plan that provides you with some specific ways of going about this.

3. When computers first appeared in the classroom in the mid-1980s, some teachers feared that they would no longer be needed and that students would learn everything from computers. Obviously, this prediction has not come true. However, the introduction of technology in the classroom has had an impact. What about teaching has/will

change because of technology? What about teaching has/will never change despite technology?

TEACHER AS RESEARCHER

Modalities

Hyerle, D. (1996). *Visual tools for constructing knowledge*. Alexandria, VA: Association for Supervision and Curriculum Development.

A helpful collection of numerous methods of representing content in graphic modes. From task-specific organizers to thinking-process maps, Hyerle describes techniques that can be utilized with old (e.g. blackboards and transparency projectors) and new technologies (e.g. computer graphic software). As you develop your own lessons for either a field experience or a peer teaching experience, use or modify one or more of these techniques to support student learning. From the alternative techniques available, be ready to defend the choice you "acted" on (the A in IDEAL).

Instructional Software

Caftori, N. (1994). Educational effectiveness of computer software. *Technological Horizons in Education Journal, 22* (1), 62–65.

This article reports on research completed at a junior high school. The researchers looked at different educational software programs (some of which are very entertaining), how they are used, by whom, and their educational effectiveness. The author expresses reservations about whether students are learning (as intended by the designers) and suggests they are merely being entertained. She provides suggestions to improve educational effectiveness of software use for both teachers and designers. After reading this article, try out one of the games mentioned. Consider ways in which you might be able to improve the effectiveness of this game if you had it in your classroom. How might you document the results?

Cooperative Learning

Bennett, N., & Diener, K. (1997). Habits of the mind: Using multimedia to enhance learning skills. *Learning and Leading With Technology, 24* (6), 18–21.

This article describes a before-school, Title 1 program in which students worked in groups to create multimedia presentations about the different biomes of the world. The authors (and project designers) cite several affective traits that they believe their students lacked, traits that are addressed in the project. List each of these "habits of the mind" and next to each hypothesize how the project or some of its aspects could help develop these traits in the students.

Harris, J. (1998). Curriculum-based telecommunication: Using activity structures to design student projects. *Learning and Leading With Technology, 26* (1), 6–14.

In this article, the author states that all tele-collaborative classroom activities fall under one of three categories: interpersonal exchange, information collection and analysis, and problem-solving. The author describes five to seven activities under each category in which "connected" classrooms can participate. A creative teacher can even initiate one of these activities. Choose one of the activity structures discussed in the article and create a project based on your curricular area of expertise that your future class can complete with the help of some on-line friends.

Always Stay Current

Scheffler, F. L., & Logan, J. P. (1999). Computer technology in schools: What teachers should know and be able to do. *Journal of Research on Computing in Education, 31* (3), 305–26.

The researchers developed a survey of sixty-seven computer competencies (such as "use computers in classroom management" and "describe how computers can assist the individual") and distributed the survey to technology coordinators, teacher educators, and secondary teachers. The respondents were asked to rate each competency on a scale of one to five. Which competencies had the five highest average ranks? Evaluate your own ability in these areas. Do you have these skills? Plan how you would acquire these skills or improve your knowledge in these areas.

CHAPTER 7

Collecting Teaching Strategies

CONVERSATION

Ginny Slater had just finished looking over the "one-minute" papers she had asked her students to do at the end of her social studies class. She could see that they were having a great deal of difficulty in distinguishing between the economic systems of socialism and capitalism and the political systems of communism and democracy. Although a couple had some familiarity because of their experiences in debate club, most of her students' understanding was sketchy; as a result, they interchanged terms, especially socialism and communism. She would need to find a way to help them clarify these concepts in their minds. She had already had them read the text, and she had also delivered her mini-lecture on the topic. So, she knew that they had "received" a good deal of accurate information. Somehow, though, they had not yet been able to internalize it, to make it their own. And they needed to because these concepts would figure prominently in the next unit on the twentieth century.

It seemed to Ginny that she would need to provide students with activities that would allow them to "manipulate" these ideas, not physically, of course, but mentally. In addition, some were very concrete learners and would need to approach the abstract terms with relevant examples. As she thought about this, she tried to define for herself what the challenge for her students really was. It seemed to be a matter of vocabulary, of her students having difficulty with the terms that she was using to describe these systems. Part of the situation was that they had internalized some inaccurate understandings of these concepts. From this analysis, then, Ginny concluded that *her* challenge was to use a teaching strategy that would focus on this instructional purpose—to develop students' concept awareness and vocabulary.

Having arrived at this conclusion, Ginny "searched" her own repertoire of teaching strategies. She had several that she had used in field experiences and in her student teaching from which she could choose. Which one would serve her instructional purpose best? She mentally ticked them off—Concept of Definition Map, Concept Attainment, Concept Circles, and Structured Overview. As she explored these alternatives, she thought about her students, their strengths and learning style preferences, and the content. She knew that her students responded to graphics, so that enabled her to exclude the Concept Attainment strategy for this effort. It was down to three choices.

She ruled out the Structured Overview strategy because she didn't feel her students were ready to consider the hierarchical and coordinate relationships among the vocabulary terms. And she worried that the Concept Circle strategy wouldn't provide them with enough explicit ways of thinking about the terms to help the majority of her students understand them any better.

Well, the process of elimination appears to work here, Ginny thought. I know that they respond to graphics, and that they need to work through their thinking in an active way. But I also know that they need my help in providing them specific cues to work with that will help them guide their own learning. I know I have my old textbook around here somewhere that describes the steps in teaching the Concept of Definition Map strategy. I'll work on planning it this weekend. . . .

DEVELOPING COMPETENCE

1. With someone else, look at and discuss photographs of events in which you both participated (photos, for example, from an album or yearbook). After reading the Activating and Organizing Prior Knowledge strategies, analyze the photo experience you had with your companion. How is it like students' probable experiences with these strategies?

2. Think about specific teachers you had throughout the grades and how they taught the meaning of new and unfamiliar subject matter terminology. How were their approaches similar or different from the strategies described in the Developing Students' Concept Awareness and Vocabulary section of this chapter?

3. Who taught you the study strategies you use in your college course work? How were you taught? Compare your answers to those we offer in the Developing Students' Learning Processes and Strategies section.

4. Most of us have short- and long-term goals for our lives. The strategies described in the Making Students' Learning Purposeful section are designed to help students' study be goal-oriented. Pull together in a summary what you know about setting life-goals with the new information here about establishing purposes for learning and studying.

5. Think of one topic that you are currently and personally interested in, one you'd like to have additional information about. How might you extend your knowledge? Who might help? How do the strategies in the Extending Students' Learning section help learners move beyond what they already know about a topic? Who assists them?

6. Most of us have participated in school group projects and have experienced various levels of cooperation among group members. In instances of high cooperation, what were the benefits to you and others in the group? Identify the students' benefits from the strategies depicted in the Enhancing

Students' Skills in the Working Cooperatively section that parallel your experience.

INTRODUCTION

The learning we champion is the result of students creating knowledge, not simply receiving and repeating it. A learner who is active, not passive, purposefully builds personal meanings. What is constructed depends on three factors: student, subject matter, and context. As you look back at Ginny Slater's efforts, you should notice her consideration of all three factors. She recognized that her students bring different backgrounds of experience to a topic and different "best ways" of learning; therefore, they construct meanings differently. When we help students recognize what they know and, further, extend what they know as they begin their study, we influence in a positive direction what they will learn about a topic. We also must recognize, as Ginny did, that the nature of the subject matter to be learned differs from one discipline to another, or from one specific content topic to another. Degrees of abstractness, patterns of ideas, and styles of presentation (exposition, narrative, argument) make study in science, for example, unlike inquiries in math. Even within the same content area, social studies in Ginny's case, many factors may affect students' understandings of the concepts that they need to learn to be successful. Finally, the learning context, all those things that happen in classrooms that affect the academic atmosphere, affects students' attitudes of acceptance and eagerness to learn. Ginny recognized this when she determined that it was important for her students to learn these concepts well because not learning them might affect their attitudes and willingness to learn later material that builds on these concepts. Because they impact the depth and richness of the meanings students construct, you need to keep the interrelatedness of these factors in mind while you plan and teach.

Along with constructivism, we wish to remind you of a twin concept that's pertinent to this chapter. Scaffolding refers to various supports teachers extend to students when they cannot complete a task alone. Part of your job as a teacher is to identify gaps in students' background and to anticipate difficulties the subject matter may pose. The supports you put in place are temporary; as students' confidence and abilities to direct their learning grow, your support fades. Your ultimate goal, of course, is student independence, to create students who are self-regulated learners. To do this, though, they may need the voice of a more competent "other," a voice that you provide as you employ specific teaching strategies to help students as they move from being supported to being self-supporting learners.

The major idea of this chapter is that planning and teaching effective lessons depends on how you implement the concepts of constructivism and scaffolding. Think of it this way: You want students to develop knowledge based on sources both in and out of themselves, and you are aware this happens most effectively in a school context of conversation and interaction (constructivism). In this setting, you are initially the guide who plans the interactions that lead students to new formulations. When students are not prepared, however, or the material is above their heads, or the assignment presents unique demands, you will need to step in to support students (scaffolding). This support is necessary but short-lived with you gradually transferring the burden and joy of learning to them. The teaching strategies in this chapter will help you to help students build facts, concepts, and generalizations on their own while you play the role of scaffold-builder. In the next chapter, we extend the discussion of constructivism and scaffolding when we explore strategies for propelling students' control of their own learning.

The teaching strategies described in this chapter are arranged by instructional purposes. **Instructional purposes** are defined as the teacher's intent with regard to the cognitive "gaps" that students must fill in order to be successful in meeting the objectives of the lesson, unit, and/or course. You will recall from chapter 4—Lesson Planning—that activities are the heart of a lesson plan. Recall further that the phases of a lesson plan are operationally defined as the teacher's intent at different points in first planning and then teaching. You are encouraged to return to chapter 4 before proceeding with this chapter. Review the three lesson plan formats presented there and especially take note of the instructional purposes, stated explicitly or implied, in the phases of the Direct Instruction, Guided Literacy, and Cooperative Learning Lesson Plans. The strategies in this chapter fit into the components of those lesson plans. As a decision-maker, it will be up to you to determine which strategies work best in which stages of the lesson plan as you build your professional repertoire.

Effective teachers know many strategies that they use to fill out their individual repertoires. In planning instruction, they explore the strategies known to them ("Explore the Alternatives, in the IDEAL model), and then choose those that best fit their students, their objectives, and overall purposes of the lesson. While you can find entire textbooks on specific strategies, it can be a bit overwhelming to wade through them to find the strategies that you will find helpful. As you grow in your own ability to plan and deliver instruction, you will borrow strategies from other teachers or seek out other sources of strategies. For now, you can begin to build your own repertoire with the strategies in this chapter.

Figure 7.1 provides you with an overview, a quick reference to each of the strategies and the instructional purpose for which it is useful. For example, if your purpose is to activate students' prior knowledge, reminding them of what they already know or have learned, you could explore several possibilities, including brainstorming, PReP, anticipation guide, and semantic map. Since you already know your instructional purpose, you've had an opportunity to narrow your choices down to ones that can be most useful for helping students to meet that specific objective. This is a much better way to approach your planning than if you were to have just read about this really neat strategy that you'd like to try and then tried to force the strategy into your instructional plans. Making instructional strategy choices based upon a clear understanding of instructional purposes will increase your chances of planning a successful lesson that increases students' achievement of your objectives. While it can seem a little overwhelming to have so many possible choices, as a new teacher, you will want to develop competence with a few of these strategies, then add to them throughout your career. Much of the fun and challenge of teaching is in collecting teaching strategies, trying them out, and modifying them to suit the unique circumstances of your students, your skills, and the content you are teaching.

FIGURE 7.1 STRATEGIES GROUPED BY PURPOSE	
Teaching Strategies and Instructional Purposes	
Purpose	Activating and organizing students' prior knowledge
Strategies	Brainstorming
	PreReading Plan (PReP)
	Anticipation Guide
	Semantic Map
Purpose	Developing students' concept awareness and vocabulary
Strategies	Concept of Definition Map
	Concept Attainment
	Concept Circles
	Structured Overview
Purpose	Developing students' learning processes and strategies
Strategies	Reciprocal Teaching
	Think-Aloud
Purpose	Making students' learning purposeful
Strategies	Questioning the author (QtA)
	Possible Sentences
Purpose	Extending students' learning
Strategies	Discussion Web
	About-Point
Purpose	Enhancing students' skills in working cooperatively
Strategies	Student Teams-Achievement Divisions (STAD)
	Teams-Game-Tournament (TGT)
	Jigsaw II
	Dyads
	Think-Pair-Share

ACTIVATING AND ORGANIZING STUDENTS' PRIOR KNOWLEDGE

When you review your notes from a college course, you probably have an "oh, yeah" reaction. Even though you haven't thought about the material for a while, you recognize it as content you've previously read or heard. As you look over it more carefully, you probably see ways in which the material "hangs together," patterns among the pieces of content. It may be that the information from which the notes were taken was presented in serial order, or as cause and effect, or as problems followed by solutions. Ultimately, looking at your notes, poring over them, reminds you of what you may already know and helps you to organize this knowledge into patterns that make it easier for you to remember. It may be that looking over those old notes makes something that you are learning today even easier to learn.

Just as looking over old notes reminds you of something you learned before, your students will need to access what they already know and organize it in ways that make it easier for them to learn new information. However, students sometimes lack the skills both to "retrieve" this information from their memories and to organize it into meaningful units. When this happens, they are likely to process new information at a superficial level, deciding to memorize it in arbitrary chunks at the expense of discovering associations and developing in-depth understandings. The teaching strategies in this section will help you to assist students with getting in touch with relevant knowledge that they likely already possess at some level, while organizing and linking it to the topic they will study. In addition to the importance for their learning, there are other pleasant by-products for students when you choose to use these strategies: 1) students' interest and motivation increase when they realize they have some knowledge of the subject already; and 2) their confidence in their capacity to learn is enhanced because they know how incoming information is linked to prior knowledge (see Activity 7.1).

Activity 7.1

Choose a strategy from the following section and use it when tutoring a student. Show a videotape of your tutoring session to your college class and be prepared to say how the strategy helped you assist students in activating and organizing their prior knowledge.

Brainstorming

In trying to help students activate and organize their prior knowledge, one of the simplest strategies to use is brainstorming. Almost undoubtedly, you have participated in some type of brainstorming exercise, either in school or out. In the classroom, the teacher announces a topic of study and the students' job is to "say whatever comes to mind" in response to the topic. Working either as individuals or members of a small group or the entire class, students generate lists of responses, avoiding lengthy discussion or debate on a single item. Listening to others stimulates an individual to think of additional responses that seem to "come out of the blue." The teacher then channels the discussion to consideration of the topic under study, saying, for instance, to an elementary grade class, "Look at all we know about trees that stay green all year around. Let's read the next section in our science books on conifers and see what additional facts we can come up with." In making this simple transition, the teacher helps students form the bridge between prior knowledge (the response list) and that day's curricular topic (conifer trees).

Vaughn and Estes (1986) have the following suggestions to ensure the success of brainstorming. First, choose a term that relates to the new topic of study but is also known to the students. If the topic in your third grade class is justice, you might begin by asking what comes to their minds when they hear the term "fairness." In order to tap into their prior knowledge, you will likely need to begin with a lower-level but related term that is closer to their third-grade experiences. Second, have students write on scratch paper their individual responses to brainstorming cues. This helps students remember their ideas as the class list is being made, and it promotes better discussion because it causes students to think before they react.

A valuable strategy when used by itself because of its ability to encourage students to generate ideas without censoring them, brainstorming is an integral part of other teaching strategies in this section. Notice how it functions in the PReP strategy that is described next.

PreReading Plan (PReP)

Langer (1981) described a PreReading Plan (PReP) that calls up a student's relevant knowledge before reading a passage, viewing a video, or learning new material in other ways. This is a three-step process (see Figure 7.2) that allows students to activate important prior knowledge, reflect on where this knowledge comes from, and see how it may change based on new information that others may present. Using this strategy also allows teachers to begin to assess whether students have the knowledge necessary to engage in the activity which comes next, or whether the teacher needs to provide them with further instruction before study of the new concept (see the Zakoluk, Samuel, and Taylor item in the *Teacher as Researcher* section for conducting your own study of estimating prior knowledge). Research by Langer (1984) revealed that the use of PReP raised students' comprehension of related material they later studied.

FIGURE 7.2   STEPS IN USING PREP

1. Teacher announces a key word to students.
   Students share their responses (as in the brainstorming strategy)

2. Teacher asks, "What made you think of [these first responses]?
   Students reflect aloud on their prior knowledge.

3. Teacher asks, "Now that you've been thinking about this for a while, have you discovered any other ideas about [the key word]?
   Students discuss changes, modifications in their thinking.

In the following illustration of PReP, the teacher has identified a lesson objective: the student will define a balanced force. Since friction, by definition, is an unbalanced force that opposes motion, the teacher has decided to approach the new concept by having students explore friction according to what it isn't, as a nonexample.

Step 1.

Teacher: "What comes to your mind when you hear the word friction? I'll write your answers on the board."

Students: *rubbing together, resistance, clash, disagreement, brakes, sandpaper, slow down motion.*

Step 2.

Teacher: "What made you think of . . . (disagreement, resistance)?"

Student: "When two people debate, there's friction because they don't see an issue the same way."

Student: "I think of resistance building up when you use sandpaper on very rough wood."

Step 3.

Teacher: "Now that you've been thinking about it for a while, do you have any further ideas about friction?"

Students: Students' memories are jogged, and they have a chance to clarify and add to the class' bank of ideas. They are challenged to further elaborate and revise earlier ideas. New ideas are added to the chalkboard list.

Based on what she learns about students' associations, the teacher either decides that: 1) yes, students have sufficient background and are ready to read a science passage about balanced force; or 2) no, they need help in building a firmer foundation under the concept before preceding. A relatively simply strategy to use, PReP's effects on achievement underscore our advice to take seriously the role of prior knowledge in all learning.

Anticipation Guide

In the strategies presented so far, students' prior knowledge is brought to the foreground through a form of brainstorming. The Anticipation Guide strategy, originally conceived by Herber (1978) and described by Readance, Bean, and Baldwin (1992), contains teacher-designed statements that actively engage students in thinking. Students predict the validity of the statements based on their experiences and best thinking. During the process, you arouse students' interest, establish the purposes for study, and encourage higher-order thinking. If you were teaching a health class, for instance, you might create an anticipation guide similar to the one in Figure 7.3. You would hand this out and discuss it prior to reading, listening, or viewing material on smoking.

To design an anticipation guide you will need to do a good deal of planning beforehand (see Figure 7.4). In step one, for instance, it is imperative that you know the material very well before you design the guide. For example, students studying the effects of smoking in a health class will likely need to focus on the following generalizations:

- Physical and psychological factors are associated with smoking.
- Nicotine has addictive effects.
- Certain behaviors encourage smoking while others discourage it.
- Smoking causes damage to body parts and systems.

As you write statements that reflect these generalizations, you will want to both invite students' opinions as well as challenge their beliefs. In the example above, most students will have heard about the negative effects of smoking, but some

---

FIGURE 7.3   ANTICIPATION GUIDE FOR HEALTH CLASS

"Smoking"

Directions: Each of the following statements concern problems associated with smoking. Put a check next to any statement with which you **agree.** Be prepared to support your views on **each statement** by thinking about what you know about smoking and its effects. You will be sharing this information with other members of your group when you discuss these four statements.

_____   1. An expectant mother who smokes has a higher risk of miscarriage than one who doesn't smoke.

_____   2. Nicotine is the only substance in tobacco smoke that is addictive.

_____   3. The cost of cigarettes tends to discourage teen-age smoking.

_____   4. Pipe and cigar smokers face a greater risk of developing throat cancer than do cigarette smokers.

FIGURE 7.4   STEPS IN DESIGNING AN ANTICIPATION GUIDE

1. Identify the major ideas students will encounter as they read, view, or listen.

2. Write declarative statements or questions related to the major ideas (see Figure 7.3 for an example of declarative statements).

3. Create three to five statements that challenge or modify your students' preexisting understanding of the topic.

4. Project the guide on the screen or hand out copies.

may question the addictive nature of tobacco. Others will be challenged by, and may challenge, the assumption that raising the cost of tobacco will discourage its use. As you discuss the guide, prior to exposing students to the content for which you are building their anticipation, it's important that students provide justification or at least a rationale for why they responded as they have. Later, after students have interacted with the source material, they come back to the guide to see if they need to change their minds regarding any of the statements. At other times they will confirm their predictions or elaborate on them. Properly modified, anticipation guides can be used successfully with students at every level and in all subject areas.

Semantic Map

We have already introduced you to three strategies for activating students' memories, but we would like to emphasize that prior knowledge can be slippery. Pieces of what we know and have experienced float in our consciousness and, without position or place, can prove difficult to work with. In the Semantic Map Strategy, the teacher helps students retrieve what they know about a subject and "tie it down" in an organized visual display. When students collaborate in constructing such a display, they see with their minds as well as their eyes. As a result, they enhance their understanding and retention of a concept as they establish anchor points for further learning. Students will be able to call upon many of the skills that they have already developed in the three previous strategies (see Figure 7.5). The graphic nature of this strategy, though, provides a different sort of learning power for many students.

Avery, Baker, and Gross (1996) describe how semantic mapping might be used in a secondary social studies classroom. You could begin by asking students to brainstorm the ideas, images, or descriptions they associate with a particular concept ("List all the thoughts that come to mind when you think of human

---

FIGURE 7.5   STEPS IN USING A SEMANTIC MAP

1. Teacher announces a key word to students.
   Students share their responses (as in the brainstorming strategy) while teacher captures all ideas on the board (see Figure 7.6).

2. Teacher leads discussion on how words on student-generated list fit together, helping students to modify or clarify their thinking.
   Students discuss categories and connections among words, providing labels for categories and lines that connect various categories to each other on the visual display of the map (see Figure 7.7).

3. Teachers and students draw their attention to the map as they go about the business of studying a particular unit or lesson, modifying it as they gain more information.

FIGURE 7.6 BRAINSTORM FOR SOCIAL STUDIES CLASS		
Terms Students Might Associate with Human Rights		
freedom of speech	no censorship	equality
free press	Saddam Hussein	voting
King	liberty	Hitler
Gandhi	justice	no searches

rights."). The class may generate a list such as the one shown in Figure 7.6. You write the concept words inside a circle on a large chart tablet or on the chalkboard. With your guidance, students discuss and group related terms into categories, provide a label for each category, and graphically display their ideas in a semantic map. Figure 7.7 shows a semantic map that might be drawn from the list of terms generated. Although such maps can be used at various points in a lesson for a variety of purposes, when used to activate and organize students' knowledge they focus students' attention on the main idea of a unit or lesson. Later, students can return to the map, add to it, and use it as a data bank for writing entries in a learning log or a summary. Or, they can use it as a review for a test.

There are many ways in which students can graphically represent relationships. They can draw circles, squares, triangles, and/or other shapes to indicate different types of relationships. They may also draw one- and two-way lines between different terms to illustrate special relationships, such as cause-and-effect or comparisons, among those terms. You can design whatever graphic representations, much like a legend on a map, that enable you to help students see the relationships between and among concepts that they have identified. Regardless of how you represent relationships, there is one indispensable element in the semantic map strategy, as well as all the strategies we have introduced in this section, and that is the importance of discussion. Discussion helps students stimulate, clarify, and give dimension to their learning. When all participate, all benefit. In addition, discussion reveals gaps in students' knowledge and misconceptions regarding the topic. Information from this type of assessment will inform you about the appropriateness of the current pace and/or the direction that you will need to go during further instruction.

DEVELOPING STUDENTS' CONCEPT AWARENESS AND VOCABULARY

Does this scenario sound familiar? On Monday, the teacher hands out a list of words for students to look up in the dictionary. For each, they are to look up the definition, copy it, and then make up an original sentence that incorporates the meaning of the word. On Wednesday, the teacher collects the definitions and sentences and assesses them for accuracy and sensibility. Finally, on Friday, the

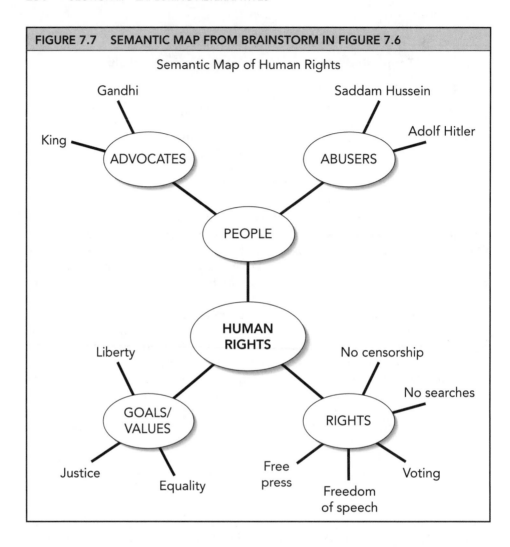

FIGURE 7.7   SEMANTIC MAP FROM BRAINSTORM IN FIGURE 7.6

Semantic Map of Human Rights

teacher administers a short-answer test (true-false, multiple choice, fill in the blanks) in which students are to connect words and definitions. The teacher grades the papers and records scores in the record book. And the whole ritual begins again the next Monday.

Variations on this scenario are played out in classrooms every day. They're testimony to the importance teachers place on vocabulary and concept development. Knowledge of words and their meanings is a large part of academic learning. Students who "own" many terms have power, and teachers recognize their responsibility for building students' muscle strength with words. As important as vocabulary and concept awareness are, though, there are difficulties that arise when teachers follow this approach. Students memorize word definitions for the vocabulary term without necessarily gaining in-depth understandings of the terms themselves. Without establishing personal meanings for concept words, students learn definitions that are empty shells. They stay in memory just long enough for the learner to pass a recitation-type quiz, and the chances for utilizing them in reading, speaking, writing, and listening are small.

Requiring students to memorize definitions, though frequently done, has few and limited benefits. Helping students to construct meanings, on the other hand, improves their comprehension of oral and written material. In this section we present a limited sample of vocabulary teaching strategies that help students clarify and extend relationships among various vicarious and first-hand experiences. Henry (1974) stated that the four mental operations basic to concept development are joining, excluding, selecting, and implying (pp. 14–15).

- The act of *joining* (bringing together, comparing, generalizing, classifying).
- The act of *excluding* (discriminating, negating, rejecting).
- The act of *selecting* (one or the other or both).
- The act of *implying* (suggesting).

As you help students take greater control of their learning of vocabulary, you should focus on these four operations. As you read the following strategies, notice how these four operations are utilized.

Before your students can clarify and extend meanings, however, they must first form an initial notion of a definition. Because the vocabulary and concepts that you will teach often deal with abstractions or experiences out of the norm for your students, you may want to try one or more of the following ideas *before* using the strategies. You can lower the abstraction level of a concept by offering a concrete example (a real pulley when studying simple machines), showing a graphic representation (a painting illustrating pointillism), or examining a word's structure (transcontinental). Piquing students' interest by focusing them on a similarity from related examples (e.g., "What attributes do a collie, golden retriever, and terrier share?") can intrigue students as they look for clues to solve "mysteries." In all such efforts, it is extremely important that you or your students put the word in a meaningful context. That is, when helping students construct a sketch of a concept, always show them the sentence or passage in which the new word will be studied, or discuss it with them so that they see the connection between the meaning of the word and the larger meaning of the passage. That way the character of the concept they are learning is influenced and situated by the meanings that surround it. These contexts often lead to subtle changes in the ways in which a particular word might act in one sentence as opposed to another. Several of the strategies lend themselves to context inspection by students (see Activity 7.2).

Activity 7.2

Select two or three concept words that students in a specific subject class need to learn. Plan for their instruction by choosing and implementing one of the vocabulary strategies in this section. Explain how your teaching of the concept meanings is aligned with your lesson objective.

Concept of Definition Mapping

Concept of Definition Mapping (Schwartz & Raphael, 1985; Schwartz, 1988) is a strategy for teaching key vocabulary and related concepts in subject classes. With repeated use and strategic coaching by a teacher, students can master it and apply it on their own as they encounter new concepts. Concept of Definition Maps are graphic structures that focus the learner's attention on key components of a definition. As they make their maps, they combine 1) the general class to which the concept belongs, 2) what it compares with, 3) the primary properties of the concept, and 4) examples of the concept. The strategy also encourages students to integrate their personal knowledge into a definition. Follow the steps in Figure 7.8 when you use this for the first time.

For example, when studying the earth's ecosystems, students might be given the concept "rainforest" to map. The textbook defines a rainforest as one of several ecosystems, communities of organisms and their environment that function as a unit. To confirm that a rainforest is, in fact, an ecosystem, they might compare it to a desert that they've studied earlier. Students will list a number of properties of a rain forest from their reading: it has at least 100 inches of rain a year; it is hot and humid; it has a dense tree cover; it has an unrivaled diversity of species. From their backgrounds, some students will know that rainforests are being heavily cleared and that their survival is in danger. They would be able to locate examples of rainforests from a world map in the textbook showing the different geographic regions (Latin America, Western Equatorial Africa, and Southeast Asia). Having finished their maps, students should write a com-

---

FIGURE 7.8   STEPS IN USING CONCEPT OF DEFINITION MAP

1. Display an example of a Concept of Definition Map (see Figure 7.9).
   - What is it (category)?
   - What does it compare to (comparison)?
   - What is it like (properties)?
   - What are some examples of it (examples)?

2. Model how to use a concept of definition map by selecting a familiar concept and soliciting the relevant information for the map from the class.

3. Present a key new word or concept from the material the students are learning.

4. Students work in pairs to collaboratively create a word map for the new concept. Students should skim the passages in which they spot the word, look at the glossary or dictionary, and then add their own background knowledge in order to complete the map.

5. Have students use their completed word maps to write a definition of the new concept.

plete definition of the new concept. Be sure to stress that the definition should include the category of the word, some of its properties, and specific examples. While definitions will almost certainly be longer than those in a dictionary, the multiple ways of connecting a word to prior knowledge and current content will help students gain a more meaningful understanding of the concept than they would if they were simply learning vocabulary off a list or out of a dictionary.

Concept maps can be used at different points in a lesson to improve students' vocabulary knowledge and comprehension in all subject areas. By weaving into definitions their own knowledge and specific examples, students feel some ownership for both the product and process of their learning.

Concept Attainment

If you were speaking to a group of peers, someone might ask, "What's it like?" or "Give me an example" to understand better a point that you've raised. In the concept attainment teaching strategy, students are led through an inductive process to compare attributes and examples of a vocabulary term until they develop a personal meaning for the concept (Gunter, Estes, & Schwab, 1990; Joyce & Weil, 1996). To use this method requires a good deal of teacher planning. As you look at Figure 7.10, notice that the first three steps are done by the teacher prior to instruction.

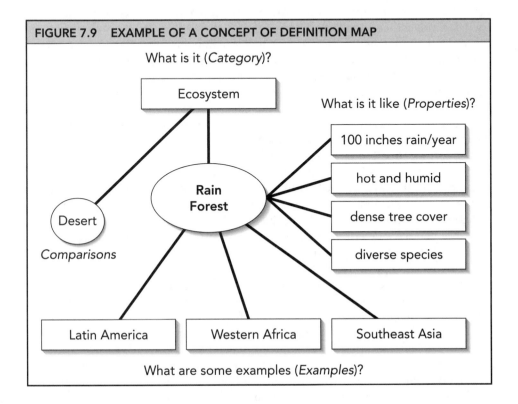

FIGURE 7.9   EXAMPLE OF A CONCEPT OF DEFINITION MAP

What is it (*Category*)?

Ecosystem

What is it like (*Properties*)?

100 inches rain/year

hot and humid

dense tree cover

diverse species

Rain Forest

Desert

Comparisons

Latin America   Western Africa   Southeast Asia

What are some examples (*Examples*)?

FIGURE 7.10 **STEPS IN USING CONCEPT ATTAINMENT STRATEGY**

During Planning Stage

1. Select and define a concept.

2. Select the attributes (e.g., the properties of the definition that make the concept unique within a larger category).

3. Develop positive and negative examples.

During Lesson

4. Introduce the process.

5. Present prepared examples and nonexamples.

6. Guide students as they develop a concept definition.

7. Allow students to provide the name of the concept based on their definition or you provide the name if they cannot.

8. Discuss the process.

The success of steps four through eight will depend upon this planning as well as your ability to determine when students have begun to grasp the concept enough to try to formulate their own definitions.

When you plan to use this strategy to supplement a subject matter lesson, the most important step is making a sound decision regarding what terms you want to teach. As a criterion, choose terms for concepts that are central to understanding the unit and lesson objectives. These concepts should have immediate applicability in your students' work within the current unit or lesson, but they should also be relevant to future investigations, too. In a U. S. History class, for instance, the term *republican* is important as students study the contrasting views of the federal government as theses were debated in the Constitutional Convention; however, the same term is important in subsequent periods in American history, even to the present time. At this step, you should also write a definition of the concept that is near the students' level of comprehension. Text or dictionary definitions sometimes contain words that themselves need to be defined.

Once you have determined the concept you will use and its definition, you will need to select the attributes of that word on which you want students to focus. For example, the concept *peninsula* can be defined as a land form that has a long, narrow portion of land that extends into the water from the mainland. The defining attributes are "long, narrow portion of land" and "extends into the water from the mainland." Both are essential in distinguishing *peninsula* from other land forms, such as islands. You need to be aware of these attributes as you develop the examples, sometimes called exemplars. Each positive example must contain all of the critical attributes. In the example about a peninsula, each example must illustrate both attributes. In contrast, a non-example will lack at least one attribute. An *island* may be a long, narrow portion of land, but it does not extend into the water from the mainland. After you have developed a series of positive and negative examples, you are ready to take them into class. Remember that it's better to have too many examples than too few.

As you introduce the process during the lesson, tell students they will be definition-makers. In that role, they will seek common characteristics among examples, contrast examples with non-examples, and hypothesize about the concept being presented. Their job is to gradually arrive at a definition of the term using their own words. Present unlabeled examples and non-examples. For example, show Florida and Italy on a map and tell students these are examples of the concept. Show Texas and Georgia as non-examples. Especially at first, it will be important for you to guide students in this process. Have students search for common features among the examples provided by contrasting examples with non-examples. Encourage students to begin guessing about the concept. What features would they put into an initial definition? Present additional examples and non-examples, asking students to test their hypothesis, modifying it as they discover more information. When it appears that their developing hypothesis is far enough along, have class members generate a summary list of features that you write on the overhead. In the peninsula example, you would expect the following list of features: a body of land, water on three sides, connected to another body of land on the fourth side. Next, have students formulate another draft of their definition for the concept, based on the features they have identified. At this point, some students may be able to name the concept, but if they can't, you may provide the name. Emphasize, however, that knowing the features of the concept is more important to their learning than knowing the name, which is really just a label for the concept.

Finally, involve the class in a discussion about the process in which they have participated. Ask them to describe their early hypotheses, what went on in their heads as they pulled features from examples and non-examples, and what parts of the strategy were most helpful in leading them to the concept. Students in the peninsula activity may say that their first inclination was to name people and places or latitude and longitude as common features. As non-examples were offered, they saw contrasts emerge, and they found themselves eliminating non-features. Eventually, they focused on the essential features of the concept.

As we mentioned earlier, finding and creating examples and non-examples for each concept to be taught takes preparation time. Of course, you will choose to teach only those concepts that are key to ascertaining core themes, principles, and generalizations. The biggest benefit for students in using this strategy is that they will know a concept from the inside out because they have been the architects and shapers of its definition.

Concept Circles

Knowing a word is not an all-or-nothing proposition. Drawing on the previous example of the concept *peninsula*, a youngster in a geography class may be able to see its outline as a mental image, but as a cartographer in adult life she may be able to describe it in much greater geologic and historical detail. The Concept Circle teaching strategy and the two strategies that follow it build on initial notions of a concept and scaffold students' understanding so they see it from different and additional perspectives.

A concept circle is a device for students to relate words and their meanings to one another. As the teacher, initially you will choose words or phrases you think students know from school study or life as well as others that are in current study materials. Then you put these words in the sections of a divided circle; students, working singly or as partners, describe the relationships among the sections. Later, as students become comfortable with this strategy, they can be the designers of the circles.

In an Introduction to Business course, the instructor presented the Concept Circle you see in Figure 7.11. Most students understood two of the terms, interest and investment, in a layman's sense. Now, however, students were being introduced to the terms with their business connotations, in a new context from the way they may have previously used these words. The other terms—time, demand deposit, and trust—had been briefly defined through examples in the textbook. At this point, the instructor decided students should enlarge their understanding of all five concepts by figuring out relationships among the adjoining terms, opposite terms, and then among all terms. When students shared their understandings of these relationships with partners and then with the class, the connections that individual students saw were reinforced or modified within the give-and-take of oral discussion and also extended by hearing the perspectives of their peers.

Structured Overview

Like the Concept Circle, the Structured Overview teaching strategy uses a visual aid that captures on a paper, chalkboard, or overhead a number of word concepts (see Figure 7.12). This allows students to more easily manipulate their elements, even if they are abstract, because of the graphical form of the printed word. In a Structured Overview, you arrange words in a diagram that depicts their relationships with each other. As students view the diagram and talk with each other and

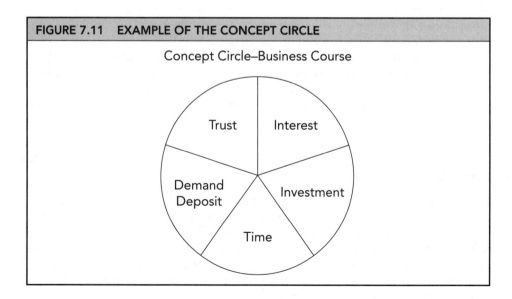

FIGURE 7.11   EXAMPLE OF THE CONCEPT CIRCLE

Concept Circle–Business Course

Trust

Interest

Demand Deposit

Investment

Time

FIGURE 7.12   STEPS IN USING STRUCTURED OVERVIEW

During Planning Stage

1. Identify concepts and their word labels that are central to the unit.

2. Arrange these key words into a diagram that illustrates their interrelatedness.

During Lesson

3. Display diagram for students.

4. Talk through the diagram—the terms and their relationships—with students.

FIGURE 7.13   SCIENCE TEACHER'S STRUCTURED OVERVIEW

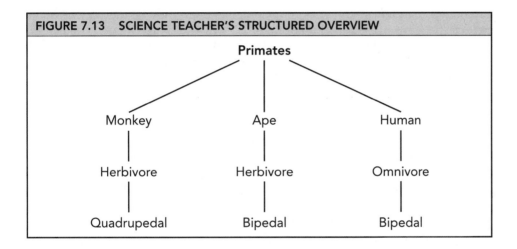

---

you, they organize related information below and beside each heading, which helps them to identify hierarchical and coordinate relationships. Here again, students construct their understandings of concepts by creating their definitions, rather than passively receiving them.

Some concepts are familiar to students while others are new to most. For example, an elementary science teacher might introduce the groups of animals that belong to the large group called *primates* (see Figure 7.13). Students already know *monkeys, apes,* and *humans.* They may not yet be familiar with *omnivore* and *herbivore* or *quadrupedal* and *bipedal.* During the planning stage, then, this teacher would need to identify these concepts as the ones that are central to the unit. The superordinate concept is *primates,* so she places it on top. *Monkeys, apes,* and *humans* are categories of primates and thus are placed below but on the same line to show equal status with each other. Lower lines might be added to show characteristics dealing with what each primate eats and how it moves about.

As we've indicated in step two of the planning stage (see Figure 7.12), when you make a structured overview, you will complete it before starting class. But resist showing it all at once. If you display it on the board, develop it one step at a time, writing down the term as you discuss it. If you have it on a transparency, uncover it one term at a time. In either case, as you reveal the graphic, facilitate a conversation with students about what they know and need to know. For instance, once you establish the definition of *herbivore* as a plant-eating animal and before revealing the word *omnivore*, ask, "What do we humans eat?" This is another example of scaffolding, building the thought bridges that students need to cover the distance between the familiar and unfamiliar. Continue to uncover new terms and discuss these with students, giving them opportunities to reinforce their understandings of these new concepts.

DEVELOPING STUDENTS' LEARNING PROCESSES AND STRATEGIES

Consider the student studying at home for a major test the next day. After a short period, she announces to her parent that she's finished with her task. The parent, questioning the short time she has been looking over the materials, wonders aloud if the student should spend more time with the study materials. "Oh, no," she replies confidently. "I know this stuff cold." After waiting a few days, the parent inquires about what grade was achieved. With a mixture of disgust and confusion, the student reports a very low grade. "But I *thought* I was prepared," she adds.

This scenario is legend in our elementary and secondary schools. We have students who don't achieve to the level of their ability because they don't know how to study the material on which they will be evaluated. Too often what passes as studying is simply passing the eyes over the material rather than digesting it. Other times students don't even know they lack appropriate study strategies. What can be done?

We believe the answer lies with you and other teachers, your students, and their homes. We can't be content with the assumption that students will pick up independent habits for learning on their own. In more cases than not, that does not happen. Many students will need purposeful, direct instruction into the types of strategies they will need to be successful in your class. You must take on the role of expert learner, using explicit forms of instruction to first demonstrate and then scaffold students' mastery of several study strategies. In chapter 8, we will elaborate on your role in collaborating with other teachers and the roles of students and home in developing these independent study skills. In the present chapter, we will focus on two teaching strategies for you to use when instructing students in the use of learning strategies. Reciprocal Teaching takes the shape of an interactive dialogue between teacher and students regarding segments of text. In the Think-Aloud strategy, teachers verbalize, in a step-by-step fashion, their own thoughts as they study and then coach students to internalize a way of thinking about some type of content or within a particular content area discipline. That is, we think differently when we are trying to analyze a poem in language arts than if we are trying to determine the appropriate theorem to use when solving a problem in geometry. In either strategy, though, you lead students' participation with your attitude about the importance of being an efficient learner while sharing your "tricks" to help them to be more successful (see Activity 7.3).

Activity 7.3

This activity might better be postponed until chapter 8 when we address specific learning strategies. However, if you choose to do it now, select one of the four learning strategies for Reciprocal Teaching (Figure 7.14). Teach the strategy using the steps in Reciprocal Teaching (Figure 7.15). Try it out on fellow class members and report how it went, especially the "modeling the process" step, which may be a new experience for you.

Reciprocal Teaching

Letting students be "the teacher" often helps them become better students. The Reciprocal Teaching strategy allows a teacher and students to share the role of instructor (Palincsar & Brown, 1984). Together they focus on segments of text and construct its meaning through interactive dialogue. During the process, participants model and practice four learning strategies: summarizing, clarifying, question-generating, and predicting. All four of these skills are important to successful study in all school subjects and are useful in first grade classrooms through graduate school with both fiction and non-fiction material (How Reciprocal Teaching works in a remedial class is the topic of Alfassi's research. See this item in the *Teacher as Researcher* section). Throughout the process, students are supported by the teacher who scaffolds their instruction and by each other.

Before you set students on their own with this strategy, give them an overview of the process by demonstrating the role of discussion leader and modeling the four strategies described below. Give time for students to practice each of the strategies under your guidance (see Figure 7.14). You will play a prominent role in the early phases of their learning by reminding, questioning, monitoring, and correcting. Later, as students' proficiency increases, your role diminishes until you become nearly invisible to students.

As students practice each of the strategies, have them use old or familiar material (a chapter they've already studied or a source written for younger or less experienced individuals). This allows them to concentrate on learning a new strategy rather than learning a strategy *and* new content at the same time. Once students have learned these four skills, you must teach them the process of Reciprocal Teaching (see Figure 7.15). These steps form the framework for the discussion where instruction occurs. Again, initially, you will be involved in teaching the process with an eye toward students' taking on the role of teacher, internalizing the processes of the strategies. As that happens, students' discussion increases while teacher talk decreases.

Depending on the age and experience of the students plus the complexity of the subject matter, the selection may consist of several sentences, a paragraph, or a section. Initially, the teacher takes on the responsibility for leading and maintaining the overall discussion. Students take turns being discussion leaders over a segment of text by creating a summary, clarifying a difficult vocabulary concept or poorly explained generalization, forming a question to ask, or making a prediction. The teacher gives feedback, provides clues, or, if needed, does more modeling. While students are discussion leaders, their peers join in a conversation by commenting on the leaders' summary, clarified concepts, generated questions, and predictions. Their intent must be to encourage through praise and self-reports ("Your summary made me think of what could be left out." or, "I wonder if your prediction would be sharper if you used the clues on the last page?"). As with any new strategy, the process must be used on a regular basis over several weeks or until the dialogues over the strategies are dominated by student talk. As regular class assignments are given, the teacher reminds students to use the strategies to better comprehend the material.

FIGURE 7.14   FOUR LEARNING STRATEGIES OF RECIPROCAL TEACHING

1. *Summarizing* involves taking one or more sentences and reducing them to the most important ideas in text. Making a summary requires distinguishing between major thoughts and supporting details. An expert summarizer recognizes clear structures for organizing material (e.g., cause/effect, problem/solution, compare/contrast, timer order).

2. *Clarifying* requires identification of obstacles to understanding and then taking action to move beyond the obstacles. Common obstacles include vocabulary concepts that are over students' heads, lack of a clear referent (the antecedent of a pronoun is not obvious), and students' inability to use context clues to suggest meaning (signal words like "on the other hand" and "finally . . .").

3. *Question-generating* relates to coming up with questions that might be on a teacher's test or on a standardized test. Learning the journalistic "w's" (who, what, where, why, and when) is one way to phrase questions regarding important text material.

4. *Predicting* entails speculation about what will be discussed next in the text. It activates prior knowledge, which gives learners confidence to "go out on a limb" and make an educated guess even on the basis of incomplete knowledge.

FIGURE 7.15   STEPS IN RECIPROCAL TEACHING

1. Students and the teacher read the selection individually.

2. Teacher models the process using one or more of the four learning strategies (see Figure 7.14).

3. Teacher guides students in taking on the role of discussion leader.

4. In groups or pairs, students take over roles of leader and respondent(s), trading off roles throughout the activity.

Figure 7.16 is an example of reciprocal teaching set in a fourth grade science classroom. Over the past two weeks, students have had training in reciprocal teaching, and have now just read a passage called "The Mechanics of Movement" on the topic of pulleys. At this point, reciprocal teaching would continue, with other students taking over the role of leader. The teacher would join the discussion to encourage participation and encourage the student leaders to keep the conversation on track.

Reciprocal Teaching is a model of constructivist learning. Students who are trained to use the strategies of reciprocal teaching use their prior experience as a

FIGURE 7.16 SEGMENT OF CLASSROOM DIALOGUE—RECIPROCAL TEACHING	
Student Leader:	The reading is about a kind of machine called a pulley. (This is the student's summary.)
Student A:	A pulley helps you lift a heavy weight.
Student Leader:	My question is whether I could lift my house using a pulley. (This student's question relates to interest; other questions could focus more on concepts.)
Student B:	I have a question, too. How does a pulley work?
Student Leader:	I'm not sure. I think you have to have a wheel, a rope, and a support for the wheel. But I'm having a hard time with the words "direction of movement." I think it means which way the load to be moved goes. (The student is both trying to clarify a word-phrase and possibly asking for further clarification.)
Student A:	I think it means a person pulls *down* on a rope while the load goes *up*. But I don't know why it works.
Student B:	I think the larger the person is, the easier it is to move a load up. The person's weight works downward, and that's a help in moving the load in the opposite direction.
Student Leader:	I think we could move the house if we used a lever. (This is the student's prediction.)
Student C:	I don't think we can. It's way too heavy for me to lift.
Student B:	Maybe we could if we had two pulleys connected together.
Teacher:	Maybe it makes a difference how high the support is.
Student A:	We want the support high above the house so we can lift it.

backdrop to creating summaries, questions, clarifications, and predictions. These are the strategies of expert learners, and with training, students become more expert in thinking and talking about text in new and productive ways.

Think-Aloud

Like Reciprocal Teaching, the Think-Aloud Teaching Strategy is a way teachers illustrate how to study by modeling their own mental processes. By talking out loud, they make their private thinking public. They share the "how, why, and when" of a learning strategy that they know students will likely need to negotiate meaning in print and electronic texts. By practicing with a fellow-student and then individually, a student internalizes the steps in a learning strategy and is ready to apply it to actual class assignments. At specific points in time, debriefing students, asking them how they have used the strategy, when, and with what success, serves to increase their metacognitive awareness of a particular study strategy.

Davey (1983), who developed the strategy, originally used it with disabled readers in intermediate and secondary grades. It has since been used by teachers at all grade levels and with students with various levels of skill sophistication. Unlike Reciprocal Teaching, which centered on the strategies of summarizing, generating questions, clarifying, and predicting, Think-Aloud works well with multi-step learning strategies. Each of the learning strategies you will encounter in chapter 8 consist of several steps and are best taught by following the scaffolding steps in Think-Aloud. It requires that you know the learning strategy very well yourself and that you are willing to offer yourself as a model learner and "study-er" to your novice students.

Teaching the steps in Think-Aloud lends itself to a direct instruction model. In your initial efforts to implement this strategy, we suggest following the steps just as they are presented here. Then, as your experiences with them accumulate, modify them to better fit your students, the material, and your own inclinations. Remember, though, that even while you may use direct instruction to teach the skill explicitly to students, your intent is to have them claim ownership of the strategy for use in their own independent study efforts.

The most important part of using this strategy is really the first step (see Figure 7.17). If you carefully observe students at work and the products of their study, you'll be able to identify their learning difficulties. Try to do this with an eye toward the skills they will need to use with topics you'll soon take up in class. For example, if you observe that your students have a difficult time remembering more than four discrete items (facts, numbers, dates), and you know that an upcoming topic in your history class will require the memorization of such items, you might decide that they will benefit from using a rehearsal strategy, such as mnemonics or visual imagery (see descriptions in chapter 8). Regardless of whether you use a strategy that you have picked up in a class, one that you learned when you were in school, or develop your own, once you have decided on the strategy it's important to be able to describe the steps clearly and concisely before you put them on display.

Once you introduce it in class and the students have copied the steps in the learning strategy from your display, then you need to talk them through the steps in

---

FIGURE 7.17   STEPS IN USING THINK-ALOUD TEACHING STRATEGY

During Planning Stage

1. Select (or determine) a learning strategy that students need for independent study.

2. Break down the strategy into a series of specific steps that students should follow.

3. Prepare a display with steps in order.

During Lesson

4. Show display and have students copy down steps.

5. Using "I" statements, model the learning strategy while referring to display.

6. Students pair up and practice steps.

7. Provide time for students to practice independently.

8. Process students' experience in working with the strategy.

9. Remind students to use the strategy as they work independently at home that night.

---

the strategy. This is primarily a "solo" step for the teacher who speaks in the first person, using a lot of "I" messages. If you were in a classroom where a teacher were using this strategy, you would likely hear, "*I* am having some difficulty deciding what is major and what is minor in this paragraph; *I'll* have to reread the material again and concentrate on sorting them out." While it's important that you model the thinking process, if you do all the talking, you run the risk of losing students' attention. Therefore, after modeling the steps of the strategy once, actively engage your students by interspersing your monologue with questions to involve them in the process. These can be quite routine questions like, "What step do I do next?" as well as evaluative ones like, "What would happen if we skipped step three?"

Once you have gone through the steps in a whole-class demonstration, have students pair up and practice the steps themselves. They should mimic your think-aloud as faithfully as possible. As they converse, you should circulate among them, listening, probing their understanding of the strategy by giving feedback (e.g., "What step are you on right now?"), and reminding (e.g., "Remember that the last step requires you to actually write down the key phrases."). When students appear to demonstrate competence with this in groups, provide time for them to practice independently. Again check up on them as they work. When the work period is near an end, debrief students, giving them an opportunity to discuss their successes and/or difficulties with the strategy. Ask questions like, "What step is easiest, hardest?" and "What will you do differently next time to make the strategy work better for you?"

As a last step, remind students to use the just-learned and practiced strategy as they embark on the next assignment. For application to be most productive, it must happen as soon as possible after training. Say something like, "As you prepare for tomorrow's essay test, remember to use this strategy. When we go over the test, I'll ask for your experience with it." The "proof of the pudding is in the eating," and students need to associate improved test scores with the use of a new method of study.

One of our profession's fondest hopes is that students acquire a need to know, the inner desire to learn. Another and related hope is that students acquire the means of learning. A familiar adage applies here: "Give a child a fish, and the child eats today; teach a child to fish, and the child eats forever." Your job is not the relatively simple one of delivering information to students. Rather, your job is the more difficult but extremely beneficial one of teaching—in a deliberative fashion—learning skills that lead to lifelong learning. You now know two teaching strategies for accomplishing that.

MAKING STUDENTS' LEARNING PURPOSEFUL

How do you know if you've arrived at your destination if you don't know what your destination is? Driving aimlessly is understandable if time, gas, and money are not concerns. In fact, seeing new scenery can be relaxing and quite enjoyable. Likewise, students sometimes study—or go through the motions of study—without a goal in sight. Their efforts are ineffective, and the results are not pleasurable. Besides, their efforts under these circumstances are inefficient; they waste time, effort, and energy. While students may not mind fumbling around on a video game for hours at a time trying to discover the right moves to be successful, most will not spend that kind of time on studying. What can teachers do to help such students?

Helping students establish a purpose for learning and studying is like giving them an internal command center that directs their work. It identifies a goal for students and maintains their attention on it. When they're aware of a goal, they're more likely to be active workers, not passive bystanders. When their work is proceeding satisfactorily, students are aware of the fact because they recognize their progress toward the goal. They're comprehending and they know it. And when work is not going well, their lack of progress sharpens their metacognitive awareness of the task, and they call themselves back to task or seek alternative routes to the goal.

The implication for teachers is to help students generate purposes for their study. The teaching strategies in this section do just that. They relate to a major teaching tool: the question. In Questioning the Author (QtA), special types of teacher-generated questions facilitate learning discussions. A second strategy, Possible Sentences, requires students to write statements, which can also be thought of as predictions to be proved or disproved (see Activity 7.4).

Activity 7.4

Plan and practice either Questioning the Author or Possible Sentences. In your report to your colleagues, describe your students' reactions (those in an actual school setting or fellow students in a simulated class). What evidence can you point to that their learning was, in fact, "purposeful"?

Questioning the Author (QtA)

In our days as elementary and secondary students, we often followed up our text readings with the "chapter checkups." The purpose of these end-of-chapter questions was to assess our understanding of ideas. Answering often involved going back into text and "skip-reading" until we spotted the information requested in the question. We then dutifully recorded these facts and details on homework paper. Until we became professionals ourselves, we never realized that making connections among ideas and applying our understanding to new problems were missing from this exercise.

QtA is a reading and discussion teaching strategy developed by Beck, McKeown, Hamilton, and Kucan (1997). In it, you ask questions called "queries" at preselected places in the text selection, so that students construct meaning *as they read*, not *after reading*, the selection. They take on the role of "revisors," persons whose job is to make the text understandable. Acting as a team, they build on each other's ideas while always referring to the text as their knowledge source. The teacher is both a facilitator and a member of the team, asking questions to prompt greater insight (Beck et al. have analyzed their implementation of QtA. Note the reference in the *Teacher as Researcher* section). Figure 7.18 shows the planning steps that you will need to go through prior to teaching this strategy in class.

Once planning is done, Beck et al. (1997) suggest that students sit in a large u-shaped group to facilitate their discussion and to allow for teacher movement among students. Then tell students that they are going to think about text in a new way. Explain that, just like all of us, authors are likely to make "mistakes" in their writing, and the problems that students have with understanding text may really be the author's inability to communicate well. Go on to model the kinds of questioning that they'll experience in QtA. Conclude the demonstration with a brief discussion to encourage students to think metacognitively about various features of the reading and thinking experience. When you move ahead to actual text in the days and weeks ahead, emphasize the inclusion of the "author" as a participant in the conversation. This personalizes text and creates interest.

Possible Sentences

Have you ever been in a contest in which you had to guess the number of objects in a glass jar? You probably used your prior experience with sizes, area, and volume to make your prediction. Then you waited with some degree of anticipation until the exact number was announced so you could assess the accuracy of your guess.

The Possible Sentences teaching strategy (Moore & Moore, 1986) capitalizes on the learning power of prediction-making and prediction-testing (see Figure 7.19). In it students are encouraged to write predictions about the probable meaning of a text passage based on what they know, or can hypothesize, about a number of key concepts or vocabulary terms. When students begin reading, they have already previewed some of the major ideas of the text, and they use reading, then, as a process for discovering the accuracy of their predictions.

FIGURE 7.18   STEPS IN PLANNING FOR QUESTIONING THE AUTHOR (QTA)

1. *Carefully read the narrative or expository selection and select the major understandings that students are to construct.* Your content analysis of the subject matter coupled with your unit and lesson objectives will guide your decisions here (a review of chapter 3 on analyzing subject matter might be in order here).

2. *Identify the stumbling blocks students may encounter.* Lack of examples or many major concepts massed on one page can hinder comprehension.

3. *Use your knowledge of the major understandings and obstacles to segment the text.* At these places, you will stop the oral reading to initiate a discussion. Segments may be any length, from a sentence that contains the gist of an explanation or argument to several paragraphs.

4. *Develop queries.* These are the key components of QtA. Questions serve to connect text and readers while they initiate construction of meaning with text. The difference between traditional questions and queries is that questions are used mostly for assessment while queries help students build thoughts.

   QtA queries deal with both lower and higher level comprehension abilities. Some sample queries for non-fiction writing are:
   - What is the author trying to say here?
   - What is the author's message?
   - Did the author explain this clearly?
   - Does this make sense with what the author said before?
   - How does this *connect* with what the author has told us?

   Queries for narratives include the following:
   - How do things look for this character now?
   - How has the author let you know that something has changed?
   - Given what the author has already told us about this character, what do you think he's up to?

As we mention in step one above, during planning it is important for you to make clear and careful decisions regarding the words that you identify. As you compile your list, some of the words on it will be familiar to students while others may be new to their experience. For example, key terms from a clothing and careers textbook passage on laundry aids might include the words *detergent, soap, synthetic detergent, syndet, hard water, soft water.* Students will bring vastly different experiences to these words and the sentences they write will underscore their individual experiences. These sentences are actually predictions about what will be said in the source. For the passage on laundry aids, for example, some students may select *hard water, soft water, soap,* and *detergent* and predict that the reading will contain a sentence like, "Whether water is *hard* or *soft* largely determines whether *soap* or *detergent* will clean clothes effectively." They may also be secure in writing, "*Detergents* are one type of *soap.*"

FIGURE 7.19   STEPS IN USING POSSIBLE SENTENCES

During Planning Stage

1. Identify six to eight terms from the material students will be reading. Choose concepts that are critical to constructing meaning from the text selection.
2. Compile a list.

During Lesson

3. Display the list on the chalkboard or on an overhead transparency.
4. Ask students to select at least two of the terms and write a sentence that could possibly appear in the reading.
5. Students now read the text selection and check the accuracy of their possible sentences.

They may not know what a *synthetic detergent*, or *syndet*, is. Therefore, in writing sentences that include them, they may have to rely on their hunches.

If you are working with younger students, you may have to help them by writing their sentences on the board for them, even if the information they contain is not accurate. Older students can work individually or in pairs. Students retain accurate sentences, those corroborated by the text, while they either modify or discard inaccurate sentences. For example, if students had predicted, "Nicotine causes body systems to slow down," it would be necessary to drastically modify and limit the statement, "Nicotine causes the heart to beat faster than normal."

Possible sentences places students in a proactive role in establishing purposes for study. They engage in using their background knowledge and best thinking to induce possible meanings. As they become more and more comfortable with the activity, some students will internalize the process and add it to their store of learning strategies.

Both of the strategies in this section aim at making learning purposeful for students. Questions and predictions, composed by the teacher or students working independently or in cooperation with each other, put learning in forward motion. Students are mentally active and interactive, striving toward a goal. Strategies in the next section help students to meet a learning goal in a purposeful way, too, but these deal more with elaborating on instructional outcomes, making them richer and more personally interesting.

EXTENDING STUDENTS' LEARNING

Learning about a topic is never finished in the sense that we can say," Now I know all there is about it." We're humbled by that realization, but we also find that there are internal rewards when we intentionally "grow our knowledge." We understand things more broadly and deeply, and we multiply the possibilities for applying our knowledge to new areas in which we are working. The following teaching strategies have the potential for extending students' learning beyond your minimum expectations for them.

Both strategies have their bases in the communication arts—reading, writing, speaking, and listening. Each employs all of the communication arts to some degree, although the emphasis differs among them. Listening and speaking are important in Discussion Web, while About-Point builds on students' abilities to read and write (see Activity 7.5).

Activity 7.5

Lead a class discussion regarding "performance indicators" for the strategies in the Extending Students' Learning section and compile a checklist of indicators. Then distribute detailed copies of the strategy you've designed to class members. Ask them to evaluate your strategy using the checklist.

Discussion Web

In every class there seem to be one or more individuals who are "verbally gifted." Given the opportunity, they speak with ease—and often. What sometimes pass as class discussions are often multiple two-way dialogues between the teacher and these students. But what about the rest of the class? They sit silently, and while some students are learning by actively listening during these exchanges, many are tuning out and, unfortunately, turning off chances to learn and achieve.

The Discussion Web by Alvermann (1991) is a teaching strategy that designs a class discussion so that all students actively participate. All students think individually about a question and possible reasons for "yes" and "no" replies. Then working with a partner and later in pairs of partners, they speak and listen to one another, constructing a chart-like web to capture and focus their interactions. Students complete the activity by engaging in whole-class discussion and/or individual responses.

Appropriate for use at the beginning of a lesson and in the middle, a Discussion Web (see Figure 7.20) works especially well when utilized near the end of one of your lessons. At that stage of lesson presentation, you will have activated students' prior knowledge about the lesson topic, helped them develop core concepts, and guided their interactions with a source that develops opposing viewpoints.

As with many of the other strategies, it is important that you plan carefully both the content and the wording of the question you ask. For instance, students in a sociology class who have discussed a chapter on issues surrounding life and death might be asked, "Should assisted suicide be legalized?" Display a Discussion Web with this question in the center. Tell students they will have to construct support for both viewpoints by citing specific reasons. After giving students time to construct their own reasons for each viewpoint, pair them up to share their reasons, encouraging them to go back to the reading as necessary. Students discussing the assisted suicide question, for example, may decide that the following reasons support it: The terminally ill would avoid acute pain, self-attempts would be avoided, and people should die with dignity. However, other reasons don't

---

FIGURE 7.20   STEPS IN USING DISCUSSION WEB

1. Introduce a question related to the reading and discussion students have just finished.

2. Display a Discussion Web with a question in the center (see Figure 7.21 for the "Living, Dying" example). Consider handing out blank webs for students to work on at the varying stages.

3. Students construct individual responses.

4. Students pair up and share their responses, taking turns writing down their ideas under the Yes/No columns.

5. Regroup students so that one set of partners is with another set; both sets share their responses and modify or add to their webs.

6. Call on group spokespersons to report on their discussions, taking turns and giving one reason per group until all ideas have been shared.

7. In class or as homework, have students respond in writing about their current thinking on the topic.

---

support it: Only a higher power can decide. We don't know how to establish criteria, and the wrong people might decide.

This first discussion should provide students with a rich opportunity to share their ideas and clarify their thinking. At that point you will combine different sets of partners to engage in this conversation again. In the example above, have the group of four compare their Yes/No reasons for, "Should assisted suicide be legalized?" They may add reasons and then work toward a consensus on the question. The group decision is written at the bottom of the web. For example, one group might conclude that although legalizing assisted suicide would help the terminally ill avoid acute pain, humans don't have the right to make that decision. Another group might reason that even though miraculous recoveries do happen, they are few in number and the greater good is saving the many terminally ill from acute pain.

When groups complete their discussions, call on a spokesperson from each group to report on their group conversations as part of whole-class discussion. Allow only one reason per group to reduce the likelihood that the last groups to report will have no new ideas to offer. Continue going around to the groups until each one has shared all of their unique reasons. During this time you may want to place these reasons on a transparency or the board as a whole-class web. As a follow-up, either as an in-class assignment or homework, have students individually write their own conclusion and their reasons for it. Encourage them to refer to the Discussion Web for arguments to include in their writing.

Discussion Webs extend students' learning through class-wide participation. As they listen and talk to each other, they look at both sides of an issue before drawing conclusions. They also develop cooperative learning skills.

FIGURE 7.21   SAMPLE DISCUSSION WEB

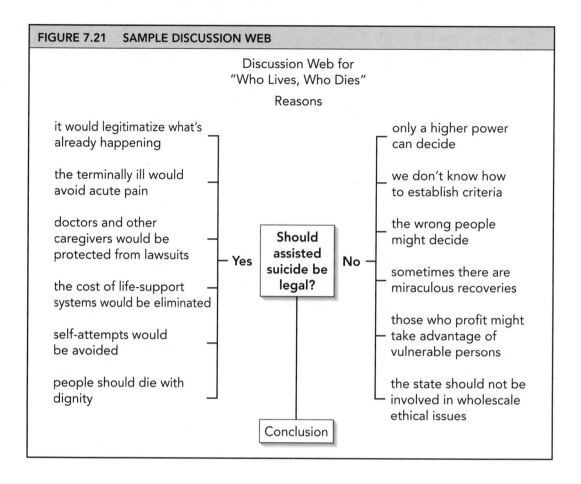

Discussion Web for
"Who Lives, Who Dies"

Reasons

it would legitimatize what's already happening		only a higher power can decide
the terminally ill would avoid acute pain		we don't know how to establish criteria
doctors and other caregivers would be protected from lawsuits	**Should assisted suicide be legal?**	the wrong people might decide
the cost of life-support systems would be eliminated	Yes ⎯ ⎯ No	sometimes there are miraculous recoveries
self-attempts would be avoided		those who profit might take advantage of vulnerable persons
people should die with dignity		the state should not be involved in wholescale ethical issues

Conclusion

About-Point

About-Point is a relatively simple way for students to summarize briefly and state the significance of a piece of text. As reported by Martin, Lorton, Blanc, and Evans (1977), students are told to pause at logical points in their reading, such as at the ends of paragraphs or sections, and to complete in writing the following two phrases:

> This section is *about* _____;
> and the *point* is _____.

What does this reading/writing sequence do for students? It helps them go beyond a mere recitation of facts and details without evaluating content. In order to do this activity, students must think about what they have just read, sifting through one or several paragraphs, and condense the material into a single sentence. Then they must reflect on its importance, tying the current material into content that had been previously read or discussed so that they can arrive at its importance (see Figure 7.22 for steps in using About-Point).

FIGURE 7.22   STEPS IN USING ABOUT-POINT

During Planning Stage

1. Determine which section of text students will use.

2. Prepare three possible About-Point statements (as described) from the first paragraph(s) and place these on transparencies. (After they have experienced the process using paragraphs, you may choose to have them use longer selections, like the section of a textbook. Depending on your students' sophistication, you may want to prepare several paragraphs or sections in this way.)

During Lesson

3. Instruct students to read the first paragraph of a selection.

4. Put the first "about" statements on the overhead and ask students to choose the best statement and discuss their reasons for the selection.

5. Follow the same procedures for a "point" statement for the first paragraph.

6. Instruct students to read the next paragraph of the selection.

7. Individually, have students generate About-Point statements for this paragraph and discuss their statements in whole-class discussion.

8. Repeat this process, having students generate About-Point statements first in pairs and then individually as they complete their reading of the selection. Monitor group and individual work.

9. Encourage students to share their statements and explain their reasoning for them at various stages during their reading process.

For example, on the topic of atmosphere, the teacher might offer these "about" statements:

- This section is about what's in the atmosphere.
- This section is about a definition for atmosphere.
- This section is about the layer of air and gases that surround the earth.

And these might be "point" statements that the teacher has prepared for students to consider:

- The point is that the atmosphere holds in heat from the sun.
- The point is that the atmosphere filters the sunlight.
- The point is that people need to protect the environment.

Your role as discussion leader at this step is very important. Refer students back to the paragraph and, if necessary, have them reread it. For the "about" statements, ask questions such as, "Which statement would the author want us to remember if we forgot all the details?" or "Which statement is like an umbrella that 'covers' all the details in the paragraph?" You want them to realize that the best "about" statement includes all of the important information and is concise and accurate. Guide students to the best "point" statement with questions such as, "What should we think or do as a result of knowing this?" or "What advice might you give someone on the basis of this information?" For "point" statements, help students do inference and application-type thinking.

When you believe that they are ready to generate their own statements, ask students for a good "about" statement for the next paragraph. Have them discuss their suggestions and develop an "about" statement. Refer them to the examples you have already discussed, the criteria you established for a good statement, and "the way their minds worked" in selecting the most appropriate choices. Then write that statement on the overhead. Follow the same procedure for developing a "point" statement for that paragraph. Have students then read the next paragraph of the selection and work with a partner to develop an "about" statement and a "point" statement. Monitor students' conversations as you circulate around the room, stopping to refocus or clarify their thinking. As you involve the class in discussing the statements developed by student pairs, encourage their metacognitive inquiry by asking student pairs to explain and defend their statements. Finally, direct students to read the remainder of the selection and write their own About-Point statements for all the paragraphs or for selected paragraphs or sections.

Using About-Point as a learning strategy will seem relevant to students. They apply it quickly and easily on text material that teachers routinely assign, the same material that will be the basis of course tests and assessments. One caution should be observed: The kinds of thinking required by About-Point do not develop overnight. While sophistication with summarization ("about") and inference ("point") are developmental, instruction aimed at enhancing a specific group of students' skills will take time and repeated periods of training. This will be time well-spent, however, since students are accountable for the outcomes related to these types of thinking both in school and in out-of-school situations.

ENHANCING STUDENTS' SKILLS IN WORKING COOPERATIVELY

You were introduced to the Cooperative Learning Lesson Plan in chapter 4. You learned that when a teacher wishes to teach subject matter and interpersonal skills together, the Cooperative Learning Lesson Plan is a wise choice. In the following section, we present overviews of teaching strategies that can enhance students' efforts in working in groups.

The lesson plan and these strategies are similar in that both serve joint academic and social goals. The goals complement each other, and students achieve in both areas. There are other similarities. In both, students come to rely less on the teacher and more on one another, thus fostering a positive interdependence. Students from culturally diverse backgrounds and those with disabilities are more easily drawn into class discussion where other students gain the skills to support their contributions, and thus spend more time in meaningful exchanges with their fellow-students. In the same vein, students who experience both Cooperative

Learning Lesson Plans and strategies are more likely to accept diversity and value individual differences than those who do not.

The differences between the plan and the strategies are ones of scope and size of membership. The plan is comprehensive. It usually has several learning objectives, is designed to last from one to three days, and involves all students in a combination of individual, small group, and whole class efforts. On the other hand, a cooperative learning strategy is narrower in its reach. Objectives are focused but few in number. A session is usually finished in a class period or less, and the class spends most of its time in small groups of four or five individuals. You may incorporate cooperative learning strategies within any of the lesson plans described in chapter 4 (Direct Instruction, Guided Literacy, or Cooperative Learning). The other option is that a cooperative learning teaching strategy may stand alone, occurring outside of a unit or lesson plan. Such occasions happen when you feel the need to build group cohesion within the class, perfect an academic skill, or in those awkward times in a school year when you've finished a unit and want to extend students' learning but don't want to start a new unit because of a pending holiday or all-school task, such as standardized testing.

We present overviews of five cooperative learning strategies below. As you read them, picture yourself organizing and leading each one. In what ways is your role different from other strategies described in this chapter? If you have not been involved in cooperative groups as a student, these descriptions may strike you as unusual and curious. Please remember the decision-making model this book is built on. You are here expanding your range of alternative approaches to teaching and learning. As always, keep an open mind to "exploring all alternatives" (see Activity 7.6).

Activity 7.6

Plan and conduct a class activity built on one of the cooperative learning group strategies described in this section. Prepare all necessary reading materials, worksheets, and discussion questions. If necessary, move classroom furniture into new arrangements. Videotape groups in action. During playback for your college class, use the pause button to stop action at preselected points. Ask classmates to identify steps in the strategy, any breakdowns in the cooperative learning process, and the various roles of teacher and students.

Student Teams–Achievement Divisions (STAD)

The first three strategies presented here are associated with the work of Slavin and his colleagues at the Johns Hopkins Center for Social Organization of Schools. They are Student Teams–Achievement Divisions (STAD), Teams–Games–Tournament (TGT), and Jigsaw II. They share several features: group membership is ideally limited to four or five persons, and groups are heterogeneous in terms of ability, sex, ethnicity, race, and special needs.

STAD (Slavin, 1991) begins after students have studied material through reading and discussion. The teacher gives out summary worksheets over the material. Students are told to study until they have mastered all the concepts and generalizations; they can use any study strategy they wish. The students are quizzed individually, and the team's overall score is determined by the extent to which each student improved his or her performance over past efforts. To level the playing field for all students, a base score is set five points below each student's average. Students can earn points up to a maximum of ten for each point that exceeds their base score. In this way, low-performing students contribute maximum points to the team by showing improvement. Slavin strongly believes that teams should receive recognition for their accomplishments outside of the class. Thus he suggests that teams with the highest scores and students who exceed their past records be recognized in a school newspaper. Results could also be announced over the public address system or in a school assembly.

Teams–Games–Tournament (TGT)

TGT (Slavin, 1991) is similar to STAD, except that students play games with others of similar performance rather than take conventional quizzes. In anticipation of the tournaments, teams hold regular practices in which students help each other master skills and concepts taught by the teacher. Each student is then assigned to a tournament table to compete with representatives of two other teams with similar performance records. Students respond to questions over material that they are currently studying; questions are written on individual cards. When each game is over, the players at each table compare their scores to determine the top, middle, and low scorers. High scorers receive six points, while middle scorers receive four, and low scorers receive two. Team scores are obtained by adding the results for teammates. These scores are added to previous game scores in the tournament for a cumulative score. As in STAD, high-scoring teams and tournament winners are announced in some type of public outlet.

Jigsaw II

The originator of Jigsaw was Aronson and colleagues (1978) at the University of Texas and then at the University of California at Santa Cruz. Jigsaw II is a modification developed at Johns Hopkins University (Slavin, 1991). In this strategy as in STAD and TGT, students work in four- to five-member teams. All students read the same text and are given a topic from the text on which each becomes an expert (Jigsaw II can even be used in math class; see the Draper item in the *Teacher as Researcher* section). Students with the same topic meet in expert groups to clarify and reinforce topic information through discussion. They then return to their teams to teach what they have learned. Individual quizzes are administered and team scores are compiled from them using the improvement score system of STAD.

Dyads

The premise of Dyads is that two heads are better than one. As conceptualized by Larson and Dansereau (1986), dyads are really "study buddies" who work together to help each other read and study text. After both have read the same passage, one, the recaller, orally summarizes what they have just read. The other, the listener, corrects misunderstandings. Then they exchange roles in a reciprocal process designed to improve the comprehension of both.

To begin, have partners individually read and study about two pages of a textbook for which they will be held accountable. Then direct them to follow the steps described in Figure 7.23.

As with all strategies and lesson plans, you can modify the dyads strategy if necessary. For instance, rather than having partners summarize an entire section or chapter, you might select for their attention only those pages that cover the most essential elements of the topic. This makes sense for young students as well as for older, slower-moving students whose capacity for summary-making is limited and who may have limited attention spans. In addition, research quoted by Larson and Dansereau suggests that students low in verbal ability perform best when paired with a more verbal partner, a situation that does not adversely affect the more verbal student. Teachers with students of widely divergent abilities and needs, including those in inclusive settings, may well want to utilize this strategy.

Think–Pair–Share

Class discussion usually means verbal interactions between a teacher and students in a whole-class setting. Even when such a discussion goes well, a small number of students quickly volunteer to respond while the majority are silent and mentally disengaged. Lyman (1992) had this scenario in mind when he developed the Think–Pair–Share teaching strategy. A three-step cooperative learning activity, it fosters involvement by all students in a task. In the first step, students think on their own about a question or problem posed by the teacher.

FIGURE 7.23   STEPS IN USING DYADS

1. With the text closed for the recaller and open for the listener, the recaller summarizes out loud everything that comes to mind. The summary should be a paraphrase and may be supplemented with a chart or drawing that illustrates major points.

2. After the recaller has completed the summary, the listener, with book open, takes on the job of strengthening the summary. The recaller does this by discussing important facts and concepts that were left out, making corrections, and relating present material to earlier material in order to understand it better.

3. Taking on the role of tutor, the recaller helps the listener correct, amplify and memorize the summary.

4. Recaller and listener switch roles and repeat the process using the next two pages of text.

Next the students pair off and exchange ideas. Finally, each pair shares its ideas with the entire class. Allowing think-time between questions and answers is a mandatory feature throughout the steps. Figure 7.24 shows the steps in a little more detail.

We sometimes carry with us an image of teacher-student exchanges that involve the teacher calling out questions in a rapid-fire manner while students all respond in an equally quick manner. There are certainly times when teachers want students to attain a certain automaticity in their responses; however, when you see these types of exchanges, by the very nature of the recitation format, teachers are asking students to respond to lower-level questions. In the steps described above, notice the importance of think-time. This allows students time in between responses to rehearse their original answer or a modified new one, create an analogy to explain their answer, or evaluate the answer just given by a class-mate. At this point, all students, not just a few, will have had the time and opportunity to share their ideas and hear the ideas of others.

Think–Pair–Share does not take much preparation time, is simple to conduct, and has numerous advantages. Besides interacting with subject ideas of merit, students receive practice with interpersonal and small-group learning skills, namely, sharing an idea, listening carefully, asking clarifying and probing questions, and paraphrasing. Using this method as described can improve the quality of responses you receive in a class period and increase the number of students capable of participating in meaningful ways.

FIGURE 7.24   STEPS IN USING THINK–PAIR–SHARE

1. Prepare students for the activity in three ways. First ask students to consider the value of wait time. Explain that everyone needs time to frame a response. It's only fair to give fellow-classmates time to "get an answer together," and three to five seconds is a minimum amount of time. Secondly, announce the signal you will use to move students from one step to the next. Thirdly, establish partner groupings and make sure partners are sitting next to each other.

2. Begin by posing a question or problem associated with the current curricular topic the class is studying. Students are to *think* silently to themselves. Allow think-time.

3. Give the signal for students to turn to their partners and *share* answers. You may also structure this step by requesting that students come to consensus, interview each other as experts, or jointly draw a cognitive map with major concept words connected with relationship lines (superordinate, subordinate, coordinate).

4. Give the signal again. Call on individual students to *share* their answers (or the answers of their partners) with the whole class. As before, be sure to allow think-time.

SUMMARY

Teachers use teaching strategies to help students construct the foundations of meaning. After choosing a strategy, teachers follow a series of steps that have been utilized by others or modify the steps to meet the unique needs of their students and the content. All the while they are scaffolding students' understanding and building on their background experiences while everyone interacts with text or other source materials and other learners. Our colleagues in the teaching profession have shared strategies in conferences, journals, and books that they have developed and perfected in classrooms.

From this growing array of field-tested strategies, we have chosen a select few that we feel will serve well a wide spectrum of student needs and interests. We made these selections on the basis of serving specific instructional purposes that are meaningful goals for any classroom teacher. These instructional purposes provided the outline of this chapter. The potential for student learning through these strategies is great. We urge you to become familiar with all of them, picking three or four to try out now during your period of initial teacher education. The caveats? Keep your lesson objectives in the foreground of your mind; choose teaching strategies that help you meet your objectives. And be flexible in strategy use. When a strategy fails to help you help students, stop and reflect on the causes of failure. Explore your alternatives by expanding your storehouse of strategies, keeping those that fit student needs, modifying others, and developing your own. After all, engaging students' minds is infinitely more important than slavishly following the steps of a teaching strategy.

The next chapter is a logical companion to this one. Since construction implies being actively involved in developing new information, we need learners who are actively involved and in control of their learning. If they are to become strategic learners, they must know strategies themselves, when to use them, and how to tailor them to fit present needs. Get ready to continue "exploring alternatives" as we think together about selecting learning strategies.

REFLECTIONS

1. Reread the conversation at the beginning of this chapter. What parts of Ginny Slater's story do you associate with specific components of the IDEAL decision-making model?
2. Look back at a specific effort you made in using one of the teaching strategies. Write a narrative of the mental steps that you went through as you decided on a strategy, used it, and then determined its effectiveness.
3. To paraphrase an old saying, "The best-laid plans designed by teachers sometimes go awry." Name several context variables that influence the success of a teaching strategy (they range from physical conditions in the room to attitudes of participants). To what degree can a teacher influence the effects of such variables?

TEACHER AS RESEARCHER

Prior Knowlege

Zakaluk, B., Samuels, S., & Taylor, B. (1986). A simple technique for estimating prior knowledge: Word association. *Journal of Reading, 30* (1), 56–60.

Knowing the adequacy and accuracy of students' prior knowledge enhances instructional decision making. Zakaluk, Samuels, and Taylor have developed a technique for estimating prior knowledge. Using a topic of your choosing, develop a prior knowledge worksheet using their technique and administer it to at least two people. Compare their scores and draw at least two implications for planning and teaching the topic.

Reciprocal Teaching

Alfassi, M. (1998). Reading for meaning: The efficacy of Reciprocal Teaching in fostering reading comprehension in high school students in remedial reading classes. *American Educational Research Journal, 35* (2), 309–332.

In an attempt to weigh the effects of two approaches to teaching remedial reading, the researcher uncovered related issues. First, summarize Alfassi's conclusions regarding the skill acquisition and reciprocal teaching approaches. Then identify the possible consequences of the different tests on the investigation's results and the implications for how remedial reading is taught.

Questioning the Author

Beck, I., McKeown, M., Sandora, C., Kucan, L., and Worthy, J. (1996). Questioning the Author: A yearlong classroom implementation to engage students with text. *The Elementary School Journal, 96* (4), 385–414.

This implementation study involved a social studies teacher, a reading/language arts teacher, and their twenty-three inner-city fourth grade students. First note how evidence regarding the effects of questioning the author was obtained. Then discuss evidence regarding teacher and student talk as well as student collaboration.

Jigsaw

Draper, R. (1997). Jigsaw: Because reading your math book shouldn't be a puzzle. *The Clearing House, 71* (1), 33–36.

With students at a field-experience school, follow the jigsaw procedures described by Draper (it's possible to adapt the math examples and problems to other subject matters). Have a co-teacher join your investigation as you both carefully observe the actions and conversations of two students as they participate in their expert and learning groups. Report your observations including differences between the students.

Selecting Materials

Teachers do research when they carefully select materials for students and themselves. Often these are written by teachers and either published commercially or shared in other ways (workshops, Internet, informal contact in the same school). "Adopt" a class of students (from a school field site or a hypothetical one from your imagination) and develop unit objectives for a topic in one curricular area. Use a Web browser, the ERIC document center, or a curriculum collection service like the Kraus Curriculum Development Library (see chapter 11 for more information on these last two resources) to locate and copy two or three units or lessons on the topic. Evaluate for (a) clarity and harmony with your objectives and (b) consistency among objectives, activities, and assessments (tests, portfolio plans, checklists, and rating scales).

CHAPTER **8**

Selecting Learning Strategies

CONVERSATION

It happened again, Terry thought. This was the third straight unit where his seventh-grade students had done poorly on their science vocabulary tests. The first two times, Terry had just assumed that the students were just getting back into the swing of things. He gave them the same "you're back in school, and it's time to buckle down" speech that his own teachers had given him in junior high. He still wasn't quite sure where the phrase "buckle down" came from, but he knew it meant that it was time to get to work. He also knew he needed to do something other than give them an inspirational lecture. Before he did anything, though, he needed to take a closer look at their tests to see where the problems were. He also wanted to talk to Marilyn, the other seventh-grade science teacher, and see if she could give him some ideas. . . .

"Marilyn, do you have a minute? I'd like to run some ideas by you about some things I've noticed about my students and their vocab tests."

"Sure, Terry, how can I help?"

"Well, I think what I need is for you to act as a sounding board for me. I've thought this through pretty carefully but I'm not sure if I'm missing something. Would you mind?"

"Be glad to. What's the problem?"

"I was getting worried and a little frustrated that students were doing so poorly on their vocabulary tests for the first several units. I spent a lot of time over the weekend looking at their tests from the most recent unit, and I tried to determine whether the vocabulary they were having trouble with were the 'big picture' terms or the words that they had to memorize that fell under them."

"So, you were seeing whether it was a 'concept' problem or a 'memorizing' problem? What did you find?"

"Definitely memorizing. Which is what led back to my old college methods book to see what kinds of strategies I could pull out that could help them to remember the terms better. You know, I probably should have sensed this before, but I thought they just weren't trying hard enough, weren't spending enough time going over the words. To be honest, I was also a little worried about all the time that it would take to teach some of the strategies we had done in methods courses. I was afraid I'd get behind, but I can't see much value in handing out these words each week if students are not going to be able to learn them."

"Gee, Terry, it sounds like you've covered a lot of thinking territory. I can really understand your concerns about the time that it takes to teach strategies. Think of it this way, though, by teaching the strategies now, early in the year, your students will be more likely to use them effectively throughout the year. I'm going to give you one piece of advice, too, something I learned as a new teacher. Less is more. It's better to teach a couple strategies that students can use over and over rather than a new strategy every week. So, what did you come up with?"

"Actually, I've been exploring alternative strategies that I know, and I found two that I thought would be helpful with the units coming up. One is Spatial Arrangement and the other is the Keyword strategy."

"Spatial Arrangement is one that I teach. My students seem to find that helpful in recalling factual information, and I've noticed that they sometimes use it in their other classes. I don't know Keyword, though. How does that work?"

"It's kind of neat. I was going to model the steps by using the word 'gymnosperm' and make up a silly word like 'gymnasium perm.' Once you do that, then you get the kids to focus on the new word. Since a gymnasium has walls but the gymnosperm doesn't have protective walls around its seed plant, I'd draw a picture of a gymnasium with all these little seeds with perms, really wild hair, and circle the whole picture in a big red circle with a diagonal line. So, they could associate the word with the gym that doesn't have walls. I figured I'd follow up by having them practice the steps of the strategy so that they could make it their own."

"Sounds great. I'd like to watch you do this if you wouldn't mind . . ."

DEVELOPING COMPETENCE

1. You are a student, and everyone knows that. But are you also a scholar? In your view, how is a scholar different from a student? Analyze our definitions of student and scholar. Do we agree with you?

2. How would you characterize your parents' assistance in helping you develop good study habits? Based on your memories of home and of those of your friends, add to the list of "keys to success" other ways that parents may help students by promoting good study habits.

3. What makes a liberal education "liberal" may be the low emphasis on memorizing information and the relatively high emphasis on reasoning with facts. Yet we make the case for teaching students how to memorize. Read our rationale with a critical eye. Do you agree with it?

4. You have years of experience taking class notes. Of the note-taking strategies described here, which have elements of how you currently take notes? What are those elements?

5. We argue that good students have a conscious "plan of attack" as they start to study. Think of someone who seemingly lacks intentional control of

his/her study. Assuming the person wants a suggestion, which of the methods of study we present would you offer? Why?

INTRODUCTION

In our teacher education classes, we introduce a variety of learning strategies to our students and suggest that they try them out as they study their college course work. They often come back to us and report their successes with the newly learned strategies. Invariably they also comment on the lack of learning strategy instruction in their elementary and secondary school days and ask, "Why didn't our teachers show us these strategies?" These students have gained a personal sense of the connection between strategy use and school achievement and are puzzled why teachers they like and respect neglected such an important part of their education.

Learning strategies refer to the techniques that students use to improve their understanding of material they are learning and reading. As we have engaged our own students in discussions about the different instructional roles teachers take on, we've uncovered several reasons why learning strategies have often been omitted in their experiences with lesson and unit presentations. The major reason seemed to be their own teachers' preoccupation with presenting the basic skills of reading and writing and the basic facts and concepts of the disciplines of English, social studies, science, and mathematics. In their zeal to have their students master these basics, teachers can sometimes forget that for most students the application of skills and the learning of subject matter beyond the school walls does not happen naturally or automatically. The other major reason that our students had not been, or could not remember being, exposed to learning strategies seemed to be that their teachers had expected them to have learned "how to do this" at some earlier time in their school experience. But with the mobility of students and the differing talents and foci of different teachers, that assumption is not necessarily either accurate or appropriate.

We are very aware that there are many demands on teachers' time, and that teachers always need to consider many factors as they plan and deliver lessons. There is no simple formula that is going to guarantee success for all students, and teachers will always need to balance coverage of material with helping students come to a deep understanding, the breadth and depth issues with which we dealt in chapter 3. However, even given this constraint, we make our college students aware that it is their responsibility to be certain that students have the learning skills necessary to succeed in their classes. When in doubt, it is better to teach a learning strategy than to assume that students already possess it.

In this chapter we will invite you to consider the differences between students and scholars, while emphasizing that one of the major differences is that scholars are able to overcome learning obstacles by choosing from a variety of strategies that they already possess. We will then introduce you to a variety of different learning strategies that you can explicitly teach your students to serve a number of school learning tasks. Finally, we challenge you to consider developing your own learning strategies to address specific learning situations that we have not addressed.

HELPING STUDENTS BECOME SCHOLARS

When we think of the word "scholar" an image comes to mind; it probably does for you, too. We have an image of a person deeply engrossed in thought with books opened and scattered about. And it may say something about us, but we also have a picture of someone older, with eyes that shine with a light of learning. So, imagine our surprise when we pulled our old dictionary off the shelf and looked up the word "scholar." The first definition, the most common usage, was "a learned or erudite person" (*American Heritage Dictionary*, 1973, p. 1162) just as our image had projected. The third definition, however, was "a pupil in elementary or Sunday school." Obviously this is an old usage of the word, but it certainly provides us with a way of thinking about students that may cause us to treat them in a different light and with higher expectations. After all, you certainly would treat "scholars" in your classroom differently from the way that you might treat your students if you thought of them as "kids."

Teachers and parents have a responsibility to help students become scholars. To explain this statement we need to draw a distinction. Students are individuals who attend school, do assignments, and take teachers' tests. They know the routines of their classrooms. In many ways, they fulfill our expectations as they perform school routines. Scholars, on the other hand, although they share these characteristics with students, have the outlook and the attributes of life-long learners. For them, loving to learn and knowing how to learn are reciprocal elements in their lives. They gain personal satisfaction from solving "mysteries," school-related ones and those that intrigue them outside of school. Their abilities to solve these mysteries increase as they add strategies to their personal repertoires and as they become more adept at using them for the appropriate purposes at the correct times. And as their strategy use becomes effective and habitual, they seek the pleasures of intellectual pursuits.

We begin this chapter by taking a close look at what teachers and parents can do to make scholars out of students, to move them toward becoming learned persons. To put this discussion in its proper context, however, we first put scholars and their student friends under the microscope. In our close-up look, we see implications for both school and home to empower students to take more control of and accept more responsibility for their own learning.

Scholars and Students

So that you can visualize the scholars we want in our schools, first picture Jamie, a typical student. When given a homework assignment, Jamie plods through the pages of the text. He runs his eyes over the print and turns the pages, working to achieve his goal of finishing the task as quickly as possible. He thinks of "studying" his textbook as something separate from learning; in the process he accumulates facts much like he collects stamps, adding each new one to his "collection," which he then puts away until he has something new again to add. Whether he's reading in social studies, science, math, or English, Jamie seldom changes his approach; he reads his science book in much the same way that he reads a short story in English, unaware that he is being both inefficient and unproductive in reading informational text in the same way that he does a narrative. And when his teacher asks him if he's well prepared and ready for a chapter test, he replies with assurance that he knows he "knows this stuff." And he honestly thinks that he is prepared and that he knows it well enough to do what will be expected of him. It's not hard then to understand his surprise and frustration when he receives a "D" as a grade.

Compare this profile of Jamie with that of his classmate, Hannah. As she begins the text assignment, she works through the material in her mind, consciously aware that she is sifting through details to arrive at the generalizations that provide the "big picture" of this particular chunk of content; she is constantly trying to connect what she is studying currently with what she has studied previously and what she knows. She also is sensitive to cues that her teacher provides, remembering the teacher announcing that the upcoming test will be mostly essay questions, which leads her to try to formulate possible test questions as she reads. Hannah sees studying as an integrative process, where her job is to combine her knowledge of the subject with knowledge from the text into a new creation. Recognizing that the text material could be organized into similarities and differences, she decides against using the strategies of memorization that she possesses and, from among others she knows, decides to use a compare/contrast notetaking system. And when asked if she's prepared for the test, she replies with confidence that she is. Unlike Jamie, when she receives her test back, Hannah is certainly not surprised by the "A" she has earned.

The differences between Jamie the student and Hannah the scholar are significant and are summarized in Figure 8.1. They are exaggerated for the purpose of illustration and differ in degree and combination from student to student. However, they typify the approaches to learning that we observe in most classrooms. Whereas Jamie is mentally passive and relatively uninvolved, Hannah jumps in and plays an active role in her own study. Regarding why he is studying, Jamie has no academic purpose in mind. In contrast, Hannah has a purpose, doing study-reading in preparation for a test and, moreover, she is conscious of her purpose. In his view, Jamie sees learning as the business of accumulating more and more facts in his fact bank while Hannah believes that to "own" knowledge she has to merge

FIGURE 8.1 CHARACTERISTICS OF SCHOLARS AND STUDENTS	
Students	Scholars
passive	active
without direction	purposeful
add information	integrate information
unaware of strategies	aware of strategies
wrongly predict success	correctly predict success

incoming with existing information. Jamie is not a strategic learner—that is, he has one learning strategy that he uses for all text reading. He rarely reflects on his own performance and is not aware that his one-strategy-fits-all-occasions approach is inappropriate. Nor is he aware that other people work with a repertoire of strategies. For her part, Hannah *is* strategic. Aware of her purpose, the nature of her task, her materials, and herself as a problem-solver, she deliberately chooses from the collection of learning strategies she possesses a notetaking system as the best alternative available to her. Finally, these two contrast greatly in terms of their perceptions of their likelihood of success. Like many younger and less academically mature students, Jamie is convinced that his study has prepared him for an exam only to find out that it hasn't. His underdeveloped metacognition has left him blissfully ignorant of the true state of his content mastery. Hannah accurately predicted her success. No doubt she attributes her mastery to strategy use and can articulate how and when to use her strategies. When strategies do not work as expected and confident that she can cope, she switches gears and tries something else.

Your goal is to help students adopt the attitudes and abilities of the scholar. This will not happen easily or all at once. Not only must you be aware that students need to be taught learning strategies, but you need to be confident that you, in fact, can teach these strategies. The time that you invest in teaching and reinforcing students' use of learning strategies will pay off many times over in increased achievement and greater confidence that your students will demonstrate.

Activity 8.1

Using the characteristics of scholars and students listed in Figure 8.1, develop a list of five to seven questions pertaining to school students' private study behaviors. Ask a classroom teacher to identify one effective independent studier and one who is relatively ineffective. Interview both students and record their answers to your questions. Summarize their responses together with selected student quotations and present them to your college class.

Guidelines for Teaching Learning Strategies

Step into most any school in the nation and ask for a copy of its mission statement and it will probably include a recommendation that students become lifelong learners (this refers to *all* students, including those with disabilities; see "Students with Disabilities" in the *Teacher as Researcher* section). Advocates of school reform (see the discussion in the Philosophies of Education section of chapter 2) from the private and public sectors almost always put "independence in learning" on their lists of how to make schools responsive to the needs of the information age. When you implement the following guidelines (see Figure 8.2), you will move these worthy recommendations into everyday reality for the students that you have in your classrooms.

Integrate Strategy Instruction into Lessons Plan to teach learning strategies concurrently with subject matter. This approach is much more effective than

---

FIGURE 8.2   GUIDELINES FOR TEACHING LEARNING STRATEGIES

1. Integrate strategy instruction into lessons.

2. Encourage students to modify strategies.

3. Debrief students on their strategy use.

4. Provide ongoing support.

5. Plan and teach sound lessons.

---

teaching study skills in isolation (this is the attitude of content reading classes in schools of education; see "Integrated Strategy Illustration" in the *Teacher as Researcher* section). When Mr. Juarez wants his fourth-grade geography students to memorize the names of the Great Lakes, he shares with them the mnemonic HOMES for remembering Huron, Ontario, Michigan, Erie, and Superior. At the same time he models a procedure and provides practice time for the teaching and learning of the steps in creating mnemonics. Mr. Juarez appreciates the fact that procedural knowledge, the "how to" of learning information, is best learned in the immediate context of subject matter instruction. Students can see the functional nature of that strategy and are much more likely to attend to it and use it for their immediate gain.

Incidentally, Mr. Juarez will probably limit the number of strategies to four or five that he will focus on throughout the year, believing that mastery of a few is preferable to superficial coverage of many. If you think about the power of this, however, by reinforcing the strategies students have already learned and adding just a few new ones each year, a school with other teachers like Mr. Juarez could devise a plan to help students build an impressive collection of strategies over the course of several years.

Encourage Students to Modify Strategies   After you have taught your students a learning strategy using either the Reciprocal Teaching or Think-Aloud teaching strategies (these were discussed in detail in chapter 7), make sure they have ample opportunities to practice the strategy so that they become familiar with its rationale and procedural steps. While providing this practice, take time to listen to students' reactions to the strategy as they have learned it. For instance, Miss Sampson taught Idea Line, a basic outlining procedure, to her lower-track freshman English class. When she was satisfied that most students had a reasonable command of it, she conducted one of her "class forums," informal conversations about class procedures, student-teacher interactions, and the like. During one of these times, she asked students their opinion of Idea Line. Although many said it was working well for them just the way it had been taught, others questioned the need for certain steps, and suggested that they alter the strategy somewhat, by either omitting or combining some steps. Miss Sampson reacted positively to the suggestions, commending students for their inventiveness, and encouraging students to try the modifications if they chose to do so the next time that they needed to use their outlining skills. What Miss Sampson knows, and what we want to impress upon you, is that strategy use is idiosyncratic. There is no one correct way to study, and once you give students a strategy, you should also give them the freedom to adjust it to fit their personal styles or needs.

Debrief Students on Their Strategy Use   When students think about how they learn, they become better learners. Ms. Taylor-Hall acts on this truism when she teaches a learning strategy. She pauses at different points in her instruction to debrief her students. That is, she asks questions and facilitates a discussion from her students about how they are experiencing the use of a particular strategy. She asks questions like: "What steps are easiest for you to do?" " Which steps are the hardest to remember?" "In what other classes might this strategy be useful?" As students answer her questions and as they learn to ask them of themselves, they become increasingly metacognitive, aware of the usefulness and limitations of each strategy.

Debriefing can also occur after students have completed a task, like memorizing facts for a quiz, taking lecture notes, or doing a research paper. How did using the strategy affect their performance on the quiz, the clarity and thoroughness of their lecture notes, and the efficiency of conducting research? Debriefing in these situations will reveal problems you may need to address, but it will also be the opportune time to help some students attribute their strategy-mediated successes to strategy use. Nothing succeeds like success, and when students recognize that their strategy efforts have paid off, they are much more likely to make the investment again.

Provide Ongoing Support   Trying out a new way of learning can be a scary proposition for some students. Realizing this, Mr. Toshiro has tried to create a classroom climate that makes his students willing to take the risk of adopting new learning strategies. During initial learning, he routinely has students work as partners or in small groups, knowing that there is comfort and security in working with others. By debriefing on problems and successes in small groups or in a whole-class setting, students can hear their fellow students' concerns and know they are not alone. In addition, Mr. Toshiro has students keep a section in their class notebooks called "Learning Strategies." In it they write entries about their efforts to make new strategies their own. Mr. Toshiro writes back, complimenting their efforts, answering their concerns, and making friendly suggestions for future reference. These entries also give him feedback about how adept students are becoming on their own and how much teacher direction they may still need. These supports continue throughout the year as he prompts students to apply the procedures and evaluate their progress.

Plan and Teach Sound Lessons   One of the most important things you can do to help students master learning strategies is to plan and teach sound lessons covering meaningful content. For example, when at the beginning of a lesson you consistently help students activate schema related to the topic, you plant the notion that skimming over a chapter, noting headings, and asking themselves, "What do I already know about these things?" is a good way to undertake a reading assignment. Or, when you have class discussions over new material and repeatedly ask about the source of an answer ("Was that answer in your head or did you find it in the story?"), you have paved the way for students to more easily learn QARS, a study method on question-answer relationships described later in this chapter. As a more competent learner in the classroom, you should provide students with a learning role model. Providing lesson structures that students can mentally "imitate" as they attempt to own the new learning strategies you teach can be a very strong influence on their abilities to internalize these strategies. Nourish your budding scholars by putting time and thought into your lesson preparation!

Parents Supporting Scholars

As we noted in chapter 1, there are a wide variety of family arrangements today. (There are also different styles of parenting. Possible connections between parental styles and students' learning strategies is the focus of Boveja's study, which you'll see in the "Parenting Styles" section of the *Teacher as Researcher* section of this chapter.) All parental figures, however, want the same thing for their children as do the schools: social and academic achievement. They know that success in school and in life for the children in their charges will depend on the ability to get along with others, develop academic concepts and generalizations, and master the strategies and skills that belong to lifelong learners. However, many interested, and potentially cooperative and helpful, parents are unaware of ways they may be able to contribute to the development of good study habits in their children. The International Reading Association distributes the brochure "Studying: A Key to Success . . . Ways Parents Can Help" that was authored by Ann Erickson, reading director for the St. Peter, Minnesota Public Schools. We present an excerpt from that brochure (see Figure 8.3), which we have modified slightly. If you are interested in using the brochure, quantities may be purchased at a nominal cost from The International Reading Association, 800 Barksdale Drive, PO Box 8139, Newark, Delaware 19714–8139, USA.

Students need to have specific learning strategies reinforced at home as well. The strategies you'll read about in this chapter and others that you teach need to be applied by your scholars as they do homework assignments, prepare for tests, and conduct the research needed for special projects. In order for parents to monitor and encourage the use of such strategies, they must first know the strategies themselves. We urge you to take the initiative in reaching out to parents in efforts to make them learning partners with their children. You can open lines to parents by sending home letters or newsletters that describe strategies their children are learning in your class. Also take direct measures. Seek the support of your building administrator and school counselor in conducting tutoring sessions for parents where you demonstrate strategies, using materials and topics of interest to adults, and where they can practice in small groups with the parents of their children's classmates. Schedule such sessions before or after school, during back-to-school nights, or in conjunction with other school events, such as academic fairs, class scheduling, and standardized test interpretation meetings. Moreover, be creative with regard to where the sessions are held. Schools may not be accessible to parents who do not have their own transportation. To overcome the problem, ask permission to use facilities closer to their homes—churches, recreation centers,

---

FIGURE 8.3   MODIFIED VERSION OF PARENT INFORMATION

Studying: A Key to Success . . . Ways Parents Can Help.

- *Find the best time for studying.* Have your child keep a time chart for one week. Help him or her record activities during non-sleeping, eating, attending school, or working hours. Then talk about times that could best be used for studying.
- *Eliminate common distractions.* These include people moving about, younger children playing, cluttered work areas, television, music, computer games, and "surfing" the Internet.
- *Avoid common interruptions.* Have a family member take messages and numbers so phone calls can be returned later. Once definite study times have been established, your student can alert friends regarding available times for visits. Avoid asking your son or daughter to do unscheduled chores during study times.
- *Provide physical conditions that help concentration.* A good light, the right room temperature, and a table or desk with adequate space are necessary. Also help your youngster find a study posture—sitting, lying down—that maintains alertness.
- *Keep supplies handy.* Keep "tools of the trade"—pencils, pens, rulers, scissors, etc.—together in one place, like a box that can be moved from place to place or a drawer or shelf. Supplies should include reference books like a dictionary and a thesaurus. Shop used book stores and discount stores for an atlas, a set of encyclopedias, and an almanac.

---

libraries, or even rooms in stores and office buildings. Civic leaders, public officials, and business leaders are aware of the importance of education to society and of their obligation to work with schools to assist students in realizing their learning potential. Reach out to them to help you help parents and students.

The more parents know about the strategies their children will be using, the more likely it will be that you will get the support from home that reinforces what you are doing in school.

TEACHING LEARNING STRATEGIES: A REMINDER

It is not enough just to describe learning strategies to students. As one of our favorite education professors impressed on us, "Telling is not teaching, and teaching is not telling." Strategy instruction must include teacher talk, of course, but it must go beyond your simply saying "do this." You will need to talk through the steps in these strategies, demonstrate them using content that is significant to your lesson objectives and, maybe most important of all, engage in lively interchanges with students about how and why they should take the time to learn some of these strategies. The learning strategies (see Figure 8.4) we offer in this chapter, along with the others you will gather and use throughout your teaching careers, must be taught in interactive ways. In other words, you will need to use a teaching strategy,

FIGURE 8.4	LEARNING STRATEGIES GROUPED BY PURPOSE
Purpose	Improving students' memorizing skills
Strategies	Spatial Arrangement Keyword Acronyms
Purpose	Developing students' note-taking skills
Strategies	Idea Line Palmatier's Unified Note-taking System (PUNS)
Purpose	Developing students' ability to summarize
Strategies	Four-Sentence Summary Guided Reading and Summarizing Procedure (GRASP)
Purpose	Improving students' research skills
Strategies	I-Search Team Research
Purpose	Improving students' methods of studying
Strategies	Question Answer Relationships (QARS) HEART Predict-Organize-Rehearse-Practice-Evaluate (PORPE)

like the ones you read about in chapter 7, to teach students how they can use a learning strategy, so that they can become more effective and efficient scholars.

We presented two such teaching strategies in the preceding chapter. Reciprocal Teaching engages both teachers and students as they take turns executing the various strategic components that they are teaching and learning; this strategy frames instruction in a true dialogue among learners. In using this strategy, students become more aware of the thought processes that guide their learning, and they discover when and where to use the strategies. You also learned about the Think-Aloud strategy. When you use this approach, you model for students a series of steps that *you* use for solving problems or overcoming obstacles. The best explanations contain explicit, detailed information that will describe the steps of the learning strategies that follow as you demonstrate how to use a particular strategy to improve students' learning of some type of content with which they will be working. The actual demonstration, or think-aloud, is followed by teacher-guided student practice, with re-explanations to partner groups, the whole class, or, when necessary, to individuals. In both of these strategies, you will begin with a great deal of teacher-directed activity, but the goal for each is to provide *all* students with ways of working with the material on their own. (*All* students includes those with disabilities. See the Scanlon et al. item in the "Students with Disabilities" section of *Teacher as Researcher*.) Now, as you proceed with this chapter, keep these two approaches to teaching learning strategies in mind and refer back to chapter 7 for full descriptions as needed.

IMPROVING STUDENTS' MEMORIZING SKILLS

American schools stress, far too much many would argue, the intake and recall of facts. You can probably testify to the frequency of tasks requiring memorization from your own experiences in K-12 classrooms. We favor attaining a balance between lower level abilities, such as memorization, and higher level, critical thinking skills to better reflect the wide range of learning situations in life. At the same time, we know that recall is important for many tests (teacher-made and standardized), as well as discussions that follow the reading of a chapter. Recalling information is also important as a foundation for forming concepts and generalizations. Therefore, in this section, we will examine three strategies that will aid your students when they are asked to memorize.

When learning new material we often rely on our senses. Think about how a newborn child relates the sight of a mother's face and the sound of her voice with security and care. Although a newborn needs to see her mother's face and hear her voice numerous times before this connection is made, it is done with the help of the senses. As a student, you might have used notecards to help you learn new vocabulary words. By writing the vocabulary word on one side of the notecard and the definition on the other side, you were able to use them as flashcards. In addition to reading the new vocabulary word, you may have said the word aloud to help you recall it on your test. If you did all of these steps, you engaged three of your senses: visual by seeing the word, auditory by hearing yourself say the word aloud, and kinesthetic by writing the word out. The following strategies rely on the use of the senses in order to improve students' ability to memorize the content that they must work with in the course of your lessons and units (see Activity 8.2).

Activity 8.2

Choose a strategy for improving students' memorizing skills. Teach it to several undergraduate students who are enrolled in courses with recall type examinations—and who are willing to participate in a follow up exercise. After they have learned the strategy and used it in preparation for an exam, interview them and audio-record their comments. What were their impressions as they were learning the strategy? How easy or hard was implementing it with actual course material? Would they use it again? Play the recording in your college class and invite discussion.

Spatial Arrangement

The first strategy, Spatial Arrangement (Bellezza 1984), is based on the sense of sight (see Figure 8.5). It involves visualizing a symbol that helps students to link their prior experiences with new ideas. This type of linking helps students to build a richer schemata for the topic.

FIGURE 8.5   STEPS FOR USING SPATIAL ARRANGEMENT

Students will:

1. Identify words, phrases, dates, etc., to be remembered.

2. Choose a spatial arrangement on and around which to place the identified items.

3. Place the items on, around the symbol.

4. Review the spatial arrangement, explaining it to yourself.

For example, if students were studying a science unit on conducting research and a lesson within that unit on the scientific method, a student might identify these phrases—create hypothesis, test hypothesis, collect data, and check results—as worthy of remembering. Since one of the tools they will be using is a microscope, students could draw a simple outline of a microscope as a symbol associated with scientific inquiry. Next, the student would write the phrase "scientific method" on the "base" of the microscope while the steps in the scientific method are placed on different parts of the microscope (see Figure 8.6). Finally, the student explains the arrangement in private and then to a friend or parent. You might also allow students to present their spatial arrangements to the class while explaining their thought processes. This will enable the students to learn the material while concurrently becoming more familiar with the strategy.

FIGURE 8.6   EXAMPLE OF SPATIAL ARRANGEMENT

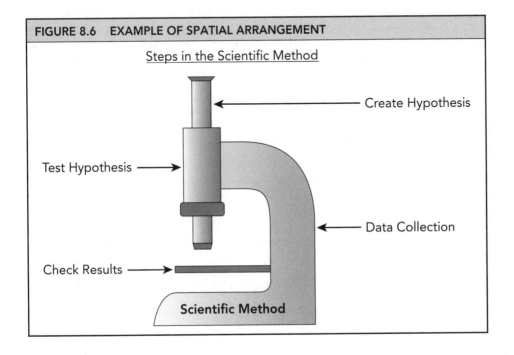

Steps in the Scientific Method

Create Hypothesis

Test Hypothesis

Data Collection

Check Results

Scientific Method

Spatial Arrangement can be used in all subject areas and works for a wide variety of types of material. The power of the graphic tool for remembering can provide students with a way of "seeing" even when the tool is not there. At the outset of teaching this strategy, you may provide students with a specific graphic tool. Later, you should encourage them to use this strategy with other material and to share with the class the kinds of graphics they have designed. Teaching your students this basic memorization strategy will enable them to organize new material in unique and personal arrangements that will aid them in the recall of needed information.

Keyword

The second strategy for memorization is Keyword (Mastropieri & Scruggs, 1991). Some students are visual learners while others are auditory learners. The Keyword strategy enables students to combine visual learning with auditory in order to rehearse new information and commit it to memory (see Figure 8.7). The goals of Keyword are to increase initial learning and aid in the retention of new, unfamiliar vocabulary words.

For example, the word "scofflaw" means "criminal," but a student might be reminded of a word like coleslaw, so coleslaw could become the keyword. After choosing a keyword, the student tries to link coleslaw (the keyword) to the definition of scofflaw (the response). Students can accomplish this in many different ways—by writing a sentence, creating a visual image, or drawing a picture in which coleslaw and scofflaw are combined. By creating a sentence such as "That person in handcuffs said, 'I do not like coleslaw,'" or drawing a picture in which a person in a bright orange suit and handcuffs is eating coleslaw, you relate the keyword to the response. By working with these images and actually talking aloud as they do, students will create powerful connections that will help them retrieve the definition from the sentence or picture they have created. In the coleslaw example, the student had to define scofflaw, so that student thought of coleslaw first. Next, after coleslaw had been retrieved, the student recreated the sentence or picture. Then, with the help of the sentence or picture, the student remembered that the definition of scofflaw is a criminal.

If your students initially think that the keyword is the definition, scofflaw *is* coleslaw, correct the problem by leading them back on track with a series of ques-

---

FIGURE 8.7 STEPS IN USING KEYWORD

Students will:

1. *Reconstruct*—Find a word that sounds like the new vocabulary word and is already familiar.

2. *Relate*—Link the keyword to the desired response by talking through the relationship.

3. *Retrieve*—Recall the word from memory.

tions and comments. Ask them who said he didn't like coleslaw, in regard to the sentence, or who was eating the coleslaw, in regard to the picture. Remind your students that the keyword is not the definition of the new vocabulary word but a word helping them retrieve the correct definition.

Using the Keyword strategy becomes a little tougher when the vocabulary words move from concrete objects, like our example above, to more abstract ideas and concepts. Although the steps are the same (reconstructing, relating, and retrieving), the strategy becomes more involved because the vocabulary is harder to visualize and the definitions are longer and more complex. Mastropieri and Scruggs recommend that you identify one instance of the new abstract word and then make that instance as concrete as possible. Then, show that instance interacting with the keyword in a sentence or picture. For example, consider the word "vituperation," which is an abstract word meaning "speaking abusively towards someone."

Here again students will follow the same steps. They will first find a keyword. For example, "operation" might work because it sounds like vituperation and is a more familiar word. Then, they "relate" by creating a sentence or picture that links the keyword (operation) with the definition (speaking abusively towards someone). A sentence could be, "The doctor yelled at the patient, 'You have to have this operation!'" or a picture in which a doctor is yelling at a patient during an operation. Finally, remembering the keyword (operation), the sentence of the doctor yelling or the picture of the doctor yelling at his patient and then remembering that "vituperation" means "speaking abusively towards someone," students can retrieve this information on a test. As you lead your students through this lesson, remind them that this is only one example of vituperation and can mean more than a doctor being abusive to a patient. After your students have mastered this example, you may want to provide them with other related examples. Vituperation could be an adult talking to a child, a boss talking to an employee, or a customer talking to a waitress.

In ways similar to Spatial Arrangement, Keyword helps the student organize new material and have it readily available for recall. However, unlike Spatial Arrangement, Keyword incorporates the sense of sound into the strategy. Allowing students to see as well as hear the information helps them remember information at a greater success rate.

Acronyms

Using acronyms is the final strategy we suggest teaching your students to help their memorization skills (see Figure 8.8). Acronyms use both sight and sound to help students memorize groups of words. Acronyms are words formed out of the first letters of the words that need to be memorized. An acronym used to help memorize the colors in the rainbow is ROY G BIV, which helps students remember that the colors are red, orange, yellow, green, blue, indigo, and violet, in that order.

In teaching this for the first few times, write down the words that need to be memorized on the board or overhead. But as students become more adept with the strategy, encourage them to determine the most important words. For example, in a fifth-grade social studies class, students needed to identify at least three

---

FIGURE 8.8 STEPS IN USING ACRONYMS

Students will:

1. Identify the words in the list of facts, names, events, etc., to be recalled.

2. Underline the first letter of each word.

3. Arrange the letters to form a pronounceable word (whether the word is "real" or a nonsense word is a matter of choice).

---

acts passed by British Parliament during the American Revolution. One student identified: Stamp Act, Intolerable Acts, and Townshend Act. This student then underlined the "S" in Stamp, the "I" in Intolerable, and the "T" in Townshend and moved these three letters to a new place on the board. The student created a word out of the letters that were underlined. The "S," "I," and "T" formed the word sit, which helped the student remember that the Stamp Act, Intolerable Acts, and Townshend Act were three acts the British Parliament passed.

An offshoot of acronyms is choosing the first letter of the terms to be memorized and creating a sentence with those letters. An example comes from a music class in which the students needed to memorize the keys on the music scale. The keys are "E," "G," "B," "D," and "F." Students used the letters to create the sentence, "*Every Good Boy Does Fine.*" The use of acronyms or a spin-off of that strategy will help your students polish their memorization skills by encouraging them to chunk a number of separate pieces of information into a more meaningful whole unit, like a sentence or word.

There is no denying the importance of recall in school learning. However we want students to learn more than memorization strategies and be able to retain the new information for long periods of time rather than just for the test. The Spatial Arrangement, Keyword, and Acronym learning strategies provide students with learning tools that will enable them to connect prior knowledge with new knowledge and become better learners. And while the skills that students develop to improve their ability to memorize will help them to do well in a variety of testing situations, remember to help students see the value in knowing these facts by having them work with them in meaningful ways in the course of your teaching.

DEVELOPING STUDENTS' NOTETAKING SKILLS

We ask students to take notes because it helps them learn subject matter. To take good notes, students must employ a variety of thinking processes. Depending on the strategies they use, notetaking can require the skills of selecting, condensing, organizing, and paraphrasing material. As students take notes from a book or lecture, they make personal sense of new material. Later, when they review their notes, they rehearse the ideas initially processed and make them even more their own.

The major tasks in notetaking are distinguishing between major and minor ideas and becoming aware of the coordination and subordination of thoughts. Because of these demands, we suggest that early grade students as well as second language learners, those with learning difficulties, and most slow-moving secondary school learners be taught informal notetaking strategies, leaving the multiple major-minor relationships of a formal system to the middle grades and above (see Activity 8.3).

Activity 8.3

Videotape yourself teaching a note-taking strategy to students. Interrupt the playback in your college class when colleagues raise their hands to identify the following: dialogue and actions involving thinking processes (coordination and subordination of thoughts, for example); the teacher debriefing students during instruction; conversation related to the psychology of notetaking.

Idea Line

Contributed by Donald Durrell (1956), the Idea Line strategy is an informal approach to notetaking that has several advantages over some more traditional methods. It reduces complexity by using single words and phrases to represent concepts and generalizations. It simplifies the major-minor idea distinction by listing ideas in vertical form, and it eases the intimidation of filling a whole sheet of plain paper by having students work on one-quarter panel of a notepage at a time (see Figure 8.9).

FIGURE 8.9   STEPS IN USING IDEA LINE

Students will:

1. Fold an 8½-by-11-inch paper into fourths (lengthwise) so that only one panel is showing at a time. The folded paper should resemble an accordion as they fold it in half and then in half again.

2. Holding the extended sheet lengthwise, draw a horizontal line an inch from the top across the paper.

3. Divide their reading assignment into sections (by section, column, several paragraphs, page, etc.). Each section (however defined) will be "outlined" on one panel only.

4. List (1, 2, 3, etc.) in a column the most important words in the section. One guideline when deciding which are the most important words to choose is to think about writing a telegram. "What is the smallest number of words that I need in order to get the message across?" Another guideline would be to ask yourself, "What words would the author think are essential?"

5. Choose the single most important word from the completed column and put a star beside it. Rewrite that word on the top line. (What students have now done is identify and categorize the major and minor ideas as represented by single words.)

FIGURE 8.10 IDEA LINE FOR SOCIAL STUDIES CLASS			
Man's Story	Old Stone Age	New Stone Age	Modern Man
1. Dinosaurs	1. Glaciers	*1. New Stone Age	1. Bronze
2. Geologists	2. Primitive Man	2. Axes, Hammers	2. Migrations
3. 100,000 Years	3. Brain	3. Pastoral	*3. Modern Man
*4. Man's Story	4. Artists	4. Nomad	4. Languages
	5. Hunters	5. Villages	5. Thinking
	*6. Old Stone Age		

Figure 8.10 shows an Idea Line that was developed by a student in a low-ability world history class. The selection outlined is from the chapter "From Savagery to Civilization." Notice that, while the words listed won't necessarily provide a great deal of detail for an outside reader, they appear to identify some of the major categories that were dealt with in the text. Even without having read a similar selection in years, you are probably able to remember back to some of your own prior experiences with these topics, and the single words may have jogged some pieces of information that you haven't thought about in a great deal of time. For the student who created the notes, obviously these will be even more meaningful.

One other advantage in using this strategy is that students can use the Idea Line to test their recall. Working on one panel at a time, students cover the main idea and attempt to recall the details. Conversely, with the details covered, they strive to remember the main idea. For further reinforcement, students can use their notes to write short summary paragraphs. They expand the main idea word or phrase into a topic sentence and expand the details into supporting matter.

Palmatier's Unified Notetaking System (PUNS)

A more formal approach to notetaking is Palmatier's Unified Notetaking System (PUNS), which was devised by Robert Palmatier (1973). PUNS provides students with a notetaking strategy that integrates the lecture, or the in-class part of students' notes, with the text or reading aspect of the class. Like the Idea Line, PUNS minimizes the major-minor idea distinction by listing ideas down the left side of a notebook page. Students are discouraged from using the back of the paper, which again limits the intimidation of trying to fill both sides of the paper. This strategy also provides an easy, systematic way in which students can organize their notes and then use them as a study guide come test time (see Figure 8.11).

Figure 8.12 is an excerpt from a student's high school biology notebook that shows how using PUNS would look in action. This student recorded notes from a lecture on a bird's nervous system. Notes such as the cerebellum "gives birds muscle coordination" and "enables it to fly," "take off and land," and "drink from

---

FIGURE 8.11   STEPS IN USING PUNS

Students will:

1. *Record*. Draw a three-inch margin on one side of an 8½-by-11-inch piece of notebook paper. Record notes from the class lecture to the right of the margin using an outline form that isolates the main topics. Leave space between topics if there is information that may be missing. Be sure to number each page as notes are taken.

2. *Organize*. Add two sections to the notes as soon as possible after the lecture. Place labels inside the left margin that act as headers and describe information in the notes. Next, insert supplemental information from the textbook into the notes. Use the back of the paper if more space is needed.

3. *Study*. Remove all pages from the three-ring binder and lay them on top of each other so that only the left margin is showing. Use the labels in the margin to recall as much information about that topic as you can. Also, use the labels to simulate test questions. Check recall by lifting the page and reading the information to the right of the margin. Set a page aside after the material on it has been studied.

FIGURE 8.12   STUDENT EXCERPT OF PUNS IN A BIOLOGY CLASS

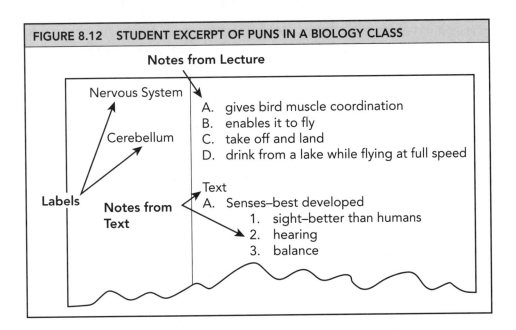

a lake while flying at full speed" appeared down the right side of their notebook pages. For the content being studied, the student placed the superordinate label of "Nervous System" in the left margin of the notebook paper. When this student later read or reread the text, she included the note that the best developed senses in birds are sight, hearing, and balance and that a bird's sight is better than humans. After finishing the unit on birds and before the biology test, this student studied her notes on the various internal systems of birds by placing the notebook pages on top of each other displaying the labels in the left-hand margin. Labels in the left margin included nervous system, digestion, respiration, and circulation. She could then test herself in much the same way we suggested in using the Idea Line notes for study.

As a further study strategy as they prepare for objective tests, you may want to suggest that your students shuffle the pages together so that they study the information at random as it may appear on a multiple-choice, true-false, and/or matching test. On the other hand, for essay tests, suggest that they group the pages together by similar labels, which can help them predict essay questions and give practice in writing answers. Obviously, if you know your tests will be a combination of both, you will want to cue your students that they would benefit by using both methods.

PUNS is a notetaking strategy that is easily taught and learned. Its flexibility allows students to record notes taken in the classroom and notes taken from the textbook. By combining information sources into a single study document, learning is made more efficient and effective. One last suggestion for you as you model notetaking strategies and subsequently work with students as they take notes: take time to discuss with them the psychology of notetaking. On what occasions do people take notes? In what ways are they helped by their notes? In school settings, should students put down notes from memory after the initial reading, or is it better to keep referring to the text for accuracy? What are some dos and don'ts of reviewing notes? This type of discussion can provide students with new frameworks to use as they consider their own metacognitive thinking as it relates to studying and using strategies.

DEVELOPING STUDENTS' ABILITY TO SUMMARIZE

A summary is a short statement that conveys the essence of a longer piece of discourse. In order to condense information, students must recognize important ideas and choose which details to include and which to eliminate. They must paraphrase an author's words, notice how material is organized, and decide to retain the original pattern of organization or impose their own structure, such as time order, cause-effect, compare-contrast, problem-solution.

Summary writing is an essential skill in composing book reports, research reports, and term papers. Moreover, teachers are increasingly employing summaries as a learning tool in day-to-day instruction. The act of constructing a summary helps students clarify information and see its internal logic, which results in their coming to greater understanding and longer retention of content they study. Therefore, students should be given a number of opportunities throughout the course of a unit to put into their own words the condensed version of the content they have been studying. You will want to consider having students write brief summaries during a lesson in order to clarify an essential concept or near the end of a lesson or unit to underscore the significance of a large amount of material.

Although it is a valuable study technique, summarization is a complex strategy to master. Applying this strategy depends in part on the material; summarizing in history often differs from summarizing in science. In addition, students must coordinate the skills of selecting and ignoring, organizing and retelling, all of which require differing degrees of cognitive sophistication. Therefore, you must also take into account students' levels of mental readiness as you decide which summarization strategies to present. Your and their initial efforts should be simple. The first strategy we offer is for primary grade students and others who can profit from an easy-to-learn formula for identifying central ideas and condensing them into a concise form. The second is for more capable younger students, as well as those in middle and secondary schools (see Activity 8.4).

Activity 8.4

Distribute copies of your plan for teaching a summarization strategy to your peers. Have them evaluate it on the criteria that apply: provision for guiding students in paraphrasing, retaining or creating a pattern of organization, selecting and ignoring information, condensing and evaluating material.

Four-Sentence Summary

Originally called "The Great American One-Sentence Summary" by its creator, this strategy has students create a summary of four sentences, each of which is a response to four sequential directives (Stanfill, 1978). Have students use it after their own reading or after hearing a story or non-fiction piece. Doing so will give them practice in selecting important ideas from source material (see Figure 8.13).

Under the first heading, "What are you summarizing," students write a sentence that summarizes the topic. For example, in a language arts class which has read the book *Lilly's Purple Plastic Purse* by Kevin Henkes (1996), one student

---

FIGURE 8.13   STEPS IN USING THE FOUR-SENTENCE SUMMARY

Students will:

1. Identify the topic being summarized. To begin, make four columns on a sheet of paper. Working from left to right, head the columns with these questions:

   "What are you summarizing?"

   "What does it begin with?"

   "What is in the middle?"

   "How did it end?"

2. Respond to each of the questions in a complete sentence.

wrote, "This book is about Lilly and how she loved school and her teacher, Mr. Slinger." Under the second heading, "What does it begin with?" he wrote, "Lilly went to school and told us why she loved it and her teacher." Continuing to the next heading, he stated that "Lilly got into trouble when she showed everyone her new purse and sunglasses without her teacher's permission." Finally, under the last heading, the student answered by writing that "Lilly went home mad at Mr. Slinger but realized she was wrong and apologized to him the next day."

As an alternative, you can teach students to roll these four sentences into a one-sentence summary. Limit them to the use of one "and" and encourage them to use "ends with" for the fourth step in the strategy. Using the *Lilly's Purple Plastic Purse* example, the one-sentence summary might be, "*Lilly's Purple Plastic Purse* is a book about a girl who loves school and her teacher, gets into trouble and becomes angry at him, but in the end she realizes she was wrong to be angry."

As we mentioned earlier, summarization is valuable in a variety of learning situations. The earlier in their schooling that students receive instruction on when to use this strategy, the better off they will be in the future. A strategy like the Four-Sentence Summary can be employed at the early grade levels and will prepare students for more complex summarization strategies such as GRASP.

Guided Reading And Summarizing Procedure (GRASP)

Guided Reading And Summarizing Procedure (GRASP) is a learning strategy meant for students who are ready for more advanced applications of summarization skills (Hayes 1989). It challenges students to condense, paraphrase, and evaluate the new material they are learning. GRASP also sharpens students' recall, organizational, and critical thinking abilities (see Figure 8.14).

After reading an article on "Healthy Lives," students used the GRASP strategy by first writing down all the information they could remember. In effect, this was a private recall exercise. As they recorded this recalled information, students cued themselves and remembered additional points from the article (see Figure 8.15). They then proceeded to reread the text selection trying to clarify their first understandings of what the article contained. This step helped students to polish

---

FIGURE 8.14   STEPS IN USING GRASP

Students will:

1. *Read the text.* In the initial reading, try to remember all the information encountered.

2. *Reread the text.* Reread the text and clarify all the information remembered from the first reading.

3. *Organize recalled information.* Identify major topics into which the information can be grouped.

4. *Turn grouped information into sentences in a paragraph.*

FIGURE 8.15 INITIAL GATHERING OF INFORMATION IN GRASP		
"Healthy Lives"		
Regular sleep	balanced diet	exercise frequently
No tobacco or drug use	8–8 ounce cups of water	breathing exercises
Vitamin and mineral supplements	drink moderately	

both recall and critical thinking skills. For example, one student in the health class remembered that the article said to exercise every day, but he had forgotten how long it said to do so. The second reading prompted him to recall this fact, and he added it to the other information.

As students began to organize the information, they noted that the article mentioned various types of food people should eat to remain healthy, so they grouped those foods into a "nutrition" category. They placed the remaining information in other appropriate groups (see Figure 8.16). In the final step, our health students first wrote a summarizing sentence for each group of information, while keeping in mind the rules of summarization: include only important information, compress information, and add words or phrases that are needed to provide clarity and coherence (Brown & Day, 1983). Students then wrote a summary paragraph that included as many sentences as there were categories of recalled data.

Working from the health information, one student summarized in the following way: "Living a healthy life includes being conscious of nutrition, managing stress, and avoiding harmful substances. Being nutrition conscious means eating a balanced diet, drinking enough water, and making sure you get enough vitamins and minerals. Managing stress levels includes regular exercise, getting enough sleep, and using breathing exercises. Avoiding tobacco, drugs, and excessive amounts of alcohol also helps you live a healthy life."

An integral part of teaching summarization is class discussion. When you model a summarization strategy and especially when students imitate you or model the strategy for each other, encourage them to talk to you and with each other. Have them examine each other's summaries and note differences among

FIGURE 8.16 ORGANIZED INFORMATION USING GRASP		
"Healthy Lives"		
Nutrition	Stress Management	Harmful Substances
Balanced diet	Regular exercise	No smoking
64 ounces of water	Regular sleep	Moderate alcohol
Vitamin and mineral supplements	Breathing exercises	No drug use

them. What thought processes did they follow? What difficulties did they experience? Being metacognitive helps them understand the nature of summaries and their composition. Our last note: Learning to be a good summarizer doesn't happen overnight. Require summaries throughout the school year. Each time the need to summarize occurs, remind students of a specific strategy and have them recall the steps in the strategy, reminding and correcting as necessary. Encourage individuals to modify steps when they have good alternatives, and support their first, often fragile, efforts.

IMPROVING STUDENTS' RESEARCH SKILLS

Research involves students in a process of inquiry which ends with a product, such as a formal paper. To be personally meaningful and to encourage students in later investigations, however, students must *begin* their research efforts with a proper attitude. To illustrate this point, contrast the activities and outlooks of two students. The first one receives a topic, proceeds to write (often copy) notes from a minimum number of sources (most notably an encyclopedia), throws the notes together, and hands in the resulting patchwork as the product of an assigned research paper. The second student discovers a topic of interest from observation and reflection, narrows it, identifies sources and tools of study, takes selective notes, orders and re-orders ideas around the topic, and finally creates a unique document. The first student sees research as gathering and compiling others' ideas. The second, working from curiosity and a need to know, sees research as a gap in knowledge that must be filled or as an intriguing problem to be solved.

In this section, we present two research strategies. In each, the instructional aims are to develop in students an intellectually healthy attitude toward research while, at the same time, helping them to master the steps of scientific inquiry. The first strategy is intended for the beginning researcher (though it need not be limited to a beginner) while the second is for the intermediate researcher (see Activity 8.5).

Activity 8.5

On your visits to a field-experience or professional development school, chronicle the experience of one student doing some sort of research. What, exactly, is the research assignment? What kinds of help does the teacher give? What problems does the student encounter? Are they solved? How? Give a report to your college class. Include by way of contrast or reinforcement suggestions for instruction made in this section.

I-Search

For most students, it's fun to tell stories, especially when the teller is the main character in the narrative. In Ken Macrorie's (1988) I-Search strategy, students tell first person stories about their search for knowledge. The "events" in their stories include the puzzle or need that led to the question they wanted to answer, identi-

---

FIGURE 8.17   SECTIONS OF AN I-SEARCH PAPER

Students will write at least four sections in the following order:

1. "What I knew"

2. "Why I am writing this paper"

3. "The search"

4. "What I learned (and/or didn't learn)"

---

fying the question, narrowing down the topic, searching sources for information, dealing with detours and dead-ends along the way, and arriving at the outcome of the search (see Figure 8.17).

The unit topic in one fourth-grade class was health, and the teacher found a variety of interests among her students. One student, Jorge, was particularly intrigued about germs (a subtopic of health), and chose to do his I-Search on that topic (see Figure 8.18 for a sample of what he wrote at each step).

FIGURE 8.18   EXCERPTS FROM JORGE'S I-SEARCH

How Germs Spread
An I-Search Report by Jorge

1. "What I knew"

    I thought I knew a lot about germs before I started this paper. Here are some facts that I know. Germs can only be seen with a microscope, germs cause tummy aches, and the fresh air and sunshine help fight against germs. I also heard some things that sounded interesting but I wasn't sure if they were true, like germs need a cold and damp place to live and multiply and sweeping or mopping the floors can get rid of germs.

2. *"Why I am writing this paper"*

    I was really curious about germs and why they needed a dark and damp place to live. I wondered if I could get rid of all of the germs. But when I started thinking about it, my teacher, Ms. King, asked me if I had two years to spend on killing all the germs! What she meant was my question might be too difficult to answer in the time our class had and that I should research a more specific question. So, I thought about it, and decided to narrow my topic to how germs spread. I asked the question, "How do germs spread?" I thought it was important to find out because I don't want anyone getting sick from my germs, and I don't want anyone spreading their germs to me.

    (continued)

FIGURE 8.18 EXCERPTS FROM JORGE'S I-SEARCH (*CONTINUED*)

3. *"The search"* (a short excerpt from a longer writing)

. . . I looked for answers in quite a few places. I found the definition of germs in the dictionary and also looked up information about germs in the encyclopedia and our textbook, but neither answered my question about how germs spread. Next, I asked my neighbor, Dr. Nelson, "How do germs spread?" He said, "Always remember to wash your face and brush your teeth because that kills the germs." Even Mrs. Garrett, our librarian, recommended some books for me to read. Then I asked my school nurse, and she gave me some pamphlets about germs. One was called "How to Stop Germs in Their Tracks," which was very helpful. . . .

4. *"What I learned (and things I am still curious about)"*

In my search, I found out that being in the fresh air and sunshine can help prevent germs from spreading, so can washing your hands after using the bathroom and washing your floors every week. That sort of answered the question I had, but it really didn't tell me how the germs spread from one person to the next. I had the problem of finding a person or book that could answer my question. Ms. King said that maybe I should search the Internet, and she gave me some addresses to look under. That might help by letting me look and see if anyone in the world had an answer to my question. She also suggested that I talk to Mr. Braine, the seventh-grade science teacher, and see if he could tell me how germs spread.

Jorge and the description of the steps he took to find out "how germs spread" is a perfect example of an I-Search. He learned how to redirect his focus when he wasn't getting the answers he needed. His learning was motivated by his desire to avoid spreading germs to other people. The I-Search allows students to take on what they are learning as their own and challenges their critical thinking and problem-solving skills. It also avoids some of the problems, such as outlining and reorganizing into major and minor points, of the traditional research paper, especially for younger and less adept students. Also, notice the narrative style in which Jorge writes. Not only does writing in a first-person narrative style add freshness to students' writing (and to your reading), it enables them to interact explicitly with their own thoughts. Jorge's completed paper not only provides a final copy of the information he has uncovered, but it also provides a record of his search efforts. In some ways the search record is more valuable than the information because he can look back on this before the next research effort and decide what procedures he wants to continue and which ones were not productive.

Throughout this book, you have been learning a decision-making process named IDEAL. Students as well as teachers need to know how to make decisions. The four steps in I-Search parallel those in IDEAL. Just as teachers "Look at the Results" of their teaching and students' learning, students using this strategy are compelled to consider what they have learned from their research efforts. Their reflection causes them to rethink the process of their inquiry, experience closure in the present story/search, and point the way to new questions. By adapting the steps to particular students or grade levels, some of us have successfully used the I-Search process with high school, college, and even graduate students. While we are certainly not advocating that you eliminate traditional research papers, we do believe that students can benefit from a number of experiences with I-Search efforts, and that these should precede and inform later research products.

Team Research

Writing a research paper is a highly involved endeavor, requiring the integration of a number of thinking and planning abilities. For many students it also inspires a great deal of anxiety as they consider all that they will have to do over an extended period of time in solitary effort. Learning in teams, however, can be a powerful and anxiety-reducing activity as students work together to master all the component parts (see "Collaborative Research" in the *Teacher as Researcher* section). There are several advantages. First, cooperative work tends to be less threatening. It also tends to promote active involvement and learning for all teammates. Because of the expectations of their peers, it also may encourage procrastinators not to wait too long before getting their information gathered. Davey's Team Research (1987) is an approach to writing research reports in which students work in teams, with systematic guided practice (see Figure 8.19).

Before we describe the steps in Team Research, we want to remind you of the Think-Aloud teaching strategy (chapter 7). Recall that it is one framework (another is Reciprocal Teaching, also in chapter 7) for modeling and providing practice opportunities in the area of learning strategies. When you use it to present Team Research to your students, you will need to modify some of the steps. The initial step, teacher modeling, will take on the character of "show and tell," with a display and explanation of documents from each step in Team Research. You will probably want to leave these displays up as students are engaged in the research process so that they can be reminded of your explanation. The team practice step of Think-Aloud will take the most time, and independent practice, a late step in Think-Aloud, will be postponed until you have evidence that individuals have sufficiently mastered the research process to successfully undertake their own research paper.

Davey reports that following the sequence of steps in conducting Team Research (see Figure 8.19) has been successfully used with middle and senior high students by teachers in English, social studies, science, and art as they undertake teamed research reports with their classes.

An example of Team Research comes from a high school political science class where the teacher assigned students to write a research paper on "systems of government." During class discussion in which they spoke from their prior knowledge, the students generated the subtopics of communism, democracy, monarchy, anarchy, and oligarchy. They then subdivided into research teams who shared the same subtopic interest.

FIGURE 8.19   STEPS IN CONDUCTING TEAM RESEARCH

Students will:

1. *Select a topic.* After being assigned a general topic, brainstorm appropriate subtopics. After the subtopics have been decided, select their subtopics of interest and, on the basis of these, form research teams of two to five members.

2. *Establish a research plan.* Meet as research teams to make decisions about the content to be studied, resources to be used, and allocation of time.

3. *Research the topic.* In teams, take notes by placing each research statement at the top of a sheet of paper. Working alone or in pairs, write short paraphrases of source materials under the correct statement headings. Citations are numbered, and notes are keyed to them.

4. *Organize an outline.* Meet in teams to evaluate and categorize what has been learned. As a team, share information, decide what to keep and delete, identify what needs to be researched further, and organize information into an outline.

5. *Write the paper.* As team members, work individually or in pairs to write the first draft. Then, work from outlines, writing one section at a time in paragraphs, concentrating on substance, not form. The second draft is an elaboration of the first, with more careful proofreading to fix sentence and punctuation errors.

The systems of government teams met to brainstorm the content they would study. They began by listing all the relevant questions they could think of for their subtopic, such as: What is a democracy? What are the differences between a true democracy and a representative democracy? Why did our founding fathers want a democracy? How would we set up a democracy in a new country? Relevant questions were written on file cards, which students then grouped into categories. They then turned the question categories into statements—characteristics of a democracy, differences among democracies, exploring democracies—which guided their notetaking process. After they identified potential and appropriate references (textbooks, biographies, websites), the teams generated a timeline with dates for completing each component task, like notetaking, outlining, and drafting. They presented one copy of their research plan to the teacher for approval and kept a second for themselves.

The democracy research team decided to work in pairs. One student pair worked on the research category "Characteristics of a Democracy." With that phrase written at the top of a piece of paper, they jotted phrases beneath it (e.g., government by the people, common people have the power, the majority rules, individuals are socially equal). They read from multiple sources and, as they learned more about the research statement, found they had to add new statements (e.g., democracies that failed, threats to American democracy, democracies in space) and collapse others.

Then the entire democracy research team met and exchanged information from their research statement papers. Together, members made decisions about deleting some material. For instance, they found that two of the student pairs found similar information in looking at "Differences Among Democracy" and "Exploring Democracies." And they discovered that they needed more information in a couple of areas. In the research team's outline, a student pair's investigation area, "Exploring Democracies," became a main topic, "Democracies Explored," and team members categorized, labeled, and placed information from their notetaking in a subtopic listing until it looked like this:

Main topics:	A.	Democracy characteristics
	B.	Democracy differences
	C.	Democracies explored
Subtopics:	1.	Past and present
	2.	Possible evolution
	3.	Brave new world

In their division of labor for the final draft, the democracy team members assigned each other the tasks of proofreading, editing, illustration, and word processing. After completing this process, the research team made an oral report to the class and entered the written report on the school's website.

To encourage a cooperative spirit among team members, Davey suggests that teachers evaluate research papers in multiple ways, finding ways to credit both group and individual efforts. Also, it is very important for teachers to be present during practice sessions to provide regular feedback. Finally, to encourage monitoring of progress by both teacher and students, Davey introduces a checklist that includes a student self-rating scale and a teacher checkoff (see Figure 8.20). The same checklist can be used later as students work independently on subsequent research projects.

While working together, however, groups of students may gather information, analyze it, and then report findings in a multimedia presentation for global as well as local audiences. In fact, by using e-mail and other means of communication, students at one school can connect with students in schools across the country and around the world to collaborate with them in all phases of research. See Figure 8.21 for websites containing exciting examples of on-line team research.

IMPROVING STUDENTS' METHODS OF STUDYING

As we define it, a "study method" is a learning strategy students use when faced with comprehending text and other source materials on their own. We give an assignment and expect students to make sense of it without guidance from parents, fellow students, or us. That's our expectation. The actual results can be disappointing, however, unless students know and use a "plan of attack" for taking in information, associating it with their own, and monitoring the adequacy of their understanding.

FIGURE 8.20   SAMPLE RESEARCH REPORT CHECKLIST

Task	Target date (for completion)	Self rating of quality (1-6)	Teacher check
Planning			
1. Brainstorm questions			
2. Categorize the questions; write them as statements			
3. Identify sources			
4. Set timelines			
Researching			
1. Read widely			
2. Take notes			
3. Make card file of references used			
Organizing			
1. List the main topics			
2. Identify subtopics			
3. Insert the details			
4. Check for completeness			
Writing			
1. Do first draft			
2. Revise			
3. Check spelling			
4. Proofread			
5. Do final copy			

FIGURE 8.21   ON-LINE RESOURCES FOR INFORMATION ON TEAM RESEARCH

Resource	Website
Classroom Connect	http://www.classroom net
Global SchoolNet Foundation	http://www.gsn.org
Scholastic Center	http://scholastic.com

In this section, we describe three proactive study methods that students can use for "attacking" subject matter and making it their own. The first involves students' recognizing basic sources of information and then searching for answers to study questions aided by their knowledge of where to look. The second is a comprehensive system that integrates several study skills and is adaptable for use in most disciplines. The third enables students to practice their critical thinking and problem-solving skills in preparation for essay exams. All three are approaches to self-regulated learning in which students take intentional control of their scholarship (see Activity 8.6).

Activity 8.6

With a peer, choose one of the methods of studying. Teach it to two different groups (different by age/grade or subject matter). Compare your experiences and report to your college class. Points of comparison might be your preparation, modifications in presentation, the "teach" itself, students' reactions, and changes in future endeavors.

Question Answer Relationships (QARS)

Raphael (1986) explained that Question Answer Relationships (QARS) can be used as a teaching tool for conceptualizing and developing comprehension questions and as a student tool for locating information and making decisions about use of a text and background information. Our interest in this section is to explain the use of QARS as a learning tool for students in independent study.

As a tool for younger students, QARS consists of two categories of sources of information. One is the text (In the Book) and the other is the student (In My Head). You train your students to recognize these categories so that when they seek answers to your questions on their own they know where to look. Using the tale of "Goldilocks and the Three Bears" as an example text, you might ask, "Where did the three bears live?" Students who are sensitive to the two categories will recognize the question as an "In the Book" one and search the written text or their oral memory of the text to find the literal answer. However, to the question, "What do you do when you're frightened, as Goldilocks was?" students will know it as an "In My Head" one, and look to their personal bank of experiences for the answer, possibly comparing what they know of Goldilocks' experience with their own.

Students in the upper elementary grades can be taught to further develop each category. "In the Book" divides into "Right There" (the answer is stated explicitly in the text within a single sentence of text) and "Think and Search" (the answer can be found in the text but requires the reader to put together information from different parts). The "In My Head" category divides into "Author and You" (the answer is not in the story and so the reader has to combine personal information with clues from the author) and "On My Own" (there's not even a clue in the text; the reader has to rely on experience alone). Figure 8.22 illustrates the QARS categories and subcategories.

Of the two teaching strategies for instructing students in the use of learning strategies presented in chapter 7, we recommend Reciprocal Teaching as the more appropriate framework for QARS. As you exchange teaching roles with your students, concentrate first on distinguishing between the "In the Book" and "In My

---

FIGURE 8.22   ILLUSTRATIONS TO EXPLAIN QARS TO STUDENTS

In the Book QARs	In My Head QARs

Right There

The answer is in the text, usually easy to find. The words used to make up the question and words used to answer the question are **Right There** in the same sentence.

Author and You

The answer is *not* in the story. You need to think about what you already know, what the author tells you in the text, and how it fits together.

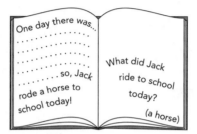

Think and Search (Putting It Together)

The answer is in the story, but you need to put together different story parts to find it. Words for the question and words for the answer are not found in the same sentence. They come from different parts of the text.

On My Own

The answer is *not* in the story. You can even answer the question without reading the story. You need to use your own experience.

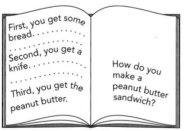

Head" categories and then the four subcategories. As you respond to students' questions, first answer them directly and then follow up with a comment on the thought processes that your questions have encouraged in students. ("To answer your question, I was very frightened once when I heard my parents' plane had engine trouble. You've asked a good question. It's an 'On My Own' one because there's nothing in the book that I can use to answer it. I only used my memories to answer.") This metacognitive awareness will strengthen students' ownership of the study method which will, in turn, increase the likelihood of its transfer and application in new situations.

HEART

In response to requests from elementary and secondary materials publishers, Santeusanio (1990) decided to draw on the research from recent decades and formulate a study system he calls HEART. This strategy takes into account the influences of prior knowledge, text structure, task demands, and metacognition on students' ability to comprehend and recall text. Teaching the five steps in one setting, although possible, is not as effective as an accumulative presentation. That is, on the first day, teach the "H." On the second day, teach "H" and "E;" then "H" and "E" plus "A," and so on. Younger and slower-learning students, especially, are more likely to master the process through this piecemeal approach. The steps follow the letters in the HEART acronym (see Figure 8.23).

Students begin using the strategy by examining the title of the chapter they are about to read. Rosa, a student in a world geography class was assigned to read a chapter titled "Maps of the World." She asked herself, "What do I already know about maps?" She took a minute to jot down her responses: Different maps convey different information; some maps have vertical and horizontal lines; we use maps when we travel, etc. Next she added to and reinforced her prior knowledge of the topic by previewing the chapter and its graphics while asking the question again.

In the next step students set purposes for their studying by taking headings and turning them into purpose-setting statements. For example, Rosa turned the heading "The Mercator and Robinson Projections" into the purpose-setting statement, "My purpose is to find the relationships between the Mercator and Robinson Projections." Besides giving Rosa a direction for study, the heading also told her how the section is organized. In this example, a sophisticated learner would probably predict that the author chose a compare/contrast writing pattern. This prediction could help with the next step.

After Rosa read the section of text, she developed her own questions based on the content she had just read. These questions were related to her purpose-setting

---

FIGURE 8.23   STEPS IN USING HEART

Students will respond to these directions:

H–determine *How much* you already know about this topic.

E–*Establish a purpose* for studying.

A–*Ask questions* as you study.

R–*Record answers* to your questions.

T–*Test* yourself.

statements (e.g., "What are the differences and similarities between the Mercator and Robinson Projections?"). She formulated additional questions that related to other important points in the section. Research shows that students like Rosa who generate their own questions from text improve their learning.

Next, she constructed "split pages" by drawing vertical lines on several pages of her notebook and writing her self-generated questions on one side and her answers on the other side. This question/answer format is reminiscent of the Idea Line and PUNS strategies for notetaking you read about earlier in this chapter and is also a way of summarizing information.

Rosa took the final step in the HEART study system by testing herself. She reviewed her questions and answers by covering the answer side of her split pages, reading her questions, reciting answers, and checking the accuracy of her responses by uncovering the answers. She continued to do this until she had learned the answers to her questions.

Predict-Organize-Rehearse-Practice-Evaluate (PORPE)

PORPE (Simpson, 1986) was developed in response to students' anxiety about essay exams. It is a strategy that requires students to engage in a series of steps that activate a number of higher order thinking skills (see Figure 8.24).

For example, in a tenth-grade American history class, students were studying the Bill of Rights. More specifically, they were taking notes on the second amendment. When asked to predict an essay question that dealt with their study of the second amendment, one student wrote, "Defend the need for the second amendment according to our founders." Once students had predicted a series of potential questions, they needed to summarize key ideas from the various sections of the unit. For each projected essay question, students created an outline that answered the question. In preparation for the history test, one student organized his notes under four separate headings: beliefs and background, historical evidence, key witnesses, and strong closing.

FIGURE 8.24   STEPS IN USING PORPE

The student will:

1. *Predict.* Generate potential test essay questions that identify major concepts in the text and lecture.

2. *Organize.* Group information that will answer predicted essay question.

3. *Rehearse.* Practice key ideas and examples, so it will be easier to recall on the exam.

4. *Practice.* Write an answer to the predicted essay question. Keep track of the time to simulate test conditions.

5. *Evaluate.* Grade the practice essay. Return to notes or text if there is confusion or points that need to be clarified.

As this history student looked through his notes during the rehearsal stage, he wasn't too sure what he meant when he wrote "James Madison: advantage" under key witnesses, so he went back to his notes to study it. Satisfied that he could now respond on that point, he prepared himself to practice. After referring back to the original question, he set his watch for forty minutes and began to write his practice essay. He remembered to restate his question in the opening of his essay: "The second amendment has its origins from the ideas of classical republicanism." When time was up, he reread his essay making sure that he had provided all the information required and that he covered all the relevant subject matter.

Enabling students to think critically and use their problem solving skills should be a major focus for you as a teacher. While there are no guarantees that the questions that students generate will actually be the ones that they will encounter on the test, PORPE provides an excellent study strategy that helps students to polish thinking and writing skills. Through this strategy, students see their writing as a unique form of feedback and a way to monitor themselves to see if in fact they are prepared for an essay exam.

As we pointed out at the beginning of this chapter, the success of these study methods, and indeed all of the strategies we have introduced so far, depends to a great extent on your teaching them in context—that is, in a real instructional unit with real content, where students have real reasons for learning. It also depends on your making good decisions about which methods to teach your students, when you should teach them, and how you should structure activities to support your students as they learn to work with these strategies.

DEVELOPING YOUR OWN LEARNING STRATEGIES

Sometimes the learning strategies that are suggested in professional journals and teacher education books like ours just do not fit the needs of your subject or your students. At those times, you can't just throw up your hands and hope that students will "get it." You will need to develop your own (which is what Elliott Ostler, a math teacher, did. See the "Teacher-Developed Strategies Section" in the *Teacher as Researcher*). That may mean combining steps from two existing strategies, sharing one that you developed for your own study, or building a new and unique one "from scratch." Whatever the situation, try building your tailor-made strategies using the steps in Figure 8.25. Following those steps is how Buckley, a teacher education

---

FIGURE 8.25   STEPS IN CREATING YOUR OWN LEARNING STRATEGY

1. Identify the learning strategy your students need.

2. Break the learning strategy down into constituent and sequential steps (notice that most of the strategies you've been introduced to in this text are four to five steps; keep the number of steps manageable for your students).

3. Rework the steps for your students, making the directions clear and direct.

student, developed his own notetaking strategy while he was tutoring in an alternative high school. You'll see the report of his experience in Figure 8.26.

FIGURE 8.26   EXCERPT FROM BUCKLEY'S TEACHING JOURNAL

Developing a Learning Strategy: Buckley's Experience

"When I worked in an alternative high school, I was assigned to tutor a young man in American history. Having been removed from two traditional high schools but determined to earn his General Education Diploma, Seymour was grateful for my help and was quite cooperative as I tried to help him.

"Seymour's teacher followed a three-phase cycle in his instruction: He'd make a page assignment from the book, have students take notes from the reading during class time, and then take a short answer, objective test over the material. His tests came straight from the book, and in order to do well, Seymour had to memorize a lot of facts, names and places, and dates. Seymour wasn't excited about the class, and although I could sympathize with him, I wanted to help him meet the reality of his situation.

"He had been taking fairly decent book notes, writing them on note paper and then attempting to memorize them before a test. He was not getting good results (D's and mostly F's), so both he and I decided that he should try another approach to his study. We decided that he'd take notes on cards at the end of each assigned section in place of notes on regular pieces of paper. I hoped this would be more productive for him but soon realized he had a problem. 'How do I know which words to write on the notecard and which ones to leave out?' he asked. Great question! He needed a detailed notetaking strategy that really got at the thought processes involved, and I needed to provide him with one.

"Since I frequently make notecards myself as I study for some college courses, I made myself think about what my head does as I construct them. I actually took notes on cards from a chapter in Seymour's book, and doing that made me conscious of the mental steps I was taking. I came up with four sequential steps:

1. *Identify major terms, places , names, dates , and other significant items.* I do this in a variety of ways. I first look for words that appear in boldface throughout the chapter. Obviously this means the author thinks such items are important. Next, I identify items that are mentioned more than once throughout the chapter (repetition is a cue to importance) as well as items in the introduction and summary. I also use my prior experience as a history major to sift out major from minor and although I'd like to see Seymour doing this too, I realized that his background information was very shallow. We'll add "schema activation and utilization" later.

(continued)

FIGURE 8.26   EXCERPT FROM BUCKLEY'S TEACHING JOURNAL (*CONTINUED*)

2. *Write a single item in the middle of one side of a notecard.* I keep the notecards in the order that the items appear in a chapter, waiting until the last step to group and regroup them. Using the same color ink helps me distinguish the item from its identifiers, which I take in a different color (see next step).

3. *Write a definition, explanation, or characteristics on the other side.* I look at an item and say to myself "What's worth *anybody* knowing about this?" The answer should be phrased in about ten words. This helps me fight through the less important details and get to the meat of the material. I try to para-phrase definitions and explanations provided by the book, and I attempt to add a significance statement when I can. For example, on the Pearl Harbor card, I wrote "Japan bombed the U.S. on December 7, 1941, causing the U.S. to enter the war."

4. *Group the notecards for study.* If my instructor gives essay-type tests, I group the cards by topic, memorizing specifics but also looking for connec-tions among the thoughts on the cards. For true-false, multiple-choice, or matching tests, however, I have a choice of grouping arrangements. Cards can be placed together on the basis of time period, a movement (coloniza-tion), or a historical pattern ("cause" cards and "result" cards bundled under the same rubber band). Once grouped, I rehearse the cards, giving myself three seconds to recall information on the other side. For even more mastery, I practice the cards two ways: looking at the item and recalling the definition, etc., and then looking at the definition and recalling the item.

"As I modeled these steps for Seymour (I used text information he had already been quizzed on so he'd be working with familiar material) and then had him practice them using a new text assignment, I found that he understood the steps. However, some of my explanations needed clarification. For example, he still had trouble paraphrasing the definitions. His tendency was to leave in unnecessary details, so I gave him some different questions to ask himself when defining a certain term. Examples are: 'Does this have anything to do with the outcome?' or 'If I remove this piece, does it change the meaning at all?' He used this strategy for the rest of the semester, and I'm happy to report that his grades improved to a C+ average. I knew he saw the worth of the strategy when he told me that he'd begun to teach the strategy to one of his friends. I also know I saw the worth in the strategy when he received his General Education Diploma in May of 1998."

Usually, you will have observed your students at work in the classroom as well as their performance on assignments and tests and will have noticed or suspected gaps in their systematic uses of learning strategies. Knowing the study demands of your units and your commitment to teaching how-to-learn skills as well as con-cepts, we hope that, like Buckley, you will be determined to work with your students during the school year on a small number of specific and critically needed learning strategies.

When you begin to break the strategy down into steps, use yourself as a model. Analyze what you do in your mind as you actively perform the strategy. Force yourself to visualize the mental steps your mind follows. This is the equivalent of taking a motion picture of your brain at work and then slowing down the film enough to capture the individual steps in order. For example, if interpreting graphs is the study skill students need, you might say to yourself, "When I interpret graphs, I begin by looking at the title of the graph. That tells me what type of information is in the graph. So my step number one is 'Read the title of the graph.'" Continue like that until you record all the steps.

Activity 8.7

Think about the learning strategies you have or are currently using. Reread the "Developing Your Own Learning Strategies" section of this chapter. Choose one of your strategies (learning from a teacher, friend, or trial and error) and delineate the steps as preparation for actually teaching it. Identify the strategy with an acronym or with your own name (e.g., "Johnson's Story Problem Attack Plan").

Before you teach this to your students, consider some critical questions: Are there too many steps for a primary school child to follow? Are there really substeps within a single step? Is the language of the steps clear and unambiguous? By answering these questions and making appropriate adjustments, you make it more likely that your students will understand and be able to learn these steps which now comprise the complete learning strategy.

SUMMARY

Learning strategies were defined as techniques used to enhance understanding and memory of the material being learned and read. Students are assisted in becoming scholars when the people at home know how to be learning partners with their students. Together with teachers who infuse learning strategy instruction in their well prepared content lessons, they are key players in students becoming independent inquirers after knowledge. Although sometimes difficult, it is up to teachers to initiate the vital home-school link.

A very important part of the teacher's job description is to help students master a limited number of learning strategies that will serve them beyond the school's walls. Reciprocal Teaching and Think-Aloud were described a second time in this chapter as two instructional frameworks you can use in teaching learning strategies to your students. Learning strategies must be presented directly and explicitly in a specified step-by-step approach in a supportive environment. Debriefing during and after strategy teaching helps students be metacognitive about the mental processes involved. However, there is no one way to study and once students know a strategy as taught, they must always be given the freedom to modify it to fit their own personal styles.

In this chapter, we looked at five different areas of learning: memorization, note taking, summarization, research, and study methods. There are valid reasons to ask students to memorize material even though we want the majority of their strategies to be composites of upper level thinking abilities. To memorize effectively, though, students need to do so purposefully and efficiently. While taking notes, it is important for students to make personal sense out of the new material they are organizing and recording. Strategies such as Idea Line and PUNS help accomplish this. Both strategies help students differentiate between major and minor details and provide them with systematic vehicles from which they are able to study. A summary is a short statement that conveys the essence of a longer piece of discourse. The strategies we present, the Four-Sentence Summary and GRASP, enable students to bypass the minor ideas and pick out the major topics. Summarizing must be more than copying another author's words out of an encyclopedia. It must help students clarify the material and understand it better. Research involves a process of inquiry and ends with a product, such as a formal paper. With the help of strategies such as I-Search and Team Research, students should work from their own curiosity and need to know, not from the burden of having to collect others' ideas. A study method is a learning strategy students use when faced with comprehending text and other source materials on their own. Too often, we expect students to do well on tests or papers when they do not know how to properly attack the subject matter. Strategies such as QARS, HEART, and PORPE are detailed plans that students use to increase their productivity while studying.

All of the strategies in this chapter, together with the tools, resources, and strategies in chapters 5–7, are a sample of the instructional alternatives you have to choose from in your planning and teaching. The next chapter continues this display of alternatives as the topic turns to assessment strategies.

REFLECTIONS

1. What school practices have you encountered that encourage or discourage the development of scholars, as defined in this chapter? Are those that Terry and Marilyn discuss in the conversation at the beginning of this chapter like or unlike those that you've seen? In small class groups, make two lists: practices that foster their development and practices that discourage it. For example, does the preparation for state-mandated proficiency tests encourage a love of learning as its own best reward? How about special classes for the "gifted and talented"?

2. It can be argued that teaching steps in a learning strategy is too much like teaching a formula, that their rigid application leads to compliance and passivity, qualities that are opposite those of a scholar. Discuss what you think the authors of this text would say in response to this argument. Then compare this with your own response.

3. Reread Figure 8.26, "Developing a Learning Strategy: Buckley's Experience." Analyze it in terms of the phases in the IDEAL model. That is, *identify* Seymour's challenge; *define* his challenge; *explore* the alternative approaches to the challenge that Buckley might have considered (as it was, Buckley skipped this step); name the learning strategy that Buckley *acted* on; and *look at the results* of Buckley's instruction (we can also refer to this phase as *reflection*; upon reflection, what comments and questions might you ask Seymour and Buckley?).

TEACHER AS RESEARCHER

Students with Disabilities

Scanlon, A., Deshler, D., & Schumaker, J. (1996). Can a strategy be taught and learned in secondary inclusive classrooms? *Learning Disabilities Research and Practice* , 11 (1), 41–57.

Students with disabilities are being placed in regular class settings for the majority or all of the school day. Can we expect secondary school teachers to teach learning strategies in their inclusive classrooms? Will students with disabilities learn strategies in this setting? Read the following research article and then, from the results of this one study, answer these questions.

Integrated Strategy Instruction

Olson, M. & Gee, T. (1991). Content reading instruction in the primary grades: Perceptions and strategies. *The Reading Teacher, 45* (4), 298–307.

Survey research is useful in sampling persons' attitudes, perceptions, and behaviors. In this source article, (a) what questions prompted the authors' investigation? (b) who was surveyed? (c) what were the responses to the survey questions?

Collaborative Research

Rekrut, M. (1997). Collaborative research. *Journal of Adolescent and Adult Literacy, 41* (1), 26–34.

When teachers embark on research projects within their schools and classrooms, they often begin by seeking out reports of similar research studies to inform their own investigations. In reading the article, pay particular attention to the section "Studies of Collaborative Research." Make a list of the investigators who researched collaborative research. For each study, name the topic of the investigator's interest. Topics will not always be named explicitly, so be ready to use your powers of inference-making!

Parenting Styles

Boveja, M. (1998). Parenting styles and adolescents' learning strategies in the urban community. *Journal of Multicultural Counseling and Development, 26* (2), 110–119.

Is there a connection between parenting styles and adolescents' use of learning and study strategies? Summarize the investigator's findings. Pay special attention to her listing of "other factors." Researchers must always be alert to the possibility that variables other than those investigated may affect the results of the study.

Teacher-Developed Strategies

Ostler, E. (1997). The effect of learning mathematical reading strategies on secondary students' homework grades. *The Clearing House, 71* (1), 37–40.

What was the purpose of this investigation? What were the results? In the "discussion" part of his research report, the investigator interprets his results, sometimes speculating on what they show, and equally important, what they don't show. What specifically did this quasi-experimental study not show?

CHAPTER 9

Planning Assessment Strategies

CONVERSATION

Michela Thomas and Wendy Wolfe are sixth-grade team teachers at Palm Middle School. Michela has taught science at the school for six years and Wendy is in her first year teaching math. During their joint planning period, the two teachers begin to prepare for parent conferences that are coming up in a few weeks.

"I'm feeling pretty discouraged about the results of the last math test," laments Wendy. "I thought the unit we just finished had gone so well. The students were so engaged in the activities. They really seemed to get the idea of perimeter and area when we drew the floor plan of our room. But when they took the test, some students didn't do very well at all. Jeff Newman's mother called last week and wanted to know why he did so poorly on the test. I had a hard time giving her an answer. To be honest, I don't know why he didn't do better. I really thought he got it!"

"Wendy, don't be too hard on yourself," responds Michela. "Teaching is a complex task. From what I see, you have done an excellent job at developing your lesson plans. It's pretty unrealistic to expect that every aspect of your teaching will be perfect the first year. Tell me a little about the math test."

"I just used the test in the teacher's manual. It was mostly story problems."

"Stop right there," smiled Michela. "I think I know the problem already. You had your students working in groups to measure the perimeter and area of the room. That type of learning activity can be very different from reading and solving story problems."

"Come to think of it," replied Wendy, "several students needed help figuring out some of the words. It almost seemed like the reading level was too difficult." Wendy shrugged her shoulders and shook her head. "So, I gave a test that was too difficult to read, and used a type of test question that was different from how we learned in class. It's no wonder they didn't do as well as I would have expected!"

"As you've just discovered," smiled Michela, "there are many assessment-related alternatives that teachers must explore. When you think about it, an assessment plan is as important as a lesson plan. Let's talk further."

DEVELOPING COMPETENCE

The field of classroom assessment is quite comprehensive. Like the unit planning, lesson planning, and other instructional decisions you have read about in previous chapters, planning for assessment requires thoughtful, logical decision-making. In fact, entire textbooks, educational courses, and even graduate degrees are devoted to the study of assessment. The intent of this chapter, however, is to provide a basic overview of some of the foundational assessment topics.

1. Through her discussion with Michela, Wendy discovers the importance of matching instructional strategies with assessment strategies. Read to elaborate upon the link between teaching, learning, and assessment.

2. Wendy has worked hard to developed her skills in lesson planning. Now, when Wendy begins to prepare for an upcoming instructional unit on the metric system, she will develop an assessment plan that coincides with her lesson plans. Based on the nature of your students and the subject matter that you teach, you should be able to develop an assessment plan by considering the balance between pre-assessments, practice assessments, and post assessments.

3. As Michela and Wendy consider how to align their assessment strategies with instruction, they will strive to develop quality assessments that are true indicators of what their students have learned. After reading this chapter you should be able to identify and follow the steps for designing valid and reliable tests.

4. The overall quality of the tests that Wendy and Michela design is a reflection of the quality of the individual test items. After completing the activities in this chapter, you will be capable of writing paper-and-pencil objective test items and evaluating them according to the formatting guidelines recognized by assessment specialists.

5. Student-created products or performances are alternatives to paper-and-pencil tests. In aligning assessment with instruction, Wendy may decide to have her students build models of various geometric forms. After reading this chapter you will be able to create a rating scale for essay tests or alternative assessments.

INTRODUCTION

Assessing student achievement is a vital component of the teaching-learning process. It makes little sense for you to plan and develop lessons without ever asking the question, "Did my students actually learn what I taught them?" Without assessment, you can never be sure of the quality of your instruction or your students' mastery of the instructional material. Surprisingly, some teachers view assessment as an afterthought. They think of testing as a one-time thing that happens at the end of instruction. Some teachers are content with simply assigning the questions at the end of a chapter, or photocopying a test from the teacher's manual. Worse yet, some use tests as threats for students to study, or they use pop quizzes as punishment when

---

FIGURE 9.1   WEB SITES WITH LINKS TO ASSESSMENT RELATED TOPICS

- Assessment and Evaluation on the Internet
  http://www.tier.net/schools/aei.htm

- Assessment Resources
  http://www.col-ed.org/smcnws/assessment.html

- Assessment Web Resources Index
  http://mac.cl.k12.md.us:2000/links/AssessmentDBLinks/
  AssessmentResources.html

- Internet Resources on Student Assessment
  http://www.iptv.org/FINELINK/hotlinks.html

---

students misbehave in class. Quality teachers, however, realize that considerable planning and decision-making goes in to assessing student achievement.

Your teacher education program may offer a specific course about assessment, or assessment may be integrated within content or methods type courses (e.g., math education, reading education, etc.). Nonetheless, you will want to expand your knowledge and skills beyond that which can be presented in an introductory chapter such as this. The websites in Figure 9.1 will link you to many Internet resources about assessment.

THE LANGUAGE OF ASSESSMENT

Like other education specialities, the field of assessment has its own very specific set of terminology, and it is important for you to become familiar with the professional language. **Assessment** refers to the whole range of information gathered and synthesized by teachers about their students. Assessment can be a somewhat informal process such as observation and discussion, or it can be a more structured process such as a comprehensive unit exam. Educators distinguish between two types of assessment—formative and summative. **Formative assessment** takes place during the process of instruction, and it is used to provide corrective feedback to a student or to modify instructional methods. For example, Mr. Halper uses homework assignments and practice exercises to identify which lesson objectives his tenth-grade American history students have mastered and which objectives need review. Mrs. Lofton, on the other hand, observes her students' responses during a class discussion to assess the effectiveness of a particular teaching strategy. Clearly, the quality of instruction and learning are greatly enhanced when teachers, students, and *parents* are given regular feedback throughout the teaching-learning process. In contrast, **summative assessments** take place at the conclusion of a lesson or unit and are primarily used to assign grades. Summative assessments can take many forms including written tests, projects, essays, and presentations. Remember, assessment is a *very* broad term that refers to a whole myriad of strategies and methods that teachers employ to examine student learning.

Measurement is a very specific type of assessment. Measurement is defined as the quantification of an attribute. Typically, measurement evokes images of using a ruler to determine the length of a room, or using various kitchen utensils to determine the amount of ingredients in a recipe, or using a thermometer to determine if you have a fever, and so on. In each of these examples, a specific number is used to indicate *how much.*

In your classroom, you are concerned with measuring student learning. In other words, you want to make a statement about *how much* a student has learned. To be precise, when teachers talk about measuring student learning they are talking about assigning a numeric value to student achievement (e.g., nineteen out of twenty questions answered correctly, 80 percent of math problems completed, etc.). Measuring student achievement is a much trickier process than measuring attributes in the physical world, where instruments such as scales and thermometers are precisely calibrated. Teachers' measuring tools are often crude in comparison. In the classroom, you will use tests or alternative assessments to measure student achievement. **Tests** are paper-and-pencil instruments that *your students* will complete. **Alternative assessments** are products or performances that your students will create combined with your assessment of the completed product (e.g., a rating scale, written comments, etc.). Tests and alternative assessments will be explored later in this chapter.

After administering a test or alternative assessment you will need to make a judgment or **evaluation** about students' achievement. Typically, teachers use letter grades (A, B, or C), grade labels (outstanding, satisfactory, or needs improvement), or written corrective feedback to make an evaluative or judgment statement about student achievement.

THE TEACHING-LEARNING-ASSESSMENT PROCESS

Now that you are familiar with the language of assessment, consider the following example that illustrates the process of teaching and assessment. Mr. Paige is teaching a unit on the Civil War. In planning for the unit, Mr. Paige has identified the lesson objectives, considered various teaching and learning strategies, identified the necessary resources, and developed the appropriate lesson plans. In essence, Mr. Paige has worked through the planning and decision-making process that has been presented in the preceding chapters. As the teaching and learning process unfolds, Mr. Paige may make the following assessments.

- "Wow, everyone was really engaged in the discussion about the Underground Railroad today!"
- "Hmm . . . I wonder why several of the groups did not seem to function effectively during the cooperative learning activity?"
- "I'm very pleased with the quality of the essays that student's wrote about reconstruction. "
- "A few of the scores on the vocabulary quiz were lower than I had expected."
- "Some students seemed confused about the causes of secession."

Activity 9.1

Form a small group or work on your own. Decide if each of Mr. Paige's statements is a formative or summative assessment. What evidence or data do you think Mr. Paige used to support his assessments? Based on the assessments, make a list of recommendations for Mr. Paige to "do next."

There are many ways to assess student learning. It is quite likely that Mr. Paige made some of his formative assessments based on casual observations during class discussions or small group work. Other assessments were made based on the results of an essay test and a project that his student created. Although there are many assessment tools that teachers employ, one of the first decisions that you will have to make is whether to develop your own assessment tool or use one that has been developed by a textbook author or publisher.

TEACHER-DEVELOPED ASSESSMENTS VS. TEXTBOOK ASSESSMENTS

Many textbooks and other curricular materials include support materials such as transparencies, student workbooks, computer software, and tests. While it might be tempting to simply adopt textbook tests, you should use caution when doing so. It may not be prudent to entrust the decision-making process to the author or publisher. After all, *you* actually developed and taught the lesson, carefully considering the appropriate teaching strategies. The textbook author has never even met your students! As Wendy Wolfe discovered at the beginning of the chapter, using the textbook questions backfired! While some textbook tests are of very good quality and follow the rules and guidelines that are recognized by assessment experts, other tests may be poorly written. As you will see as this chapter unfolds, there is considerable skill involved in developing quality assessments. Whether teachers decide to develop their own assessment tools or modify and adapt those included with textbooks, they must consider both the type and format of the assessment.

TYPES OF ASSESSMENTS

There are three types of assessments that teachers use to measure student achievement: 1) pre-assessments, 2), practice assessments, and 3) post assessments. Pre-assessments and practice assessments are used to make formative decisions about student achievement. Post assessments are the only type of assessment that should be used to make summative decisions (e.g., to assign a grade).

Pre-assessments are administered prior to instruction, and they are used to assess the knowledge and skills that students should have mastered prior to a lesson. Ms. Jones, a third-grade teacher, is preparing to teach multiplication of two digit numbers. Before beginning this unit of instruction, she needs to know which students have mastered basic facts, a second-grade skill. Even though this was a second-grade skill, it is likely that some students may need review before going on to a more complex skill. Ms. Jones could decide to administer a pre-assessment before she begins instruction on the new unit. The results will help her identify which of her students may need to review. A **pre-assessment** can also cover material that is the focus of the current lesson. For example, Mr. Pennel, a tenth-grade biology teacher, is preparing to teach a lesson on the animal kingdom. He examines the objectives for the unit and constructs a test that addresses these objectives. Mr. Pennel can use the results to identify students who may or may not have prior knowledge and skills and to identify specific objectives that may have been encountered during previous instruction. Although a pre-assessment can be very helpful, students can become unduly stressed because it is likely that they will not know many of the answers.

The second type of assessment is a **practice assessment.** Practice assessments are administered after instruction. Teachers use the results of practice assessments to identify learning problems and instructional weaknesses, and students use the results of practice assessments to identify areas in need of further study. A few weeks into a unit on capitalization, Ms. Martin administers a test to her twelfth-grade English class. The test covers several capitalization rules. The results of the practice assessment indicate that her students have mastered all but two of the lesson objectives that were covered on the test. As a class, Ms. Martin will review the two objectives that were not mastered. In addition, Ms. Martin shares the results of the practice test with her students so they know which objectives they may need to review. Ms. Martin was careful to format the practice assessment in a manner similar to the unit post assessment. She included several multiple choice and short answer test items. She also included a paragraph that contained capitalization errors for her students to correct, similar to what they will encounter on the post assessment. Ms. Martin knows that practice assessments are very useful for relieving test anxiety. When students know "what the test will look like," they are more relaxed when they take the actual test. Practice assessments are formative assessments and should not be used to assign grades. Practice assessments can be administered in class, or they can be assigned as homework.

A **post assessment** is used after instruction has been completed, and the results are used to calculate student grades. Quizzes are a type of post assessment that are administered after a short period of instruction. A unit test is administered at the completion of an instructional unit. Midterm and final exams are administered at the midpoint and end of a grading period. In some high schools, teachers are required to administer semester exams.

ASSESSMENT FORMATS

In making decisions about assessing student learning, a teacher must carefully consider both the *type* of assessment and the *format* of the assessment. Pre-assessments, practice assessments, and post assessments can be formatted in a number of ways. Paper-and-pencil objective tests, (e.g., multiple choice, alternative response, matching, completion, and short answer), essay tests, student-created products, and skill performances are very common assessment formats. Guidelines for developing these assessment formats will be presented in a later section of this chapter. First, let's consider some general aspects of designing classroom assessments.

DESIGNING CLASSROOM ASSESSMENTS

Teachers, students, and parents alike want assessments to be fair. They want to make correct, accurate decisions about student learning. When teachers and students talk about *fair* assessments, they are actually talking about assessments that are valid and reliable. Actually, a more precise statement is that the *scores* on the assessments are valid and reliable, not the test or rating scale itself. In conversation, however, many educators are more casual and speak of the validity or reliability of the test itself.

Validity and Reliability Defined

The term **validity** refers to the appropriateness of the inferences made from the assessment results. In other words, does the assessment measure what it is supposed to measure. Classroom teachers are interested in one specific kind of validity called **content validity.** The scores on a classroom assessments have content validity if they measure the subject matter and learning processes that are the focus of instruction. To ensure that assessment tools has content validity, the test items or rating scale components must match the lesson or behavioral objectives that have been the focus of instruction. There are other types of validity, such as predictive validity and construct validity, but these types of validity do not apply to teacher-developed classroom assessments.

The term **reliability** refers to the consistency or stability of assessment scores. Consider the following example. If you wanted to measure your weight, you would step on the bathroom scale. If you stepped on and off the bathroom scale a number of times, the scale should read the same weight. Perhaps if you were to lean in a particular manner or step on the scale in a different place each time, your weight could vary by a very small amount. Overall, you would weigh the same each and every time you stepped on the scale. Your weight is a reliable measure. What if the scale was broken? What if every time you stepped on the scale your weight varied by several pounds? Your weight would no longer be reliable. The same applies to assessment scores. You want to be assured that a student's assessment score will remain stable and consistent if the student were to re-take the assessment a number of times. Of course you would never re-administer a test or recode a rating scale several times to determine if the assessment scores are reliable. Instead, by striving to develop assessments that have content validity you are likely to develop assessment tools that will result in reliable scores.

The Process of Assessment Development

Mrs. Bedford teaches English at Valley Middle School. Follow the planning of Mrs. Bedford as she begins to design a vocabulary test for her students. You may be surprised at the amount of time and consideration that Mrs. Bedford puts into designing assessments that are likely to produce a valid and reliable measure of her student's achievement.

1. *Identify the type of assessment.* The first thing Mrs. Bedford considers is whether the test will be a pre-assessment, practice assessment, or post assessment. She will consider whether the assessment task is formative or summative, whether she wants to know the skills and knowledge that students are bringing into the unit, or what they have learned following several weeks of instruction. The type of assessment determines the lesson or behavioral objectives that will serve as a foundation for the vocabulary test items themselves.

2. *Identify the lesson or behavioral objectives that will be measured.* The lesson or behavioral objectives that Mrs. Bedford has written for the unit of instruction serve as a foundation for her assessment. For example, a pre-assessment might reflect lesson objectives that are a review from the previous unit. A practice assessment could be composed of a sample of objectives from throughout the unit, or a limited set of objectives from one aspect of the unit. A quiz (post assessment) typically reflects a small number of objectives from one aspect of the instructional unit; whereas an essay test (post assessment) may reflect a more comprehensive sampling of the objectives. When selecting the objectives, Mrs. Bedford will consider the balance between subject matter (declarative knowledge) and learning processes (procedural knowledge). She will feel confident that her assessments have content validity when there is an appropriate balance between subject matter and learning level. Once Mrs. Bedford has identified the objectives she will consider the format of the assessment tool.

3. *Determine the appropriate format.* Mrs. Bedford will examine the nature of the objectives to determine the format of the assessment tool. Less complex objectives that require her students to simply state or recall factual information readily lend themselves to objective paper-and-pencil test items such as multiple choice, matching, or short answer. More complex objectives that require her students to produce more comprehensive responses lend themselves to essay tests, or perhaps her students will create a product or demonstration that will reflect their mastery of the objectives. Assessment formats will be discussed later in this chapter.

4. *Consider the amount of time available for assessment.* The amount of time available for assessment is an important consideration. For example, primary students have a shorter attention span than upper elementary students; thus primary elementary teachers may have only ten to fifteen minutes available for a paper-and-pencil test. In contrast, upper elementary students have a longer attention span and a test may take twenty minutes or more. If necessary, Mrs. Bedford's middle school students can use the entire fifty minute class period to complete the vocabulary test. This does not necessarily mean her students will be tested for the entire fifty minute time period. Typically, she will take attendance, make

announcements, and provide some type of overview to her class. She must also keep in mind that her students work at different rates. Some will finish quickly, while others may need considerably more time to finish. Her students will need less time to complete objective paper-and-pencil test items and more time for assessment with lengthy reading passages, or for essay tests. Mrs. Bedford has used a number of practice assessments during the unit and has a fairly good sense of the amount of time her students will need. It is important for students to have sufficient time to complete in-class assessments and review their answers. Sometimes product assessments are completed outside of class, and students are given several days or longer to complete the assignment. Performance assessments, on the other hand, must be completed during class time so Mrs. Bedford can observe and record the skill level of her students.

5. *Construct the assessment tool and instructions.* As she begins to develop her assessment tools, Mrs. Bedford will consider the guidelines that measurement experts have recommend. (Some of these guidelines are included in the following sections, and several excellent references are noted in the *Teacher as Researcher* section at the end of this chapter.) Mrs. Bedford likes to have one of the other English teachers in her building "proofread" her tests for clarity. This will help to avoid the likelihood that her assessment tools will contain errors that may confuse her students and create unnecessary anxiety, which in turn can inadvertently affect their achievement . In addition, Mrs. Bedford will pay careful attention to the directions for completing the assessment. The directions should state precisely how students should respond, and she will tailor the amount of detail provided in the instructions to match her student's prior experience with the format. For example, multiple-choice test items typically require less-detailed directions than an essay test item, while directions for writing a report or creating a project may be much more detailed. Once again, practice assessments have provided Mrs. Bedford with an ideal opportunity to teach her students how to respond to various assessment formats, and for her to evaluate the clarity and completeness of the instructions she has developed.

6. *Administer the assessment.* Mrs. Bedford will consider a number of other factors as she prepares to administer an assessment. First, she will consider the physical setting—making sure that there is ample space, proper lighting, a comfortable temperature, and reasonable air circulation. During the assessment, she will monitor any distractions from hallways, adjacent rooms, or outside the building. Next, Mrs. Bedford will consider the psychological atmosphere associated with assessment. These factors can affect results as much as the physical conditions of the assessment environment. If her students feel tense, overanxious, or pressured, their performance may be hindered. She will create a positive atmosphere by explaining the reason for the assessment, adequately preparing her students, and providing ample practice time prior to the actual assessment. If Mrs. Bedford's students are emotionally or physically unable to complete a assessment

during the scheduled time period, she will provide an alternative time. For example, a student who is ill or is worried about a lost pet will not perform at his or her best; thus, the assessment will not be a valid indication of the student's ability. Finally, Mrs. Bedford will keep in mind that her students may be tempted to "copy" off one another. Rather than be disheartened to discover that a student has cheated or worse yet, be put in a very compromising position should she need to confront the student, Mrs. Bedford will elect to structure the administration procedures to *prevent* the likelihood of cheating taking place. She may choose to rearrange the classroom seating, and she will most definitely monitor the class as they complete the assessment rather than grading papers or writing lesson plans. The best way to deal with cheating is to prevent it from happening.

General Guidelines for Developing Assessments

Once you decide on the type of assessment and the lesson objectives that will be the foundation of the assessment, the next thing you must do is decide on the appropriate format. You may elect to use traditional paper-and-pencil objective or essay tests, or you may choose an alternative assessment method such as a product or performance assessment. Your choice of assessment format will be based on the nature of the subject matter, the time available for assessment, and the characteristics of your students. Before considering each of the assessment formats in more detail, let's look at three general considerations that apply to all of the formats.

First, and most importantly, **assessments must match the lesson or behavioral objective.** This alignment between what was taught and what is assessed is one way to ensure that measures of student achievement are valid. Consider the following examples:

- *Lesson Objective: The student will be able to interpret tables and graphs.*

To assess whether students have mastered this objective, you would provide your students with an example of a table or graph, and then ask them questions about the information contained within the example. The objective implies that students will be asked to make judgments or statements about the information, not merely label the parts.

- *Behavioral Objective: Given temperature and rainfall weather data, the students will construct bar graphs that are labeled with the unit of measurement.*

To assess whether your students have mastered this objective, you would provide your students with temperature and weather data, perhaps collected from the daily newspaper, from an Internet site, or from classroom weather instruments that the students have been learning to use. Furthermore, your students may need rulers, colored pencils, or graph paper. In addition to constructing the bar graphs, you would expect your students to provide appropriate labels.

You can see from these two examples that behavioral objectives are more detailed than lesson objectives and provide a very explicit link between teaching and assessment. Whether you prefer to use lesson objectives or behavioral objectives, the important thing to consider is that test items are a key link between instruction and assessment. When assessments and lesson or behavioral objectives are clearly related, assessment results are more likely to be valid, providing you with an accurate picture of both the ability of your students work and the quality of your teaching.

A second general consideration is that **assessments should match your students' characteristics.** Vocabulary, reading level, and the context of the assessment must be appropriate for their age and experience. For example, a reading passage about a camping adventure in the rugged mountains of Alaska in which students are asked to identify the main idea, may become an inordinately complex task for students who have no prior knowledge about Alaska, or who have never been camping. You should pay careful consideration to the *fit* between assessments and your students' characteristics if you use assessments that have been developed by textbook authors and publishers.

Finally, **assessments should be clearly written** and **checked for spelling, grammar, or typing errors and for content matter that may be biased or offensive.** A good way to perfect your assessment development skills is to have a teaching colleague proofread newly created items. In addition, student "assistants" from other classrooms can provide excellent feedback about vocabulary or wording that may be confusing.

USING PAPER-AND-PENCIL TESTS TO ASSESS STUDENT LEARNING

Paper-and-pencil tests are a very popular assessment format. The tests consist of objective test items such as multiple choice and short answer, essay questions, or a combination of both. Now, let's look at these assessment formats in greater detail.

Objective Tests

Objective tests include alternative choice, multiple choice, matching, fill-in-the-blank, and short answer items. These formats are called objective because teachers can grade them *objectively*. In other words, there is little if any interpretation necessary on the part of the teacher to determine if students answered an objective test item correctly. The student's answer is quite clearly correct or incorrect.

Alternate choice test items require students to select one of two alternatives: true-false, yes-no, fact-opinion, or other similar sets of choices. Figure 9.2 is a checklist for constructing alternate choice test items, and Figure 9.3 provides several examples of correctly formatted items. A limitation of alternate choice questions is that students are just as likely to guess correctly as incorrectly; however, clustering the items together as illustrated in the second set of questions in Figure 9.3 is more likely to reveal a pattern of student knowledge because students are unlikely to guess all items correctly.

	FIGURE 9.2 CHECKLIST FOR ALTERNATIVE-CHOICE ITEMS
✓	Word statements in a positive manner, and avoid the use of negative statements.
✓	Each statement should focus on a single most important idea.
✓	Avoid questions that are meant to trick students. A test item should be false because it contains an important concept that is incorrect, not because it contains an insignificant error.
✓	Test items should be brief, but not at the expense of clarity. To avoid providing clues, true and false test items should be approximately the same length. Lengthy test items are correctly guessed true more often than false.
✓	Avoid using textbook wording. Statements taken directly from a textbook provide clues and are frequently guessed true correctly.
✓	Avoid terms such as *all, always, never, only, and none.* These statements are typically false and provide clues to students.
✓	Avoid the use of words such as *sometimes, often, maybe, should, may, some, and generally.* These statements are typically true and provide clues to students.

FIGURE 9.3 CORRECTLY FORMATTED ALTERNATIVE RESPONSE TEST ITEMS

True/False Questions

T	F	James Madison was President of the United States.
T	F	Paul Revere was Vice-President of the United States.
T	F	John Quincy Adams served two terms as President.

Fact/Opinion Questions

Fact	Opinion	1. California is the most scenic state.
Fact	Opinion	2. Cats make better pets than dogs.
Fact	Opinion	3. Oranges are a good source of vitamin C.
Fact	Opinion	4. Alaska is the largest state.

Multiple choice test items consist of two parts—the stem and a set of three or more responses. The stem presents a statement or question, and should be written in a complete sentence whenever possible. Stems that are only a short phrase do not provide enough information to guide the student's thinking process. The set of responses consist of one clearly best answer and at least two incorrect answers. The incorrect answers are called **distractors** or **foils**. Figure 9.4 is a checklist for writing multiple-choice items and Figure 9.5 displays several correctly formatted multiple-choice items. Note that the set of responses is listed vertically underneath the stem, rather than listing several responses horizontally across the test. The vertical list of responses is much easier for students to read.

Matching test items require students to match information in two columns. The list of items in the first, or left column, is called the premises. The premises are a set of words or short phrases that prompt the student to think about a matching response. The premises should "go together"—meaning that there should be a common theme or topic among them. The second list of items, or right hand column, is called the responses. The response should be listed in a logical order (e.g.,

FIGURE 9.4	CHECKLIST FOR WRITING MULTIPLE CHOICE TEST ITEMS
✓	The *stem* should be a complete thought or question.
✓	When possible, the *stem* should be stated positively. If negative words must be used, they should be highlighted in some way.
✓	The *responses* should be approximately the same length and should be grammatically compatible with the stem.
✓	The *responses* should contain similar subject matter.
✓	The *responses* should be listed in chronological, hierarchical, alphabetical, or some other systematic order to avoid providing clues. Most attempts at listing responses in random order actually provide clues because students become quite adept at identifying response patterns (e.g., "Response 'c' hasn't been used yet so I'll pick 'c'.")
✓	Avoid *responses* such as "all of the above", "none of the above", "A and B", "A, C, but not B", etc. In most cases, these types of responses serve no purpose other than to confuse students.
✓	Avoid *responses* that are not plausible or are silly. It is perfectly acceptable to have a different number of responses for each multiple choice question. If you cannot identify at least 2 plausible distractors, then use an alternative test format.

FIGURE 9.5   CORRECTLY FORMATTED MULTIPLE CHOICE TEST ITEMS

1.   What happens to the temperature of a gas when it is compressed?

    (a)   Increases
    (b)   Decreases
    (c)   Fluctuates between increase and decrease
    (d)   Remains the same

2.   What type of material is oak?

    (a)   Closed-grain wood
    (b)   Hardboard
    (c)   Open-grain wood
    (d)   Soft wood

3.   Identify the measure of central tendency that is calculated by summing the scores and dividing by the number of observations.

    (a)   Mode
    (b)   Median
    (c)   Mean

4.   Which of the following is **NOT** a synonym for the word *anxious*?

    (a)   Apprehensive
    (b)   Calm
    (c)   Nervous
    (d)   Uneasy

---

alphabetical, chronological, etc.) so students can easily skim through the list. Avoiding a one-to-one match between the premises and responses helps to reduce the likelihood that students will "guess" matches correctly simply through the process of elimination. Figure 9.6 is a checklist for writing matching test items and Figure 9.7 is an example of a correctly formatted item.

    Completion test items, or fill-in-the-blank items, are complete statements with one or more key words omitted. Students respond to this type of question by supplying a missing word or words. Students must be provided with adequate subject matter in the statement to guide their response; thus, it is important that the missing word or words be placed as close to the end of the sentence as possible. The wording in completion items should be carefully reviewed to avoid situations in which more than one answer is correct. Figure 9.8 is a checklist for writing completion test items, and several correctly formatted items are displayed in Figure 9.9.

    Short answer test items are questions that require students to provide a word, phrase, or a simple short sentence or two in response to the question. Short answer test items differ from completion items in that they require the student to answer a

FIGURE 9.6   CHECKLIST FOR MATCHING TEST ITEMS

✓	Label the premise and response columns and refer to the labels in the directions.
✓	Both columns should contain homogeneous material.
✓	The *premises* should contain the more difficult (or lengthy) material.
✓	The *responses* should be systematically ordered (i.e., alphabetically, chronologically, etc.)
✓	The premise and response columns should have an unequal number of items. Provide specific directions to indicate whether responses will be used more than once.
✓	Limit the number of items to approximately six to eight (less for younger students).

FIGURE 9.7   CORRECTLY FORMATTED MATCHING TEST ITEM

Directions: Match the inventors with their inventions by placing the letter for the inventor in the space before their invention. Some of the inventors will not be used.

Inventions

_____ 1. Atlantic cable
_____ 2. cotton gin
_____ 3. electric starter
_____ 4. sewing machine
_____ 5. steam engine
_____ 6. wireless telegraphy

Inventors

A. Colt
B. Edison
C. Field
D. Howe
E. Kettering
F. Marconi
G. Watt
H. Whitney

question, rather than simply filling in a missing word. Keep in mind that short answer items are objective test items and should be written in such a way to illicit one clearly correct response. It is this characteristic that differentiates short answer test items from essay test items, which call for a much more individualized response from students. Figure 9.10 is a checklist for writing short answer items, and several correctly formatted short answer items are presented in Figure 9.11.

	FIGURE 9.8 CHECKLIST FOR WRITING COMPLETION TEST ITEMS
✓	Place a blank at or near the end of the sentence. Sufficient content should be provided in the statement to direct students' attention to the concept of interest. Blanks at the beginning of the sentence are too confusing.
✓	Remove only key word(s) from the sentence.
✓	Eliminate the possibility of more than one correct answer.
✓	Avoid providing clues by using 'a(n)' rather than 'a' or 'an' as the final word before the blank.
✓	Paraphrase statements taken from instructional materials. Using statements taken directly from a textbook provides clues.

FIGURE 9.9   CORRECTLY FORMATTED COMPLETION TEST ITEMS

1. A multiple choice test item consists of a stem and three or more _____.

2. A sentence that tells what a paragraph is about is called a(n) _____ sentence.

	FIGURE 9.10 CHECKLIST FOR WRITING SHORT ANSWER TEST ITEMS
✓	Provide a blank for each item to suggest the expected length of the response.
✓	Specify the units required in the response (i.e., inches, cm, dollars, etc.)
✓	Keep the focus of the question specific to ensure that response can be evaluated objectively.

Activity 9.2

Use the checklists in the preceding sections to evaluate the objective test items in Figure 9.12. Each of the items contains one or more formatting errors. Verify your evaluation of the items with the evaluation in the Appendix. Then, work in pairs to write some objective test items of your own and evaluate each other's items.

FIGURE 9.11   CORRECTLY FORMATTED SHORT ANSWER TEST ITEMS

1. Calculate the perimeter for the following figures.

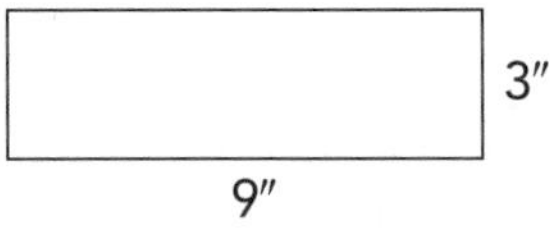

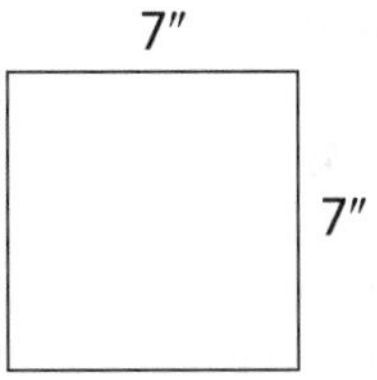

_____feet _____inches   _____feet _____inches

2. Briefly define the term measurement.

_____

_____

Essay Tests

Essay tests require students to produce a unique written response to a question or set of directions. This is in contrast to the short answer objective test items in which the expected response will vary little from student to student. Furthermore, short answer test items address a single lesson or behavioral objective, while essay questions typically reflect a synthesis of many, if not all, of the objectives that comprise an instructional unit.

When you think about essay tests, you might picture students sitting at their desks and writing furiously in an attempt to fill up a blank page, hoping to remember the facts and details that may have been hastily memorized the night before. In fact, this is a very limited view of an essay test. First, the purpose of an essay test is *not* for students to simply recall or restate factual information. Second, essay tests can take a number of forms such as a term paper or a report, a poem, a newspaper editorial, a business letter, and so forth. Finally, essay tests can be administered during a single class period, or they can be completed outside of class. The following examples illustrate the variety of essay test options:

- Mr. Chin's twelfth-grade psychology class has been studying the stages of human psychological development. On an essay test, Mr. Chin will present an example of a situation that involves a psychological phenomenon (e.g., joy, separation, anger, etc.) and ask his students to write a brief paragraph to illustrate how people at various life stages (e.g., toddler, teenager, adult, etc.) would respond to the situation.

- Ms. Lee's ninth-grade English class has been studying various forms of poetry. At the conclusion of the unit, Ms. Lee will require her students to submit an original haiku, sonnet, and limerick poem.

FIGURE 9.12   INCORRECTLY FORMATTED OBJECTIVE TEST ITEMS

Can you spot the errors in the following alternate choice items?

T   F   On multiple choice tests more than one correct answer should not be included.

T   F   "The Raven" was written by Edgar Allen Poe.

T   F   It is possible to determine whether a solution is acid by the red color formed on litmus paper when it is inserted into the solution.

T   F   All birds can fly.

Can you spot the errors in the following multiple choice test items?

1.   Australia   *Complete thought or question*
  (a)   is an island continent.
  (b)   imports coffee from the United States
  (c)   has a larger population than the United States.
  (d)   was discovered by Marco Polo.

2.   Which of the following is not an example of a mammal?
  (a)   Monkey
  (b)   Penguin
  (c)   Whale
  (d)   None of the above

3.   Which one of the following people signed the Declaration of Independence?
  (a)   Leonardo DaVinci
  (b)   Paul Revere
  (c)   Paul Bunyan   *silly*
  (d)   Thomas Jefferson

Can you spot the errors in these completion test items?

1. _____ discovered the polio vaccine. *put blank at end*
2. The first American astronaut to walk on the moon was _____.
3. A neutron is a _____ consisting of a _____ of _____.
  too many blanks

Can you spot the errors in this matching item?

Match the following:

_____ 1. The oldest town in the U.S.   (a) St. Augustine
_____ 2. A famous Quaker   (b) Boston
_____ 3. A city in Virginia   (c) Cartier
_____ 4. First French Explorer   (d) Pilgrims
_____ 5. He founded Connecticut   (e) Thomas Hooker
_____ 6. They landed at Plymouth Rock   (f) Jamestown
                                              (g) William Penn
  Premise   *Response*

Can you spot the errors in these short answer test items?

1. If Sandy can run one mile in twelve minutes, how long will it take her to run six miles? _____
2. Define what is meant by the term 'measurement'.
  Doesn't ask question, asks for definition

- Mrs. Damian's fifth-grade science class has been studying the scientific method. On an upcoming essay test, Mrs. Damian will provide several examples of science problems. Her students will be asked to select a problem that is suitable for the scientific process and describe the steps that they would follow to solve the problem.

Activity 9.3

Consider the previous three examples of essay tests by Mr. Chin, Ms. Lee, and Mrs. Damian. In a small discussion group provide a rationale for deciding whether the essay tests should be a: (a) pretest, practice test, or post test, (b) completed in class or outside of class, and a (c) formative or summative assessment.

Like objective tests, essay test questions and directions should be based on the lesson or behavioral objectives for a particular unit, match learner characteristics, and be clearly written. In contrast to objective tests, essay tests pose several unique challenges. First, essay tests require longer, more elaborate responses so it follows that the test directions require considerably more detail. Second, more complex directions and lengthy responses may precipitate the need to *teach* students *how* to answer essay questions; hence, practice tests can be a very useful instructional strategy. Third, essay tests can be challenging to grade. The use of a rating scale will help you to focus on the important aspects of written responses rather than being swayed by lengthy or creative responses that do not really address the question asked. Providing copies of the rating scale to your students along with the written instructions is a very effective way to communicate your expectations. Finally, you must decide and clearly communicate to your students how spelling and grammar will be evaluated.

Figure 9.13 is a checklist for writing essay questions and Figure 9.14 is an example of a set of written directions and corresponding rating scale that Ms. Hernandez

FIGURE 9.13	CHECKLIST FOR WRITING ESSAY QUESTIONS
✓	Develop a rating scale or checklist for scoring tests.
✓	Distribute copies of the rating scale prior to the test to provide guidance to students.
✓	Provide students with guidance to indicate the depth or breadth of the expected response (e.g., length of response, time limit, or possible points, etc.)
✓	Consider using practice tests as an instructional strategy with students who have limited experience responding to essay formats.
✓	Determine in advance the emphasis that will be placed on spelling, grammar, and proofreading, and clearly communicate this information to students.

FIGURE 9.14   DIRECTIONS AND RATING SCALE FOR AN ESSAY TEST

Directions: Select <u>one</u> of the following issues listed below and write an editorial for or against the issue.

Topic #1–Mandatory social service requirement for high school graduation
Topic #2–Compulsory school uniforms
Topic #3–Lowering the drinking age to 18

Requirements: Your responses should be: (a) be limited to one type-written page, (b) proofread for spelling, grammatical, and typing errors, and (c) include the following four components:

1. An introductory paragraph that identifies the issue and provides background information.
2. At least three arguments for or three arguments against the issue. For each argument provide a rationale to support your contention.
3. At least three references that support your opinion.
4. A concluding paragraph that summarizes your opinion.

Editorial Rating Scale

	Points Awarded	Comments	Score
Introduction	3 points = all criteria met 2 points = some criteria missing 1 point = many criteria missing 0 points = not included		
Arguments & Rationale	3 points = all criteria met 2 points = some criteria missing 1 point = many criteria missing 0 points = not included		
References	3 points = all criteria met 2 points = some criteria missing 1 point = many criteria missing 0 points = not included		
Summary	3 points = all criteria met 2 points = some criteria missing 1 point = many criteria missing 0 points = not included		
Proofreading Spelling Typing Grammar	2 points = no errors 1 point = some errors 0 points = many errors		

Total Score_____

might use during a unit on expository writing that is part of the ninth-grade English curriculum. Ms. Hernandez has explicitly stated the required components of the assignment and included a sample of the rating scale she will use to grade the assignment. Note the match between the requirements and the criteria listed on the rating scale. Furthermore, her lesson objectives would also align with both the directions and rating scale. Ms. Hernandez is likely to use a full-page rating scale for each assignment, which would afford her more space for writing comments.

USING ALTERNATIVE ASSESSMENT METHODS TO ASSESS STUDENT LEARNING

Alternative assessment implies that student learning is assessed by some method other than the objective and essay paper-and-pencil tests that we have just described. Although there are any number of alternative methods for assessing student learning, we have chosen to group alternative assessment methods in two broad classifications: product assessment and performance assessment. Alternately, some educators use the term **authentic assessment** to refer to alternative assessments that more resemble students' real-word experiences than paper-and-pencil tests.

Product Assessments

Imagine the following classroom scenarios. Students in Mr. George's sixth-grade social studies class will work in collaborative groups to create a relief map of a Central American country. Ms. Slonsky's art students are creating pen and ink drawings. Students in Mrs. Rayburn's math class are constructing bar graphs that depict the average daily rainfall. In each of these classrooms, the outcome of student learning is a unique tangible product—an alternative to a paper-and-pencil test. Instead of *students* completing a paper-and-pencil test, the *teachers* will complete a rating scale or compose written comments to assess their students' achievement of the learning objectives. Thus, **product assessments** consist of three components—the directions you provide to your students to outline the nature of the product they will develop, the product itself, and the rating scale or comments you complete. Like paper-and-pencil tests, products assessments will be valid and reliable indicators of student achievement when they are based on the lesson or behavioral objectives that have been identified for a particular unit.

   Product assessments are rather similar to essay tests in a number of ways. First, product assessments tend to reflect a synthesis of more complex lesson objectives. Second, product assessments require more detailed instructions for students, and a rating scale for the teacher to use for grading purposes. Third, developing and grading product assessments can be challenging because it is much easier to be swayed by neat, creative, and elaborate projects rather than focusing on the underlying lesson objectives. Fourth, product assessments often take more time to complete, and may be assigned as out-of-class projects. There is a greater temptation for help from parents, which can be problematic for those students whose parents are unable for a number of reasons to provide assistance. Unlike essay tests, product assessments may be fragile, large in size, or in some other manner, more difficult to store or transport.

Product assessments are particularly popular because there is a high level of student engagement and because products most resemble real-world activities. However, product assessments pose a unique challenge because it is tempting to confuse a product assessment with an enrichment activity. For example, Mr. Constantine's fourth-grade social studies class has nearly completed a unit on the early American settlers, and small groups of students are constructing dioramas to depict a historical scene from that era. Mr. Constantine has elected to use this as an enrichment activity—to reinforce learning and engage students in the learning process, and to promote cooperation and social skills among the students. On the other hand, Mr. Constantine could have used the dioramas as a product assessment. Had he chosen to do so, he would have had to identify the lesson objectives that would have been the foundation for the projects, and based the grades on how well the dioramas indicated each student's attainment of the objectives. Had this been the case, Mr. Constantine probably would have needed to have students write a paragraph or so explaining how the diorama depicted the objectives, give oral reports, or had student conferences. Because the assignment was completed in class, he did not have to consider how much help parents provided. He would, however, have to decide if each student in the group should get the same grade.

Activity 9.4

Mrs. Lopez teaches seventh-grade English at Forrest Middle School. Her students are completing a unit on Greek mythology, and she has assigned them the task of creating posters of various mythological characters. The posters will be used in a hallway display in the Language Arts wing of the school. Would you advise Mrs. Lopez to use this assignment as a product assessment or simply an enrichment activity. Present a rationale to support your decision.

Performance Assessments

Performance assessments require students to demonstrate their mastery of lesson objectives by completing a physical activity. Like product assessments, performance assessments consist of three components: the directions that you give your students for performing the task, the performance itself, and your assessment of the performance—be it a rating scale or written comments. Performance assessments can be almost solely a motor skill such as executing a standing broad jump in a physical education class. More often, performance assessments reflect a combination of motor and cognitive skills. For example, Mrs. Rosenthal's health class is studying basic first aid methods. At the end of the current unit, she will expect her students to demonstrate the proper procedures for administering CPR. Before her students can demonstrate the physical skills of checking for an open airway and circulation, or proper hand placement, they will need to have mastered a number of lesson objectives from the cognitive domain such as listing the sequence of steps, and the number of breathes for children and adults. Thus, she is teaching and assessing both a cognitive and physical skill. She might elect to teach the cognitive skills related to circulation and respiration first, or she might actually teach both together. The nature of her students, their prior knowledge and understanding, and the complexity of the material are all things she will consider in deciding how best to integrate all components of the task.

Performance assessments pose some unique challenges for teachers. First, physical tasks are often completed in a very short period of time. Unless a videotape of the performance is made, you may miss or forget important aspects of the performance, especially if there are detailed aspects of the performance that are of interest to you. Second, because students are assessed individually, there can be some nervousness associated with the assessment. They may need considerable practice time or the opportunity to "try again." Finally, your class management skills must be finely tuned. In a class of twenty students, what will the remaining nineteen students be doing if only one student at a time can demonstrate CPR. Similar to other test and assessment formats, performance assessments must be based on the lesson or behavioral objectives if valid and reliable decisions about student achievement can be made. Thorough directions and rating scales are necessary components of performance assessments.

Activity 9.5

For each of the following performance objectives, decide if the task is *primarily* physical or a combination cognitive and motor skill. For those tasks that you have classified as psychomotor, list several of the underlying cognitive skills that students will need to master before they can successful *perform* the task.

Playing a musical instrument   Swimming the backstroke
Sculpting a bowl from clay   Performing a dramatic play

To learn more about alternative assessment, browse the websites listed in Figure 9.15 or search the more general assessment websites identified in Figure 9.1 earlier in the chapter.

ASSESSING LESSON OBJECTIVES FROM THE AFFECTIVE DOMAIN

Lesson objectives from the affective domain describe students' feelings, attitudes, and values of the learner. Sometimes affective objectives will be the direct focus of instruction and at other times, affective objectives will be likely outcomes, but not

---

FIGURE 9.15   INTERNET SOURCES ABOUT ALTERNATIVE ASSESSMENT TOPICS

- Assessment and Rubrics
  http://www.grand.k12.ut.us/curric/rubrics.html

- Alternative Assessment
  http://www.mel.lib.mi.us/education/edu-assess.html

- Alternative Assessments and Portfolios
  http://scrtec.org/track/tracks/f00133.html

- Resources for Alternative Assessment
  http://www.district44.dupage.k12.il.us/assess.html

---

objectives that you will directly teach or assess. Consider the following two-learner objectives from the affective domain:

- *The student will appreciate reading poetry for enjoyment.*

After completing a poetry unit Ms. Nathan hopes that her fifth graders have a greater appreciation and interest in poetry, that they will perhaps choose to read or write poems simply for enjoyment. But she certainly cannot *grade* her students on their feelings about poetry. The very notion of assigning a student a lower grade, or deducting points because they did not develop a love of poetry is absurd. She cannot directly teach a love of poetry. Although Ms. Nathan sought a particular outcome, she did not directly assess or take direct intervention should the objective not be met.

- *The student will choose to follow classroom rules.*

In contrast, at the beginning of the school year Mr. Thome and his seventh graders developed a set of classroom rules. Together, they discussed the importance of the rules and the logical consequences for not following the rules. A copy of the rules is posted in the classroom, and each student signed a personal pledge to follow the rules. For the most part, the students obey the rules but lately the class seems to be having some trouble with verbal harassment. There is considerable teasing taking place. Mr. Thome has decided to hold a special class meeting to review this behavior. For the most part the teasing has stopped, but there are still a few students who continue this inappropriate behavior. He makes some phone calls home and sets up conferences with parents. In contrast to Ms. Nathan, Mr. Thome has a professional obligation to directly teach *and* assess the objective.

In both cases, assessing learner objectives from the affective domain have similar challenges. First, affective objectives can be difficult to define. What *precisely* does "appreciate poetry" or "respect others" *mean*? Second, affective outcomes cannot be directly assessed. Rather, it is the overt behaviors associated with the value or feeling that can be assessed. Although Ms. Nathan's students may select a poetry anthology from the library or verbally express their interest in poetry, she can never know whether these behaviors are a true indication of their appreciation of poetry, or if they are simply trying to please her. Mr. Thome's student's may not call each other names in school to avoid the consequences of having their parents come to school, but they may not have necessarily embraced the value of respecting others. Name calling may still be taking place off the school grounds. Finally, affective objectives are difficult to teach. Simply telling her students about the joys of poetry, or lecturing his students about why teasing is unacceptable, is not instructional strategies that are likely to ensure that Ms. Nathan's or Mr. Thome's students will embrace the affective objectives their teachers have identified.

Depending on the subject matter that you teach and the characteristics and needs of your students, your emphasis on lesson objectives from the affective domain may vary from a more informal emphasis to a more direct emphasis where you will actually use instructional strategies such as modeling behaviors, role-playing, and class discussions.

PORTFOLIO ASSESSMENT

Teachers have always collected and displayed examples of student work. Think back when you were in school—perhaps during parent conferences your teacher shared some examples of your work with your parents. During open house, the bulletin boards and showcases around your school were brimming with examples of student work. More recently, using examples of student work in a *systematic* and thoughtful way to make assessments about student learning has received renewed interest and is commonly referred to as **portfolio assessment.**

Consider Mr. McBride's ninth-grade English class. His students are creating a writing portfolio and they will select pieces of their writing that they feel illustrate their attainment of the unit objectives and their growth over time. In addition, they can include a few of their favorite pieces. Their portfolios will include a brief narrative to explain why they selected the individual pieces, how each writing sample illustrates what they have learned, and how their skills and knowledge have developed during the semester. The writing pieces will be assembled in a notebook. Mr. McBride will have developed a clear set of directions to guide students as they develop their portfolios, and he will provide feedback and guidance throughout the semester. Once the portfolios are submitted, he will use a rating scale, or scoring rubric, to evaluate each students achievement of the unit objectives. In addition to writing samples, the students will be directed to include several of the post tests that were administered during the semester.

Mr. McBride is doing more than simply collecting samples of student work. Rather, the portfolios that his students are assembling are characterized by three features that are the mainstays of portfolio assessment—a clear cut purpose behind the items to be included in a portfolio, student participation in selecting the components, and pieces that show growth over time.

There are several distinct advantages to portfolio assessment. First, portfolios encourage students to become more active participants in the learning and assessment process. Second, the focus of assessment becomes academic growth—rather than a *snapshot* of achievement at one point in time. Finally, portfolios may give a more realistic picture of student achievement because assessment is based on a series of assignments that may more closely resemble authentic tasks. Portfolio assessment is characterized by a number of challenges as well. On the surface, portfolios look easy and straight forward but as you can see, there is far more to portfolio assessment than merely compiling student work. To be meaningful measures of student achievement, portfolios assessment must be planned and implemented in a systematic way. Your students will need to be *taught* how to become active participants in this method, and you are likely to need additional time to develop and grade them.

STANDARDIZED TESTS

No doubt, you have taken standardized tests throughout your school years. Not only did you take standardized achievement tests during your primary and secondary school years, but it's likely that you took a standardized test such as the SAT or ACT as a entrance requirement for college. And, you may be required to take the National Teacher Exam (NTE) as a requirement for your teaching certification and the Graduate Record Exam (GRE) as an entrance requirement for graduate school.

Although there are a number of different types of standardized tests, the two kinds used most commonly in schools are **proficiency achievement tests** and **norm-referenced achievement tests.** Proficiency tests require students to meet or exceed a particular score in order to *pass,* or be deemed *proficient* in the subject matter covered on the test. Some school districts or states require students to pass proficiency tests as a requirement for high school graduation. Norm-referenced achievement tests compare student performance to other students in the same grade. Student achievement on the test is classified as below average, average, or above average when compared to a similar group of students. Due to the expense, time, and expertise needed to develop and score standardized tests, individual school districts rarely take on this task. More often than not, standardized tests are developed by a team of measurement and curriculum experts at large test development companies or state departments of education.

Your personal experiences may have fostered various ideas and opinions about standardized tests. You might remember feeling very anxious about taking these tests because of the important decisions hinging on the results. You may have felt quite elated when you received the test results, or you might have felt disappointed, or perhaps you thought that there had to be something *wrong* with the test because your score did not seem to match the good grades you got in school. Whether you have positive or negative feelings about standardized testing you have the following professional responsibilities:

- Learn about the tests that are administered in your school district. When are they administered? What subject matter is covered? Consider the testing dates and content matter when you are developing your curriculum plans. Teaching a particular topic several weeks *after* it is tested is a disservice to your students.

- Provide parents and students with appropriate and timely information about the test. What is the purpose of the test? When will the test be administered? How long will the test take? When will the results be available?

- Prepare students to take the test. Many testing companies provide practice tests so students can become familiar with the test format. Teaching your students effective test-taking strategies (e.g., getting a good night's sleep before the test, how to approach difficult questions, whether to guess, etc.) is simply *good* teaching.

- Maintain a positive testing environment. Over-dramatizing or dismissing the importance of the test can affect student performance. You may have your own opinions about the value or worth of standardized tests, but you owe it to your students to encourage their best performance.

- Be prepared to interpret test results for parents and students. Standardized test scores are reported in one or more special type of scores such as sta- nines, percentiles, percentile bands, or grade equivalent scores. Materials published by the test developers, assessment experts at your school dis- trict, and assessment textbooks can be valuable resources for learning more about standardized test scores.

ASSESSING CHILDREN WITH SPECIAL NEEDS

Not only are you likely to find that your students have a range of learning abilities and styles, you may also find that one or more of your students will be identified as a special needs student. Special needs students may be classified as learning disabled, developmentally delayed, or with physical disabilities such as loss of hearing or sight. It is quite likely that you will need to develop and modify teach- ing and assessment strategies to meet the instruction needs of your special needs students. For example, a student with a hearing disability may wear a special receiver while you wear a microphone. A student who is visually impaired may use a magnifier to read, or use instructional materials that are written in large print, or listen to books that have been recorded on tape. You may need to read a test aloud to a student who has difficulty reading, or accept answers orally from a student who has difficulty writing. A student who is easily distracted may need to take a test in a small group, or individually. Many teacher-education programs and state teacher certification requirements include at least one course that specif- ically addresses the instructional needs of children with special needs. In addition to course work, most school systems have instructional experts who will provide you with assistance.

ASSESSING PRE-K AND EARLY ELEMENTARY STUDENTS

The examples we have presented so far are geared toward students who can read and write. What about younger children who have not reached the developmental level where they can read and respond to a test in the same way as older children? The *process* that teachers of young children follow to develop assessment methods is the same process all teachers follow—but the unique characteristics of young children limit some of the assessment *choices* that other teachers might have.

In her pre-K classroom, Ms. LaRocca is preparing to assess her students' discrimination skills. First and foremost, she must consider the lesson objectives that have been the focus of instruction during the past week or so. Because her pre-K students neither read nor write, Ms. LaRocca must rely primarily on some type of performance or product assessment. Similar to the tasks that her students have *practiced during instruction*, she will give each child a set of wooden blocks that they will be asked to sort by color and shape. Ms. LaRocca will only be able to observe a small group at a time—sitting with three or four children at one of the work centers in the classroom. While she is working with each group, the remainder of the class will be working on a craft project with Mrs. Michaels, the teaching assistant. Since Ms. LaRocca will need to provide oral directions to her students, she has jotted down some notes to ensure that her instructions are consistent across groups, and she has created a checklist for recording each child's success with the task. She may also decide to jot down anecdotal notes that she might want to refer to later. In this instance, Ms. LaRocca has elected to use a somewhat formal assessment approach that entailed developing a set of written instructions (that she read aloud) and a checklist for recording each student's progress. In other instances, her assessments may be based on naturalistic observations throughout the school day.

SUMMARY

In this chapter we have explored many assessment and testing alternatives. The Educational Resources and Information Center (ERIC) sponsors several Internet sites that you may find useful, and they are listed in Figure 9.16. The ERIC Clearinghouse on Assessment and Evaluation is a large database that you can search for assessment related information. ERIC sponsors a Listserv that will allow you to dialogue with teachers and assessment experts, and it publishes an on-line journal called *Practical Assessment*.

Developing and administering the appropriate assessments are only a part of the assessment process. Whether you elect to use an objective test, an essay test, or an alternative assessment method, the next step is to use the results of assessment to make decisions about what your students have learned, the quality of your teaching, and the quality of your tests. Chapter 10 examines these topics.

Although assessment is only one component of the instructional process, it is a complex and comprehensive field in and of itself. There are many good references that address

---

FIGURE 9.16   INTERNET ASSESSMENT RESOURCES SPONSORED BY ERIC

- ERIC Clearinghouse on Assessment and Evaluation
  http://ericae.net/

- Educational Assessment in Grades K-12 Listserv
  http://ericae.net/k12assess/

- Practical Assessment, Research and Evaluation: A Peer-Reviewed Electronic Journal
  http://ericae.net/pare/

these and other assessment topics in considerably more detail, and a number of them are listed at the end of this chapter. As you complete your teacher education course work, assume your first classroom, and eventually join the ranks of experiences teachers, you will, no doubt, revisit the topic of assessment.

REFLECTIONS

1. Michela Thomas and Wendy Wolfe provide their sixth-grade students with feedback from formative assessments. They recognize this as a sound strategy for helping their students to identify their strengths and weakness, and ensuring their comfort with a particular test item format. With this in mind, Michela and Wendy have developed a set of homework assignments that *parallel* the upcoming proficiency test that their sixth-grade students will be required to take. A few of Michela's and Wendy's colleagues have criticized them for "teaching to the test," while others have supported their sound teaching practice. What do you think the phrase "teaching to the test" means? How would you reply to Michela's and Wendy's critics?

2. Jack Corraro teaches five sections of English literature at Cummings High School, with twenty-five to thirty students in each of his sections. At the beginning of the semester, Jack administered mostly essay tests. Although he feels that essay tests are probably a more appropriate format, he has resorted more and more to using objective tests. With essay tests he was spending nearly an entire weekend reading and grading papers. Although objective tests have cut his grading time in half, he is not convinced that objective questions are *always* the best format to use. Can Jack reach a balance between using essay tests and the time it takes to grade them? What suggestions would you give him?

3. Think back on some of the tests *you* have recently taken. Were your test scores valid and reliable indicators of your achievement? What was it about how the test was designed or administered that may have contributed to or detracted from the *fairness* of the test?

TEACHER AS RESEARCHER

Paper-and-Pencil Assessment

Stiggins, R. J. (1997). Essay assessment: Vast untapped potential. In *Student-centered classroom assessment, second edition* (pp. 133–158.) Upper Saddle River, NJ: Prentice-Hall, Inc.

The author upholds that essay tests are an excellent option for evaluating student learning. Despite their advantages, there are a number of flaws that often characterize essay tests. What suggestions does Stiggins provide for ensuring the quality of essay tests?

Alternative Assessment

Adams, T. L. (1998). Alternative assessment in elementary school mathematics. *Childhood Education, 74* (4), 220–225.

The author provides examples of how journals, observations, interviews, self-assessments, and surveys can be used to assess a wide range of mathematics-related learning objectives. What do you see as the strengths or limitations of adapting these suggestions for a subject or grade level that is of interest to you? Are there particular methods that may be more suitable than others?

Assessing Attitudes

Cutforth, N., & Parker, M. (1996). Promoting affective development in physical education: The value of journal writing. *The Journal of Physical Education, Recreation & Dance, 67* (7), 19–24.

The authors describe how journal writing in their physical education classes promote respect and sensitivity toward others, responsibility, cooperation, and fair play among their students. What are some of the advantages that journal writing has provided for students *and* teachers? Consider the subject and grade level you are most interested in teaching and identify some attitudes that your students could write about in a journal.

Popham, W. J. (1994). Educational assessment's lurking lacuna: The measurement of affect. *Education & Urban Society, 26* (4), 404–16.

Although educators have given assessment issues considerably more notice in the past decade, nationally-recognized assessment specialist James Popham contends that the assessment of student affect has received scant attention. How does the author suggest that affective outcomes should be addressed instructionally? How should affective outcomes be measured?

Portfolio Assessment

Barton, J., & Collins, A. (Eds.) (1997). *Portfolio assessment: A handbook for educators.* Menlo Park, CA: Innovative Learning Publications.

This book was written by eleven classroom teachers who have developed and used educational portfolios in their classrooms. Examples range in grade from kindergarten through high school and across a variety of subject areas. Select and read a chapter that best matches a subject or grade level of interest to you. In what ways was the teacher's approach to assessment different and/or similar to paper-and-pencil and alternative assessments?

Assessing Students with Special Needs

Lustig, R. L. (1989). *Assessment of learners with special needs.* Boston: Allyn and Bacon.

Unlike similar texts of this nature that are written primarily for special education teachers, this book provides a much more comprehensive view of assessing learners with special needs and considers many practical and informal methods that any classroom teacher can use. Assessment in specific content areas such as spelling, handwriting, language development, and mathematics is addressed. A chapter on social skills and affective assessment is included.

Salend, S. J. (1995). Modifying tests for diverse learners. *Intervention in School and Clinic, 31* (2), 84–90.

This article suggests specific modifications and techniques that classroom teachers can use to adapt their tests to meet the needs of diverse learners. Consider the subject matter or grade level that is of most interest to you. In what ways are you likely to modify your assessment methods for students with physical or learning disabilities?

SECTION IV

IDEAL

Acting on the Plan

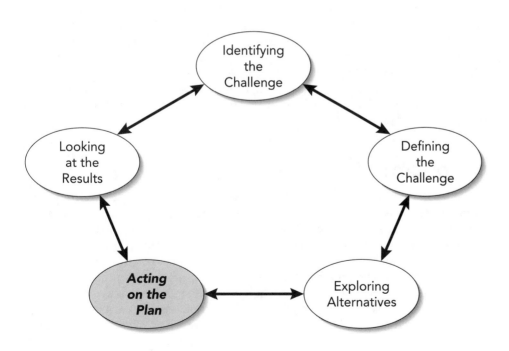

There comes a time when the formal planning of a lesson is done, and it's time to try it out in the classroom. You've identified the challenges in front of you: dealing with the characteristics of your students and the requirements of the curricula. You've defined in exact terms what you want your specific group to learn and analyzed the unit and lesson formats by which to deliver the instruction. Furthermore, you've explored the "tools" of questioning, direction-giving, and grouping arrangements together with instructional resources, teacher, learner, and assessment strategies. Sometimes the planning process has been messy; your mind has gone forward and backward as you considered students, curricula, instructional options, and assessment in numerous combinations. This is typical of most good decision-makers, who most likely have come up with a Plan A and Plan B, at the very least. And because they have thought through all of the possibilities that they could anticipate, they probably feel reasonably comfortable about the probability of Plan A being successful. They also probably feel even more comfortable because, in the process of defining the challenges and exploring alternatives, they have considered the potential obstacles to their success and already have a way of working through those obstacles—Plan B. Let's do it, they'll say.

In teaching, the first three stages of the model are done during your planning stage. At some point, though, the show must go on. You must act on the plans that you have made. And while it is important that you plan for all the possible roadblocks to delivering a successful lesson that you can, even veteran teachers cannot anticipate every possible thing that could go wrong. In this section, we take a break from the chapter arrangement to tell you about Annie, a first-year teacher. You'll hear her voice and see her actions as she experiences decision-making from planning to teaching—actually "doing it"—to looking at the results of teaching. You'll also hear the voices of two other important people in Annie's professional life, a mentor and an evaluator. We'll also offer our observations and interpretations at the end of the section. We hope this experience, although vicarious, will give you a more personal feel for the material in the first nine chapters as well as for some of the ideas and techniques you will encounter in chapters 10 and 11.

INTRODUCTION

Annie is a first-year teacher and has been enjoying teaching fourth grade, although it has been stressful at times just as student teaching was. She talks frequently with Lydia, her mentor teacher, and confides that she looks forward to her second year when she can rely on a file of "tried and true" lessons. Overall, however, the year has gone well. The students are most often cooperative, and they know how to settle down when they know that Annie means business.

What follows are scenes from Annie's story as she plans, delivers, and then reflects on her lesson. Included is a relatively new reality in many teachers' careers: required classroom observations as one part of certification and licensure decisions.

As you read, you'll see that the scenes are dated over a five month period to give you a sense of Annie's planning and teaching over time, as well as the process of a performance assessment as a part of certification or licensure. Some of the scenes are also titled with the phases of the IDEAL decision-making model even though, as we've said all along, making instructional decisions is often recursive, going back and forth among the phases.

DECEMBER 9   Identifying the Challenges of Learners and Curricula

Annie was straightening the desks in her classroom when her mentor, Lydia, peeked in the door.

"Hi, Annie, how was your day?" Lydia inquired.

"Fine. Adam tried to push my buttons just once today, but I could tell what he was up to and I stopped him in his tracks."

"Good for you. You know that ability to 'tell what he is up to' will develop with time and pretty soon Adam will be complaining that you've got eyes in the back of your head. Keep him guessing!"

Annie felt temporarily assured. Lydia had been teaching for twelve years. Besides helping Annie weed through much of the school's paperwork requirements and offering advice for handling tough student situations, one of Lydia's most important jobs as Annie's mentor was to give her the emotional boost she needed to continue with energy through the school year. Now was the time to start thinking about a future event.

Lydia asked, "Well, I don't know if this is the best time to bring this up, but have your considered what you will prepare for your PRAXIS lesson?"

Oh, the PRAXIS lesson. Annie had tried to put it aside in her mind during the first months of the school year, but now it was time to bring it to the front burner. Sometime in January, an educator trained in the PRAXIS III system of evaluation would come to the school to interview and observe her teach a lesson. And a good evaluation was critical for Annie to obtain her state's license to teach. Her state grants a provisional license upon completing the bachelor's degree. The only way to convert that provisional license to the "real thing," her first Professional License, is to have a successful evaluation. Obviously, she had to take this observation quite seriously.

The school principal had assigned Lydia to be Annie's mentor. Although assigning mentor teachers to new teachers had been a practice at the school for years, the mentoring role had been refined now that the state had implemented the PRAXIS III performance assessment as licensing requirement. Lydia had attended workshops on mentoring to help her better understand what new teachers would be expected to accomplish and how she could best assist novice teachers. She had observed two of Annie's lessons last month and had discussed them with Annie as a way of preparing her for the PRAXIS III observation process.

With Christmas break coming up, Lydia knew it was time to begin discussing the preparation for this important lesson.

"I haven't had much free time to think about it," Annie began.

"That's understandable."

"But I was thinking that a science lesson might be fun and get the students excited. Besides, by January, we'll be far enough along in the curriculum for a more sophisticated science concept like energy. I've found out that the students can handle a fairly abstract concept if I go about it right and use concrete examples. You know, that excites me. I'm ready for it."

"Yes, I agree," replied Lydia. "Why don't you start putting some things down on paper, and we can sit down together and look at it. Would Thursday after school be O.K.?"

"As long as a faculty meeting isn't called," Annie grinned.

DECEMBER 12   Defining the Challenge of What to Teach and How

Annie and Lydia sat together in Lydia's room and Annie shared the notes she had brought along. She explained her preliminary lesson ideas.

"I looked ahead in the science text and also checked the Graded Course of Study. The text has a chapter coming up on energy and the Graded Course of Study has an objective for students to demonstrate their understanding of energy. I could see doing something that's visual with that topic—pictures that illustrate examples of energy. And for my approach, maybe I could use concept attainment. The kids seem to react well to an inductive approach, especially when they're dealing with things they can visualize. What do you think?" Annie asked.

"Sounds good so far. I could even see you making several instructional resources that would illustrate various examples of energy. But let's go back to the beginning. Your concept is energy. What is the definition you want the students to obtain?"

"Well, for fourth graders, I think it's sufficient for them to know that energy is power in motion. They've already been exposed to the definitions of power and motion. What I want to do in this lesson is to get them to recognize both attributes so that eventually they'll include both in a definition of energy that they'll compose. I'll present examples and non-examples of both attributes. At the end of my presentation and class discussion, I'll assess their understanding of the concept by having them create their own examples in cooperative groups."

With this preplanning done, Annie and Lydia agreed that Annie would continue to develop this lesson at home over the next night or two while the ideas were still fresh. Lydia suggested that Annie be certain to address the issues of what form of media would be best for displaying her pictures, how student grouping arrangements would change over the course of the lesson, what activities the students would engage in, and how student learning would be evaluated. Annie arranged to share these plans with Lydia in a few days.

Annie discusses her upcoming lesson with her mentor, Lydia

DECEMBER 16   Exploring Alternative Ways of Teaching

Annie stopped into Lydia's classroom after school to report her progress.

"I was on quite a roll this weekend working on this lesson," Annie began. "Here's what I have so far. I think I'll begin the Anticipatory Set with whole-class instruction in order to give everyone a similar frame of mind and pique their curiosities. First I'll explain the steps in my lesson so they know what to expect. Then I'll show about three pictures that illustrate energy, but I won't use the word energy itself. Instead, I'll tell them that even though the pictures are different, they show the same scientific idea and challenge them to figure out what the common attributes are. We'll take what time we need for discussion, and for me to guide their observations, so that they come to identify the common attributes of power and motion. With that done, I'll show about three more pictures, one at a time, all of which will be non-examples of energy, asking of each, 'Is this picture like the first three?' I'll need to plan some good questions so they see that one or the other or both of the attributes are missing. We'll finish up this section by writing the attribute words, "power" and "motion," on the board.

"If they haven't guessed at this point that the scientific word we're talking about is energy," Annie continued, "I'll tell them, write it on the board, and ask the class to define energy for me. It'll be a matter of putting the attribute words in the right order, and if I'm patient and provide enough cues, I think they'll do it just fine!

"Finally, in cooperative groups, I'll have them draw original pictures of energy. I'll assign roles to all the group members like artist, author, and presenter. When they're done, each group will present its pictures to the class, explaining how the pictures display energy, namely, that they show power in motion. There! So what do you think?"

"This is really coming together nicely." Lydia said. "You still need to work on the minute details of how to display your pictures at the beginning of class, and you need to determine how your students will earn a grade for this activity."

"Well, I've been thinking about the pictures. The easiest thing for me to do would be to cut out pictures from magazines and mount them on hard board material like foam core, but that technique would not exactly show the evaluator that I know how to use technology. Besides, I want to model, using our classroom technology resources, products like the ones I'll expect my students to make."

"Good point," said Lydia. "Besides, the magazine pictures might be a little too small for the entire class to see and that would definitely be a problem for the students as they try to unravel the concept from your clues. I'm sure the evaluator would catch that as a problem, too."

"I think the better idea would be for me to scan in the pictures and to bring the pictures into a slide presentation software package," Annie said. "That way, if a student wanted to talk about a picture I had already shown, I could easily bring it back up again. During their group time, they could also bring it up on the computer if they needed to refer to an example."

A few years ago, all of the teachers in Annie's elementary school were equipped with classroom computers—five per classroom. The school owns three projection pads that connect to the computer and sit on top of the overhead projector, which can be signed out in advance. The flatbed scanner is housed in the library, but for a special lesson, can be moved into a classroom.

"And what about the students? How would they display their work?" Lydia inquired.

"Hmm. If we have the time, I could have them scan their work, too."

"I think that all of their pictures would make a nice slide show on 'What Is Energy?' It would also look great in your portfolio."

"Yes! And I could have them type in their explanations, as well, to create a sort of class 'interactive book.'" Annie blurted. She was really getting excited.

Annie prepares her lesson on energy

"And that would be your assessment tool of their learning. Just write some assessment criteria for each of the aspects you want them to address and I think you've got a great lesson here."

JANUARY 12   The Pre-Observation Interview

Annie received a phone call from her PRAXIS III evaluator last week. During the call, she and Gary, her evaluator, determined that January 13 would be the day of her observation. Since then, she and Gary have been e-mailing details such as time and place of arrival and time of lesson. Since Gary lives and works only forty-five minutes away, he was willing to stop by the after-noon before the lesson to complete the Pre-Observation Interview. Prior to the interview, Annie completed and faxed to Gary the Class and Instruc-tional Profiles. On the Class Profile, Annie needed to complete a good deal of data regarding the number of males and females in the class as well as racial and ethnic distribution figures. She needed to identify any students in the class who had special needs. On this form, Annie reported that she had one student in the class who appeared to display some symptoms of dyslexia while he was in first grade and one student who was working with a tutor since she was falling behind in math. And of course there was Adam, who has been on Ritalin since he was diagnosed as hyperactive last year. Annie also described students' background knowledge in the subject mat-ter and what pertinent lessons were taught prior to this lesson.

Activity IV.1

Consider a class that you've observed in the field or consider one of your own classes from college. Answer the following questions from the PRAXIS III Class Profile about that class: How many total students were there? How many were males and how many females? How many students had limited English language proficiency? What terms that describe ethnic/racial background would describe the students in the class? What type of learning exceptionalities (visually or audibly impaired, developmentally, emo-tionally, behaviorally, learning, or physically disabled, or gifted) are represented by those in the class? How does the teacher become familiar with what the students already know? What are the most important classroom routines, procedures, rules, and expectations for student behavior?

On the Instruction Profile, Annie answered nine questions about the lesson she had prepared. Since she had already planned this out, she found the questions were all straight-forward and didn't take much time to complete.

INSTRUCTIONAL PROFILE

What is your goal for student learning in this lesson? That is, what do you intend students to learn?

The students will compare and contrast examples and non-examples of energy.
The students will compose a definition of energy.
The students will apply their understanding of energy by creating unique graphic examples.

Why have you chosen this goal?

Energy is a building block for many scientific concepts. To know potential energy, kinetic energy, and work, for example, students must first have a fairly good notion of energy. In addition, the concept of energy is in the fourth grade

Course of Study and, therefore, teachers in fifth grade and beyond will expect that their students have been introduced to this concept.

How will you group students for instruction?

The lesson will begin in a whole-class arrangement. Once the students have demonstrated an initial grasp of the concept by creating a class definition, they will move into cooperative groups to apply their understanding of it by creating unique examples. In the lesson that follows this one, the students will present their slides in a whole-class presentation arrangement.

Why have you chosen these groupings?

Whole-class instruction is best for getting everyone started off on the right foot. I can see who's catching on and give extra attention to those who aren't. Also, whole-class is more efficient for giving instructions for the cooperative group activity. As a follow up to whole-class, cooperative groups are the most effective grouping because they increase the chances of students talking and learning from each as they construct additional layers of meaning for energy.

What teaching method(s) will you use for this lesson?

I will use the concept attainment strategy. I will develop and present examples and non-examples of the concept of energy and have students discuss them until they see its attributes. From there, they'll compose a tentative definition and construct their own examples to further develop the concept, confirm it, and make it their own.

Why have you chosen this method?

I want my students to develop a conceptual understanding of what energy is. It's an abstract term and sometimes students at this age have difficulty with abstract terms. By having them see visual examples, I can make the concept more concrete. And by having them generate their own, I can check to see that they understand.

What activities have you planned?

I've thought about what I want my students to do, the general sequence, and the approximate amount of time I'll allocate for each activity.

<u>Activity</u>	<u>Time Allocated</u>
Review previous material.	5 minutes
Show examples and non-examples of energy. Identify attributes and develop tentative definition through guided observation and discussion. Have students write tentative and final definitions in notebooks.	15 minutes
Give cooperative learning directions. Allow students time to draw and scan their examples. Discuss examples, attributes, and definition.	25 minutes

What instructional materials will you use, if any?

I will use a computer slide show to display the examples and non-examples. I will also use the board to write key terms and ideas that the students or I generate. The students will use paper and crayons to create their own examples. One member of each cooperative group will use the computer and scanner to transfer a drawing to the students' slide show.

Why have you chosen these materials?

The computer slide show displays the pictures very large on the classroom screen so that all students can see them. The slide show software is very easy to use and allows me to move forward or backward, if needed. After the lesson, if I think that a picture needs to be added, I can easily do that without redoing the entire slide show. The disk is also easy to store. I think that the computer and scanner are important tools for the students to use so that they will have the skills to use this equipment in other situations. As for the chalkboard, I think that placing key terms and ideas on the board during class discussion helps visual learners keep focused on the development of ideas. The paper and crayons allows the students to use their creativity to express their growing understanding.

How and when do you plan to evaluate student learning on the content of this lesson?

During this lesson, I intend to evaluate student learning formatively by determining if the students are reacting appropriately to the examples and non-examples. I also intend to circulate around the room during their cooperative learning activity to be certain that the students are on-task and that the pictures they create are appropriate based on the attributes in the definition. I will also be able to determine how well the students have learned the concept as each group explains its contribution to the class slide show.

The cooperative learning activity will be worth 60 points:

> 15 points–producing three examples (5 points each)
> 10 points–drawing the example for the class slide show
> 10 points–scanning the example for the class slide show
> 10 points–writing the description for the class slide show
> 10 points–presenting the example to the class
> 5 points–completing the cooperative group evaluation form

Why have you chosen this approach to evaluation?

During my whole-class presentation, I think that I need to gather enough information from my students to know that they are not getting lost. I also think that I need to circulate around the room to make sure that the students are not working on something else or having only one or two students do all the work. We've been working on oral presentation skills, so I think that the class presentation is an important tool to have each group share what they created and for all the students to learn from each other. Therefore, the things that the students must do to complete the presentation have to be worth enough points that they are motivated to see it through to the end.

After the school day ended, Annie met Gary in the front lobby of the school. The two found a comfortable corner in the school library to talk. Gary began the conversation by handing Annie the profiles she had faxed last week.

"Please look these over," Gary stated. "Have there been any changes in them since you completed them?"

"No. Not that I can see," replied Annie.

The rest of the interview went equally smooth, with Annie discussing how today's lesson fit into the sequence of instruction that had gone before and how she will build on this lesson in the future. As Annie responded, Gary wrote her responses on a separate form created for the Pre-Observation Interview. Ten minutes later, Gary finished his questions and the form was complete.

"Thank you, Annie. I look forward to observing your lesson tomorrow. It sounds interesting. Will you show me to the front door? We can confirm the time of the lesson and location of your classroom as we walk."

JANUARY 13   Acting on the Plan by Teaching the Lesson

Annie's students were moving busily around the room near the end of a cooperative math lesson when she saw Gary at the door of her classroom. She welcomed him and showed him where he could sit and take notes during the lesson.

"O.K., boys and girls, please place your reports in my box and return to your seats as soon as possible," Annie began. "I have a visitor I want you to meet."

Adam asked Annie if "that man" was Annie's husband. "No, Adam." Leave it to Adam! The majority of the students were in their seats, while some were finishing putting away their materials.

"Let's get to your seats quickly. We have so much to do today. Marcus, in your seat, please. Katie, sit down, please. Reshawn . . . Thank you."

Finally, all the students were seated. Annie could still hear mumbling, but it subsided as the students settled down and turned their attention to the teacher.

"I would like to introduce Mr. Rivani. He's visiting our class today and is interested in seeing what exciting things we will be doing in our science lesson.

"Now, then, who can tell me what we have been talking about in our science lessons since we've been back from winter break? Ariel?"

"Things that move?" Ariel replied

"Right, and we called that . . . what?"

"Motion." said Ariel.

"Right again. And, class, what was the other science idea we looked at? Yes, Jamie?"

"The ability to do something. Like when I put a box on the shelf over my bed, that shows that I have the ability to use my muscles. We said the science word for that is power."

The observation day; Annie begins her lesson

"All right, fourth graders! You have good memories," said Annie. "Now, I have selected several pictures for us to look at. What I want you to do is to look at each picture and tell me what you see. Just one hint: Remember the two things we just talked about."

Annie wrote "motion" and "power" on the board. Then she turned on the overhead projector and moved to the computer on the cart. She used the mouse to start the slide show. The first picture was of a football player running.

"Who can tell us about this picture? Chris?"

"He's running down the field; maybe he'll make a touchdown," Chris said.

"Well, maybe he will. Now, what science word would 'running' be? Go ahead, Chris."

"Well, running is moving, so I guess 'motion' would be the best word."

"Very good thinking, Chris. And what was the other science term we just reviewed and how might that be seen in this picture? Sharon?"

"Power. He's got power in his muscles to move him down the field."

"Very good, Sharon. Now, class, I'm going to show you three more pictures, and you see if they show us the same two things that we saw with the football player."

In succession, Annie showed slides of a rocket ship, a gymnast on a balance beam, and a bowler sending a ball into the pins. After each one, she engaged her students in identifying the attributes of motion and power. Then she asked questions to help the students induce a tentative definition of energy.

"O.K., fourth-grade scientists," Annie said, "you've told me that all four of these pictures show us motion. . . . .and power. Does anyone have a guess about the science word that uses both of these words? No? Well, the word is 'energy.' I'll write it here on the board. I'll bet we can use our 'thinking' minds to make up a temporary definition for energy. Later on, we'll write a final definition. But for right now, we already have two important words to use in it. Somebody finish this sentence for us: Energy is . . . ."

The class struggled at this point. Although students quickly suggested "power" and "motion," the relationship between them did not emerge immediately. Annie felt her questioning abilities being put to the test.

"What's the relationship between the football player's muscles and his running? Shawn?"

"His muscle power makes him move."

"Right! And think about the other pictures. What's the relationship between the fuel and the rocket? The gymnast's skills and her handstand?"

Eventually, Annie's students recognized that motion and power work together. It expresses itself in different ways but there is an aspect of movement in power. Annie wrote the tentative, "temporary," definition on the board and students copied it into their notebooks: Energy is power in motion.

"Let's look at three more pictures. Tell me if they are like or not like the first three."

From her slide show, Annie showed three pictures one at a time—a wall, a statue, and a "No Parking" road sign—all non-examples of energy.

"What do you see in this picture? Kirsten?"

"A wall. A simple old wall."

"Class, is this old wall like the football player, the rocket, or the gymnast?"

Several students offered their observations, and Annie responded by asking, "Why do you think so? Can you tell me more?" Some of the first-named contrasts were obvious: a football player is alive, but a wall is not. A "No Parking" sign gives a message, but a rocket does not. To further develop and consolidate students' perception of energy, Annie realized she needed to be more direct and guide their reasoning back to the attributes of power and motion.

"Recall the football player? What did we say he had? Yes, Tressa?"

"He had power and motion. But this old wall doesn't have either one. It doesn't have power, and it doesn't have motion."

"Neither power, nor motion . . . mmmmm. O.K. Then, what can we say about the statue and the "No Parking" road sign?" Annie asked.

Class conversation continued. Using a variety of question types, Annie helped students appreciate the attributes of energy in the examples by noticing their absence in the non-examples. As a check on their progress, she presented a few more pictures representing examples and non-examples in a mixed list. Addressing the entire class, she had students raise their hands if they saw an example of energy and keep their hands down if they saw a non-example. This way, she could assess at a glance who had caught on and provide immediate, additional instruction when she needed to. Concluding this segment, Annie directed students back to their notebooks where she had them record the examples of energy they had seen and talked about. She also had them reread their temporary definition. After a brief discussion, all agreed that it was sound and could stand as their final definition. They then went into the final phase of instruction.

"O.K.," Annie began, "now in your cooperative groups, I want you to think of at least three other examples of energy that you can see. But before you get into your groups, please listen to the rest of the instructions."

Annie turned on the overhead again to show the last slide, the instructions for the activity, the roles of the group members, and the evaluation criteria.

"You will list three more examples in your notebooks, but then you will choose one of the examples to draw. One member of the group will draw the picture you all have chosen of something showing energy. Another member will write what it is and explain why it is an example of energy. A third member will be the technician and scan the picture, and the fourth member will present the group's picture and explanation to the class when the class slide show is ready to be presented, probably tomorrow afternoon. This activity is worth sixty points. You will get fifteen points for showing me three examples, ten points each for the drawing, the scanning, the description, and the presentation, and five points for the completion of a cooperative group work evaluation form from everyone in the group. Remember, since this is a group project, everyone in the group has a job to complete. But at the same time, everyone is responsible for seeing to it that all the jobs are completed, and done well. Are there any questions? Yes, Alex?"

"Do the pictures have to be colored?"

Annie circulates around the room observing students' work

"Yes, so either the one who draws the picture will add color using markers or crayons or the technician will add color using the computer. Any other questions? So, for the rest of this lesson, be sure to have your picture drawn and scanned. I'll assemble them into the class slide show today after school. We'll show it to the class and make our presentations tomorrow. Let's get started!"

The students got to work as Annie circulated around the room making certain that examples were accurate, that students were

Students scan their work for the final slide show

aware of the time, and that they were on task. As groups were ready with their drawings, Annie sent them to the scanner and attached computer she had brought in for the lesson. To the first student to complete the scanning, Annie gave the additional task of staying at the scanner to watch that the graphics were labeled and filed appropriately and to keep waiting technicians in an orderly line. As things got noisier, Annie reminded the groups to read and refine their explanations and to be sure that all members of the group had read it and agreed to its wording.

While Annie was assisting a group, she happened to look up in time to see Adam at the teacher's computer. His eyes were fixed on the screen as his hand reached for the mouse.

"Adam!"

She moved immediately over to him. He released the mouse as he saw her approaching. Annie gently moved him away from the computer and back to his group.

Annie redirects Adam away from the computer

"What is your role in the group?" Annie asked Adam.
She knew he was the drawer.
"Is your drawing finished?" Annie inquired.
"Yes, and it's already been scanned, too," Adam said.
"Good, now why don't you take one of the other examples that your group came up with and draw one of those as well. When you're finished, I'll put it up on the front board near the word 'energy' as an example of energy."
Annie gazed around the classroom and was pleased and relieved to see that the rest of the class was still active and on task. As time went on,

Students share their work with Annie

some groups started to get noisier as they completed the required tasks. Annie went over to those groups and asked to see their drawings. She asked the students to explain why their drawings were good examples of energy. The students complied but she could tell she was testing their attention spans. A student came up to Annie to show her his drawing. Annie complimented him and asked why the picture was a good example of energy.

Twenty-five minutes after the start of the activity and forty-five minutes after the time the class started, Annie walked over to Gary.

Annie discusses her lesson with the observer, Gary

"I will be reassembling them in a few minutes to take them to the art room," Annie said.

"That's fine. I'll step out until school lets out," Gary said. "You said we could complete the Post-Observation Interview then, right?"

"Yes, that will be fine. I need to make the energy slide show, but if we run long, I can always get it done during their gym class tomorrow."

"Sounds good. I'll see you then."

Gary stepped out of the classroom unnoticed by most of the students. Annie collected the students' notebooks and lined them up for their walk down the hall. Inside, she felt incredibly relieved that the observation was over and that the lesson had gone well.

AFTER SCHOOL   Looking at the Results During the Post-Observation Interview

After dismissing the students at the end of the school day, Annie began to think back on the energy lesson and prepare for the Post-Observation Interview. She had had post-observation sessions with Lydia often over the last few months, so she hoped that there wouldn't be any surprises. When Gary arrived, the two sat down in a comfortable corner of the room. Luckily, Gary's questions were predictable.

"In light of your instructional goals, how do you think the lesson went?" Gary began.

"Did the students learn what you wanted them to learn? . . ."

"Were the teaching methods effective? . . ."

"If you could teach this class period over again to the same class, what would you do differently or the same? . . ."

Most of the answers that Annie gave reflected her opinion that, overall, the lesson had gone well and that the students left the lesson understanding that energy is power in motion. The materials she had selected proved to be effective because they helped students distinguish examples from non-examples by identifying attributes of energy. The cooperative group segment did what it was supposed to do: By having students create original examples of the concept, they further clarified and personalized it. Drawing out concept attributes had been a challenge, she confessed, and although helping students develop a concept inductively gave her the sense that she was really teaching, she would need to work on this competency in the future. In response to Gary's question about Adam and his problem of staying on task, Annie explained that Adam had been a challenge to her the entire year and that her technique of keeping him occupied in a productive manner and enlisting the assistance of his parents had been fairly successful. Clearly, though, she needed to learn additional ways of channeling students' energy. At that, they both chuckled, as Gary stood and walked toward the door.

"Well, thanks, Annie. You should hear about the results in a few weeks. I hope this experience wasn't too stressful for you."

"Not really. I'd like to think that between Lydia's observations and yours, I've become a better teacher this year. This process has really forced me to think about not only what I do in the classroom, but also why."

APRIL 26

Annie entered Lydia's classroom with an envelope and handed Lydia the contents. Lydia perused the contents.

"All scores within passing limits," Lydia smiled. "Congratulations, I knew you could do it!"

Activity IV.2	

Before you go on to read the discussion which follows, get a copy of the PRAXIS III/ Pathwise criteria and evaluate Annie's lesson, either by yourself or as a member of a small group. While it is obvious that you cannot gain the full flavor of the classroom and her lesson just by reading excerpts, you should be able to identify some areas of strength that Annie has demonstrated. When you're finished, compare your thoughts to ours in the next section. It's moments of reflection like this, whether done individually or with other teachers, that improve our decision-making in planning and teaching.

AUTHORS' DISCUSSION

Annie's lesson was a good one for several reasons. First of all, Annie attempted to tie together what was learned previously with her plans for this lesson by having the students recall what they had been learning. Annie could have actually done more in her Anticipatory Set to connect previously learned concepts with the concept being discussed in this lesson without ruining the discovery portion of the lesson, and a good supervisor or mentor will help a new teacher do this. In Annie's case, someone who better understands the curriculum at that grade level, such as Lydia, can best assist Annie in doing this honing.

Secondly, Annie is a skilled beginning teacher in her questioning abilities. She didn't just ask quick "yes" or "no" (convergent) questions, but instead asked open-ended (divergent) questions that required more thought, such as, "What do you think is the relationship between. . . . . . . ?" and "Then, what can we say about the statue and the 'No Parking' road sign?" Furthermore, Annie encouraged students to justify and explain their responses by saying, for example, "Why do you think so?" and "Can you tell me more?" Annie also effectively used the raising of hands to collect some formative assessment information about whether students were grasping the concept. Simply relying on the correct answers of four or five students is not enough to know if everyone is understanding and learning.

Annie also took time before going into the small group portion of the lesson to bring some closure to the whole-class portion by having the students compose a tentative definition of energy. Taking time to do this helps students synthesize what's gone on to that point while it provides a "foreshadowing" direction to what comes next.

Annie's transition into the cooperative group activity was generally effective because of two actions she took. First, she made certain to clearly define her expectations for the academic portion of this activity. She punctuated these expectations by having them summarized on the screen. Secondly, she avoided a mistake many new teachers make; she communicated these expectations for the group work to her students *before* the students broke into their groups. This minimized the numbers of questions from students and clarifications from Annie once the group work began. Also, Lydia was right to have Annie specify her evaluation criteria since this enabled the students to know exactly what was expected of them by the end of the lesson. However, this is one portion of the lesson that she could have improved upon. If you'll remember back to chapter 4, one of the requirements of a true cooperative learning lesson is a social skills goal and preparation for the students to develop the social skill. Annie prepared a group activity but not really a cooperative one. Given Annie's concerns about the noise level and Adam's wandering, she might be wise to prepare students for working on a social skill that involves on-task behavior or use of "group talk" noise levels. Explicitly preparing students for these skills prior to engaging in the lesson would likely have headed off these problems before they became issues of concern for her. As she engages in future planning, then, Annie might want to consider these issues and plan explicitly for them, beginning with identifying the behaviors to be worked on in her learning goals.

Most likely Gary would have positively evaluated the methods and resources that she chose; their visual appeal captured students' attention and were essential to concept development. Annie's use of concept attainment with its concrete examples and non-examples was a very appropriate choice of teaching strategy for such a complex, abstract concept as energy. The evidence of the effectiveness of this strategy was shown in the responses of the students. Tressa, for example, could "see" the football player and the wall and thus commented on the absence and presence of critical attributes.

During the course of the lesson and during the Post-Observation Interview, Annie was able to demonstrate that she understood the learner characteristics of one of her special needs students, Adam. She demonstrated that she was able to accommodate his needs during one of the most challenging portions of the lesson for him by redirecting his energy in a positive manner and providing him with a meaningful task and an appropriately motivating reward. She recognized, however, that her repertoire is limited and that she needed to find other strategies to help Adam. This recognition demonstrates her developing sense of efficacy in the classroom but also shows one disadvantage that most new teachers have, her shortage of specific strategies to assist students with special needs.

Annie's lesson preparation is typical of many complex lessons such as this one. Most good lessons are not simply planned within minutes. Annie's conversation with Lydia helped her verbalize her ideas and determine if they sounded reasonable, not only to Lydia, but to herself as well. Experienced teachers like Lydia can help new teachers see possible pitfalls in their plans and consider alternatives. Often, veteran teachers enjoy listening to the fresh ideas of a novice teacher and sometimes infuse some of those ideas into their own lessons. Good teachers, both novice and veteran, revise even good lessons constantly. They prefer to teach one lesson at least twice in one day or one course or grade at least two years in a row in order to test a revision to a lesson or a course.

Many of the teaching skills Annie exhibited may take several years for other new teachers to acquire, but they serve as a model of a lesson that incorporates some of the decision-making approaches and instructional design principles described in this book. Of course, exemplary lessons do not occur everyday for the first-year teacher. In fact, they might, at best, occur once a week. But for an important event like a PRAXIS III lesson evaluation, even first-year teachers can design and deliver a lesson that includes most of the elements of a positive learning experience. First learn the evaluation criteria on which you will be assessed and consult with a mentor you respect and trust. Then give yourself the time to consider student needs, curricular expectations, alternative strategies, resources, and assessments. You will have built a solid foundation for present and future growth.

SECTION **V**

IDEAL

Looking at the Results

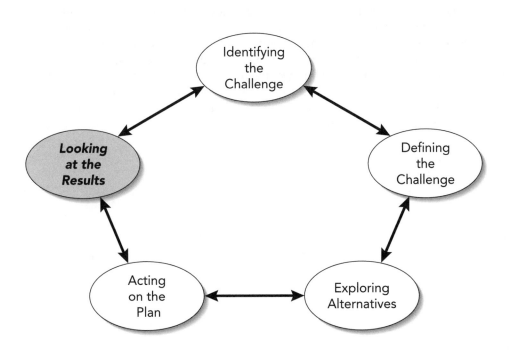

In many ways, from the time you begin the IDEAL problem-solving method, you are continually looking at results. If you look at the two-way arrows, you could think of that process of working in both directions as one way in which all good decision-makers look at the results of their identification of the challenge *while* they are defining it, and so on. This particular step, however, is a very conscious one in which you engage *after* you have acted on your plan. You need to take in the whole of the experience and consider very consciously and deliberately how successful you were. If you believe you were successful, you will want to remember that plan for a later time; and if you were not, you will want to consider what you would do differently the next time you are faced with this same situation. Often, the reality is somewhere in between wildly successful and chaotically unsuccessful. In these cases, you may want to think about how you might do things *differently*, all the time looking at how successful your students are at meeting significant objectives for their learning. Regardless of how you assess your plan, you will need to think about what evidence you are basing your evaluation of success.

The thought process that we've just described is what effective teachers do in explicit ways during the course of the school year. They take the time to reflect upon what they have done well, and what they have not done as successfully as they'd wanted, in teaching lessons and units. The major criterion that they use to determine success is the achievement of their students as measured by their cognitive and social growth. But they also have other sources of feedback that they use as they consider how well they have met the goals of their plans.

The two chapters in this section will provide you with some sources that you can consider as you think about your own teaching successes. Building on the skills of creating assessment instruments that you began to develop in chapter 9, chapter 10 focuses your attention on using the results of those instruments to evaluate your students' successes in meeting your goals and theirs. In chapter 11, we invite you to consider how you can use a variety of sources of information to begin to build a schema that allows you to evaluate the success of your own teaching of lessons, units, and courses.

CHAPTER **10**

Evaluating Student Achievement

CONVERSATION

Mary Ellen Watson and Tony Marino are team teaching a social studies unit on early American settlers, and earlier in the day they administered an objective paper-and-pencil test on the settling of the thirteen colonies. After school that afternoon, they met to reflect on the test results. Each takes a stack of papers and compares them to the answer key, putting a check by the correct responses. After half an hour or so they have completed the initial step of grading of the tests.

"What do you think Mary Ellen?" queries Tony. "How do you think everyone did?"

"Well Tony," responds Mary Ellen, "overall it looks like the test results are really good, actually better than I had expected! I was really pleased to see that Jonathan Allen and Suzy Keith seemed to do particularly well. I know they used the Reciprocal Teaching strategy to review for the test and it really seemed to pay off. How about your stack?"

"Same here. I'm really encouraged by the results. But, I noticed that a lot of students seemed to miss that short answer question about the Jamestown settlement," replies Tony as he flips through a test paper. "Yes, here it is. The second question on page two."

"I think you may be right," confirms Mary Ellen. "That seemed to be a difficult question for my group, too. And, I'm not sure if we spent enough time on the mapping lesson last week. There seemed to be some confusion about how to use the map key."

"Well then," replies Tony, "let's get started on the item analysis. Then we can finish up the grading and be ready to return the papers tomorrow. I know the students will be anxious for the results, and I told Mrs. Hargrove that I would try and call her tonight and tell her how Michelle did."

"O.K., here's a copy of the chart we developed for recording student responses. Why don't you read me your results and I'll start the tally," requests Mary Ellen.

DEVELOPING COMPETENCE

1. Tony and Mary Ellen were pleased with the results of assessment because their students performed better than they had expected. After reading this chapter, you should be able to set realistic expectations for student achievement.

2. "A chain is no stronger than its weakest link." Similarly, the quality of a test rests on the quality of the individual test items. As you examine the results of assessment, consider how you can evaluate the quality of test items.

3. With the results of the social studies test in hand, Tony and Mary Ellen will don *detective hats* to determine why the achievement of a few specific students differed markedly from their *typical* performance. Read to discover how teachers probe beyond test results to more fully understand the nature of student achievement.

4. The mother of one of Mary Ellen and Tony's students has requested a conference to discuss her son's test grade. Her son did not do particularly well on the test, and the mother would like to know how she can help her son study the material he does not understand. After reading this chapter, you should be able to use assessment results to differentiate learning objectives that your students have mastered from those in need of remediation.

5. As the grading period comes to a close, Mary Ellen begins to tally-up her students' scores on the assessments she administered throughout the term in preparation for filling out report cards. Your work with this chapter should enable you to develop a two-step process for assigning report card grades.

6. Assessing and grading student achievement is an important and necessary part of teaching. Report card grades in particular are often used to make decisions about students beyond the scope of your classroom. Identify steps that you can undertake to avoid unfair grading practices.

INTRODUCTION

The process of assessing student learning can take many forms. Assessment tasks can range from an informal process such as a somewhat casual observation of cooperative learning groups, to a more formal process such as developing and administering an essay test. Regardless of the assessment method, the *outcome* of assessment will be key information and data that you will use to make subsequent instructional decisions. In this chapter we will look specifically at how test results are used to evaluate the quality of the test itself, the achievement of your students, and the effectiveness of your teaching skills.

SETTING EXPECTATIONS

Before you can evaluate the quality of a paper-and-pencil or alternative assessment method, student performance, or your teaching, you must have some general expectations against which you can compare the results. The three most important criteria that you should consider are the learning characteristics of your students, the nature of the subject matter, and your knowledge and experience with the instructional unit.

If the students in your class usually display a rather wide range of abilities—some performing at grade level, some below, and some above—then it would be reasonable to expect a rather wide range of performance on tests. If your students are more similar in ability—an advanced placement chemistry class or a basic level math class, for example—then it would be reasonable to expect that the performance of the class as a whole would be fairly similar. In setting initial expectations, we are not advocating that you set such rigid expectations that you conclusively label a class or a particular student as "below average" or "remedial" or "gifted." Rather, you simply need to have a *general sense* for how the class or an individual student is likely to do.

A second consideration is the nature of the instructional material. Subject matter and learning tasks that are a review from previous lessons or are not particularly complex should be generally easy for students. On the other hand, novel or especially difficult subject matter or learning tasks may be quite challenging.

Finally, you should consider your own experience and knowledge with the instructional material. If this is the first time you have taught the subject or tried a particular teaching strategy, chances are that *you* will be learning along with your students. Even experienced teachers get better with practice! In fact, secondary teachers who teach several sections of the same class each day look at the results of their teaching throughout the day, making modifications accordingly.

Activity 10.1

The students in Mrs. Friedman's fifth-grade math class have a wide range of learning abilities. Some of the students are very bright and qualify for the gifted program, most seem about average, and some receive special learning assistance. Consider the learner characteristics of Mrs. Friedman's class and make some initial predictions about how the students in her class might perform on the following tasks:

- A review unit on adding fractions with like denominators
- A new unit on adding fractions with unlike denominators
- A challenging unit on adding complex fractions

LOOKING AT TEST QUALITY

When you think about it, the quality of an assessment tool that you develop is no better than the quality of the individual components that comprise the assessment. Even though you may have spent considerable time developing your assessment tools, carefully checking them against the recommended guidelines and perhaps getting input from a colleague, the final evaluation of the quality of your assessment tools actually comes *after* your students complete the tasks.

Assessment experts have developed a number of very specific statistics that they use to evaluate the quality of assessment tools. These statistics can be adapted for both paper-and-pencil and alternative assessments; however, we have chosen to use objective paper-and-pencil tests in the examples that follow. Our purpose here is to examine these concepts in a somewhat more intuitive manner rather than investigating some of the more detailed mathematical calculations.

Difficulty of Individual Test Items

By the very nature of the material being tested and the ability level of your students, some test items are likely to be easier and others will be more challenging. The difficulty index is a test statistic that identifies the percent of students who answer a question correctly.

Figure 10.1 is a tally form that Mrs. Friedman developed to calculate the **difficulty index** of each item on a recent test she administered, and she has completed the analysis for the first five test questions.

In this instance, the test consisted of ten questions. As she scores the tests for each of her twenty students, Mrs. Friedman keeps a running tally of the number of students who answer each of the questions correctly. For example, eighteen

FIGURE 10.1	TALLY FORM FOR TEST ITEM DIFFICULTY		
Test: _Fraction Unit #3_		Date: _3-7-99_	
Number of Students: _20_		Number of Test Questions: _10_	
Test Questions	Tally of Correct Responses	Difficulty Index	Evaluation
#1	ⅢⅢ ⅢⅢ ⅢⅢ |||	18/20 = 90%	easy
#2	ⅢⅢ ⅢⅢ ⅢⅢ ⅢⅢ	20/20 = 100%	easy
#3	ⅢⅢ ⅢⅢ ⅢⅢ	14/20 = 70%	moderate
#4	ⅢⅢ ⅢⅢ |||	13/20 = 65%	difficult
#5	ⅢⅢ ⅢⅢ ⅢⅢ ⅢⅢ	20/20 = 100%	easy
#6	ⅢⅢ ⅢⅢ ⅢⅢ ⅢⅢ		
#7	ⅢⅢ ⅢⅢ ||		
#8	ⅢⅢ ⅢⅢ ⅢⅢ		
#9	ⅢⅢ ⅢⅢ ⅢⅢ ||		
#10	ⅢⅢ ⅢⅢ		

students answered the first question correctly, twenty students answered the second question correctly, and so on. In the third column of the form, Mrs. Friedman calculated the difficulty index by dividing the total number of students in the class by the number who answer the question correctly (e.g., eighteen out of twenty students answered question one correctly, twenty out of twenty answered question two correctly, etc). Thus, she concludes that 90 percent of the students answered the first question correctly, 100 percent answered the second question correctly, and so forth. In the last column, Mrs. Friedman classifies the difficulty of each item. The following criteria can be used to classify the difficulty level of test items. These criteria are somewhat subjective, and you may need to modify the upper and lower values based on your knowledge of your students and the test material.

Difficulty Index		Classification
80% – 100%	⇒	Easy
65% – 79%	⇒	Moderate
50% – 64%	⇒	Difficult
Below 50%	⇒	Very Difficult

Once she has classified the difficulty of each test item, Mrs. Friedman must decided whether the difficulty level of each question is reasonable. In doing so, she must once again consider the learning abilities of her students and the nature of the subject matter. Remember that Mrs. Friedman's class has a fairly wide range of learning abilities. Let's assume that the test she has administered is a review unit on adding fractions with like denominators. With this information in mind, Mrs. Friedman *expects* that the test items should be relatively easy. Looking at Figure 10.1, we can see that questions one, two, and five were classified as easy and that question three was moderately easy. No surprises here! But what about question four? This question was classified as difficult—an outcome that differs from Mrs. Friedman's initial expectations.

A test item that is more difficult than expected *could be* a signal that the item was poorly formatted, not written clearly, or that instruction may have been inadequate. In the same manner, test items that are easier than expected *might* mean that a clue was provided and students were able to guess the item correctly. Remember that Mrs. Friedman *expected* that the test question should be relatively easy for her students. If Mrs. Friedman determines that the reason her students did poorly on question four is because of an inherent problem with the item itself or perhaps with ineffective instruction, she will not *count* the question in the overall test scores. Thus, her students would *not* be penalized for a poor quality test item. We are certainly not advocating that you *throw out* test questions simply because they are difficult for your students. Rather, we are suggesting that you honestly look at the quality of your test items and classroom instruction. Test scores should be valid and reliable indicators of what your students have learned, not some other factor.

Activity 10.2

Calculate the remaining difficulty indexes for questions six through ten in Figure 10.1 and use the suggested criteria to classify the level of difficulty. Assume that Mrs. Friedman's fifth-grade math class has a wide range of learning abilities and that the unit test covers relatively *new material* on adding fractions with unlike denominators. Are any of the difficulty indexes different from what she might expect. If so, what factors might explain the discrepancy? How would her expectations change if the unit test covered *very challenging subject matter* on adding complex fractions?

Multiple-Choice Distractor Analysis

A **distractor analysis** is a test item evaluation method that lets you look at the quality of multiple choice items. This method entails counting the number of students who choose the correct answer and each of the distractors. Figure 10.2 is an example of a distractor analysis that Mr. Bobinsky completed for a recent test he administered in his sixth-grade art class.

For the first test question, he notes that twenty of the twenty-five students in the class, selected red, the correct response, five students mistakenly choose green, and none of the students selected lavender, orange, or white—the other distractors. Mr. Bobinsky considers two possible explanations for this response pattern. First, if the question is relatively easy and he believes that his teaching was good, he would *expect* most of the students to answer the question correctly. It would follow, then, that the correct answer would be selected more frequently than the distractors. But, if the test item covers subject matter that Mr. Bobinsky

---

FIGURE 10.2 DISTRACTOR ANALYSIS FOR MULTIPLE CHOICE QUESTIONS			
Test:___Art Unit #5___ Date:_3-25-99_ Number of Students:_25_			
1. Which of the following is an example of a primary color?	# of Students	2. Which of the following is an example of a secondary color?	# of Students
A) Green	5	A) Black	2
B) Lavender	0	B) Blue	4
C) Orange	0	C) Grey	8
*D) Red (correct answer)	20	D) Pink	5
E) White	0	*E) Purple (correct answer)	6
Total Number of Students	25	Total Number of Students	25

knows to be more difficult, it could be that the distractors are not particularly attractive to students. Remember, the idea behind distractors is to present options that appear realistic to students. If Mr. Bobinsky concludes that the distractors are not appealing, he will want to revise them the next time he uses this test question.

Activity 10.3

Consider the results of the distractor analysis for the second question in Figure 10.2. What conclusions would you draw about the difficulty of the test item, the quality of the distractors, and/or the quality of instruction?

Student Feedback

If you are surprised by the difficulty of a particular test item or disappointed in the quality of responses, you may find that your students themselves can provide useful feedback. Depending on the age and maturity of your students, you may be able to simply ask students why they found the item so challenging, or why they responded in the manner that they did. This approach may be more effective when used with an individual student or with a small group, rather than enlisting the entire class to *critique* a particular test item. When you invite students to be a part of the assessment process then testing can be seen as less threatening, and your students will become more active participants in the learning process.

Overall Analysis of Student Response Patterns

No doubt, it would take you a considerable amount of time to systematically analyze the quality of each and every test item. The important thing to keep in mind is the general response patterns that you expect. Patterns of student success may be indications of their keen intellect and your skillful teaching, and there is certainly nothing more professionally satisfying than celebrating your students accomplishments. But, performance that is much better than you would expect may be an indicator that your test items are too easy, provide clues, or that cheating may have taken place. In the same manner, it is disheartening when your students do not perform particularly well. Student performance that is not as good as you expected may be an indication of poor quality test items, inadequate instruction, or a lack of preparation on the part of the students. Be thoughtful and reflective as you look through student work, rather than simply marking the correct or incorrect answers. Look for patterns in the way that your students respond and consider if your students' successes or challenges are reasonable given the nature of the subject matter, their ability level, and your familiarity with the subject, instructional method, or assessment method format.

LOOKING AT STUDENT ACHIEVEMENT

Once you have evaluated the quality of a test and if appropriate, adjusted for poor quality test items, you are ready to consider student achievement. Looking at student achievement is a two-step process. First, you will make an overall evaluation of your class's performance and then you will consider the performance of individual students. Once again, you must begin this process with some general expectations of how you expect the class as a whole, and individual students in particular, to perform.

Class Achievement

Mrs. Friedman has completed her evaluation of the geometry test that she administered to her eighth-grade students last week. Satisfied with the quality of the test, she has tallied the total scores and assigned grades. The results are displayed in Figure 10.3.

FIGURE 10.3 RECORD SHEET FOR UNIT GEOMETRY TEST							
Test: Geometry Unit #3 Date: 3-25-99 Total Possible Points: 32							
Name	Raw Score	Percent Correct	Grade	Name	Raw Score	Percent Correct	Grade
Abner, Betty	30	94%	A	Montoya, Jesse	23	72%	C
Bitner, Ellen	27	84%	B	Nelson, Sherrod	25	78%	C
Corsaro, John	28	88%	B	Peterson, George	30	94%	A
Exter, Jackie	24	75%	C	Rosario, Richard	31	97%	A
Guardino, Marie	29	91%	A	Santos, Eric	27	84%	B
Hawkins, Bill	32	100%	A	Scheldorf, Anna	28	88%	B
Jacor, Ronald	21	66%	D	Tanner, Paul	25	78%	C
Kelley, Patricia	29	91%	A	Vincent, John	27	84%	B
Lester, Marcia	27	84%	B	Winston, Beth	30	94%	A
Molowsky, Ann	26	81%	B	Ziff, Ben	29	91%	A

Raw Score Average: 27
Percent Correct Average: 86%

Letter Grade Totals: A–8
B–7
C–4
D–1

Of the twenty students in Mrs. Friedman's class, fifteen students earned As or Bs, four students earned Cs, and only one student earned a D. Should Mrs. Friedman be pleased with the class's performance? The answer to this question depends on the answer to a number of other questions. What is the overall ability level of the class? How challenging was the subject matter? How satisfied was Mrs. Friedman with the quality of her instruction?

Assuming that her students are somewhat heterogenous in their learning ability and the geometry unit was not particularly difficult, Mrs. Friedman should be relatively satisfied with the results. This is not to say that she will ignore the fact that one student, Ronald Jacor, earned a D on the test—but at this point she is simply looking at the overall performance of the class. When her class performs as she would expect, Mrs. Friedman has evidence to support that her instruction was effective for most students.

Activity 10.4

Imagine that the students in Mrs. Friedman's geometry class are honors students, and that the learning tasks addressed on the test are relatively easy. What expectations would she have about class performance? Would the test results in Figure 10.3 support her expectations? What reasons might explain the discrepancy between her expectations and the test results?

Looking at the grades that her students earned is one way that Mrs. Friedman considers class achievement. In some cases, especially when the class may not have done as well as she would have expected, Mrs. Friedman will take a more in-depth look at the results. Rather than simply counting the number of correctly answered questions, she may elect to consider her students' achievement of the lesson objectives that were covered on the test. Figure 10.4 is a record sheet that Mrs. Friedman developed for this task.

There were six lesson objectives that were covered on the test. (If we were to examine the actual test, we would see that there were several test questions for each of the lesson objectives.) Based on the pattern of correct responses, Mrs. Friedman has noted which lesson objectives each student has mastered. It follows then that the students who did quite well, mastered all, or nearly all, of the objectives. In addition to this achievement pattern, some additional information is evident. Clearly, lesson objectives three and six were more challenging for the class *as a whole*. In reflecting back upon the unit, Mrs. Friedman must try and decide *why* these two objectives were problematic, and *what* action she should take. For example, perhaps there were a number of interruptions during the two days when lesson objective three was addressed in class (e.g., a fire drill, shortened class schedule due to an assembly, etc.). Or, maybe she tried a new, and perhaps ineffective, strategy for teaching this objective. If lesson objective three is important, then Mrs. Friedman will need to re-teach it. In contrast, perhaps lesson objective six covers enrichment material that is not as important. In this instance, Mrs. Friedman may elect not to re-teach this material.

FIGURE 10.4	RECORD SHEET FOR UNIT GEOMETRY TEST						

Test: Geometry Unit #3   Date: 3-25-99

Name	Grade	Lesson Objective #1	Lesson Objective #2	Lesson Objective #3	Lesson Objective #4	Lesson Objective #5	Lesson Objective #6
Abner, Betty	A	✓	✓	✓	✓	✓	✓
Bitner, Ellen	B	✓	✓		✓	✓	
Corsaro, John	B	✓	✓		✓	✓	✓
Exter, Jackie	C	✓	✓		✓		
Guardino, Marie	A	✓	✓	✓	✓	✓	✓
Hawkins, Bill	A	✓	✓	✓	✓	✓	✓
Jacor, Ronald	D		✓		✓		
Kelley, Patricia	A	✓	✓	✓	✓	✓	✓
Lester, Marcia	B	✓	✓		✓	✓	
Molowsky, Ann	B	✓	✓		✓	✓	
Montoya, Jesse	C	✓	✓		✓		
Nelson, Sherrod	C	✓	✓		✓	✓	
Peterson, George	A	✓	✓	✓	✓	✓	✓
Rosario, Richard	A	✓	✓	✓	✓	✓	✓
Santos, Eric	B	✓	✓	✓		✓	
Scheldorf, Anna	B	✓	✓		✓	✓	✓
Tanner, Paul	C	✓	✓		✓		✓
Vincent, John	B	✓	✓	✓	✓	✓	✓
Winston, Beth	A	✓	✓	✓	✓	✓	✓
Ziff, Ben	A	✓	✓	✓	✓	✓	✓

Individual Student Achievement

After considering the overall performance of the class, Mrs. Friedman considers individual student performance. Once again, her consideration of individual student achievement is based on her general expectations for each student. For example, Bill

Hawkins earned a perfect score on the test. Because Bill typically earns As in class and is, in fact, enrolled in a special program for gifted math students, his perfect score is exactly what Mrs. Friedman would expect. On the other hand, Jackie Exter is usually an A student as well, but earned a C on this particular test. She recalls that Jackie was absent for several days with the flu, and in talking with Jackie, she also learns that Jackie and her family were out of town the weekend before the test to attend an aunt's wedding. Jackie was simply not able to devote as much time as she would have liked to prepare for the geometry test. Mrs. Friedman elicits the help of Bill Hawkins who has the same study hall time as Jackie. Bill is happy to review the material with Jackie, and Mrs. Friedman provides them with some practice problems that address lesson objectives three, five, and six—the objectives that Jackie did not master.

Mrs. Friedman is particularly concerned with the performance of Ronald Jacor. Over the past month or so, she has noticed a rather disturbing trend. Once a better-than-average student, Ronald has been absent considerably more often, has even fallen asleep in class a few times, and has been late in turning in his homework. Although Mrs. Friedman has tried to engage him in conversations about the change in his work habits, Ronald has seemed uncomfortable and simply says that he'll work harder. In a phone conference with Ronald's mother, Mrs. Friedman learns that there are a number of changes at home as well, and they both agree to schedule an appointment with Ronald's guidance counselor.

LOOKING AT YOUR TEACHING

As Mrs. Friedman examines student achievement she is, at the same time, reflecting upon her teaching. Like the process she uses to assess student achievement, she takes both a formative and summative approach to evaluating her teaching skills. From a formative stance, she makes mental notes at the end of each day—noting if her students seem to need a lot of clarification, or ask a lot of questions, or are particularly motivated, etc. In this way she can *fine tune* her teaching throughout the instructional unit. From a summative stance, Mrs. Friedman can use assessment results to make a more final judgment of her teaching. The topic of evaluating your teaching is addressed in more detail in chapter 11.

ASSIGNING GRADES

It is no wonder that beginning and experienced teachers alike acknowledge that assigning grades is one of the most important decisions they make. Right or wrong, grades are used as a criteria in many situations—being promoted from one grade level to the next, awarded a scholarship, admitted to college or graduate school, getting a job, etc. It goes without saying that the process of assigning grades must be done with considerable care. In essence, assigning grades is a two-step process. The first step entails assigning a grade to individual classroom assignments, and the second step involves combining the grades of many different assignments—most often for report cards or progress reports.

Grading Individual Assignments

Your approach to grading individual assignments will depend on the grade level you teach, the nature of the assignment, and perhaps the grading requirements of your school. With these factors in mind, you will either calculate a quantitative index, assign a grading label, compose written comments, or use a combination of these approaches.

A **quantitative index** is a numeric indication of achievement, such as the number of questions answered correctly or the number of points earned. Both of these indexes can be easily converted to a percentage. For example, if Belinda spelled nineteen out of twenty words correctly this would be equivalent to 95 percent. Or, if Carol earned thirty-seven out of forty-three points on an essay test this would be equivalent to 84 percent of the possible points. A relatively long-standing grading practice is to use the percentage correct as a criteria for assigning a grade label. **Grading labels** can consist of letter grades, word labels, or other symbols such as check marks. Figure 10.5 displays some examples of grade labels.

A long-standing practice in education is to assign a letter grade based on the percentage of questions a student answers correctly or the percentage of points the student earns. Let's say that you use the following percentage scale for assigning letter grades:

Sample Grading Scale		
90 – 100%	⇒	A
80 – 89%	⇒	B
70 – 79%	⇒	C
60 – 69%	⇒	D
Below 60%	⇒	F

According to this grading scale, Belinda would earn an A on her spelling test, and Carol would earn a B on her essay test. You may decide to use different percentages to distinguish your letter grades, or you may be expected to use set per-

FIGURE 10.5 GRADING LABELS			
Letter Grades	Labels	Symbols	Symbols
A	Outstanding	✓+	☺
B	Good	✓	
C	Satisfactory		
D	Needs Improvement	✓−	☹
F	Unsatisfactory		

centages and letter grades that have already been established at your school. The use of letter grades can be problematic if they are not assigned according to defined criteria, such as a quantitative index. Although you will probably be able to read through a stack of student work and rather easily distinguish quality work from that which is sub-standard, you *should not* simply mark a paper with an "A" or a "D" based on your *intuition* alone. Letter grade, or other grade labels for that matter, will be more truthful indicators of your student's achievement when they are assigned in a systematic way.

Written comments can be used to supplement quantitative indexes or grade labels, or in place of them. The purpose of written comments is to provide substantive feedback that will support the further academic growth of your students. Comments such as "good work" or "needs improvement" do not provide much direction. In contrast, comments such as "logically organized paragraph" or "check for addition errors" are more focused observations.

Cumulative Report Card Grades

Depending on your school district, you will be asked to complete a report card at various times throughout the school year. Sometimes report cards are completed every nine weeks (four times per year), and in other school districts it may be every six weeks (six times per year). In the early elementary grades, report cards often consist of a list of competencies that you will be asked to rate as satisfactory or unsatisfactory. In the upper elementary grades through senior high school, you will most likely be asked to assign a letter grade to represent your students' achievement. Although many schools are experimenting with alternative methods of evaluating student achievement, the use of letter grades is still predominant in schools today. In addition to report cards, you may be asked to complete a progress report during the time between report cards. Check with your principal, team leader, or other administrator to find out about the report card and progress report practices that are used in your school district. You will need to pay particular attention to the dates that report cards and progress reports are completed, the criteria and subjects that you will be expected to assess, the manner in which you will report student achievement, and if relevant, the grading scale you will be expected to use. Considering these things *before* the school year begins will facilitate your long-range planning and help avoid any unexpected surprises.

The grades you report on report cards and progress reports are *cumulative* in that they represent a summary of your students' achievement to date. Reporting cumulative grades means that you will need to combine grades across many assignments. In combining grades you will need to consider how much emphasis individual assignments should contribute to the overall grade.

Mr. Benson teaches eighth-grade civics at Jacobs Middle School. During the first grading period, his students will be required to submit weekly homework assignments, take quizzes approximately every other week, and complete four post tests. Mr. Benson has decided to place the following emphasis on each of the assignments.

Assignment	Emphasis
Homework	10%
Quizzes	20%
Objective Test #1	20%
Objective Test #2	20%
Individual Research Report	15%
Group Project	15%
Total	100%

Mr. Benson considers homework a practice exercise, and he encourages the parents of his students to get involved by helping or checking homework. His students are also urged to work in study groups, and he schedules after-school tutoring sessions twice a week. Because homework assignments may reflect the collaborative thinking of many, Mr. Benson gives less weight or emphasis to homework.

Quizzes, on the other hand, are taken in class. The quizzes are not particularly complex, each covering one or two lesson objectives, and they are formatted in a manner similar to the homework assignments. Still, they reflect the individual achievement of each student so Mr. Benson gives them slightly more weight than homework assignments. Over the course of the grading period, the students will take two objective paper-and-pencil tests, write an individual research report, and complete a group project. Mr. Benson has given the two in-class objective tests slightly more emphasis. These two tests cover more lesson objectives than the research report or group project; hence, they are more comprehensive. Also, in-class tests are more of a reflection of achievement of each individual student. In contrast, students will submit draft copies of each section of the research report to Mr. Benson for a preliminary review, and they are expected to seek assistance from the librarian. Likewise, the group project reflects the collaborative efforts of several students. At the beginning of the school year, Mr. Benson will communicate the grading system to his students and their parents so there will be *no surprises* later in the semester.

RECORD KEEPING

Accurate record keeping is a critical aspect of teaching. The grade level and subjects you teach will play a big part in determining the exact nature of the records that you keep. Achievement data, tardy and attendance counts, lunch money tallies, permission slips, locker numbers and combinations, emergency contact numbers, home phone numbers and addresses, and school identification numbers are just some examples of the information that you are likely to manage.

At the beginning of the school year you may be issued an *official* grade book. You may be required to use specific codes for marking attendance-related information, and you may be required to mark attendance in ink to prevent this information from being altered. You will want to check with your principal, team

---

FIGURE 10.6 COMPUTERIZED GRADE BOOKS AND INFORMATION AVAILABLE ON-LINE

- eGrader
  http://www.learninggate.com/lgi/home/home.asp?Stamp=376868

- Think Wave Educator
  http://www.thinkwave.com/educator.html

- Grade Guide
  http://www.alberts.com/AuthorPages/00004782/Prod_239.htm

- GradeQuick
  http://www.jacksoncorp.com/gquick.html

- Pretty Good Grading Program
  http://www.pggp.com/

---

leader, or other administrator to determine the record keeping practices that are used in your school and district.

You have a professional and legal responsibility to keep accurate and timely records. The image of a teacher sifting through stacks of papers in order to fill in blank spaces in a grade book the night before report cards are due is not a particularly flattering one. Furthermore, your attendance and achievement records are legal documents that could be called into a courtroom to provide legal evidence of the whereabouts or achievement of a student. At the conclusion of the school year, your grade book or lesson plan book may be collected by your principal as a legal record of the school year activities. It goes without saying that you must keep your records in a secure place. The use of computerized grade books make grading and record keeping much easier. Some of the websites identified in Figure 10.6 provide grade book software that you can actually download and use free of charge. Other sites provide trial copies or general information of software that is available for purchase.

In addition to the records that you are *required* to keep, it is likely that you will want to develop some individualized record keeping strategies. For example, Mr. Benson keeps a notebook with student phone numbers and addresses in his brief case, and he carries this with him back and forth from his home to school. Because he likes to make regular phone calls to parents to keep them apprized of school activities, he finds that having this information readily accessible facilitates this task. He developed a recording form so he can jot down the essence of each conversation, creating a permanent record rather than having to rely on his memory.

COMMUNICATING ASSESSMENT RESULTS

Most school systems have regularly scheduled parent conferences once or twice during the school year. The conferences usually take place over several days, and a number of scheduling changes may be made to the normal school day. For example,

---

FIGURE 10.7   INTERNET SITES ABOUT PARENT CONFERENCES

- 10 Tips for Parent-Teacher Conferences
  http://www.nysut.org/dept/nyt/98-99/981007parentconference.html

- Making Parent-Teacher Conferences Work
  http://www.pta.org/programs/tchwk5.htm

- Toward More Productive Parent-Teacher Conferences
  http://npin.org/pnews/1998/pnew1198/int1198c.html

- The Importance of the Parent-Teacher Conference
  http://npin.org/pnews/pnewo97/pnewo97e.html

---

at Mrs. Reisen's school the Friday before parent conferences is designated as a teacher preparation day and students will not be in attendance. Instead, the teachers in Mrs. Reisen's school will use this time to prepare their written conference reports, share assessment information with other teachers, and make phone calls to parents to confirm meeting times. During the week that conferences are scheduled, Mrs. Reisen's students will be dismissed after lunch on Wednesday and Thursday, and will not attend at all on Friday. Mrs. Reisen and her colleagues will meet with parents Wednesday and Thursday afternoon and evening, and then again on Friday morning. Each parent conference is scheduled for a fifteen minute time period. Mrs. Reisen will introduce herself and welcome those parents with whom she has not met previously, making parents feel welcome and creating a positive atmosphere. She will begin each conference by sharing a personal and positive observation about the student. Then, she will describe several of the student's strengths, followed by some suggestions for improvement. Mrs. Reisen will be careful to leave enough time to answer parents' questions. Parent conferences and report cards should *not* be the only time you share assessment information with parents. Regular communication through written notes, phone calls, or class newsletter will go a long way in developing a strong support system with parents. Figure 10.7 lists a number of websites that provide suggestions for facilitating parent conferences.

GRADING DILEMMAS

Although there are many grading-related decisions you will make, there are several specific situations that can be particularly challenging. First, you will need to consider how to assess assignments that are completed outside of class, such as homework or projects. Providing your students with practice work or sufficient time to complete more lengthy or complex assignments is certainly a sound educational practice. Yet, while some students will diligently complete their homework assignments, others may be tempted to copy the homework of another student. Likewise, some parents may provide a great deal of assistance in completing projects, while other parents do not. Without a grade, many students would not complete homework or other projects; yet, the more impact that an out-of-class assignment has on a student's grade, the more likely that someone other than the student may be helping with the assignment.

A second practice centers around extra-credit assignments. If one of your students does poorly on a test or assignment it makes sense to give the student an opportunity to review and possible re-learn the material. But the practice of regularly assigning extra-credit might actually be rewarding students for effort rather than achievement. Furthermore, extra-credit assignments that are completed outside of class may reflect assistance from parents or other students.

A third issue associated with grading is the practice of administering unannounced tests. This is *never* a justifiable practice. The typical reason that teachers give for this practice is that *pop quizzes* motivate students to study on a regular basis. This is a poor practice for several reasons. Unannounced tests create undue anxiety and frustration, and students learn to associate tests with negative feelings. Furthermore, low scores on an announced test do not necessarily indicate low achievement. It may be that the student was ill the night before, had family responsibilities, or had other school assignments. Announcing test dates encourages regular study habits and ensures that test scores are a valid indication of student achievement.

Finally, using grades as a punishment for unacceptable behavior is not appropriate. A teacher who takes points off for assignments that are turned in late, for talking in class, messy handwriting, or any number of other behaviors not directly related to the lesson objectives, confuses student achievement with lack of maturity or judgment. Grades should not be used as punishment for inappropriate behavior.

SUMMARY

In this chapter you have seen how the results of assessment are used to make many instructional decisions. Assessment results can be used to evaluate the quality of your assessment tools, the achievement of your class as a whole and the achievement of individual students, and to provide feedback about your teaching. Letter grades are a common method for describing achievement—both for individual assignments and for cumulative report card or progress report grades.

Looking at the results of assessment may seem like the culminating step in the teaching process. In fact, teaching and assessment are a recursive process in that the results of assessment are used to begin the instructional process all over again. Learning to use the result of assessment in a thoughtful and systematic manner will help you to become a better teacher—to better understand the achievement of your students and to refine and develop your own personal skills and knowledge.

REFLECTIONS

1. After last month's social studies test, Mary Ellen Watson and Tony Marino determined that one of the test questions was not written very clearly, which explained why the item was so difficult for their students. Much to the relief of their students, Mary Ellen

and Tony elected not to *count* the test item towards their grade. Now, after the current test, several students are quite upset that he did not eliminate several questions that they claim were confusing. How would you suggest that Mary Ellen and Tony respond to their students? How might they avoid this situation from happening in the future?

2. Mrs. Willis, Julie's mother, has called to set up a conference with you. She is concerned about Julie's scores on the district proficiency test that was administered last month. Mrs. Willis would like some help interpreting the test report that she received in the mail, and she wants to know why Julie's test scores were so low when she is getting As and Bs in your class. What sorts of things are you likely to do to prepare for the conference? What reasons might explain the discrepancy between Julie's test scores and class grades?

3. After looking at the results of a recent science test, Mrs. Li notes that two of the lesson objectives were quite difficult for the majority of her students. She would like to spend some time reviewing and re-teaching these objectives but she is concerned that she might *get behind*, especially with the district proficiency test just a few weeks away. Should Mrs. Li go back and review the objectives or move forward? What factors do you think that Mrs. Li should consider in making her decision to review or move forward? What if only three or four students missed the objectives? Would your decision change?

TEACHER AS RESEARCHER

Evaluating the Quality of Tests

Brown, W. R. (1998). Test mapping: Planning the classroom test. *The Clearing House, 71* (3), 153–155.

The author suggests nine criteria that teachers can use as they *develop* their assessment tools. How can these criteria be used *after* you have administered the assessment to *evaluate* the quality of the assessment process?

Griswold, P. A. (1990). Assessing relevance and reliability to improve the quality of teacher-made tests. *NASSP Bulletin, 74* (523), 18–24.

Assessing the relevance and reliability of classroom assessments is an important skill for teachers to develop. What non-technical and non-statistical suggestions does the author provide for evaluating the quality of teacher made tests.

Grading and Report Cards

Kagan, S. (1995). Group grades miss the mark. *Educational Leadership, 52* (8), 68–71.

The benefits of group work are often tempered with the challenge of grading them. Grading group projects can be problematic. Do you agree with the author's contention that giving the same grade to all members of a group is unfair and undermines the positive outcomes of cooperative learning. What are some possible alternatives to group grades?

Allison, E., & Friedman, S. J. (1995). Hassle-free report-card reform. *Education Digest, 60* (8), 55–58.

The authors describe one school district's efforts to adopt a nontraditional report-card format. Do you think the objections of parents and school board members were warranted? What suggestions are provided for dealing with objections from outsiders with regard to alternative grading methods?

Communicating Assessment Results

Austin, T. (1994). *Changing the view: Student-led parent conferences.* Portsmouth, NH: Heinemann.

The author describes the student-led quarterly conferences that she uses with her sixth-grade students and their parents. Through the use of portfolios, her students reflect on their own learning and become more active and responsible participants in the learning process.

Rose, M. C. (1998). Handle with care: The difficult parent-teacher conference. *Instructor, 108* (3), 92–95.

Ideally, parent-teacher conferences should be a pleasant and positive experience. There may be times, however, when you may need to be prepared to talk with parents about their child's negative behavior or poor achievement. Understandably, parents may become defensive or even hostile. What steps can you take to facilitate potentially hostile conferences?

CHAPTER **11**

Evaluating Teaching

CONVERSATION

It was finally Friday. The past week had been almost overwhelming for Sarah; so many weeks had seemed that way lately. As a first-year teacher, she was busy all the time with planning and delivering lessons. She hadn't been overjoyed, then, by Mrs. Washington's suggestion that she consider "testing out" her theory about how much more students would enjoy reading and how much more they would get out of it if they could respond to outside readings in ways different from the traditional book reports that the English department had been requiring for years. For the past several days her students had been presenting their responses, and she had just collected the interest survey. She was poring over students' comments, looking back at their descriptions of the experiences that they had had as she tried to get a sense of whether this project had indeed increased their enjoyment. As Sarah looked back at the projects, she felt the students had certainly shown more personal connections than any previous reports she had assigned. However, Sarah also wanted to be able to give Mrs. Washington a sense of how the students had evaluated this project.

Mrs. Washington had been a great mentor for Sarah, allowing her to make informed choices in curricular decisions and giving her the opportunity to practice what she had been learning in her college methods courses. This particular curricular decision had been based on something Sarah had read about Howard Gardner's multiple intelligences. She also had thought about her educational psychology course and the importance her psych prof had attached to the need to gather objective data to support or refute what "common sense" told us.

"So, how did it come out?" Mrs. Washington asked.

"Well, by and large, I thought it went really well. Students seemed to engage with the works they read on a much more personal level. That was what I meant when I said that they would "get more" out of their reading. Before, with the book reports that I had assigned, they seemed to be going through the motions. A lot of the plot summaries seemed to be done as paraphrases of the book jackets. Until this project I had never seen the different talents that some of these students possessed. Like Juan, his writing has always been on the rough side, but the mural that he drew for *One Hundred Years of Solitude* (García Márquez, 1991) captured the mystical quality of the work and still allowed someone who hadn't read it to recognize the importance of family as one of the connecting strands. He was absolutely glowing after all the positive feedback from his peers.

"I'm still not sure if they liked it any more than the book reports. A couple students said it was a lot more work, but I'm not sure whether that meant they liked it or not. I'll know more when I look at the interest inventories at home this weekend."

DEVELOPING COMPETENCE

1. Think back to the ways in which your teachers evaluated your work in high school and grade school. Jot down a list of all the sources you remember. After reading, consider what sources of information you can add to this list that teachers use as feedback as they evaluate their lessons and their units. Why is it important that teachers solicit multiple sources of feedback as they evaluate the successes and areas of improvement in their lessons? units?

2. Consider a time when you met a challenge and accomplished a goal you set for yourself. Think about the activities—mental and/or physical—you went through as you engaged in *identifying* this challenge, *defining* it, *exploring* alternative plans for meeting the challenge, *acting* on your plan, and then *looking* at the results. How important was the last step, looking at the results, for helping you to realize how much you had accomplished? As you take this problem-solving mentality into the classroom, what are the professional benefits to be gained by teachers from evaluating lessons and units? What are the benefits to be gained by their students?

3. As you reflected on your success in the previous question, what were the standards you used to know that you had accomplished your goal? After reading, explain how the various frameworks described—INTASC, Pathwise, Framework for Teaching—could assist you in setting standards for reflecting on your future work as a teacher?

4. This text has focused mainly on the teaching act as it revolves around the skills and techniques that teachers use to build effective units and lessons. There is a great deal more to building a teaching career. What other responsibilities and roles can you think of that teachers respond to? After reading, identify which sources that you've read about can provide new teachers with some guidance in beginning their practice and explain how these might prove helpful.

5. Remember back to a time when a teacher's presence in a classroom had a positive influence on your learning, either helping you with difficulties in a subject or exciting you to go beyond the constraints of the lesson or unit being taught. What did the teacher do to influence you so strongly? Would you say that this teacher possessed a sense of "self-efficacy"? What would you consider to be the impact on student learning of a teacher with a strong sense of efficacy?

INTRODUCTION

Dr. Carmen Giebelhaus, who worked in the Division of Professional Development and Licensure for the Ohio Department of Education, trains prospective mentor-teachers in the use of the Pathwise system as a framework for working with new teachers as they take on the task of planning, delivering, and evaluating lessons. When the mentors raise "What if . . . ?" questions—questions about the things their mentees might do that might not have a clear-cut right or wrong answer—Giebelhaus responds that these are the perfect times to "enter into a conversation about teaching and learning" with the novices.

It may seem a bit odd to you that we should introduce the last chapter by indicating that we are "entering into" a conversation about teaching and learning. You might be thinking, "Goodness gracious (or something to that effect), aren't you finished yet!" However, as we hope you have determined by now, teaching is such a complex act that the conversation is never truly completed and any teaching episode gives a teacher new material for further conversations. Just as the IDEAL model connects "Looking at the Results" back to "Identifying the Challenge," as you reflect upon the successes and concerns of any teaching event, whether that is a lesson, unit, or an entire semester or year, you naturally arrive at the starting point. You should start to ask yourself important questions, such as: What should I keep doing that I have already done? What should I change? How do I know what I should keep and what I should change? How will I know if changes were successful?

This chapter will provide you with some ways of thinking about lessons and units that expand upon what you just read in chapter 10. You will be introduced to, or be reminded of, some sources of information that you want to consider as you enter into conversations on teaching and learning with yourself and other professionals. Finally, we will suggest some activities that you may want to consider as opportunities to further your teaching career in ways that can be energizing and professionally satisfying.

REFLECTING ON YOUR OWN TEACHING

In this section, you are asked to look back at the effects of what you have done. The teaching day moves so quickly that it is often difficult to take time out to reflect on the successes and concerns you might have about individual students or student groups or your own teaching practices. Schon (1987) discussed two types of reflection processes in which professionals engage—reflection-in-action and reflection-on-action. **Reflection-in-action** takes place while lessons are going on. Because of the complexity of teaching, the pace, multiple activities and individual student differences to name a few, teachers cannot simply fall back on some type of predetermined response to a situation. Teachers must act, reflect on the effects of that action, and be prepared to modify their behavior or future actions based on that reflection. At any given moment, for instance, while you are engaged with a small group of students, a child may shout out for help. This child could really need your help, or he could be trying to draw your attention, or he could be practicing a play in which his character needs help. You will need to quickly assess the situation to determine which of these situations is taking place. If it is a play, for example, you may choose to ignore the behavior because it's fine within the context of the activity, or you may determine that this behavior is distracting others and make eye contact or say something to the child. Regardless of which decision you make, you will need to evaluate the effects of your decision and be prepared to act in some other way if necessary.

Reflection-on-action provides you with an opportunity to consider the effects of your decisions after the event has taken place rather than while it is ongoing. As a professional, you should make these systematic "reality" checks on yourself so that you can consider how you might proceed in re-teaching a particular concept the next day or what skills students still need to develop after they have completed a unit. You should make both of these types of reflection a part of your professional repertoire. At first, you will probably need to set specific time aside for reflecting-on-action in specific and systematic ways. Eventually, though, this will become an internalized piece of your practice.

In the conversation at the beginning of this chapter, Sarah is engaging in this latter form of reflecting. She has gathered some evidence, both informal—her own perceptions of the success of the lessons—and formal—the students' writing about their experiences in the interest survey she created. With these sources of information as her foundation, she is looking back at and reflecting on the successes and concerns of the project her students had just completed. Effective, experienced teachers like Mrs. Washington, Sarah's mentor, realize that they must consistently and systematically reflect upon their teaching practices with an eye constantly focused on students' achievement of the goals that they are trying to meet. It is in the act of reflecting that novice teachers grow in their professional duties and responsibilities. Those duties and responsibilities go far beyond designing, teaching, and evaluating lessons and units and, while that has been our main focus throughout this book, we feel we would be remiss if we didn't recognize and draw your attention to some aspects of a larger view of teaching. The remainder of this chapter, then, is organized to proceed from evaluating lessons to units and to yourself as a professional.

EVALUATING LESSONS

When teachers close the doors in their classrooms, they have a great deal of autonomy and freedom in how they "teach" their classes. For the most part, unless the noise level is so high or enough complaints are lodged, most teachers and administrators have little or no knowledge of how well any individual teacher is teaching on any given day or, for that matter, throughout most of the year. This opportunity to do something meaningful on your own, to be your own boss most of the time, is one of the aspects of teaching that makes it most appealing; it is also one of the factors that makes it very difficult to exert quality control over teachers. It is our belief that teachers are responsible, both professionally and ethically, to make sure that the decisions that they make about teaching and learning are done in accordance with accepted practices and always in students' best interests. (One way of looking back at the success of lessons is in terms of "best practice." The Zemelman, Daniels, and Hyde reference in the "Reflecting on Teaching" section of *Teacher as Researcher* provides you with some standards to use in reflecting on practices in particular content areas.)

To make good decisions, you need to consider the aftermath of your teaching, reflecting on both strengths and weaknesses and adjusting your teaching appropriately. Expert teachers do this automatically, often making adjustments so flawlessly within teaching episodes that an observer does not even realize that any changes from the plans have been made. To do that effectively as a novice, however, you will need to reflect, often very consciously and systematically, on your lessons by using many different sources of information. While the primary sources will be your students, there are many other possibilities available to you, though you may have to seek these out.

Students as a Source of Feedback

Effective teachers know that their first source of feedback about the success of any lesson are the students who experienced it. In commenting on expert teachers, Darling-Hammond and Ball (1997) contended that teachers' "skill in assessing their students' progress depends [not only] on how deeply they themselves know the content, [but also on] how well they can understand and interpret students' talk and written work" (pp. 2–3). As a novice, you need to do a great deal of preparation to constantly add to your own knowledge base, regardless of your grade level or content area; but you will also need to carefully consider what students say and produce before, during, and immediately following your lesson in order to determine the appropriate starting place for and the appropriate pacing of a day's lesson.

Informal, Subjective Observations   Teachers gain a good deal of information as they teach by scanning the room, looking at the eyes of their students. Speak to veteran teachers and they might tell you that this is the major method that they use while a lesson is in progress. And there appears to be some basis for effective teachers to feel this is an appropriate method. A growing body of research suggests that interpreting visual cues in a classroom is one important factor in making appropriate instructional decisions, as well as in managing classrooms. In one study (Carter, et al., 1988) in which a variety of teachers were asked to respond to slides of science and math classrooms, the authors noted that experts "appeared better able to weigh the import of one piece of information against another, to form connections among pieces of information, and to represent management and instructional situations into meaningful problem units" (p. 25). To be effective, you will need to develop your informal observation skills, focusing on audio and visual cues. As a new teacher, however, you will not have developed your skills to a high enough level to count on this type of assessment as your major source of feedback. Therefore, you will probably want to consider more conscious methods as you develop your "teaching schema."

More Formal, Objective Observations   To begin to develop your observational skills, we suggest you take a bit more systematic approach. There are a number of other methods that you may want to use that will provide you with some information about the successes or gaps in a particular lesson. One teacher we know asks students exit questions nearly every day. For instance, at the end of a lesson on the Industrial Revolution, he may ask students to identify new technologies that appeared at this time and the impact that these had on the economy of the day. He tries to sample different students each day to get a sense of the success of that day's teaching and learning. He then uses this information as a sort of "reality" check on himself, often beginning the next day's lesson by referring to what he learned about the students' perceptions of the previous day's lesson. This may call for reteaching a specific concept, or it may prompt him to assess more explicitly the students' development of the concept. Regardless, this teacher believes in the importance of sampling student perceptions as he reflects on a day's work.

What you will need at this point are ideas, ways in which teachers, especially new ones, can go about gathering information while they develop their observational skills to such a point that they can feel comfortable counting on them like a "sixth sense." Sharon McNeely (1997) has written just such a useful resource of more formal, objective techniques available for you as a new teacher to use as you look at your students (see a further description of McNeely's work in the "Reflecting on Teaching" section of *Teacher as Researcher* at the end of this chapter). In fact, this resource provides checklists that you can use or adapt to look at a variety of student behaviors that can offer you insights into how successful your teaching of a lesson really was. McNeely describes techniques that classroom researchers have used for years as they have built the knowledge base for effective teaching about which you have read and to which we have referred throughout this book. She gives specific procedures that you can follow that will allow you to devise your own checklists that you can use to investigate student behaviors.

For example, you may be interested in evaluating the success of one of your lessons in terms of how well you attempted to meet students' individual cognitive needs according to Piaget's theory of cognitive development. You could use the checklist from Form C3B (see Figure 11.1) to check off specific behaviors you observe for individual students, especially those for whom you might be most concerned. Obviously, students may not have an opportunity to exhibit all of the behaviors during any one lesson, but your objectives will indicate which behaviors should most likely be demonstrated. Over the course of time, keeping records like this can certainly provide you with insights about the kinds of lessons and instructional activities that are most successful for different students.

Using checklists like this and other explicit forms of recording observations will facilitate your own development as an observer of student behaviors. Until you become adept at "reading their eyes," these are more accurate and helpful methods to use as you develop your own teacher skills. And it is important that you assess students' perceptions of a day's lesson before you determine to forge ahead with your unit plan. When it is most important to get student information, however, you will be wise to devise systematic, formative assessments.

FIGURE 11.1   FORM C3B: SOME INDICATORS OF COGNITIVE DEVELOPMENT APPLYING PLAGET'S THEORY

School: _____ Room: _____ Teacher: _____

Grade level: _____ Subject Matter: _____ Number of Students: _____

Date: _____ Start Time: _____ Finish Time: _____ Total Observation Time: _____

Room Set-up/Special Information: _____

Definition of Observation: _____

_____ simple reflexive moves

_____ imitations centered on own body

_____ retrieves partially hidden objects

_____ retrieves hidden object from first place hidden

_____ searches in many places for hidden object

_____ engages in deferred imitation

_____ unaware of other's viewpoints

_____ inanimate objects have lifelike qualities

_____ judges based on current perceptions

_____ centers on one aspect of a situation

_____ focuses on present, not past and future

_____ cannot go backward through a series of steps

_____ wrong linking of events as cause and effect

_____ cannot group objects into categories

_____ knows mass stays same as shape changes

_____ understands relations of distance and time

_____ coordinates several features of a task

_____ arranges items in logical series

_____ can work backwards through a problem

_____ can infer relationships among objects

_____ can group objects into categories

_____ tests hypothesis in an orderly manner

_____ evaluates abstract verbal statements

(*Source:* Sharon McNeely, Observing Students through Objective Strategies. Copyright (c) 1997 by Allyn and Bacon. Reprinted by permission.)

Systematic Formative Assessments   Subjective and objective observations are important to use in assessing the success of a lesson, especially in terms of student learning. At their best, however, these observations, like in the exit interviews or the checklists, only sample specific individuals. At their worst, teachers, especially novices, may misinterpret their scanning of faces and continue on with a lesson while leaving students behind. One way to combat these two possible problems is to use **systematic formative assessments,** which are techniques designed to determine students' development of your objectives *while* students are still developing the behaviors.

The difference between a systematic formative assessment and the subjective and objective observations described earlier is that formative assessments do not just choose a couple of students and assume that they reflect the learning of all students. The systematic nature of this technique requires that you be guided by three principles as you plan for formatively assessing students' learning. These are:

- Formative assessments should measure *all* students;
- They should be done in a relatively time-efficient manner; and
- They should be non-punitive.

Let's look at each of these separately.

The first principle is one that sets formative assessments apart from subjective and objective observations. If you were to do an interview with several students as they leave your classroom, you would certainly have some important pieces of information upon which you might evaluate the success of your lesson plan. However, in a class of twenty-five or more, that information would naturally be limited. You may have spoken only to those who "didn't get it" or those who did; the majority of your students may have had a vastly different experience. If you decide to reteach a concept on the basis of these three or four students, you run the risk of providing a less-than-meaningful experience for the majority. That is why a true formative assessment must measure all students who experienced the lesson or portion of a lesson that you want to assess.

Obviously, you could not stop the class to interview, even briefly, all of the students in the room. That brings us to the second principle, time efficiency. We intentionally use the term "relatively" here. What is time efficient under one circumstance would be time "wasteful" under another. For example, if students were actively engaged in producing individual projects related to your unit objectives, you might be able to justify brief individual interviews with every student. Using this method assumes that you are able to monitor student activity even while conducting these interviews. More often, you may choose to do something that requires much less time. For instance, something as simple as a thumbs-up or thumbs-down in responding to questions that you ask of the entire class. One other possibility is to have students write a "one-minute" paper at the end of the day or lesson in response to a specific or open-ended question you devise. As long as you read the responses and then make appropriate adjustments, like reteaching or spending extra time with a small group of students who have not yet mastered the content or skill, on the basis of the information, this too can be an effective formative assessment because it does not take away from instructional time.

Activity 11.1

Brainstorm with others in your content-area discipline and/or certification level (early childhood, middle school, etc.) and generate a list of formative assessment strategies. Be prepared to justify every choice in terms of the three principles above. Display your techniques on butcher paper and/or create a database of ideas that you can share with your classmates.

Finally, a formative assessment should be non-punitive. Remember, the intent of these measures is to assess students' development of your objectives *while* they are "under construction." You are trying to gather information for yourself as you determine how well you have taught (and students have learned) the previous material, what to teach now, how long to spend on any one chunk of content or skill, and when to move on. Therefore, a pop quiz, while it may be very appropriate for students' accountability in some ways, should not be considered a formative assessment because it does penalize individual students who have not yet mastered the content or grade.

Let's consider this a bit further. You have likely been in a class in which a teacher was delivering a lesson that was based on material that students were to have read the night before. The teacher had prepared lesson objectives, asked a couple of questions and observed students looking around at the floor, their books, anywhere but at the teacher; no one volunteered, and the students who were called on could not respond appropriately. At this point, the teacher may have said: "Take out a sheet of paper and number from one to ten." Is this teacher really trying to assess student mastery of the objectives? Certainly not. She may be sending a message, and she will probably find out who read and who didn't; she probably already has a good idea about that anyway based on what has already taken place. The point is, if you want to hold students accountable for reading and you find that quizzes are an appropriate method of doing this, then do it. Just don't call it a formative assessment. Your purpose here in quizzing is quite different from the intent of a formative measure. (You may want to look back at chapters 9 and 10 as you consider the differences in assessment strategies designed to measure your teaching and those you might use to assess student achievement.)

Mentors

While students will generally act as your first line of information about the success of a lesson, there are times when you may not be able to receive all that you need from them to improve your practice. That is when you may need to turn your attention to a teacher-expert, like a mentor. In the conversations at the beginnings of each chapter in this text, you have been reading about mentors and seeing the types of relationships that they may have with novice teachers. As we hope the conversations have indicated, mentors are there to support your efforts at improving your teaching skills. They will generally observe individual lessons that you teach and structure a conversation with you shortly after their observations in order to provide you with feedback. Generally, a mentor will work with a new teacher during an induction year. A number of studies (Huling-Austin 1988; Looney 1997) indicated that connecting with mentors can increase the retention rate of new teachers by providing them with support in areas, like classroom management, discipline, and understanding the school culture, that they really need and for which education courses like the one you are taking now cannot fully prepare you. (The Lucas article in the "Mentors and Mentoring" section of *Teacher as Researcher* describes the process in which both parties engage as mentors support their mentees' development).

By definition, a **mentor** is a wise and trusted counselor, someone who can provide you with support as you attempt to learn the basics of your first year in a district. There is an implied relationship here between an expert and a novice. Depending on the quality and training of the individual involved, the mentor may provide very specific tips on techniques you can try or how to streamline some of the procedural and clerical concerns that affect most new teachers. In other cases, the mentor may actively listen to you as you work through your own decision-making process. As effective teachers, mentors recognize that there are many ways that teachers can go about their practice and still be successful. The effective mentor will provide you with feedback that may help you to think about issues in your lesson or unit planning that you had not considered, thus giving you an opportunity, either to avoid a mistake or learn from one that you have already made. (The qualities that a "good mentor" possesses is the subject of the Rawley article in the "Mentors and Mentoring" section of *Teacher as Researcher*.)

More and more, schools are recognizing the benefits of mentors for their new teachers and are instituting their own mentoring programs as a part of their systems. It is certainly a question you may want to ask when you are interviewing for your first job. Whether there is an official mentoring program or not, it is worth your while to find a colleague, who is respected and whom you can trust, in your school with whom you can carry on professional conversations. In one study of mentoring programs, Barnes (1993) noted that sometimes the most effective mentors are college faculty or field supervisors with whom you have already worked and in whom you have gained trust. Be aware of that as you continue your education and strive to maintain a professional relationship with these important people. They can act as an important part of your network and can act as a "critical friend" as you consider a wide variety of teaching issues.

EVALUATING UNITS

It is important that you evaluate how well students have mastered specific objectives and content before you move on. At some point, however, you will feel comfortable that students have shown sufficient progress that you want to evaluate them on a larger chunk of learning, the unit. In chapter 9, you read about the multiple sources available to you to measure students' achievement of educational objectives. As you look back at the success of your teaching of a particular unit you will want to consider the information you have gathered from these and many other sources as you evaluate the success of your teaching.

Student Information

Teachers often look at unit test scores in terms of how well their students have done on the content of the unit as a whole, particular pieces of the unit, or in terms of the skills they were helping students to develop. (The focus on looking back at student attainment of objectives was dealt with in Chapter 10.) Be careful, though, not to limit the type of information student tests and projects can provide you. For instance, the first time you looked at the summative evaluation instruments that your students completed, you were probably doing so to evaluate *their* success in learning. As you look at this information again, you will want to do so with an eye toward *your* success in teaching.

Student tests, projects, or exhibitions provide you with a great deal of information about the success of your teaching. As you look at these, try to determine patterns of errors, both for individual students and for groups or the class as a whole. After discovering any patterns that may exist, determine the relative importance of this piece of content or skill. Is this skill fundamental to what students will be doing in the next unit? If so, then you will need to reteach it as a planned part of the learning experiences of the next unit. If not, then you may be able to hold off on reteaching until it becomes important to students' success. In this way, though the test may have been a summative instrument for the previous unit, you can still allow it to function as a diagnostic instrument for what you still need to teach.

How might this play out in a classroom? Let's say that David, a second grader, takes a timed math facts test. He has five minutes to complete one hundred two-addend, single-digit addition problems. In that time span he completes seventy problems, missing four, but leaving thirty blank. His teacher writes on his paper "–34" and "You need to study your addition!" in big, red letters. As a summative measure of David's automaticity in doing these types of addition problems, she has made a professional judgment as to the quality of his work and what he needs to do. He has not met her standard of 90 percent accuracy, which she has identified as the criterion for mastery. But let's take another look (see Figure 11.2). What do you notice? What we noticed was that David appeared to work across the page at first, then down the page (or vice versa). When we questioned David regarding the order in which he attempted these problems, he confirmed our initial suspicion. If you look at the problems he attempted, he certainly was meeting the standard. Of the errors in problems that he attempted, two of them were clearly wrong. However, two of the errors seemed to indicate that he subtracted rather than added, still an error for what he was supposed to do but a qualitatively "better" error than the first two.

So, does David really need to study his addition facts? Not necessarily, though it certainly wouldn't hurt. What the teacher may need to teach David is a learning

FIGURE 11.2   DAVID'S MATH FACTS TEST PAPER

100 Addition Problems

(-34)

You need to study your addition facts!

7	6	5	3	4	8	2	3	8	0
1	3	2	1	5	1	0	4	2	6
8	9	7	4	9	9	2	7	10	6

3	4	3	2	0	4	4	0	2	1
3	1	7	2	1	4	6	9	6	8
6	5	10	4	1	8	10	9	8	9

1	2	6	2	2	4	3	2	5	1
9	3	1	8	7	1	6	4	5	1
10	5	7	10	9	5	9	6	10	2

3	5	3	7	0	9	4	6	5	3
6	4	2	2	6	1	1	2	1	5
9	9	5	9	6	8	5	8	6	6

4	2	2	0	5	1	6	4	0	2
6	5	4	3	5	7	2	4	9	5
10	9	6	3	10	✗	✗	✗	✗	✗

1	0	3	2	4	0	1	1	3	1
8	1	5	4	6	3	9	1	2	4
9	1	8	6	✗	3	✗	✗	✗	✗

4	3	4	2	6	8	0	5	3	8
5	5	1	3	1	2	4	1	5	0
9	8	3	5	7	✗	4	✗	✗	8

2	2	9	1	4	2	1	2	6	8
7	4	0	4	3	6	5	2	4	0
9	6	9	✗	✗	✗	✗	✗	✗	8

1	3	2	4	6	0	1	5	8	3
4	6	5	3	1	8	3	2	2	3
5	9	7	✗	7	✗	✗	✗	✗	✗

6	7	1	8	3	2	7	4	5	8
2	3	4	0	4	1	0	6	1	2
8	10	5	8	7	✗	✗	✗	✗	✗

strategy that he can employ in doing timed math tests so that he can finish all of the items. (Learning strategies were addressed in chapter 8). In a timed situation, he would be better served by going left to right, so that he can see the next problem as he finishes the previous one, rather than down the page, since his hand will be covering the next problems all the way down the page. Looking at the test in this way provides us with a very different judgment of David's skills, on the one hand, and on what it is that we need to teach, on the other. If we find that the majority of students have had the same problem, then it may be worth a whole-class lesson in test-taking strategies prior to the next timed test. If only a handful had this problem, then we might just work with them in a small group and send some reinforcement work home for them to practice.

Activity 11.2

Look back at David's paper in Figure 11.2. Referring back to the "Developing your own Learning Strategies" section of chapter 8, design a strategy that you could teach David and other students who struggle with this type of test behavior. Share the strategy and any materials you design with your classmates.

In addition to using test and projects as diagnostic instruments for teaching in future lessons and units, you can use some of the same techniques that we previously mentioned in the formative assessments section of this chapter. In this case, though, you can use these formative assessment strategies to find out information about students' perceptions of the strengths of particular lessons within the unit and changes they would like to see made in procedures that you used throughout the unit. Providing students with a one-minute paper topic on "What to Keep" and "What to Change" would give them an opportunity to give you feedback on their experiences in the unit. When entrusted with this type of responsibility, we have found that students tend to rise to the occasion, offering insightful comments for you to consider. Regardless of what students say, it is still up to you to make professional decisions about your own practices, but offering them an opportunity on a number of occasions throughout the year to provide you with feedback may give you important pieces of information that can improve future units.

School Sources

We have already mentioned the use of colleagues as mentors or peer coaches. Using these people, or other departmental or grade level colleagues, who know how the curriculum fits together, can provide you with a good sounding board for evaluating how your own unit plans fit into the "scheme of things." Your school also provides a number of other resources that you may be able to use as you evaluate your unit planning and delivery. In some schools, there may be a collection of model units for different grade levels or content areas (here, again, we want to remind you of the Zemelman et al., source in the "Reflecting on Teaching" section of *Teacher as Researcher*). These may be bound in notebooks or filed in cabinets at a common site. These can be invaluable resources for you to check against your own plans. Schools should also have copies of the state curriculum models. Especially in this age of high stakes testing, you want to be certain that your units cover the objectives that may be tested on a proficiency exam that might determine a student's opportunity to graduate.

Still, your best resource should be the Graded Course of Study (GCS), as we mentioned earlier (see chapter 2). As a new teacher you will probably rely on it as a source for planning, but sometimes veteran teachers slowly move away from the curriculum. One of us was recently at a high school where the chair of the English department and his colleagues were developing a year-end exam for ninth-grade students. The department chair felt it was necessary because every ninth-grade teacher seemed to be doing something very different with the content, some breaking from the established curriculum in significant ways. These breaks can seriously affect students, since the teachers at the tenth-grade level expect that students have been introduced to certain content and skills upon which their tenth-grade experiences can build. You can avoid these sorts of problems simply by checking the extent to which each of your units matches the performance objectives in the local GCS.

Other Professional Resources

So far, outside of the GCS, we have mentioned mostly "people resources" that you can check with as you evaluate your teaching of lessons and units. In addition to the GCS or Scope-and-Sequence guides that your district provides, you have some other professional resources that you can access that can provide you with information about which you can think as you reflect on how to improve your units and lessons. Though there are many more than the ones we will mention here, four sources that you may want to consider are learned societies, the Internet, ERIC, and Kraus Curriculum Guides.

Learned Societies   As we mentioned in chapter 2, learned societies help curriculum designers to identify important content within their particular disciplines. In addition to this important function, they provide teachers with forums for sharing ideas about teaching, both in terms of content and methods. Each content-area discipline, like the National Council of Teachers of English (NCTE) for English/Language Arts, and a number of age or grade levels, like the National Middle School Association (NMSA), have organizations devoted to trying to improve teaching. Most of these associations have journals that you receive as a part of your membership dues. These journals present articles of interest to teachers that will often provide you with insights into what other teachers are doing to help students develop a specific skill or work with a particular content area. Don't think that you need to wait until your first job to join, either; many of the learned societies also offer student memberships that provide you with member benefits at a discount price. See Figure 11.3 for a list of addresses for a number of the major organizations.

FIGURE 11.3 PARTIAL LISTING OF MAJOR LEARNED SOCIETIES		
Organization	Website	Address
American Educational Research Association (AERA)	www.aera.net	1230 17th St. Washington, DC 20036
Association for Supervision and Curriculum Development (ASCD)	www.ascd.org	1703 N. Beauregard St. Alexandria, VA 22311
Council for Exceptional Children (CEC)	www.cec.sped.org	1920 Association Dr. Reston, VA 20191
International Reading Association (IRA)	www.ira.org	800 Barksdale Rd. P.O. Box 8139 Newark, DE 19714
Music Educators National Conference (MENC)	www.menc.org	1806 Robert Fulton Dr. Reston, VA 20191
National Arts Education Association (NAEA)	www.naea-reston.org	1916 Association Dr. Reston, VA 20191
National Association for the Education of Young Children (NAEYC)	www.naeyc.org	1509 16th St. N.W. Washington, DC 20016
National Council for the Social Studies (NCSS)	www.ncss.org	3501 Newark St. N.W. Washington, DC 20016
National Council of Teachers of English (NCTE)	www.ncte.org	1111 W. Kenyon Rd. Urbana, IL 61801
National Council of Teachers of Mathematics (NCTM)	www.nctm.org	1906 Association Dr. Reston, VA 20191
National Middle School Association (NMSA)	www.nmsa.org	4151 Executive Pkwy. Suite 300 Westerville, OH 43081
National Science Teachers Association (NSTA)	www.nsta.org	1840 Wilson Blvd. Arlington, VA 22201

The Internet   As a teacher in the twenty-first century, you will need to become both familiar and comfortable with using the Internet. It is hard to envision all of the ways in which this resource will change the ways that teachers go about their business, but it is already impacting what teachers need to know so that they can keep up with their students. Many of the associations mentioned in the previous section host their own websites with links to sites that can provide you with lesson and unit plans. For instance, one of us recently accessed the National Council of Teachers of Mathematics website (http://www.nctm.org/) and within four mouse clicks was at a linked site that had links to middle school math activities and projects for the Internet, individual lesson plans and collections of plans, as well as "fun sites for kids." You could also join a listserve that deals with your subject area or grade level. After joining, you could post questions or comments on the listserve and even receive feedback about plans you were thinking about doing or ones that you have already tried. In any case, the Internet can provide you with access to virtual "mentors" who are willing to share their insights with you as you build your own practice.

Activity 11.3

Spend a session or two "surfing" the World Wide Web. Try using keywords that relate to a general grade level (e.g., primary, secondary) and content area. See how many sites you can find that provide specific lesson or unit plans. Report back to the class. Consider creating a class data base of sites that appear to be educationally sound and helpful or create your own webpage with links to these sites.

Educational Resources Information Center (ERIC)   If you haven't yet used the ERIC system, you probably should. The ERIC databases are designed specifically for educators. Many campus libraries provide access to this resource, either in the form of CD-ROMs or through Internet access. If you have access to an Internet Service Provider, you can connect to ERIC from home (http://ericir.syr.edu//ERIC/). By simply typing in a few keywords you will have access to hundreds if not thousands of articles by educators on topics of interest to you. ERIC searches will provide you with abstracts of articles that you can scan to determine if you want to pull up an entire article, either in a journal, on microfiche, or in a full text file (if that is available for you through your library). In addition, you can order copies of articles, as well as annotated bibliographies on many topics, directly from the clearinghouse. As with Internet searches, the better you become at limiting your searches, the easier it will become for you to be more efficient with your time. Here again you can quickly find many articles that will provide you with information that you can use as you plan lessons and units.

Kraus Curriculum Guides   One interesting resource that may be overlooked are the Kraus Curriculum Guides. If you are fortunate enough to be on a campus that subscribes to these guides, you will find that they have literally thousands of recent curriculum guides from across the country. Many of the guides provide district or state model curricula, but some provide lesson and unit plans that are currently being used in local districts. Many large university libraries will carry a number of the individual guides on microfiche. An index provides you with information about what each guide contains and, by accessing several that appear to deal with unit plans, you can gain valuable information as you set about planning for students.

EVALUATING YOURSELF AS A PROFESSIONAL

We have said it before, but we're going to say it again. Expert teachers evaluate themselves on the basis of how well their students achieve. In addition to this criteria, though, there is a large and growing amount of scholarship that revolves around the skills that exemplary teachers share and can demonstrate. Since the 1980s, this body of knowledge has been transformed into a variety of frameworks that teachers can use to help them guide their development as professionals. These frameworks provide teachers with a shared vocabulary for discussing their professional activities. Some, like the PRAXIS/Pathwise framework, are being used for assessing teacher performance in order to certify or license new teachers. As such, these frameworks may be more useful for evaluating novice teacher performance. Others, like the process for being certified by the National Board for Professional Teaching Standards (NBPTS), are standards that can be used for evaluating the long-term development of a teacher's practice. In either case, the activities required to meet these standards can provide professional teachers with one other source of information about their own professional skills.

PRAXIS III/Pathwise

The PRAXIS III Performance Assessment was developed by Educational Testing Service (ETS) based upon an extensive review of research into teacher performance (Dwyer, 1994). Its purpose was to assess the performance of beginning teachers in their own classrooms with the intent of providing states or local agencies with one measure that they may use in licensing or certifying a beginning teacher. Pathwise is a companion to PRAXIS III, acting as a formative measure to PRAXIS III's summative. In the hands of a trained mentor, the use of Pathwise can provide new teachers with the skills they need to pass a PRAXIS III assessment and, more importantly, feedback that can assist them in developing their skills as a new teacher.

PRAXIS III/Pathwise looks at teaching in terms of four domains (see Figure 11.4) that relate to what teachers do before, during, and after they teach. Just as we have suggested you do, this assessment uses multiple methods of collecting data. Teachers fill out several documents prior to a lesson that demonstrate their planning and understanding of their students. A trained observer then watches teachers as they deliver the same lessons they had planned. Both before and after teaching, teachers and observers participate in a structured interview. These multiple sources are then used by the observer to determine the degree of proficiency demonstrated by teachers as weighed against each of the nineteen criteria. Again, ETS has set the level of proficiency to be that which novice teachers can demonstrate. The assumption is that the competent novice has the foundation to become an effective veteran.

A Framework for Teaching

Building upon the research that went into the PRAXIS III instrument, and having participated in the validation of it, Danielson (1996) created "A Framework for Teaching" that she believed would help both novices and veterans alike to enter into the conversations about teaching and learning that we mentioned at the start

FIGURE 11.4   PRAXIS III/PATHWISE PERFORMANCE ASSESSMENT CRITERIA

Domain A–Organizing Content Knowledge for Student Learning

A1   Becoming familiar with relevant aspects of students' prior knowledge, skills, and cultural experiences.

A2   Articulating clear learning goals for the lesson that are appropriate for the students.

A3   Demonstrating an understanding of the connections between the content that was learned previously, the current content, and the content that remains to be learned in the future.

A4   Creating or selecting teaching methods, learning activities, and instructional materials or other resources that are appropriate for the students and that are aligned with the goals of the lesson.

A5   Creating or selecting evaluation strategies that are appropriate for the students and that are aligned with the goals of the lesson.

Domain B–Creating an Environment for Student Learning

B1   Creating a climate that promotes fairness.

B2   Establishing and maintaining rapport with students.

B3   Communicating challenging learning expectations to each student.

B4   Establishing and maintaining consistent standards of classroom behavior.

B5   Making the physical environment as safe and conducive to learning as possible.

Domain C–Teaching for Student Learning

C1   Making learning goals and instructional procedures clear to students

C2   Making content comprehensible to students.

C3   Encouraging students to extend their thinking.

C4   Monitoring students' understanding of content through a variety of means, providing feedback to students to assist learning, and adjusting learning activities as the situation demands.

C5   Using instructional time effectively.

Domain D–Teacher Professionalism

D1   Reflecting on the extent to which the learning goals were met.

D2   Demonstrating a sense of efficacy.

D3   Building professional relationships with colleagues to share teaching insights and to coordinate learning activities for students.

D4   Communicating with parents or guardians about student learning.

(*Source:* Reprinted by permission of Educational Testing Service, the copyright owner.)

of this chapter. She, as so many others, recognized that "[b]ecause teaching is complex, it is helpful to have a road map through the territory, structured around a shared understanding of teaching" (p. 2). She also recognized that there were many other frameworks from which one could choose, but she contended that the choice of the particular framework was not as important as the value of conversations that could take place when teachers were sharing a common language.

As with the PRAXIS III criteria, Danielson built her framework upon the same four building blocks: Planning and Preparation; the Classroom Environment; Instruction; and Professional Responsibilities. She fleshed these out just a bit more, providing five to six components for each of the four domains, but essentially provided teachers with very similar areas of concern. Where her framework differed was in the criteria that determined level of performance. For each component she provided four levels of performance: unsatisfactory, basic, proficient, and distinguished. This greater ability for the instrument to differentiate among performance levels may make this a more useful instrument for you as you attempt to chart your continued growth as a professional, allowing you to see substantive differences in your performance in specific areas over the years. Figure 11.5 provides a look at the differences in performance for one component.

Interstate New Teacher Assessment and Support Consortium (INTASC)

One of the criticisms levied against PRAXIS III, and that will probably be the same for *A Framework for Teaching,* is that these frameworks are content-neutral. That is, they provide for a generic teaching model that may not be as appropriate in some contexts as others. Certainly our own experiences with Pathwise lend credence to this concern. The framework seems to be much easier to use within a traditional classroom, much more difficult to use under certain conditions, such as performance classes like drama and art, or in some contexts in vocational or physical education classes. As of this writing, INTASC is engaged in developing frameworks that are content-specific. However, they still base these content-specific frameworks on ten principles that apply to effective teaching (see Figure 11.6).

As you can see from looking at the figure, the principles themselves sound very similar to the PRAXIS III standards, which are similar to the *Framework for Teaching.* The contrasts lie in the subtle and different ways in which people define these terms. The importance of these frameworks for you at this time is to be aware that they are there. If you are fortunate, you will go through a formal induction year in the first district in which you are hired, and the district will have made a choice as to which framework the teachers there agree best fits the unique nature of what they do in that setting. At the very least, we suggest that you familiarize yourself with the standards from one or more of these frameworks. You can then compare your own development in terms of specific standards that have been researched and identified as meeting "best practice" standards for teaching. You may also find that one of these is more helpful for you when you are first beginning but that a different one provides you with more thought-provoking standards as

FIGURE 11.5   COMPONENT 3C: ENGAGING STUDENTS IN LEARNING

Element	Level of Performance			
	Unsatisfactory	Basic	Proficient	Distinguished
Representation of Content	Representation of content is inappropriate and unclear or uses poor examples and analogies.	Representation of content is inconsistent in quality: Some is done skillfully, with good examples; other portions are difficult to follow.	Representation of content is appropriate and links well with students' knowledge and experience.	Representation of content is appropriate and links well with students' knowledge and experience. Students contribute to representation of content.
Activities and Assignments	Activities and assignments are inappropriate for students in terms of their age or backgrounds. Students are not engaged mentally.	Some activities and assignments are appropriate to students and engage them mentally, but others do not.	Most activities and assignments are appropriate to students. Almost all students are cognitively engaged in them.	All students are cognitively engaged in the activities and assignments in their exploration of content. Students initiate or adapt activities and projects to enhance understanding.
Grouping of Students	Instructional groups are inappropriate to the students or to the instructional goals.	Instructional groups are only partially appropriate to the students or only moderately successful in advancing the instructional goals of a lesson.	Instructional groups are productive and fully appropriate to the students or to the instructional goals of a lesson.	Instructional groups are productive and fully appropriate to the instructional goals of a lesson. Students take the initiative to influence instructional groups to advance their understanding.

(continued)

FIGURE 11.5   COMPONENT 3C: ENGAGING STUDENTS IN LEARNING (CONTINUED)

| Element | Level of Performance | | | |
	Unsatisfactory	Basic	Proficient	Distinguished
Instructional Materials and Resources	Instructional materials and resources are unsuitable to the instructional goals or do not engage students mentally.	Instructional materials and resources are partially suitable to the instructional goals, or students' level of mental engagement is moderate.	Instructional materials and resources are suitable to the instructional goals and engage students mentally.	Instructional materials and resources are suitable to the instructional goals and engage students mentally. Students initiate the choice, adaptation, or creation of materials to enhance their own purposes.
Structure and Pacing	The lesson has no clearly defined structure, or the pacing of the lesson is too slow or rushed, or both.	The lesson has a recognizable structure, although it is not uniformly maintained throughout the lesson. Pacing of the lesson is inconsistent.	The lesson has a clearly defined structure around which the activities are organized. Pacing of the lesson is inconsistent.	The lesson's structure is highly coherent, allowing for reflection and closure as appropriate. Pacing of the lesson is appropriate for all students.

(*Source:* Reprinted with the permission of Charlotte Danielson (1996). *Enhancing Professional Practice: A Framework for Teaching.* Alexandria, VA: Association for Supervision and Curriculum Development.)

FIGURE 11.6   INTERSTATE NEW TEACHER ASSESSMENT AND SUPPORT CONSORTIUM (INTASC) STANDARDS

Principle	Description of Teacher Performance
1	Understands the central concepts, tools or inquiry, and structure of the disciplines taught; creates learning experiences to make them meaningful to students.
2	Understands how children learn and develop; provides learning opportunities that support their development.
3	Understands how students differ in their approaches to learning; creates instructional opportunities adapted to diverse learners.
4	Understands and uses a variety of instructional strategies.
5	Creates a learning environment that encourages positive social interaction, active engagement in learning, and self-motivation.
6	Uses knowledge of communication techniques to foster active inquiry, collaboration, and supportive interaction.
7	Plans instruction based on knowledge of subject matter, students, the community, and curriculum goals.
8	Understands and uses formal and informal assessment strategies.
9	Reflects on teaching.
10	Fosters relationships with colleagues, parents, and agencies in the larger community.

(*Source:* Reprinted with the permission of INTASC (1992). *Model Standards for Beginning Teacher Licensing, Assessment, and Development: A Resource for State Dialogue.* Washington, DC: Council of Chief State School Officers.)

you grow. Whichever is true, these frameworks provide you with one more source of feedback as you evaluate your lessons, units, semesters, or career.

Creating a Professional Portfolio

As you evaluate your growth as a teacher, you will find that the systematic gathering of artifacts from your teaching will help you reflect on your development. There is no one way to do this, and you will probably find that this portfolio is a constantly evolving collection. Getting into the habit of collecting important pieces of information, cataloging them, and reflecting upon their significance will enable you to be prepared for many opportunities in teaching as they present themselves. It could help you in finding a job and preparing for an interview. As your career continues, you can use your portfolio as a way of documenting your accomplishments, possibly using it to gain certification from the National Board for Professional Teaching Standards (NBPTS).

Activity 11.4

If you have not already done so, begin to collect materials that you can use for a professional portfolio. Your instructor may choose to have you share your portfolio of a collection of materials from this semester and/or from other education work you have done. Consider carefully how you will organize these materials and how you will present them. If there is not enough time to share these in class, consider sharing with a teacher, possibly a cooperating teacher within one of your field experiences, or other students to gain some feedback about how this appears to present you as a blossoming professional.

There are many different suggestions of the kinds of artifacts that one should collect into a professional teaching portfolio (Danielson, 1996; Edgerton, Hutchings, & Quinlan, 1991; National Board for Professional Teaching Standards, 1998; Osterman & Krug, 1995). At this stage in your career, it's probably more important that you collect a number of items. Figure 11.7 indicates some of the types of materials that you may want to include. As you consider these choices, be sure to reflect on why you are choosing each item and what that particular item says about you. Items should complement each other rather than duplicate.

As you consider how you will present these materials, think about what you are saying about yourself as you contemplate your delivery system. We have seen students who have done their portfolios in Hyperstudio and sent them out on

---

FIGURE 11.7   ARTIFACTS FOR TEACHING PORTFOLIOS

- 2- to 3-week unit plan
- Individual lesson plans (using different whole lesson formats)
- Description of a specific class and reflections on adjustments you made, resources you used with them
- Video record
- Artifacts of in-class assignments, homework, evaluation instruments
- Samples of students' work
- Reflective narrative (possibly in conjunction with the video or lesson plans)
- Records of classroom observations
- Letters or testimonials of teaching competence, reliability, and professionalism
- Logs of family contacts, contributions to schools, professional development, and/or classroom investigation or action research
- Student evaluations or comments
- Philosophy of teaching and learning
- Classroom management procedures and policies
- Documentation of professional work experiences or school related experiences
- Documentation of special skills (e.g., coaching, directing, etc.) or certifications (e.g., CPR, Water Safety Instructor, etc.)

floppy disks or on CD-ROMs, indicating their technological skills. One prospective high school English teacher we know sent hers out to principals in the form of a newspaper, showing that she had page layout skills and indicating her interest in working as an advisor for the newspaper or yearbook. Others have simply brought an organized set of materials with them to their interviews so that, when the conversation came around to a specific topic, they could quickly access an artifact that showed their past success.

THE TWO E'S OF TEACHING: ETHICS AND EFFICACY

As we stated in the introduction of this chapter, in many ways you are just beginning to enter into a discussion of teaching and learning. We hope that this discussion will continue to frame the work that you do throughout your professional career, enabling you to find the same excitement and joy that we have each found in teaching. As you go out to continue this discussion in your course work and in the schools you find yourself, we want to leave you with two last thoughts, what we call the two Es of teaching: ethics and efficacy. Both of these are about the manner in which teachers behave in their classrooms and in their professional lives. The former is a code of behavior for you to follow, while the latter is about the effect that your presence has on the students you have been called to teach.

The Ethics of Teaching

There is much more to becoming an effective and respected teacher than the ability to plan, teach, and evaluate lessons and units. One characteristic that the general public expects of its teachers is that they will behave in an ethical manner. According to Strike and Soltis (1985), **ethics** "concerns what kinds of actions are right or wrong, what kind of a life is a good life, or what kind of a person is a good person. . . . [Ethical claims] do not tell us how the world is, but how it ought to be" (p. 7). As you enter the teaching profession, we believe that it is important for you to consider the ethical implications of what you do and strive to behave in such a way that you demonstrate your commitment to making schools the way they ought to be, rather than allow them to remain the way they are.

But, what does it mean to act in an ethical manner as a teacher? Certainly, newspapers in most states publish stories of teachers who have acted unethically. You have probably read of teachers who have taken sexual advantage of their students or some who have physically or psychologically abused students in their charges. You may have also experienced teachers who have had "pets" that have been granted privileges that other students do not have or teachers who have graded students on factors, such as being a star athlete or the child of an influential person in town, other than the quality of work they have turned in. This is the way school *may be* in some places, but we think you would agree it is not the way it *ought to be*. These negative examples demonstrate unethical behavior, but they do not answer the question we asked at the beginning of this paragraph. One resource you could use to answer it is the Code of Ethics of the Education Profession (National Education Association, 1975), which is shown in Figure 11.8.

Just as you have read about the various frameworks that you can use to help in a self-evaluation, the Code of Ethics provides you with a framework to think

---

FIGURE 11.8   CODE OF ETHICS OF THE NATIONAL EDUCATION ASSOCIATION

Preamble

The educator, believing in the worth and dignity of each human being, recognizes the supreme importance of the pursuit of truth, devotion to excellence, and the nurture of the democratic principles. Essential to these goals is the protection of freedom to learn and to teach and the guarantee of equal educational opportunity for all. The educator accepts the responsibility to adhere to the highest ethical standards.

The educator recognizes the magnitude of the responsibility inherent in the teaching process. The desire for the respect and confidence of one's colleagues, of students, of parents, and of the members of the community provides the incentive to attain and maintain the highest possible degree of ethical conduct.

The Code of Ethics of the Education Profession indicates the aspiration of all educators and provides standards by which to judge conduct. The remedies specified by the NEA and/or its affiliates for the violation of any provision of this Code shall be exclusive and no such provision shall be enforceable in any form other than the one specifically designated by the NEA or its affiliates.

PRINCIPLE I–Commitment to the Student

The educator strives to help each student realize his or her potential as a worthy and effective member of society. The educator therefore works to stimulate the spirit of inquiry, the acquisition of knowledge and understanding, and the thoughtful formulation of worthy goals.

In fulfillment of the obligation to the student, the educator—

1. Shall not unreasonably restrain the student from independent action in the pursuit of learning.

2. Shall not unreasonably deny the student's access to varying points of view.

3. Shall not deliberately suppress or distort subject matter relevant to the student's progress.

4. Shall make reasonable effort to protect the student from conditions harmful to learning or to health and safety.

5. Shall not intentionally expose the student to embarrassment or disparagement.

(continued)

> **FIGURE 11.8   CODE OF ETHICS OF THE NATIONAL EDUCATION ASSOCIATION**
> **(*CONTINUED*)**

6. Shall not on the basis of race, color, creed, sex, national origin, marital status, political or religious beliefs, family, social or cultural background, or sexual orientation, unfairly—
   a. Exclude any student from participation in any program.
   b. Deny benefits to any student.
   c. Grant any advantage to any student.

7. Shall not use professional relationships with students for private advantage.

8. Shall not disclose information about students obtained in the course of professional service unless disclosure serves a compelling professional purpose or is required by law.

PRINCIPLE II–Commitment to the Profession

The education profession is vested by the public with a trust and responsibility requiring the highest ideals of professional service. In the belief that the quality of the services of the education profession directly influences the nation and its citizens, the educator shall exert every effort to raise professional standards, to promote a climate that encourages the exercise of professional judgment, to achieve conditions that attract persons worthy of the trust to careers in education, and to assist in preventing the practice of the profession by unqualified persons.

In fulfillment of the obligation to the profession, the educator—

1. Shall not in an application for a professional position deliberately make a false statement or fail to disclose a material fact related to competency and qualifications.

2. Shall not misrepresent his/her professional qualifications.

3. Shall not assist any entry into the profession of a person known to be unqualified in respect to character, education, or other relevant attribute.

4. Shall not knowingly make a false statement concerning the qualifications of a candidate for a professional position.

5. Shall not assist a noneducator in the unauthorized practice of teaching.

6. Shall not disclose information about colleagues obtained in the course of professional service unless disclosure serves a compelling professional purpose or is required by law.

7. Shall not knowingly make false or malicious statements about a colleague.

8. Shall not accept any gratuity, gift, or favor that might impair or appear to influence professional decisions or action.

—Adopted by the NEA 1975 Representative Assembly

about what it means to behave in an ethical way as a teacher in two dimensions, your commitment to students, and your commitment to the profession.

Commitment to Students   As we stated at the opening of this book, students have to come first as you look at your teaching. So, too, does the NEA Code of Ethics begin with your commitment to students. The statements that you see under Principle I provide you with some clear guidelines about what you should and should not do in order to meet the ethical standards of the profession in your commitment to students. If you look back to the examples of unethical behavior in the paragraph above, you can probably see that these examples are in opposition to one or more of these guidelines. For instance, psychological abuse could be in the form of condescending or unduly critical comments to students' responses to questions or in the process of learning activities. For a teacher to make these kinds of comments to students clearly violates guideline number five by "intentionally expos[ing] the student to embarrassment or disparagement." It may also violate guideline number four if you think of this kind of comment as creating psychological "conditions harmful to learning." From those previous examples, it is also obvious that a sexual relationship with a student is unethical because it stems from a teacher's professional relationship being used for private advantage.

You should also be aware that, while unethical behavior is not always illegal, it may be. For example, imagine if you had had trouble with a particular student one day and needed to write an office referral on him. In the referral, you described the behaviors of this child and your previous steps to stop his inappropriate behavior, very appropriate steps for you to take. However, while you are in the process of writing the referral, a parent with whom you've been working and with whom you've developed a good, personal relationship stops by to see you and asks how you're doing. You mention what a frustrating day it's been because of this student and show her the referral. This may not seem like a significant breach of ethics, but it does violate guideline eight since your sharing your frustration and the referral with a parent does not serve a "compelling educational purpose." What may not seem like a "big deal" also violates the Buckley Amendment of the Educational Rights and Privacy Act of 1974, which requires that you protect the privacy of student records. If the parent also shares this story with a neighbor, you may be running the risk of embarrassing the student and, when it gets back to the school, you may find yourself in a difficult professional situation.

The previous example is not meant to worry you about sharing information about a student. It should be taken as a cautionary tale, though. There are many times that sharing information can help the students in your charge and numerous people with whom you will come in contact who may need the unique insights you possess. If you are ever in doubt about what information you can share, you will want to talk to someone, like your mentor or principal, for guidance so that you don't engage in behavior that could undermine your professional reputation and negatively impact your integrity. In any case, you will want to begin your career upholding the highest professional standards of ethical behavior in regards to your commitment to your students.

Commitment to the Profession   According to the Code, you also have a second commitment, and that is to the profession. In this, too, the standards insist upon personal integrity in your day-to-day work. The public trusts teachers to work with this nation's most valuable resources, its children, and demands from teachers professional behavior necessary to maintain that trust. Every year, teachers lose their teaching certificates or licenses because they make false statements on official documents or misrepresent their qualifications. These are the most obvious cases of a teacher engaging in unethical behavior, but the guidelines provide you with some other issues to consider.

After the issue of appropriate dealings with students, probably one of the most important ones to think about as you prepare yourself to join a school is how you deal with your colleagues and other school personnel. We have seen many teachers burn themselves in the flames of political and personal controversies that sometimes take place in the social institution of a school. As a new teacher, you will find yourself working with many diverse people in your daily responsibilities. We hope that you will personally develop rewarding relationships with most of these people. The reality of working with as many professionals as you will over the years, however, increases the likelihood that you will encounter some teachers or other colleagues with whom you do not get along for a variety of possible reasons. We have been in schools where the backstabbing among staff members makes these schools dreadfully depressing places to be. If you conduct yourself in an ethical manner, you will certainly not engage in this type of behavior of making diparaging or malicious comments about your colleagues. More importantly, you will feel worthy of the trust that the public endows upon you as you act as a role model for your students.

Activity 11.5

With several peers, identify and discuss some of the experiences with the best teachers you and they have had in schools. As you discuss these stories, put a line down the middle of a sheet of paper and, on the left-hand side, jot down the personal and professional qualities that these teachers exhibited. On the right-hand side, match these up to the number(s) of the principle(s) or to the description of behavior in the preamble that indicate the ethical manner in which these teachers behave. Share your experience with your class as a whole.

Teacher Efficacy

You have just spent a good deal of time reading about multiple sources of feedback that you can use to improve your planning of lessons and units, as well as evaluating your continuing growth as a teacher. All of the sources in the world, however, will not help you to become a better teacher unless you believe that you can use that information to improve the skills and knowledge of the students in your classes. **Teaching efficacy** relates to teachers' abilities to establish and maintain a positive influence on students' achievement in their classroom. Efficacious teachers see student gaps in knowledge and skills as challenges for them to encounter. These challenges compel expert teachers to call upon all of the scholarly and experiential knowledge that they have developed over their careers with one goal in mind: to help each child begin to reach his or her potential, as a learner, as a member of a community, and as a human being, just to name a few. Efficacious teachers tend to have an **internal locus of control** (refer back to chapter 1 where we discussed this term in regards to children's learning). They believe that their internal resources, their intelligence, their persistence, their insight, not external factors, like a child's poverty level or home life, determine how successful lessons, units and years will be for the children in their classrooms.

There is a great deal of research, conducted over the past thirty years especially, that demonstrates the connection between teacher efficacy and student achievement (Ashton & Webb, 1986; Guskey & Passaro, 1994). A sense of teaching efficacy has been correlated with student achievement and appears to be one of the few personal characteristics that has made such an impact (Guskey & Passaro, 1994). If you develop in the same way that many preservice teachers do, your own sense of teaching efficacy will also increase as you gain experience in schools, in student teaching, for instance. You are also likely to increase your sense of efficacy by working in schools that hold high expectations for students and in which teachers have a strong educational leader who helps them in meeting instructional and management challenges (Hoy & Woolfolk, 1993). For us, however, we believe that the National Board for Professional Teaching Standards (1998) says it both simply and convincingly. Of the five general propositions that guide their mission, the first one states: Teachers are committed to students and their learning. If this statement also guides your practice, you will do whatever it takes to help your students learn and grow. You will try everything you know how to do, and if that doesn't work, you'll learn other things to try. You will continue to work with all children and be guided by the belief that all students can learn.

SUMMARY

Well, that's about it. You're now more prepared to go out and begin your own conversations on teaching and learning, with your students, your colleagues, and other professionals. Between the four of us, we have over 100 years of teaching, and each one of us has used nearly every one of the resources that we have mentioned in this chapter, as well as the techniques and procedures we have introduced to you in the remainder of this book. Still, to this day, we find the need to talk things over with our students, our own mentors, and trusted colleagues. As we have looked back at our own teaching of lessons and units, we have found the need to give ourselves reality checks, to see if we are being as effective as we can be. Sometimes we are, but sometimes we've needed to change the ways we went about doing something in order to meet more appropriately our students' needs. It is this need for reflection, along with the knowledge and belief that we can make a difference for every student that comes our way, that makes what we do so rewarding. We believe that you too will find this to be true. Our final hope is that, through reading this book and working through the challenges that present themselves as you go about planning, delivering and evaluating lessons, one of the professional "voices in your head" will be ours. Now go out there and teach those kids something!

REFLECTION

1. Look back to the conversation at the beginning of this chapter. If you were Sarah, what would you be looking for over the weekend that would help you to determine whether or not the project was successful? What standards do you think she should use to determine whether students "got more" out of their reading?

2. Think about a time that you have been asked to "teach" someone something. When you were successful, how did you know that you were successful? What sources of feedback did you look back at that convinced you of your success?

3. Now, think about a time that you were asked to "teach" someone something when you did not feel as if you were terribly successful. How and when did you realize that your teaching was not going smoothly? As you look back on this experience, if you had it to do over again, what would you do differently? Why?

4. During a field experience, identify a particular concept (e.g., questioning strategies, formative evaluation, etc.) with which you have dealt this semester. Observe your cooperating teacher's use of this concept and record your observations. When the lesson is finished, share with the teacher your observations, and ask her to reflect on what was happening at the time that caused her to make the choice that she did. What other possible choices could she have made? under what circumstances?

TEACHER AS RESEARCHER

Reflecting on Teaching

McNeely, S. L. (1997). *Observing students and teachers through objective strategies.* Needham Hts, MA: Allyn and Bacon.

This resource provides numerous checklists or other frameworks that you can use as you observe students and other teachers. Most lists are tied explicitly to a theoretical or research-supported foundation. Try using several of these in the course of a field experience. What kinds of information were you able to gather? What factors (e.g., school setting, individual student, your own knowledge base, etc.) caused you difficulties in gathering this information? In what ways did using these forms assist you in looking at or reflecting on the quality of instruction that took place?

Zemelman, S., Daniels, H., & Hyde, A. (1993). *Best practice: New standards for teaching and learning in America's schools.* Portsmouth, NH: Heinemann.

Regardless of grade level, the authors cover the major content areas by describing learned society guidelines for specific disciplines and then providing real-life examples of these programs in action. After reading the description of best practice in one of the content areas, you (alone or with peers) could create a matrix in which you identify key characteristics an observer could look for in determining to what extent a teacher is engaging in best practice.

Mentors and Mentoring

Lucas, C. A. (1999). Developing competent practitioners. *Educational Leadership, 56* (8), 45–48.

The author describes the Beginning Teacher Support and Assessment/California Formative Assessment and Support System for Teachers (BTSA/CFASST), which is an assessment process that is built on the premise of teachers' needing time for reflection and a period of years to build strong practices. As you read this article, you will note that a modified version of the IDEAL model is embedded within the description of the development cycle. Ask peers who are student teaching or newly-hired to describe their own experiences in taking on a teaching challenge. Compare that to the process of development of teaching strategies described in the article.

Rawley, J. B. (1999). The good mentor. *Educational Leadership, 56* (8), 20–22.

The author identifies six characteristics of good mentors and describes the impact that these qualities have on the mentor-protege relationship. If you know people who have recently begun teaching jobs where they have a formal mentoring program, ask them to describe their mentor-mentee relationship and determine how many of these traits are exhibited. If you don't have access to new teachers, talk to your friends who are student teaching and see if these qualities are apparent in their cooperating teachers.

Appendix

EXPERT EVALUATION OF INCORRECTLY FORMATTED OBJECTIVE TEST ITEMS (SEE FIGURE 9.12)

Alternate Choice Test Items

1. **Problem:**   Item is worded in a negative manner.

   Solution: Rewrite as a positive statement.

2. **Problem:**   This is a trick question. Although Poe did write "The Raven," his middle name is spelled incorrectly. The correct spelling is Edgar All<u>a</u>n Poe.

   Solution: Rewrite with focus on an substantive idea, rather than a spelling error.

3. **Problem:**   The statement appears to be taken directly from the textbook.

   Solution: Rewrite by paraphrasing.

4. **Problem:**   Statement uses the term *always* which provides a clue that the statement is likely to be false.

   Solution: This statement does not lend itself well to the alternate choice format. Rewrite the question in another format (e.g., multiple choice, short answer, etc.).

Multiple-Choice Test Items

1. **Problems:**   The stem should be a complete thought or question.
   The responses are not similar in content.
   The responses are not listed in a systematic order.

   Solution: Rewrite stem so it is a complete thought or question.
   Rewrite responses along one specific topic (e.g., all geography).
   Alphabetize the responses.

2. **Problems:**   The stem is worded in a negative manner.
   The use of 'none of the above' is confusing.

   Solutions: Rewrite the stem or highlight the negative word (e.g., underline, all caps, bold, etc.).
   Replace 'none of the above' with a plausible distractor.

3. **Problem:**   Two of the distractors are implausible or silly.

   Solution: Replace with plausible distractors.

Completion Test Items

1. Problem: The blank is misplaced.

   Solution: Rewrite so blank appears at the end of the statement.

2. Problem: There is more than one plausible answer (e.g., brave, born in Ohio, Neil Armstrong)

   Solution: Add the word 'named' at the end of the statement, or rewrite as the following short answer question. "Name the first American to walk on the moon."

3. Problem: There are too many blanks in the statement and not enough substantive information to guide the student's response.

   Solution: Rewrite statement with only one blank or consider a different item format.

Matching Test Item

Problems: The premises are not similar in content or topic.
The responses are not listed in a systematic order.
Premise and response columns are not labeled.
Directions are not included.

Solutions: Rewrite premises so they address a single concept or topic (e.g., cities, colonists, explorers, etc.).
Alphabetize the response column.
Label the premise and response column.
Provide directions.

Short Answer Test Items

1. Problem: The unit of response is not indicated; thus 72 minutes or 1 hour 12 minutes are both correct hours.

   Solution: Identify the unit of measure for the correct answer.

2. Problem: There is no guidance provided for students to indicate the breadth or depth of the expected response.

   Solution: Provide a blank or in some other manner indicate to students how detailed of a response is expected (e.g. write a one-sentence definition.)

Bibliography

Adler, M. J. (1982). *The paideia proposal: An educational manifesto.* New York: Collier.

Alvermann, D. (1991). The discussion web: A graphic aid for learning across the curriculum. *The Reading Teacher, 45* (2), 92–99.

Alvermann, D. E., & Phelps, S. F. (1998). *Content reading and literacy: Succeeding in today's diverse classrooms* (5th ed.) Needham Heights, MA: Allyn and Bacon.

American Association for the Advancement of Science. (1993). *Benchmarks for science literacy.* New York: Oxford UP.

Anderson, J. (1983). *The architecture of cognition.* Cambridge, MA: Harvard University Press.

Anderson, J. (1987). Skill acquisition: Compilation of weak-method problem solutions. *Psychological Review, 94,* 192–210.

Anderson, L. W., & Sosniak, L. A. (Eds.). (1994). *Bloom's taxonomy—a forty-year retrospective.* Ninety-third Yearbook of the National Society for the Study of Education Part II. Chicago: The National Society for the Study of Education.

Apple, M. W. (1991). Regulating the text: The socio-cultural roots of state control. In P. G. Altbach, G. P. Kelly, H. G. Petrie, & L. Weis (Eds.), *Textbooks in American society: Politics, policy and pedagogy* (pp. 7–26). Albany, NY: SUNY Press.

Aronson, E., Blaney, N., Stephan, C., Sikes, J., & Snapp, M. (1978). *The jigsaw classroom.* Beverly Hills, CA: Sage Productions.

Ashton, P. T., & Webb, R. B. (1986). *Making a difference: Teachers' sense of efficacy and student achievement.* New York: Longman.

Avery, P. G., Baker, J., & Gross, S. H. (1997). "Mapping" learning at the secondary level. *The Social Studies, 87* (5), 217–223.

Barbe, W. B., & Milone, M. N. (1980). Modality. *Instructor, 89* (6), 44–47.

Bare, P. A. (1997). When parents don't speak English. *Principal, 76* (2), 42–43.

Barnes, C. P. (1993). *Beyond the induction year.* (ERIC Document Reproduction Services No. ED 356 225).

Barr Media Group (Producer). (1992). *Threatened* [Videodisc]. (Available from Barr Media Group, 12801 Schabarum Ave, P.O. Box 7878, Irwindale, CA 91706–7878).

Beck, I., McKeown, M., Hamilton, R., & Kucan, L. (1997). *Questioning the author: An approach for enhancing student engagement with text.* Newark, Delaware: International Reading Association.

Bellezza, F. (1983). The spatial-arrangement mnemonic. *Journal of Educational Psychology, 75* (6), 830–837.

Berlin, J. A. (1987). *Rhetoric and reality: Writing instruction in American colleges, 1900–1985.* Carbondale, IL: Southern Illinois UP.

Bloom, B. S. (Ed.). (1956). *Taxonomy of educational objectives: Handbook I: Cognitive domain.* New York: David McKay.

Bransford, J. D., & Stein, B. S. (1984). *The IDEAL problem solver: A guide for improving thinking, learning, and creativity.* New York: W. H. Freeman and Co.

Brown, A. L., & Day, J. D. (1983). *Macrorules for summarizing text: The development of expertise.* Urbana-Champaign, IL: Center for the Study of Reading, University of Illinois.

Brown, S. I., & Finn, M. E. (1988). *Readings from progressive education: A movement and its professional journal.* Landham, MD: United Press of America.

Bruner, J. (1960). *The process of education.* Cambridge, MA: Harvard University Press.

Bruner, J. (1972). Nature and uses of immaturity. *American Psychologist, 27* (8), 687–708.

Buchberg, W. (1996). *Quilting activities across the curriculum.* New York: Scholastic.

Bullock, L. M. (1992). *Exceptionalities in children and youth.* Boston: Allyn and Bacon.

Burden, P. R., and Byrd, D. M. (1994). *Methods for effective teaching.* Boston: Allyn and Bacon.

Burns, R. (1993). *Parents and schools: From visitors to partners.* Washington, D.C.: National Education Association.

Canney, G. F., Kennedy, T. J., Schroeder, M., & Miles, S. (1999). Instructional strategies for K–12 limited English proficient (LEP) students in the regular classroom. *The Reading Teacher, 52* (5), 540–544.

Carey, L. M. (1994). *Measuring and evaluating school learning* (2nd ed.). Needham Heights, MA: Allyn and Bacon.

Carter, K., Cushing, K., Sabers, D., Stein, P., & Berliner, D. (1988). Expert-Novice differences in perceiving and processing visual classroom information. *Journal of Teacher Education, 39* (3), 25–31.

Casement, W. (1987). Bloom and the Great Books. *The Journal of General Education, 39* (1), 1–9.

Chapin, S. H. (1996). External and internal characteristics of learning environments. *Mathematics Teacher, 89* (6), 112–15.

Clark, M.L. (1991). Social identity, peer relations, and academic competence of African American adolescents. *Education and Urban Society, 24* (1), 41–52.

Collins, A., Brown, J. S., & Newman, S. E. (1989). Cognitive apprenticeship: Teaching the crafts of reading, writing, and mathematics. In L. Resnick (Ed.), *Knowing, Learning, and Instruction: Essays in Honor of Robert Glaser.* Hillsdale, NJ: Lawrence Erlbaum.

Commission on the Reorganization of Secondary Education. (1918). *Cardinal Principles of Secondary Education*. Washington, DC: U.S. Government Printing Office.

Cooter, R. B., Jr., & Flynt, E. S. (1996). *Teaching reading in the content areas: Developing content literacy for all students*. Englewood Cliffs, NJ: Prentice-Hall.

Cyrs, T. E., & Smith, F. A. (1990). *Teleclass teaching: A resource guide*. Las Cruces, NM: College of Human and Community Services, New Mexico State University.

Dale, E. (1969). *Audiovisual methods in teaching* (3rd ed.). Hinsdale, IL: The Dryden Press.

Danielson, C. (1996). *Enhancing professional practice: A framework for teaching*. Alexandria, VA: Association for Supervision and Curriculum Development.

Darling-Hammond, L., & Ball, D. L. (1997). *Teaching for high standards: What policymakers need to know and be able to do*. Prepared for the National Educational Goals Panel.

Davey, B. (1983). Think-aloud: Modeling the cognitive processes of reading comprehension. *Journal of Reading , 27* (1), 44–47.

Davey, B. (1987). Team for success: Guided practice in study skills through cooperative research reports. *Journal of Reading, 30* (8), 701–705.

Deschemes, C., Ebeling, D. G., & Sprague, J. (1994). *Adapting curriculum and instruction in inclusive classrooms*. Bloomington, IN: The Center for School and Community Integration, Institute for the Study of Developmental Disabilities.

De Vaney, A. (1994). *Watching Channel One: The convergence of students, technology and private business*. Albany, NY: State University of New York Press.

Dewey, J. (1899). *The school and society*. Chicago: U of Chicago P.

Dewey, J. (1902). *The child and the curriculum*. Chicago: U of Chicago P.

Dick, W., & Carey, L. (1996). *The systematic design of instruction* (4th ed.). New York: Harper Collins.

Dockterman, D. A. (1991). *Great teaching in the one computer classroom*. Cambridge, MA: Tom Snyder Productions.

Dreeben, R. (1968). *On what is learned in school*. Reading, MA: Addison-Wesley.

Duffelmeyer, F. A. (1994). Effective Anticipation Guide statements for learning from expository prose. *Journal of Reading, 37*, 452–457.

Durrell, D. (1956). *Improving reading instruction*. Yonkers-on-Hudson, NY: World Book Co.

Dwyer, C. A. (1994). *Development of the knowledge base for the Praxis III Performance Assessment*. Princeton, NJ: Educational Testing Service.

Ecology treks [Computer software]. (1993). San Mateo, CA: Sanctuary Woods Multimedia.

Edgerton, R., Hutchings, P., & Quinlan, K. (1991). *The teaching portfolio: Capturing the scholarship in teaching*. Washington, DC: American Association for Higher Education.

Educational Testing Service. (1995). *Pathwise orientation guide*. Princeton, NJ: Educational Testing Service.

Faggella, K., & Horowitz, J. (1990). Different child, different style. *Instructor, 100* (2), 49–54.

Fischer, L., Schimmel, D., & Kelly, C. (1995). How does copyright law affect me? *Teachers and the Law* (4th ed.). White Plains, NY: Longman.

Flood, J., Lapp, D., Flood, S., & Nagel, G. (1992). Am I allowed to group? Using flexible patterns for effective instruction. *The Reading Teacher, 45* (8), 608–616.

Fosnot, C. T. (1996). *Constructivism: Theory, perspectives, and practice.* New York: Teachers College Press.

Freire, P. (1970). The adult literacy process as cultural action for freedom. *Harvard Educational Review, 40* (2), 363–381.

Gagné, R. M. (1965). *The conditions of learning.* New York: Holt, Rinehart, and Winston.

Gagné, R. M., Briggs, L. J., & Wager, W. W. (1992). *Principles of instructional design* (4th ed.). Fort Worth: Harcourt Brace Jovanovich College Publishers.

García Márquez, G. (1991). *One hundred years of solitude.* (G. Rabassa, Trans.). New York: HarperPerennial. (Original work published 1967).

Gardner, H. (1983). *Frame of mind: The theory of multiple intelligences.* New York: Basic Books.

Gardner, H. (1993). *Multiple intelligences: The theory in practice.* New York: Basic Books.

Good, T. L., & Marshall, S. (1984). Do students learn more in heterogeneous or homogeneous groups. In P. Peterson, L. C. Wilkinson, & M. Hallman (Eds.), *The social context of instruction: Group organization and group processes* (pp. 15–38). Orlando, FL: Academic Press.

Goodwin, S. S., et. al. (1983). *Effective classroom questioning.* (ERIC Document Reproduction Services No. ED 285 497).

Great Lakes National Program Office. (1990). *Great minds? Great lakes.* (Document No. 905/M/90/004). Chicago: Environmental Protection Agency.

Gunter, M., Estes, T., & Schwab, J. (1990) *Instruction: A models approach.* Boston: Allyn and Bacon.

Guskey, T. R. (1997). *Implementing mastery learning.* Belmont, CA: Wadsworth Publishing Company.

Guskey, T. R., & Passaro, P. D. (1994). Teacher efficacy: A study of construct dimensions. *American Educational Research Journal, 31*, 645–674.

Harrow, A. J. (1972). *A taxonomy of the psychomotor domain: A guide for developing behavioral objectives.* New York: David McKay.

Hayes, D. (1989). Helping students GRASP the knack of writing summaries. *Journal of Reading, 33* (2), 96–101.

Henkes, K. (1996). *Lilly's purple plastic purse.* New York: Greenwillow Books.

Henry, G. H. (1974). *Teaching reading as concept development: Emphasis on affective thinking.* Newark, DE.: International Reading Association.

Herber, H. (1978). *Teaching reading in content areas* (2nd ed.). Englewood Cliffs, NJ: Prentice-Hall, Inc.

Hirsch, E. D., Jr. (1996). *The schools we need: And why we don't have them.* New York: Doubleday.

Hodgkinson, H. (1993). American education: The good, the bad, and the task. *Phi Delta Kappan, 74* (8), 619–623.

Hopstock, P., & Bucaro, B. (1993). *A review and analysis of estimates of the LEP student population*. Arlington, VA: Special Issues Analysis Center, Development Associations, Inc.

Hout, M., & Lucas, S. (1996). Narrowing the income gap between rich and poor. *The Chronicle of Higher Education, 42,* B1–B2.

Hoy, W. K., & Woolfolk, A. E. (1993). Teachers' sense of efficacy and the organizational health of schools. *Elementary School Journal, 93,* 355–372.

Huling-Austin, L. (1988). *A synthesis of research on teacher induction programs and practices.* (ERIC Document Services No. ED 302 546).

Hunter, M. (1994). *Enhancing Teaching.* New York: Macmillan.

INTASC (1992). *Model standards for beginning teacher licensing, assessment, and development: A resource for state dialogue.* Washington, D.C.: Council of Chief State School Officers.

International E-mail Classroom Connection. [On-line]. Available: http://www.stolaf.edu/network/iecc. St. Olaf, MT: St. Olaf College.

Joyce, B. R., & Weil, M. (1996). *Models of teaching* (5th ed.). Boston: Allyn and Bacon.

Johnson, D. W., Johnson, R. T., & Smith, K. A. (1991). *Active learning: Cooperation in the classroom.* Edina, MN: Interaction Book Company.

Johnson, D. W., Johnson, R. T., & Smith, K. A. (1995). Cooperative learning and individual student achievement in secondary schools. In J.E. Pederson and A.D. Digby (Eds.), *Secondary schools and cooperative learning.* New York: Garland Publishing.

Kemp, J. E., Morrison, G. R., & Ross, S. M. (1994, 1997). *Designing effective instruction.* New York: Merrill.

Kemp, J. E., & Smellie, D. C. (1994). *Planning, producing, and using instructional technologies.* New York: Harper Collins College Publishers.

Kilpatrick, W. H. (1918). The project method. *Teacher's College Record, 19,* 319–335.

Kolb, D. (1985). *Learning style inventory.* McBer and Company, 116 Huntington Ave., Boston, MA 02116.

Krathwohl, D. R. (1964). *Taxonomy of behavioral objectives: Handbook II: Affective domain.* New York: David McKay.

Langer, J. A. (1981). From theory to practice: A prereading plan. *Journal of Reading, 25* (2), 152–156.

Langer, J. (1984). Examining background knowledge and text comprehension. *Reading Research Quarterly, 19* (4), 468–81.

Langer, J., & Purcell-Gates, V. (1984). *Knowledge and comprehension: Helping students use what they know.* Washington, D.C.: National Institute of Education. (ERIC Document Services No. ED 250 654).

Laosa, L. M. (1984). Ethnic, socioeconomic, and home language influences upon early performances on measures of abilities. *Journal of Educational Psychology, 76,* 1178–1198.

Larson, C., & Dansereau, D. (1986). Cooperative learning in dyads. *Journal of Reading, 29* (6), 516–520.

Learning in Focus (Producer). (1980). *William Faulkner's "Barn burning"* [videorecording]. (Available from Monterey Home Video, 23038 Dorothy, Ste. 1, Agoura Hills, CA 91301.).

Loewen, J. W. (1995). *Lies my teacher told me: Everything your American history textbook got wrong.* New York: Touchstone.

Looney, J. (1997). *Mentoring the beginning teacher: A study of influencing variables.* Paper presented at the Annual Meeting of the Eastern Education Research Association, Hilton Head, SC, February 1997. (ERIC Document Services No. ED 411 238).

Lyman, Frank T. (1992). Think-pair-share, thinktrix, thinklinks, and weird facts: An interactive system for cooperative thinking. In N. Davidson, & T. Worsham (Eds.), *Enhancing thinking through cooperative learning.* New York: Teachers College Press.

Macrorie, K. (1988). *The I-search paper.* Portsmouth, NH: Boynton/Cook.

Manning, M. L. (1993). *Developmentally appropriate middle level schools.* Wheaton, MD: Association for Childhood Education International.

Marshall, G. (1990). Drill won't do. *The American School Board Journal, 177* (7), 21–23.

Martin, D., Lorton, M., Blanc, R., & Evans, C. (1977). *The learning center: A comprehensive model for colleges and universities.* Grand Rapids, MI: Central Trade Plant.

Mastropieri, M. A., & Scruggs, T. E. (1991). *Teaching students ways to remember: Strategies for learning mnemonically.* Cambridge, MA: Bookline.

McNeely, S. L. (1997). *Observing students and teachers through objective strategies.* Needham Heights, MA: Allyn and Bacon.

Moore, D., & Moore S. (1986). Possible sentences. In E. Dishner, T. Bean, J. Readance, & D. Moore (Eds.), *Reading in the content areas: Improving classroom instruction* (2nd ed.). Dubuque, IA: Kendall/Hunt.

Moore, D., Readance, J., & Rickelman, R. (1989). *Prereading activities for content area reading and learning* (2nd ed.). Newark, DE: International Reading Association.

National Board of Professional Teaching Standards (1998). *The five propositions of accomplished teaching.* [On-line]. (Available http://www.nbpts.org/nbpts/standards/five-props.html).

National Center for Education Statistics (1998). *America's children: Key national indicators of well-being* (NCES 98140). Washington, D.C.: National Education Data Resource Center.

Newman, F. M., & Wehlage, G. G. (1993). Five standards of authentic instruction. *Educational Leadership, 50* (7), 8–12.

Newman, J, W. (1998). *America's teachers: An introduction to education.* New York: Longman.

Ohio Department of Education. (1994). *Science: Ohio's model competency-based program.* Columbus, OH: State Board of Education.

Orlich, D. (1993). Social challenges to America 2000. *Social Education, 57,* 359–360.

Osterman, D. N., & Krug, D. A. (1995). *Put the professional portfolio into focus for individual and special education applications.* (ERIC Document Services No. ED 385 023).

Palinscar, A. S., & Brown, A. L. (1984). Reciprocal teaching of comprehension-fostering and comprehension-monitoring activities. *Cognition and Instruction, 1* (2), 117–175.

Palmatier, R. (1973). A notetaking system for learning. *Journal of Reading, 17* (1), 36–39.

Pasch, M., Langer, G., Gardner, T. G., Starko, A.J., & Moody, C. D., (1995). *Teaching as decision making: Successful practices for the elementary teacher* (2nd ed.). New York: Longman.

Piaget, J., & Inhelder, B. (1969). *The psychology of the child.* New York: Viking Basic Books.

Potter, L. (1996). *How to improve parent-teacher conferences: A guide for parents from the principal.* Washington, D.C.: National Institute of Education. (ERIC Document Reproduction Service No. ED 393198).

Pressley, M., & Woloshyn, V. (1995). *Cognitive strategy instruction that really improves children's academic performances* (2nd ed.). Cambridge, MA: Brookline Books.

Raphael, T. E. (1986). Teacher question answer relationships, revisited. *The Reading Teacher, 39* (6), 516–522.

Readance, J. E., Bean, T. W., & Baldwin, R. S. (1992). *Content area reading: An integrated approach.* Dubuque, IA: Kendall/Hunt.

Rosenshine, B. V. (1987). Explicit teaching. In D.C. Berliner, & B.V. Rosenshine (Eds.), *Talks to teachers: A festschrift for N. L. Gage.* New York: Random House.

Rosenshine, B. V. (1987). Teaching functions in instructional programs. *The Elementary School Journal, 83* (1), 335–351.

Rowe, M. B. (1974). Wait-time and rewards as instructional variables: Their influence on language, logic, and fate control. Part 1: Wait-time. *Journal of Research in Science Teaching, 11,* 81–94.

Santeusanio, R. P. (1990). Content area reading and study. In C. Hedley, J. Houtz, & A. Baratta (Eds.), *Cognition, Curriculum, and Literacy.* Norwood, NJ: Ablex.

Schaeffer, M. B., & Hook, J. G. (1996). Multi-age grouping: The one room school revisited? *Rural Educator, 18* (1), 10–12.

Schon, D. (1987). *The reflective practitioner.* New York: Basic Books.

Schwartz, R. M. (1988). Learning to learn: Vocabulary in content area textbooks. *Journal of Reading, 32,* 108–117.

Schwartz, R., & Raphael, T. (1985). Concept of definition: A key to improving students' vocabulary. *The Reading Teacher, 39,* 198–205.

Shannon, C., & Weaver, W. (1949). *The mathematical theory of communication.* Urbana, IL: University of Illinois Press.

Shores, L. (1960). *Instructional materials: An introduction for teachers.* New York: The Ronald Press Company.

Shulman, L.S. (1987). Knowledge and teaching: Foundations of the new reform. *Harvard Educational Review , 57* (1), 1–22.

Simpson, M.L. (1986). PORPE: A writing strategy for studying and learning in the content areas. *Journal of Reading, 29* (5), 407–414.

Sizer, T. R. (1992). *Horace's school: Redesigning the American high school.* Boston: Houghton Mifflin.

Slavin, R. E. (1987). Ability grouping and student achievement in elementary schools: A best-evidence synthesis. *Review of Educational Research, 57,* 293–336.

Slavin, R. E. (Ed.). (1989). *School and classroom organization.* Hillsdale, NJ: Lawrence Erlbaum.

Slavin, R. E. (1990). Achievement effects of ability grouping in secondary schools: A best-evidence synthesis. *Review of Educational Research, 60,* 471–500.

Slavin, R. E. (1991). *Student team learning: A practical guide to cooperative learning* (3rd ed.). Washington, D.C.: National Education Association Professional Library.

Slavin, R. E. (1995). *Cooperative learning: Theory, research and practice* (2nd ed.). Boston: Allyn and Bacon.

Stanfill, S. (1978). The great American one-sentence summary. In O. Clapp (Ed.), *Classroom Practices in Teaching English.* Urbana, Ill: National Council of Teachers of English.

Steinberg, L. (1996). *Beyond the classroom: Why school reform has failed and what parents need to do.* New York: Simon and Schuster.

Strike, K. A., & Soltis, J. F. (1985). *The ethics of teaching.* New York: Teachers College Press.

Taba, H. (1962). *Curriculum development: Theory and practice.* New York: Harcourt Brace.

Tyler, R. W. (1949). *Basic principles of curriculum and instruction.* Chicago: University of Chicago Press.

U.S. Department of Commerce, Bureau of the Census (1997). Resident population—selected characteristics, 1790–1996 and projections 2000 to 2050. *Statistical Abstract of the United States 1997* (117th ed.) Washington, D.C.: U.S. Government Printing Office.

U.S. Department of Education (1987). *What works: Research about teaching and learning* (2nd ed.). Washington, D.C.: U.S. Government Printing Office.

U.S. Department of Education, Office of Special Education and Rehabilitative Services (1996). *Eighteenth annual report to congress on the implementation of the individuals with disabilities education act.* Washington, D.C.: U.S. Government Printing Office.

Valauskas, E. J., & Entel, M. (1996). *The Internet for teachers and school library media specialists.* New York: Neal-Shuman Publishers.

Vaughn, J., & Estes, T. (1986). *Reading and reasoning beyond the primary grades.* Boston: Allyn and Bacon.

Viadero, D. (1996). Mixed bag. *Teacher Magazine, 9* (1), 20–23.

Vygotsky, L. (1962). *Thought and language.* Cambridge, MA: MIT Press.

Wade, S. E., & Reynolds, R. E. (1989). Developing metacognitive awareness. *Journal of Reading, 33* (1), 6–14.

Wiles, J., & Bondi, J. (1998). *Curriculum development: A guide to practice* (5th ed.). Upper Saddle River, NJ: Merrill.

Wittrock, C.F. (1978). *Relationship between personal values, aptitudes, and year-end grade averages for secondary students in selected vocational education classes.* Cincinnati, OH: University of Cincinnati.

Wood, D., Bruner, J., & Ross, G. (1976). The role of tutoring in problem solving. *Journal of Child Psychology and Psychiatry of Allied Disciplines, 17,* 89–100.

Woolfolk, A.E. (1995). *Educational Psychology* (6th ed.). Boston: Allyn and Bacon.

Woolfolk, A.E. (1998). *Educational Psychology* (7th ed.). Boston: Allyn and Bacon.

Index